THE
AVOIDABLE
WAR

THE
AVOIDABLE
WAR

The Dangers of a Catastrophic
Conflict between the US and
Xi Jinping's China

KEVIN RUDD

PUBLICAFFAIRS

New York

PublicAffairs
Hachette Book Group
1290 Avenue of the Americas, New York, NY 10104
www.publicaffairsbooks.com
@Public_Affairs

Printed in the United States of America

First Edition: March 2022

Published by PublicAffairs, an imprint of Perseus Books, LLC, a subsidiary of Hachette Book Group, Inc. The PublicAffairs name and logo is a trademark of the Hachette Book Group.

The Hachette Speakers Bureau provides a wide range of authors for speaking events. To find out more, go to www.hachettespeakersbureau.com or call (866) 376-6591.

The publisher is not responsible for websites (or their content) that are not owned by the publisher.

Library of Congress Control Number: 2021952259

ISBNs: 9781541701298 (hardcover), 9781541701304 (e-book)

LSC-C

Printing 6, 2023

Dedicated to our three little grandkids, Josephine, Mackie, and Scarlett, and to precious grandchildren the world over as our generation contemplates decisions that will determine whether these little ones get to live in poverty, fear, and war—or prosperity, freedom, and peace.

Contents

★ ★ ★ ★ ★
Introduction:
On the Danger of War

I wish I did not have to write this book. I am just old enough to remember marching as a small child in our annual ANZAC Day parade—the Australian equivalent of Memorial Day—in our tiny country town with my father, who had fought in World War II. I also remember marching beside men in their seventies, by then a little unsteady on their feet, who had fought back in World War I. One of them, my father confided in me, still suffered from shell shock.

There was nothing inevitable about the Great War from 1914 to 1918. It came about because of the flawed decisions of political and military leaders in July and August 1914. That's what led to the slaughter. Those decisions cost approximately 40 million lives, including 117,000 Americans and 60,000 Australians. The decisions about how to punish the losers of that war set the fuse for the next global conflagration, one so horrific that when it was done, as many as 85 million—approximately 3 percent of the world's population—lay dead.

When I think of the collective killings of the last century, I fully acknowledge that my mindset forces me to make every effort to do whatever can be done to avoid yet another episode of global carnage on an industrial scale. In doing so, however, we must not only maintain the peace but also preserve the national and individual freedoms that our forebears fought to secure over the many centuries that have passed since the Enlightenment.

We must be ever mindful of the debacle of Neville Chamberlain's proclamation, having handed the Sudetenland to Hitler in Munich in 1938, that he'd come home to London bringing "peace with honor" and urged the people of Britain to "go home and sleep quietly in your beds." The uncomfortable truth is there can never be peace at any price.

This brings us to the unfolding crisis in the relationship between China and the United States. The 2020s loom as a decisive decade in the overall dynamics of the changing balance of power between them. Both Chinese and American strategists know this. For policy makers in Beijing and Washington, as well as in other capitals, the 2020s will be the decade of living dangerously. Beneath the surface, the stakes have never been higher or the contest sharper, whatever diplomats and politicians may say publicly. Should these two giants find a way to coexist without betraying their core interests—through what I call managed strategic competition—the world will be better for it. Should they fail, down the other path lies the possibility of a war that could rewrite the future of both countries and the world in a way we can barely imagine.

A Student of China and America

I have been a student of China since I was eighteen years old, beginning with my undergraduate degree at the Australian National University, where I majored in Mandarin Chinese and classical and modern Chinese history. I have lived and worked in Beijing, Shanghai, Hong Kong, and Taipei through different diplomatic postings and have developed many, many friendships right across greater China. I have traveled back to China and Taiwan on innumerable occasions over the last forty years, including in my role as prime minister of Australia, personally meeting with Xi Jinping and other senior Chinese leaders many times. I admire China's classical civilization, including its remarkable philosophical, literary, and artistic traditions, as well as the economic achievements of the post-Mao era in lifting a quarter of humanity out of poverty.

At the same time, I have been deeply critical of Mao's depredations of the country during the Great Leap Forward of 1958, which left some thirty million dead from starvation; the Cultural Revolution, in which Mao eliminated his political enemies through Stalinesque show trials, leading to millions of deaths and the destruction of priceless cultural heritage at the same time; and human rights abuses that continue to this day. My undergraduate dissertation at the Australian National University, "Human Rights in China—The Case of Wei Jingsheng," forced me to retrace the sad and sorry history of the concept of rights throughout both the classical and the Communist periods. I had simply read too much—and seen too much—over the years to politely brush it all under the carpet. I am still haunted by the thousands of young faces in Tiananmen Square in late May 1989, when I spent the better part of a week walking and talking among them—before the tanks moved in on June 4. That's why I could not avoid the whole question of human rights when, nearly twenty years later, I returned to Beijing as Australia's prime minister on my inaugural visit. I traveled to Peking University to deliver a public lecture in Chinese on the very first day of my visit, where I argued that the best classical traditions of friendship within the Chinese tradition (the concept of *zhengyou*) meant that friends could candidly speak to each other without rupturing the relationship. Within that frame, I raised human rights abuses in Tibet in the middle of my speech. The Chinese foreign ministry went nuts. So, too, did the more supine members of the Australian political class, business community, and media, who did what they always do: they asked, "How could you upset our Chinese hosts" by mentioning the unmentionable? The answer was reasonably straightforward: because it happened to be the truth, and to ignore it was to ignore part of the complex reality of any country's relationship with the People's Republic.

I have also lived for a number of years in the United States. I have a deep affection for Americans, a profound interest in American history, and a deep admiration for the country's extraordinary culture of innovation. I am intimately aware of the differences between the two countries, but I've also seen the great cultural values they have in common—the love of family, the importance that both Chinese and Americans attach to the education of their children, and their vibrant entrepreneurial cultures driven by aspiration and hard work. No approach to understanding US-China relations is free from intellectual and cultural prejudice. For all my education in Chinese history and thought, I am inescapably and unapologetically a creature of the West. I therefore belong to its philosophical, religious, and cultural traditions. The country I served as both prime minister and foreign minister has been an ally of the United States for more than one hundred years and actively supports the continuation of the liberal international order built by the United States out of the ashes of World War II. At the same time, I have never accepted the view that an alliance with the United States mandates automatic compliance with every element of American foreign and security policy. This has been demonstrated by the fact that despite pressure from Washington, my political party, the Australian Labor Party, opposed both the Vietnam War and the invasion of Iraq. Nor do I have a rose-colored view of American domestic politics and its endemic problems of uncontrolled campaign finance, the corruption of the redistricting system, and the politics of voter suppression. Nor am I complacent about the unsustainable economic inequalities that we find increasing across American society and that have fueled a new wave of populist extremism.

The judgment I bring to bear on US-China relations also reflects my personal loathing for jingoistic nationalism, which, regrettably, has become an increasingly prominent feature of many aspects of both Chinese and American public life. This may be emotionally satisfying to some and politically useful for others in eliciting widespread popular support for a given course of action, but its inability to bring about any good is of little interest to demagogues. Above all, what history teaches us is that nationalism is a very dangerous thing in the conduct of international relations.

A History of Mutual Distrust

The current state of US-China relations is the product of a long, complex, and contested history. This complexity has been compounded over the last 150 years by each side blaming the other for the relationship's failings. What emerges across the centuries is a recurring theme of mutual noncomprehension and deep suspicion, often followed by periods of exaggerated hopes and expectations that then collapse in the face of fundamentally different political and strategic imperatives.

In its most narrow conception, the modern relationship between China and the United States has relied on common economic self-interest. At other times, this has been supported by a sense of strategic condominium against a common enemy, at first the Soviet Union and, after 9/11, to a much more limited extent, militant Islamism. More recently, a further pillar was added with shared American and Chinese concerns for global financial stability and the impacts of climate change. Human rights have always remained an underlying point of friction in the relationship, waxing and waning in significance over the last half century of diplomatic engagement. Despite occasional flirtations by the Chinese Communist Party (CCP) with various forms of political liberalization, particularly during the 1980s, there has been, at best, a sullen tolerance for each other's political systems. Across the overall history of the modern relationship, these various pillars (economic, geostrategic, and multilateral), when taken together, have supported the relationship in a way that's been relatively robust. But one by one, over the last decade, each pillar cracked, so much so that by the 2020s, they crumbled under their own weight, having virtually exhausted their individual transactional utility.

Most Americans, including educated elites, struggle to understand the nature of the domestic politics and policy decision-making processes in the People's Republic of China. This is understandable given the linguistic, cultural, and philosophical divide between the two countries. This leads to the most basic American perception of China of all—namely, a profound sense of difference, mystery, and confusion about what China is about, what it is becoming, and what this may mean for American interests, values, and the future of US global leadership. Again, this is not surprising. Americans have been asked to come to terms with a people, culture, and political system that lies way beyond traditional American frames of reference. Once we cross the Dardanelles into Asia, whether it's the Near East, the Middle East, or the Far East, the more familiar cultural lens of

Europe soon disappears. Americans struggle to comprehend these ancient civilizations that do not share common assumptions about the past, or for that matter the future, and that are the product of a collective cultural heritage. On China in particular, the lack of American familiarity with the Chinese cultural canon, its logographic language, its ancient ethical concepts, and its contemporary communist leadership can cause Americans to feel deeply uncertain and distrustful about this newly emerged rival for the mantle of global leadership.

This deepening chasm of distrust did not develop overnight. It has been growing over many years, fueled by a vast array of accumulated political and strategic perceptions. There is a deep belief in the capitals of both countries that the diplomatic formulations used by each side about the other are no longer believable, that they are a diplomatic fiction, detached from the world of strategic fact, where an entirely different reality has unfolded. Washington no longer believes in China's self-proclaimed "peaceful rise." The US national security establishment, in particular, now holds the view that the CCP has never had any compunction about lying to deceive its political or strategic adversaries. It sees such language as little more than a diplomatic ruse to disarm the politically gullible while spreading China's influence, backed by military power, throughout the region and the world. It points to island reclamation in the South China Sea, the building of Chinese naval bases around the Indian Ocean, and Chinese cyberattacks on the US government as evidence of the reality of Chinese aggression.

Each side points to the other as the guilty party. If Washington protests that it has no interest in "containing" China's rise, Beijing isn't buying it. As evidence, China points to increased arms sales by the US to Taiwan despite American promises to reduce these under the terms of the three joint communiqués of 1972, 1979, and 1982; the trade war that Beijing sees as a concerted effort to cripple its economy; and the American campaign against Huawei, which it sees as an effort to stymie China's technological advance. Beijing reads Washington's insistence on freedom of navigation for itself and its allies in the South China Sea as hostile and aggressive interference in Chinese sovereign waters. Given the depth of this bilateral trust deficit, there is a limit to what strategic dialogue can achieve. Pious statements that we must "rebuild strategic trust" are greeted with laughter and derision in both capitals. As one senior American military commander said to me recently, "In dealing with China, strategic trust is a much-overrated thing." And his People's Liberation Army (PLA) counterparts have much the same view about American trustworthiness.

Thucydides's Trap

If a primary factor dissuading China from engaging militarily against the United States in the past has been a Chinese belief that it was too weak to do so, that hesitancy is fading with the rapid modernization of the PLA. The precarious evolution of the US-China balance of power is what Harvard's Graham Allison (a good friend of mine) has described as an emerging "Thucydidean dynamic." In Thucydides's *History of the Peloponnesian War*, the ancient historian concluded that "it was the rise of Athens and the fear that this instilled in Sparta that made war inevitable." Allison explains that Thucydides's Trap is "the natural, inevitable discombobulation that occurs when a rising power threatens to displace a ruling power." In Thucydidean logic, the threat of such displacement causes structural stress in the relationship, which makes a violent clash the rule, not the exception. According to Allison's model, based on his examination of multiple historical case studies, war is more likely than not. Embedded in Allison's logic is the implication that there are also real and perceived tipping points in the great power relationship in question, which means the question for policy makers is what to do to either preempt them or respond to them before it's too late.

At this stage in the unfolding dynamics of the US-China relationship, it is relatively easy to envisage a flow of events that mutates into a sort of Cold War 2.0, which, in turn, runs the risk of triggering a hot one. These days, the early stages of such conflict could be entirely cyber in nature. For example, hackers could disable the other side's infrastructure, from pipelines and electric grids to air traffic control systems, with potentially deadly results. Dangerously, there is as yet no clear international or even bilateral agreement between the two countries on what cybertargets, if attacked, would trigger a war or that should be off-limits during war to protect civilian life. More conventional military exchanges are also within the realm of the possible. America has Asian allies it has sworn to protect; China's ambitions push up against those alliances. From Taiwan to the South China Sea and the Philippines to the East China Sea and Japan, China is increasingly testing the limits of America's defense commitments.

While Beijing's chief aim for the modernization and expansion of its military has been to prepare for future Taiwan contingencies, China's growing military, naval, air, and intelligence capabilities represent, in the American view, a much broader challenge to US military predominance across the wider Indo-Pacific region and beyond. Of greatest concern to the United States is the rapid expansion and modernization of the Chinese navy and its growing submarine capabilities, as well as China's development, for the first time in its history, of a blue-water fleet with force-projection capabilities beyond its coastal waters. This has enabled China to expand its strategic reach across the Indian Ocean, enhanced by a string of available ports provided by its friends and partners across Southeast Asia, South Asia, and all the way to East Africa and Djibouti in the Red Sea. Added to this is a wider pattern of military and naval collaboration with Russia, including recent joint land-and-sea exercises in the Russian Far East, the Mediterranean, and the Baltic. These have caused American military thinkers to conclude that Chinese strategists have much wider ambitions than just the Taiwan Strait. Chinese technological advances in space, cyberspace, and artificial intelligence have also led some in Washington to conclude that whatever Chinese declaratory policy might be, its strategic ambitions extend both globally and regionally. The reported success of Chinese intelligence operations in penetrating American computer systems to steal sensitive defense plans and personnel records, as well as the theft of sophisticated US military technologies, have heightened American concerns.

In many respects, therefore, many of the elements of Thucydides's Trap are already present in the US-China relationship of today.

The Rise of Xi Jinping

Changes in the objective balance of power are one element of the strategic equation. The other is the changing character of China's leadership. A pattern has emerged in recent years of a new, more confident, assertive, and even aggressive leadership that no longer accepts its previous subordinate military and economic status. In the first decades of post-Mao reform, from the 1980s to 2012, when Xi Jinping became leader, Beijing hewed to the maxim set out by the architect of reform and opening, Deng Xiaoping, as a guide to the PRC's actions in the world: "Hide your strength; bide your time; never take the lead." Xi has consigned that maxim to oblivion. China, having become far more powerful, is removing the mask of modesty and restraint that its leaders had carefully crafted for themselves over the previous thirty-five years. Such evasion is no longer required when, as Xi told a gathering of central and provincial party leaders in 2021, "time and momentum are on our side."

While the ideological framework established over decades by the CCP remains the scaffolding on which all Chinese policy is ultimately constructed, not since Mao has China had a leader as powerful as it has right now. Xi Jinping sits at the apex of the Chinese political system, and his influence permeates every level of party and state. His acquisition of power has been politically astute and brutal in its method. To take but one example, the anticorruption campaign he has wielded across the party has helped "clean up" the country's almost industrial levels of corruption. It has also afforded him the additional benefit of "cleaning out"—via expulsion from the party and sentences to life imprisonment—nearly all his political rivals and critics who might otherwise have threatened his supreme authority.

For Americans, who idealized Deng Xiaoping—twice *Time* magazine's Man of the Year—and imagined that as China transformed its economy from the socialist planning model to one with a free market, it would one day become a liberal democracy, China's new leadership represents a radical departure. As Washington sees it, Xi Jinping abandoned any pretense of China ever transforming itself into a more open, tolerant, liberal-democratic state. He has also adopted a model of authoritarian capitalism that is less market-driven and prioritizes state enterprises over the private sector, and he is tightening the party's control over business writ large. Even as Beijing appears determined to rewrite the terms of the international order, America also sees Xi as fanning the flames of Chinese nationalism in a manner that is increasingly anti-American. The US sees Xi as determined to alter the strategic and territorial status quo in the western Pacific and establish a Chinese sphere of influence across the Eastern Hemisphere.

Washington has also concluded that Xi decided to export his domestic political model to the rest of the developing world by leveraging the global gravitational pull of the Chinese economy in order to maximize China's political and foreign policy influence. The ultimate objective is to create an international system that is much more accommodating of Chinese national interests and values. Finally, unlike in decades past, the United States has concluded that these changes in China's official worldview are underpinned by an economically, militarily, and technologically powerful Chinese party-state that is increasingly on a self-selected collision course with America. That means that Washington, as a matter of strategic logic, will either have to submit to Chinese interests, accommodate them, or actively seek to resist and, if possible, defeat them.

Of course, the Chinese strategic lens on this unfolding reality is grounded in a radically different worldview. Xi's view is that there is nothing wrong with China's political-economic mode and that while Beijing offers it to others in the developing world to emulate, it is not "forcing it" on any other state. By contrast, Xi points out the considerable failings of Western democracies in dealing with core challenges, such as the COVID-19 pandemic, populist protectionism, and the gathering momentum of antiglobalization. Xi argues that China has modernized its military in order to secure its long-standing territorial claims, particularly over Taiwan, and he makes no apology for using the gravitational pull of the

Chinese economy to advance its national interests across the board. Nor does he apologize for using his newfound global power to rewrite the rules of the international system and the multilateral institutions that back it, arguing that this is precisely what the victorious Western powers did after World War II.

The CCP's goal under Xi is also to pull China's per-capita GDP up to "the level of other moderately developed countries" by 2035. Chinese economists typically place that somewhere between $20,000 and $30,000, or a level similar to South Korea. This would require a further doubling or tripling of the size of China's economy. Such ambitions add further evidence to the likely extension of Xi Jinping's political career, given the party's controversial 2018 decision to remove the two-term limit for five-year presidential terms that was written into the 1982 Chinese State Constitution. This was done by Deng to prevent the rise of another absolute ruler, such as Mao, whose political campaigns led to much suffering and death. Normally, by this stage of the Chinese political process, well past the midway point of a leader's second term, a successor would have been designated. As of now, there is none. Xi will be nearly seventy by the expiration of his second term as president, general secretary of the party, and chairman of the Central Military Commission in 2022—and eighty-two at the end of 2035. Given his family's longevity (his father lived to eighty-eight, and his mother is still alive at ninety-one at the time of writing), it is prudent to assume that Xi could remain, in one political form or another, as China's paramount leader through the 2020s and well into the 2030s. It is therefore likely to be on his watch that China finally becomes the largest economy in the world, however calculated, supplanting the United States after more than a century of global economic dominance. With this shift in the global balance of power, Xi will likely feel emboldened to pursue a growing array of global ambitions over these next fifteen years—none more consequential to him than to see the return of Taiwan to Beijing's sovereignty.

A substantial portion of this book is therefore devoted to defining Xi's core priorities, which will likely be the main lens for Chinese policy making in the decades ahead. To my mind, they can best be understood as ten concentric circles of interests, starting with the most vital (which are, not coincidentally, those closest to home) and expanding outward from China to encompass greater and more global ambitions. This layered exploration is woven into the structure of the chapters that follow, in what I hope will give readers a better understanding of how the world looks from Xi's desk in Zhongnanhai. As noted earlier, Chinese political thought is not frequently well understood in the West. That is why a large part of this book is dedicated to understanding Xi Jinping's worldview. It is fundamental to any analysis of the likelihood of war and how we might avoid it.

Xi's View of the United States

In the eyes of China's leadership, there is only one country capable of fundamentally disrupting Xi's national and global ambitions. That is the United States. There are, of course, many domestic political and economic factors that can get in the way of the realization of Xi's China Dream of "the great rejuvenation of the Chinese nation." But among the external forces that lie beyond Chinese control—and while great powers such as Russia, Japan, and even India could complicate or even impede China's rise—only the United States could wield sufficient strategic and economic power to potentially derail it. That's why the US continues to occupy the central position in Chinese Communist Party strategic thinking. This covers what we might call Chinese "grand strategy." But it also covers each individual area of potential Chinese vulnerability, including the military, foreign policy, the economy, trade, investment, technology, capital flows, currency exposure, international development aid, global reputation on human rights and democracy, the rule of law, and, of course, Taiwan.

Xi personally is no neophyte in his understanding of America. He visited America during his earlier political career: once as a junior official, where he famously homestayed with a family in rural Iowa in the 1980s, and then more than twenty years later when, as Chinese vice president, he was hosted by then US vice president Joe Biden on a weeklong visit to various American cities and states. In 2010, Xi sent his only child to Harvard University for her undergraduate degree. Xi also had rolling engagements hosting visiting American delegations throughout his political career, both in Beijing and in the provinces. But despite his daughter's English language fluency, Xi himself neither speaks nor reads English—which means that his understanding of America has always been intermediated through official Chinese sources of translation, which are not always known for accuracy, subtlety, or nuance. And official briefings, generated from China's foreign policy bureaucracy and intelligence community, have a traditional frame for looking at America that is rarely benign. This is also compounded by a real fear of Xi on the part of Chinese officials and a career-preserving desire to provide analyses that conform to what they believe he wants to hear. Still, Xi's direct experience of America exceeds the direct experience of China of any American leader, including Joe Biden. No American leader has ever spoken or read Chinese, and all have been similarly reliant on intermediate sources. As a Mandarin speaker, I was fortunate as foreign minister and prime minister of my country to be able to communicate directly with my counterparts and other Chinese officials in their own language. More Western political leaders will need to do so in the future.

For many reasons, much of the American strategic community discounts the idea of China's peaceful rise or peaceful development altogether. Instead, there is a deep view that some form of armed conflict or confrontation with Beijing is inevitable—unless, of course, China were to change strategic direction. Under Xi Jinping's leadership, any such change is deemed to be virtually impossible. In Washington, therefore, the question is no longer whether such confrontation can be avoided, but when it will occur and under what circumstances. And to a large extent, this mirrors the position in Beijing as well.

Managed Strategic Competition

There is, therefore, both a moral and a practical obligation for friends of China and friends of the United States to think through what has become the single hardest question of international relations of our century: how to preserve the peace and prosperity we have secured over the last three-quarters of a century while recognizing the reality of changing power relativities between Washington and Beijing. We can allow the primordial dimensions of Thucydidean logic to simply take their natural course, ultimately culminating in crisis, conflict, or even war. Or we can identify potential strategic off-ramps, or at least guardrails, which may help preserve the peace among the great powers while also sustaining the integrity of the rules-based order that has underpinned the stability of the wider international relations system since 1945.

Therefore, to borrow a question from Lenin himself: "What is to be done?" As a first step, each side must be mindful of how their actions will be read by the other through the prism of their accumulated national perceptions—in other words, what buttons light up in the decision-making processes on one side when a particular action is taken by the other. At present, both sides are bad at this, often reflecting a combination of mutually assured noncomprehension and mirror imaging that has long characterized large parts of the US-China relationship. If we are serious about the possibility of developing a joint strategic narrative that might be capable of governing the future of the relationship peacefully, we must, at a minimum, be mindful of how strategic language, actions, and diplomatic signaling will be interpreted within each side's political culture, systems, and elites. It is this sort of awareness that can help us navigate the practical complexities of competing national interests, values, and perceptions within a stable, albeit still competitive, strategic framework.

Developing a new level of mutual strategic literacy, however, is only the beginning. What follows must be the hard work of constructing a joint strategic framework between Washington and Beijing that is capable of achieving the following three interrelated tasks:

1. Agreeing on principles and procedures for navigating each other's strategic redlines (for example, over Taiwan) that, if inadvertently crossed, would likely result in military escalation.

2. Mutually identifying the areas of nonlethal national security policy—foreign policy, economic policy, technology development (for example, over semiconductors)—and ideology where full-blown strategic competition is accepted as the new normal.

3. Defining those areas where continued strategic cooperation (for example, on climate change) is both recognized and encouraged.

Of course, none of this can be advanced unilaterally. It can only be done bilaterally by senior negotiators who have been charged by the two countries' presidents with an overarching responsibility for the totality of the relationship, not just discrete and individual parts of it. In the case of the United States, this would be the national security advisor, given their coordination role across the full range of government agencies. For China, it would probably devolve to the director of the foreign affairs office of the Central Committee, or else the vice chairman of the Central Military Commission, or both. These same individuals would also be charged with operationalizing any joint strategic framework that they negotiated and agreed to around the core principles of managed strategic competition described above. As with all such agreements, the devil will, of course, lie in the detail—and in its enforcement. Such a framework would not depend on trust. It would rely exclusively on sophisticated national verification systems already deployed by each country. In other words, the integrity of these arrangements would not rely on Ronald Reagan's famous "trust, but verify" approach, which Reagan insisted on with the Soviet Union, but rather on "verify" alone.

A joint strategic framework of this type will not prevent crisis, conflict, or war. But properly negotiated, effectively implemented, and reinforced with effective deterrence, it would reduce their likelihood. Of course, it would also not prevent any premeditated covert attack by one side against the assets of the other as part of a complete violation of the framework. Indeed, such a framework would rest on the assumption that it would not be in the interests of either side to initiate any such unilateral attack for the foreseeable future. But where a joint framework could assist lies in managing escalation or de-escalation in the event of accidental incidents at sea, in the air, or in cyberspace. Were there to be a breach of any of the framework's subsidiary agreements on strategic redlines (for example, a cyberattack), then the matter would immediately be referred to the principals of both sides for clarification prior to any further escalation being undertaken.

I'm not so naive as to believe that any agreed-upon joint framework arranged on managed strategic competition assumptions would prevent China and the US from still strategizing against the other, deploying their assets and statecraft as best they could to maintain (or obtain) long-term primacy. But the United States and the Soviet Union, following the near-death experience of the Cuban Missile Crisis, eventually agreed on a political and strategic framework to manage their own fraught relationship without triggering mutual annihilation. Surely it's possible to do the same between America and China in the arguably less trying geopolitical circumstances of today. It is from this hope that the idea of managed strategic competition comes.

Certainly, the rest of the world, and not just Asia, would welcome a future where the strategic temperature came down and where they are not forced to make binary choices between Beijing and Washington in an increasingly bipolar world. These countries would prefer a world in which there is a global order in which each country, large and small, has confidence in its territorial integrity, political sovereignty, and pathway to national prosperity. They would also prefer a world whose stability was underpinned by a functioning international system that was also empowered to act on the great global challenges of our time that no individual nation can solve alone. What happens next between China and America will decide if that is still possible.

The Danger That Is Nationalism

There is no time to waste. Hypernationalists are gaining ground in the politics of both capitals. Self-described realists with confrontationist agendas seek to influence their respective national security policies. Liberal internationalists, let alone multilateralists, are usually written off as weak-kneed. The United States, under first the Trump administration and now the Biden administration, has formally concluded that after forty years, strategic engagement between China and the United States has outlived its usefulness as a strategy. Instead, we have entered a new, uncharted era where there are, as yet, no new rules of the road. China has reached a similar conclusion. The time has therefore come to craft some new ones before it's too late.

The purpose of this book is not to provide advice to either side on how to prevail against the other in some sort of final economic, technological, and military shootout at the O.K. Corral. There are plenty of people already doing that, both publicly and privately, as they happily embark on the slippery slope of decoupling, containment, confrontation, and perhaps ultimately the unthinkable itself. Rather, the purpose of this book is to provide a joint road map to help these two great nations navigate a common pathway to the future—not through wishful thinking, nor stern moral lectures about the importance of peace, but rather through a comprehensive realist framework anchored in the enduring principles of diplomatic negotiation, verification through intelligence, effective deterrence—and, most importantly, mutual respect.

The book is not intended as an academic text. There are no footnotes, nor is there a bibliography. Even less is it a populist polemic seeking to appeal to a mass audience, drawing on the depressingly familiar, ancient alchemies of xenophobia, nationalism, and political opportunism. Instead, the book is aimed at the intelligent general reader, of whom there are still many in both China and the United States, who is not seeking simplistic answers to complex questions of the type we are wrestling with here. It reflects my analysis of what is going on in the relationship, the factors that are driving it in an increasingly confrontational direction, and my thoughts on what can be done about it before it's all too late.

In my view, there is nothing inevitable about war. To believe that would deny the agency of leadership, instead making us captive to some deep, imaginary, irreversible forces of history. As noted above, Allison quotes Thucydides's observation that "it was the rise of Athens, and the fear that this instilled in Sparta, that made war inevitable." But Allison's textual analysis of the classical Greek concluded that "inevitable" was perhaps better rendered as "probable." And Allison's analysis of sixteen historical engagements between rising and established powers over the last five hundred years concluded that one-quarter of them did not result in war. In other words, both from the classical texts and more recent modern examples, war under these circumstances may be probable—*but it is by no means inevitable.* History should always be our guide but never our master.

We, too, may not prevail over the drumbeats of war. Leaders can make that choice. It is never forced upon them. The argument of this book is that our best chance of avoiding war is to better understand the other side's strategic thinking and to conceptualize a world where both the US and China are able to competitively coexist, even if in a state of continuing rivalry reinforced by mutual deterrence. A world where political leaders are empowered to preside over a competitive race rather than resorting to the lethality of actual armed conflict. Indeed, if we can preserve the peace for the decade ahead, political circumstances may eventually change; strategic thought may evolve in the face of new, much broader planetary challenges; and it may then be possible for leaders to imagine a different way of thinking (the Chinese term is *siwei*) that prioritizes collaboration over conflict in meeting the existential global challenges confronting us all. But to do that, we must first get through the current decade without destroying each other. We are governed by a generation with little lived memory of the horrors of war. They should understand that history teaches us that if war were to break out, our world would never be able to return to the way things were before. War changes everything in the most destructive and unexpected of ways. That's why straining every conscious and creative sinew is required to preserve the peace for the period ahead. We owe this to future generations as well as to the generations past, including my father and the men who marched to war beside him, to whom we vowed "never again."

1

★ ★ ★ ★ ★

A Short History of the US-China Relationship

Chinese leaders have long made it their business to understand America in a manner that their American counterparts have rarely felt the need to reciprocate. This is because the Chinese Communist Party, since its founding in 1921, has believed that its ultimate survival and success depends on understanding those countries and forces in the world capable of destroying it, principal among which is the United States. By contrast, even today, among American political elites, with few notable exceptions, there is little sense of urgency to understand the domestic drivers of China's international policy behavior. Whereas understanding China may have been seen by some Americans as *important* for US national interests, very few have seen this as *essential*, let alone *existential*. Moreover, because America's geopolitical footprint is so large, the US-China relationship—which has long seemed problematic but rarely critical—has had to compete for attention for decades: first with the Soviet Union and then with rolling crises in the Middle East.

Belatedly, that may now be changing. This is driven in recent years by a destabilizing mix of ill-considered strategic panic and domestic political opportunism in a race to the bottom on who can sound the toughest on China during a given election season. The policy appetite and political space for a more rational American approach, the product of seasoned analysis of China's and America's changing political, economic, and strategic circumstances over time, remains limited. Indeed, in the view of the American strategic establishment, China has been transformed from a strategic partner to a strategic competitor—and, for most parts of the American elite, to a strategic adversary—all roughly in the handful of years since Xi Jinping came to power in China in 2012. By contrast, China, under the Communist Party, has long exhibited a deep strategic realism toward America where the limitations of strategic and economic collaboration with Washington have always been recognized, particularly given the underlying Marxist-Leninist nature of the Chinese party and state.

When the American republic was in its infancy in the immediate aftermath of the Revolutionary War, China was at its height as the largest, wealthiest, and most populous country on earth. The Qing dynasty (1644–1911) extended the territorial reach of the Celestial Kingdom to its greatest extent since China first became a unified kingdom in 221 BCE. Under the Qianlong Emperor (1735–1796), the Chinese economy represented 40 percent of global GDP, despite the fact that relatively little of China's wealth was derived from external trade.

Some earlier eras, including the Han (206 BCE–CE 220), Tang (618–907 CE), and Song (960–1279 CE) dynasties, as well as the Mongol Yuan (1279–1368) and early Ming (1368–1644), witnessed considerable political and economic engagement with the rest of the world, including when the Silk Road was at its height and China's flourishing commercial sea routes were connecting its merchants with their central Asian, Middle Eastern, and European counterparts. But even during these high periods of China's international commerce, historians have calculated that probably no more than 25 percent of GDP came from sectors of the economy involving trade.

Given the history of periodic political and military incursions, China has long been suspicious of foreign "barbarians" of any stripe. Chinese official culture has also long taken pride in its ability to Sinify intruders within a generation of their arrival through the inherited norms, practices, and procedures of China's formidable Confucian bureaucratic state.

On multiple occasions, foreign conquerors, including the Mongol Yuan and Manchu Qing dynasties, had little choice but to first adopt Chinese practices and norms in order to rule the vast Chinese state and then find means of accommodation between their own ethnic practices and those of the Confucian state. Still, the fact that multiple ruling dynasties had themselves been the product of invasion by non-Han peoples living along China's borders made China's leaders all the more aware of possible threats from abroad.

Over the millennia, China also developed its own philosophical and religious traditions (Confucianism, Taoism, and Legalism) without reference to the wider world. All three predated the arrival of Buddhism from the Indian subcontinent during the Han dynasty (at approximately 150 BCE), and successive Chinese dynasties then spent a thousand years varying between attempting to assimilate it entirely and attempting to eliminate it. They finally resorted to the next best thing to Sinifying it, which was subordinating this new foreign teaching to the political imperatives of the Chinese Confucian state. Islam had traveled along the Silk Road during the Tang dynasty (around the mid-seventh century), but its primary impact was limited to minority ethnic communities along China's western borders and some other pockets, with little penetration of the vast Han majority. Christianity, having arrived first in the seventh century with the Nestorians and then again in the seventeenth century with the Jesuits before the arrival of Protestant missionaries in the nineteenth, had fared considerably worse, leaving little appreciable imprint on the Middle Kingdom, at least until the last decades of a declining Qing empire.

China, therefore, as seen through the framework of its national historiography, had been a relatively successful self-contained, self-referential political, economic, philosophical, cultural, and religious system. Foreigners, by contrast, were viewed with a combination of suspicion and condescension: as episodic invaders; culturally inferior; and, in most practical respects, irrelevant to China's essential national needs. It was within this wider frame that, by the mid-nineteenth century, neither the West nor the British, let alone their distant American cousins, loomed large in the collective Chinese imagination.

The Opium Wars

This isolated status quo, however, would be turned on its head in the decades following the First Opium War (1839–1842), when Britain forced China to open its ports to international trade, imposed a series of unequal treaties on the Qing (including granting foreigners in China impunity from Chinese law under the principle of extraterritoriality), and gradually forced China to accept foreign missionaries. While the Americans may have been officially squeamish about the colonial methods used by their European cousins in forcing open China's doors, they were soon demanding the same access to the country—both for commerce and Christian evangelism. American businesspeople were no more noble than any other country's. Boston merchants did a significant trade in opium, sourced from Ottoman suppliers, and then plied across the Pacific to China's newly opened treaty ports.

During the course of the nineteenth century, America's trade and investment interests in China continued to grow. However, China represented only about half the overall value of America's economic engagement with Japan. Together, China and Japan made up an even smaller proportion of total US trade and investment than did Europe, which had captured the vast bulk of American economic interests abroad. By contrast, over the course of the next one hundred years, American Protestant missionaries became the dominant Christian presence in China. Beyond their core mission of saving human souls, American missionaries also led the way in the establishment of Western hospitals, colleges, and universities in the late Qing and (after the revolution that overthrew the Qing in 1911) early Republic of China. Tens of thousands of young Chinese professionals were trained and educated either through American philanthropic institutions in China or, increasingly, at America's public universities. Relatively quickly, America became the single largest foreign destination other than Japan for Chinese students studying abroad.

As anticolonialists themselves (at least in their conception), the Americans brought to China a different sensibility than the Europeans did. Nonetheless, while the US government regularly protested the growing depredations of Western colonialism in China, its diplomatic emissaries continued to insist on equal treatment for its nationals to ensure that American interests would not be sacrificed at the altar of political purity. Indeed, in the aftermath of the Boxer Uprising of 1900 (a violent antiforeign and anti-Christian movement that attacked foreign legations with the tacit support of the Qing), the US sent troops to help put down the Boxers' siege of the foreign legations in Beijing. They took part, with the armies of seven other imperial powers, in the brutal foreign occupation of Peking and in the extraction of exorbitant financial indemnities from the Qing government, equal to six times the court's annual revenue at the time, to be paid in silver over the following forty years.

Washington, however, under pressure from American missionaries objecting to the indemnity, later remitted a large part of its share back to the Chinese government to fund scholarship programs for Chinese students going to America. Yet this did not fundamentally ameliorate Chinese perceptions of America's semicolonial behavior in China or place the United States in a significantly more benign light than the other imperial powers of the time.

With the dawn of what would in time come to be called the American Century, the fundamental dynamics of the relationship changed as the US supplanted Britain as China's principal interlocutor with the West. The United States had become one of four major powers with which the new republican government—itself unstable and under constant threat from local warlords—was forced to deal to secure its territorial integrity. Imperial Russia effectively annexed more than a million square kilometers of territory from the Qing dynasty through a series of unequal treaties. Imperial Japan, following the Sino-Japanese War of 1894–1895, seized de facto control over the Chinese tributary state of Korea (which it would then annex in 1910) as well as Taiwan. France effectively took control of China's southern tributary state of Annam (Vietnam). America, however, maintained an official stance of supporting the continuing "integrity of the Chinese Empire," in contrast to its continuing dismemberment by the colonial powers. Still, Washington proclaimed its open-door policy, under which the United States would not allow American traders, investors, or missionaries to be squeezed out by those of the other, openly imperialist powers.

Nonetheless, given its foreign and domestic circumstances, the late Qing reformers and the early Republican revolutionaries increasingly looked to America to assist China in resisting further external territorial depredations and in reforming its national political institutions. American strategy, however, continued to be divided between higher political principle and basic commercial instincts. American liberal intellectuals, such as John Dewey, provided guidance on the formation of the new legislative and executive institutions of the fledgling Chinese republic. Despite such well-intentioned private interventions, the official American response to the needs of the emerging Chinese state ranged from ambivalence and indifference to outright hostility. US policies toward China were also influenced by questions of race. The Chinese Exclusion Act, passed by the US Congress in 1882 and made permanent in 1902, was an explicitly racist piece of legislation effectively banning further Chinese immigration to the United States on the grounds that their presence was seen as a "threat to the working conditions of the white man." Other federal and state acts that explicitly targeted Chinese immigrants followed. In reaction to both the Chinese Exclusion Act and anti-Chinese violence in the US, a large-scale movement to boycott American goods erupted across China in 1905.

When the US finally entered World War I in 1917, Washington prevailed on China's recently established Republican government to also declare war on Germany. As a result, Beijing dispatched hundreds of thousands of Chinese laborers to the western front to dig trenches, build field hospitals, deliver ammunition, and work in French factories to relieve the Allies' manpower shortages. Thousands of them lost their lives in the war. All this was on the understanding that the former German territories in the Chinese province of Shandong would be returned to China once the war was won.

After Germany was defeated, President Woodrow Wilson announced his Fourteen Points for the Paris Peace Conference and the postwar international order that was to follow, including the right for all peoples to self-determination. For doing so, he was heralded as China's hero across Chinese domestic public opinion. Chinese patriots believed their country would be able to recover Qingdao and other German-occupied parts of their country where local people had lived like second-class citizens. Chen Duxiu, dean of letters at Peking University, who went on to become a founder and first secretary-general of the Chinese Communist Party in 1921, described Wilson as "the number one good man in the world." Chinese university students were reportedly able to recite Wilson's Fourteen Points by heart. But when the "Big Three" met at Versailles (Wilson, British prime minister David Lloyd George, and French prime minister Georges Clemenceau), they rejected all of China's key demands—including the abolition of the unequal treaties, the ability to control its customs revenue rather than have the treaty powers collect it on China's behalf, and the return of Germany's possessions in Shandong. Back in China, America's betrayal triggered a wave of disillusionment, anger, and protest. The insult was made worse by Wilson's decision to cede the Shandong territories to the Japanese for fear that if the US alienated Japan, Tokyo might not join his prized creation, the League of Nations. (Japan had fought on the side of the Allies in the war and had preemptively occupied the German concessions.)

The decisions made in Paris immediately sparked widespread protests in China and radicalized Chinese politics. America's status, in the eyes of China's emerging political class, collapsed overnight from national savior to spineless hypocrite. Mao Zedong (1893–1976), who had been one of many young Chinese who had been initially inspired by Wilson's commitments to China, now described the United States and the other Western powers as a "bunch of robbers" who "cynically championed self-determination."

Had Woodrow Wilson stood up to Japan at Versailles, the twentieth-century history of China may have been significantly different.

Enter the Chinese Communist Party

A principal political beneficiary of the Versailles Treaty was the newly formed Bolshevik government in Moscow. Lenin refused to attend the peace conference or sign the treaty. The new Soviet government also unilaterally repudiated Russia's extraterritorial rights in China, automatically securing acclamation from all of China's newly emerging political parties. Chinese students protesting over the Paris treaty took to the streets in what became known as the May Fourth Movement—an intellectual watershed moment for Chinese politics, including the subsequent foundation of the Chinese Communist Party. Li Dazhao, who, along with Mao and Chen, became one of the first members of the CCP, commented that World War I was won by Lenin, Trotsky, and Marx rather than Woodrow Wilson. At the party's founding in Shanghai in July 1921, two members of the Kremlin's Comintern, dedicated to promoting world communism, were also in attendance.

By 1922, however, Moscow's representatives from the Comintern were providing financial and military assistance to both the ruling Nationalist Party (the *Kuomintang*, or KMT) and the CCP. The new republic was in danger. Warlords were carving up the country into personal military fiefdoms. Moscow insisted that the KMT include the Communists in the government in those parts of the country it controlled and helped establish a military academy for training both CCP and KMT forces so that they could jointly defeat the warlords and reunite the country.

An appeal by Sun Yat-sen, the first (provisional) president of the Republic of China, to President Warren Harding in 1921 to help save China's infant republic at "the most critical time of her existence," meanwhile, fell on deaf ears. Instead, Washington granted diplomatic recognition to a series of warlord commanders who controlled Beijing during the 1920s. Sun had previously supported America's democracy as a model for China's future political development. Now, he found himself with nowhere else to turn other than Moscow. Sun dispatched his deputy Chiang Kai-shek to lead a four-man military commission to Moscow to seek strategic support. Thus began what would become a one-hundred-year-long political competition between Moscow and Washington for influence over China's future domestic and foreign policy direction.

Over the next thirty years, between the Treaty of Versailles and the proclamation of the People's Republic in 1949, China's future was largely shaped by three great powers: Japan, the United States, and the Soviet Union. Japan's invasions of China in 1931 and 1937 rendered it effectively impossible for Chiang Kai-shek's KMT government to modernize the Chinese economy, bring about basic social reforms, or begin any transition to liberal-democratic institutions. In the meantime, the Soviet Union continued to nurture close political and operational relationships with both the KMT and the CCP. However, after 1927, when Chiang sought to eliminate the Communists, Moscow's support for the party during the course of the ensuing civil war eventually became complete. As for the United States, the KMT government looked to Washington as the only possible strategic counterweight against Japan on the one hand and the Soviet-backed CCP on the other.

Once again, however, the United States proved an unreliable ally. It was not until after the Japanese invasion of the Chinese far northeast, or Manchuria, in 1931 that the US finally agreed to an American "civilian mission" to help train the fledgling Chinese air force. Still, President Herbert Hoover reminded Americans that "Japan in Manchuria did not challenge the deep interests or values of the United States." Even following the full-scale Japanese invasion of China in 1937, US aid to the Republic of China continued to be unofficial—primarily in the form of the Flying Tigers, under the command of Claire Chennault, a retired US Army Air Corps officer who was an advisor to Chiang Kai-shek. However, US assistance fell short of Chiang Kai-shek's military and financial needs in dealing with the combined challenges of a Japanese invasion, continued predations by warlords, and a growing Communist insurgency.

In the end, fearing it risked outright war with Japan, the Roosevelt administration held back from offering official military support for Chiang despite professing sympathy for China. Indeed, until America's entry into the war in 1941, 80 percent of all foreign aid to China came from the Soviet Union. Even after Pearl Harbor, Roosevelt pursued a policy of Europe first, regarding China as a secondary theater of operations and, therefore, warranting no serious US troop presence. Although Republican China lost more than three million troops and eleven million civilians during their fourteen-year war against Japan, thereby pinning down the bulk of the Japanese army in the Asian theater in a rolling war of attrition across the Chinese mainland, the US refused to make any significant military deployments to China itself. Instead, the US focused on its maritime campaign, including its island-hopping strategy across the western Pacific, before destroying Hiroshima and Nagasaki with nuclear weapons in 1945 and finally bringing the war with Japan to an end.

The same equivocal American approach to the KMT continued after the war, when the Truman administration never effectively resolved the question of whether, and to what extent, the US would intervene to defend Chiang against Mao's resurgent Communists. The US extended a series of significant Treasury loans to a cash-strapped KMT government that was wrestling with postwar hyperinflation and a chronically unstable currency. But as soon as the war with Japan was over, Truman announced the ending of all military assistance to Chiang. Meanwhile, the Soviets were in the process of rearming Mao's forces and secretly relocating them to Manchuria in preparation for the final phase of the civil war against the KMT.

American postwar diplomacy, primarily through the Marshall Mission of 1945 to 1947 (when General George Marshall was dispatched to China by President Harry Truman to act as a mediator) focused on the fool's errand of trying to reconcile Nationalist and Communist forces in a democratic government of national unity supported by an integrated Chinese army under Chiang's control. The naivety of US policy was underlined when full-scale civil war erupted in the summer of 1946, by which time Communist forces, armed and equipped by the Soviets, were at full strength and about to begin their sweeping march south. US military and financial aid to the Nationalists resumed but was insufficient to make a material difference to the war's outcome. In Washington, the view of the State Department and others across the Truman administration was that the Nationalists were hopelessly corrupt and that a Communist victory would not necessarily be catastrophic to American interests. Mao had also assured the wide-eyed American journalists, to whom he granted carefully arranged interviews in the CCP's Yan'an stronghold, that he was not a Soviet proxy, that a Communist regime would be politically democratic and economically pragmatic, and that it would welcome continued US trade and investment. This included Edgar Snow, a pliant journalist whose best-selling 1937 book, *Red Star Over China*, had a strong impact on raising American opinion of the revolutionaries. US policy, therefore, fell between two stools: not materially supporting Chiang sufficiently to deliver victory over the CCP while sufficiently committing itself to Chiang, at least symbolically, to earn the enduring enmity of Mao and the Communists, who concluded that their only reliable ally was the Soviet Union.

The uncomfortable truth was that Mao had long seen the United States as no better than the other imperialist powers. According to Mao's writings as early as 1923, the Chinese people had "a superstitious faith in the United States," and Americans were "naïve people" who failed to understand that "America was actually the most murderous of hangmen." His reasons were the familiar ones—the US had failed to repeal the unequal treaties, had insisted on extraterritoriality for its nationals, and had been of negligible assistance in effectively confronting Japan's territorial ambitions. But Mao also recognized a second and much more lethal threat to Marxist ideology: the potential impact of American political ideals and ideas within China itself. First- and second-generation American missionaries had attracted millions of Chinese converts (far more than the Europeans had) and established hundreds of charitable institutions across the country to help the poor. Popular admiration of the efficient and uncorrupt American-trained advisors working across multiple branches of the KMT administration in Nanking was substantial. Above all, there was the continued popular appeal of the American democratic-capitalist model to Chinese political elites, notwithstanding the equivocal nature of US official support for China's national aspirations. This was reinforced by the still significant cohort of returning Chinese students from US academic institutions, many emboldened with new ideas on the transformation of China into a modern liberal state.

All of these, Mao concluded, were corrosive to CCP claims to comprehensive ideological legitimacy. In 1937, he wrote that American "liberalism is extremely harmful in a revolutionary collective. . . . It is an extremely bad tendency." Therefore, from its early years to the present, the Chinese Communist Party has seen the United States, uniquely among the Western democracies, as hostile to its ideological interests and a continuing challenge to its efforts to secure and sustain political power.

The United States and the People's Republic

Following the Communist victory in 1949, the next quarter century of the US-China relationship became its most acrimonious. For all its reservations about Chiang and the KMT, the US continued to support him after he fled with his army and supporters to Taiwan, determined to make the island his political and military base for "recovering the mainland." In the United States, the domestic political debate for the next decade was dominated by the Cold War, McCarthyism, and a viciously partisan fight between Republicans and Democrats over "who lost China." Meanwhile, Chinese domestic politics were driven by the convulsions of the Great Leap Forward, the Cultural Revolution, and Mao's doctrine of continuous revolution, which saw millions of deaths, social fracturing, and the near collapse of the Chinese economy.

Chiang's establishment of the Republic of China on Taiwan was a direct affront to Mao. But facing the considerable challenges of rebuilding a war-torn country and establishing an entirely new form of government there, Mao did not want to risk a general war with the United States. So when North Korean leader Kim Il-sung asked for his help in dislodging the Americans from South Korea, Mao gave conditional assent. He said he would come to North Korea's aid if the Americans crossed the thirty-eighth parallel. When they did, he sent hundreds of thousands of Chinese troops to fight them—but not as the People's Liberation Army. Instead, they were called "volunteers" so that the fledgling People's Republic would not have to officially declare war on the US.

While Chinese troops were fighting American forces in Korea, China's propaganda apparatus launched a "hate America" campaign on the home front to "cure three diseases: *kongmei bing* (the disease of fearing America), *chongmei bing* (the disease of worshiping America), and *meimei bing* (the disease of flattering America)." The party also used the campaign to discredit American-trained intellectuals who had stayed in China after 1949, requiring them to make public confessions of their ideological heresies while professing afresh their love for the party.

This demonization soon became mutual as American troop losses in Korea mounted, concerns over the brutal treatment of thousands of American POWs grew, and McCarthyism amplified the threat of the "yellow peril," the "red peril," and the domino theory of prospective Chinese domination of all East Asia. It was during this period that America developed its postwar alliance structure across the region, involving Australia and New Zealand (1951), Japan (1952), South Korea (1953), Taiwan (1954), the Philippines (1951), Thailand (1962), and South Vietnam (1956), as well as (modeled along NATO lines) the multilateral Manila Pact, or Southeast Asian Treaty Organization, of 1954. These polarizing years were also punctuated by multiple crises across the Taiwan Strait during which President Dwight Eisenhower repeatedly threatened China with nuclear annihilation. By the 1960s, the US-China relationship reached its historical low point, creating deep, scarifying, personal, and institutional memories on both sides of the Pacific with lasting resonances to this day.

Strategic enmity between the two nations continued until Richard Nixon and Henry Kissinger's "opening" to China in 1971, aided by Zhou Enlai's "ping-pong diplomacy" and Mao Zedong's positive response to it. This radical change in course was the product of a rapid deterioration in

Sino-Soviet relations over the previous decade, sparked by Nikita Khrushchev's 1956 denunciation of Joseph Stalin after the Soviet leader's death. This infuriated Mao, who considered Stalin (an early supporter of the CCP) "the greatest genius of the present age." More importantly, Mao saw Khrushchev's criticism of Stalin's dictatorial abuse of power and cult of personality as a potential threat to himself—particularly if his Chinese comrades ever became tempted to follow suit. Even as US-Soviet tensions reached a peak with the Cuban Missile Crisis, Sino-Soviet relations were rapidly deteriorating to the point of lethal military conflict on their shared border. While American schoolchildren were practicing duck-and-cover drills, citizens in Beijing and elsewhere were mobilized to dig vast networks of bomb shelters as China raced to test its own A-bomb—a defense not just against the Americans but also against the Soviets. Meanwhile, the withdrawal of Soviet economic aid and technical advisors in 1960 left China's industry and economy in increasingly desperate circumstances.

The opening to America was, therefore, in part a reaction to domestic political and economic developments within China itself, including the economic implosions of the Great Leap Forward and the Cultural Revolution (1966–1976), and in part a reaction to China's strategic exposure to the Soviet threat. Nonetheless, the normalization of US-China relations during the course of the 1970s had nothing to do with any Communist Party reappraisal of the virtues of American liberalism or Western democracy. These remained anathema to party orthodoxy. Instead, it reflected China's desperate financial and economic circumstances and a deeply pragmatic response to the withdrawal of Soviet economic aid and technical advisors, as well as the large-scale deployment of Soviet forces and escalating military clashes along the Sino-Soviet border.

In the United States, a parallel sense of pragmatic opportunity emerged. Following the "missile gap" debate of the 1960s and Soviet equivocation under Leonid Brezhnev on the desirability of strategic arms control negotiations with the US, Washington concluded that a political opening to Beijing would significantly advance a range of American strategic interests. Developments in Vietnam accelerated this process, as Nixon and Kissinger saw Beijing as a potential ally in permanently "freezing" the Vietnam conflict between north and south along the same lines that had been achieved in Korea. This would enable Nixon to bring about the withdrawal of American forces from a deeply unpopular war while achieving "peace with honor." Vietnam would also become a factor in Beijing's consideration of the advantages of full normalization with Washington in 1979, after the Soviet-backed regime in Hanoi unceremoniously removed the Beijing-backed Pol Pot regime in neighboring Cambodia in 1978, leading to a full-scale Sino-Vietnamese border war the following year.

Diplomatic Normalization

Diplomatic normalization between China and the United States was finally achieved in 1979, seven tortuous years after the negotiation of the Shanghai Communiqué of 1972. The main sticking point between the two nations was Taiwan—as, indeed, it has been ever since. The US insisted unsuccessfully that China renounce the use of force in any attempt to compel reunification with Taipei. At the same time, the US passed the Taiwan Relations Act, under which Washington would continue to provide military assistance to Taipei, an action that came close to derailing diplomatic recognition altogether. Taiwan aside, as a result of diplomatic normalization with the US, China had achieved its core strategic goals: a steady flow of military intelligence from Washington on Soviet and Vietnamese troop deployments; the sale of US and allied military hardware to the PLA; and Beijing ultimately being granted "most-favored nation status," which allowed China the same trading relationship with America as the latter had with its friends and allies around the world. Thus began China's decades-long march toward economic modernization—a process in which access to American technology, markets, and capital was fundamental. Playing the "China card" also strengthened Washington's negotiating hand with Moscow, causing the Soviet Union to soon begin long-delayed strategic arms control negotiations with the US.

But while this transition from a quarter century of strategic enmity to an embryonic strategic rapprochement between China and the United States was remarkable, the underlying expectations in each capital were radically different from the outset. The CCP saw its new relationship with Washington as a temporary arrangement until such time as the Soviet Union was no longer a threat to Chinese security and until China itself could build its national economic and, in time, military strength. On the other hand, over the years that followed, Washington nurtured much deeper aspirations that China's opening to the United States would presage the development of a massive new market for American exports and investment and that China's evolution into a market economy would eventually create the foundations for a more open, even liberal, society. In many respects, the seeds of the current crisis in US-China relations originated in these different expectations. To put it another way, from the outset, Beijing saw the relationship as a *transactional* one, as a means of enhancing China's national security and prosperity. Whereas Washington came to see it, at least in part, as *transformational*, carrying with it the deeper objective of changing the fundamental nature of Communist China itself.

Deng Xiaoping, Economic Reform, and the Road to Tiananmen

Mao may have begun the process of normalization, but by the time it happened in 1979, the CCP (and thus the PRC) was under the collective leadership of Deng Xiaoping. The age of "reform and opening the door to the outside world" was now well and truly underway. Deng had, in fact, been Mao's faithful lieutenant in the vicious purge of suspected capitalists and party critics in the 1958 antirightist campaign. So much so that Mao warned him to cool his ardor: "If we kill too many, we will forfeit public sympathy, and a shortage of labor power will arise." Yet after the Great Leap Forward caused three years of famine, Deng was part of a group of leaders who reintroduced small-scale markets and gave farmers the right to grow their own food—a crime for which he was eventually accused of being a capitalist roader during the Cultural Revolution. After his emergence as China's paramount leader after Mao's death, Deng brought back an even wider range of market-based reforms, transforming the Chinese economy in ways that left many in the West starry-eyed. Despite this, Deng never committed to any form of political liberalism. He had no qualms about suppressing the Democracy Wall movement of 1979–1980, sending its leaders off to lengthy prison sentences, presaging how he would act with overwhelming force in the violent suppression of hundreds of thousands of protesters in Tiananmen Square a decade later in June 1989.

Deng saw China's modernization not as any kind of political, let alone ideological, transformation but as a pragmatic economic move in the tradition of the various national self-strengthening movements from China's imperial past. While opposed to the political and economic chaos brought about by Mao's mass movements during the Great Leap Forward and the Cultural Revolution, Deng had no interest in any form of fundamental democratic reform. While Deng may not have seen the United States as a source of political reform, he did see it as a source of foreign trade, investment, technology, training, and modern financial and economic management. While not an orthodox Marxist, Deng remained a fully committed Leninist. Unsurprisingly, he was determined not to cede the party's political power for the sake of American economic engagement or common strategic endeavor against the Soviet Union. Even as he began his reform and opening campaign in 1979, he vowed from the outset adherence to the Four Cardinal Principles and that China would forever "uphold the dictatorship of the proletariat" and "the leadership of the Communist Party." In Deng's words, while it was important for China to "open the windows wide to breathe the fresh air," the party's responsibility was to continue to "swat away the flies and insects that came with it." For the party, that meant remaining ever vigilant against the importation of Western liberal-democratic ideas, ideals, and institutions.

The fact that most US administrations after Nixon did not see the relationship in the same brutally pragmatic terms as the CCP was not entirely naive. Indeed, it was broadly consistent with long-standing development theory that irrespective of what the party might want or say, market reforms would increase living standards and create, in time, a burgeoning middle class that would eventually demand a political voice of their own. According to this theory, over time, the resulting democratization of China would also cause Beijing to acquiesce, accept, and gradually become full participants in the overall fabric of the liberal international order led by the United States. At the outer reaches of this reasoning rested the view that if China eventually surpassed the United States in aggregate economic power, as the US had surpassed the UK a century before, this transition would again be peaceful because the shared values underpinning the global order would remain broadly constant.

The bilateral trade and investment relationship grew rapidly as Beijing imported advanced computer systems, aircraft, and automobiles from the US. China's economic transformation to become the world's factory was fueled by its access to a vast American consumer market and new sources of foreign direct investment. Military collaboration between Washington and Beijing reached its height during the 1980s, as American and Chinese forces worked together to arm the mujahideen in Afghanistan against the Soviet occupation. A joint listening station was also established near the Soviet border to help China monitor Soviet troop deployments. Indeed, the flow of American military hardware and intelligence steadily grew to assume the operational characteristics of a substantive strategic alliance.

However, in the decade following diplomatic normalization, the deep underlying tensions already at work across the wider fabric of the US-China relationship came to the surface. The political relationship during this period remained fraught as the Communist Party wrestled with the effects that the opening to America was having on Chinese students, intellectuals, and policy elites. Exposed to a wide range of heterodox ideas, many challenged various aspects of Marxist-Leninist orthodoxy and one-party rule, including in art, literature, and film. In 1983, Deng authorized a "campaign against spiritual pollution." Four years later, after the purge of leading reformist General Secretary Hu Yaobang, Deng launched another campaign against "bourgeois liberalization," culminating in the removal of Hu's replacement, Zhao Ziyang, just before Deng sent in the military to repress the Tiananmen protesters in 1989—a bloody crackdown that stunned the world and left Chinese citizens dead in the hundreds, if not thousands. I met both Hu and Zhao on a number of occasions during my time in the Australian Embassy in Beijing. Hu, despite having risen through the ranks of the Communist Youth League, had become a pioneering liberal reformer during the golden decade of Chinese reformist experimentation in the 1980s. Hu enjoyed the patronage and, importantly, the protection of Deng for nearly a decade against the powerful group of conservatives remaining in the party center. Like Deng, Hu was barely five feet tall. His native dialect was an almost impenetrable Hunanese, and he was a colorful, internationally active political live wire. We entertained him at the Australian Embassy before he embarked on one of his first visits abroad—to Australia. The embassy was overrun with official food tasters (an important legacy of both a Leninist and Confucian state) to ensure we were not about to poison the party's senior leadership over lunch.

Zhao, in the many meetings I observed with him, was just as personable as Hu but was a more conventional politician from central casting of Chinese mandarins and more seasoned in dealing with foreign barbarians such as ourselves. Both, however, eventually fell, having pushed the reformist envelope too far even for Deng's tastes, at a time when Deng still had to be mindful of the body of political opinion within the central leadership that was ever prepared to critique him from the left. Indeed, Tiananmen marked the end of China's first phase of reform, when, at least for a season, all things seemed possible under heaven.

Until Tiananmen, successive US administrations by and large tended to avert their gazes from Deng's politics and the enduring Leninist nature of the CCP. But even after 1989, American sanctions, to the extent they were applied, were only temporary. The larger consideration for the US was the continued strategic and economic relationship with Beijing, its continued utility against the Soviet Union, and an eternal American corporate optimism for the prospects of a burgeoning Chinese market.

Resolution of the Sino-Soviet Border Dispute

By the 1980s, however, one of the foundational pillars of the US-China relationship faltered. The ascent of Gorbachev in 1985; a final agreement on the Sino-Soviet border in 1989 after three hundred years of dispute, conflict, and war; and then the collapse of the Soviet Union in 1991 fundamentally changed China's strategic landscape. While politically and ideologically, the CCP was horrified at the domestic implosion of Soviet Communism without the Americans dropping a single bomb on Moscow, the Soviet collapse effectively eliminated Moscow as a long-term threat to Chinese national security. Importantly for this account, one of the principal strategic rationales for the normalization and development of US-China relations in the early 1970s disappeared, leaving little beyond mutual economic self-interest to take its place.

In fact, Beijing's rapprochement with Moscow began several years earlier, as the CCP leadership grew to fear excessive dependence on Washington, especially as it sought to modernize its military. US sanctions on China's export of nuclear and missile technologies to Iran, Pakistan, and North Korea incurred the wrath of a cash-strapped PLA interested in expanding its export income. Furthermore, as tensions eased between Beijing and Moscow after 1991, the Russians proved willing, once again, to become suppliers of advanced weaponry to their Chinese neighbors, thereby providing fresh orders for Russian armaments factories that were desperate for work.

Meanwhile, the strategic relationship between Washington and Beijing was reaching a breaking point. First, a crisis erupted in 1996, when China launched missiles into waters around Taiwan in an effort to discourage the democratic election of independence-minded candidates in the island's first direct democratic presidential election. This prompted the Clinton administration to dispatch two carrier battle groups to the Taiwan Strait as a demonstration of American political and military support for Taipei. Then, in 1999, amid the Balkan War, five US guided missiles struck the Chinese Embassy in Belgrade, killing three Chinese journalists. Washington claimed it was an accident, but neither the outraged Chinese leadership nor the public ever accepted the explanation and to this day continue to strongly believe that the attack was deliberate. By the end of the 1990s, the US-China strategic relationship was beginning to nosedive.

At the same time, Moscow's post–Cold War relationship with the US was unravelling, as the Russian economy lurched from crisis to crisis during its "cold turkey" experiment with American capitalism. As various of its former republics applied for NATO membership, Russia's strategic interests were also being shredded through the dismemberment of what it had for decades seen as its imperial territory. These concerns were validated from Moscow's perspective with NATO's military intervention in the Balkans in the 1990s, as the Russians had long considered the region within their sphere of geopolitical influence.

The gradual strategic realignment that followed had a profound impact over time on the future trajectory of the US-China relationship. The CCP concluded, under Jiang Zemin, Hu Jintao, and then most decisively under Xi Jinping, that China now had more in common with Russia than the United States, even if US investment and trade, along with the education of China's future elite in American universities, remained critical to China's economic prospects.

From Tiananmen to WTO Membership

Despite growing concerns by the American public, the administrations of both George H. W. Bush and Bill Clinton ultimately pushed human rights concerns to the side after Tiananmen to promote America's growing trade and investment relationship with China. Both administrations overtly justified this course of action by insisting, despite the evidence of Tiananmen, that Chinese economic reform, development, and prosperity would lead to political reform. America's business community, which viewed its growing presence in the massive Chinese market as an unparalleled opportunity, advocated in favor of this view and helped provide the necessary political and economic ballast to restabilize a rocky post-Tiananmen relationship.

Three years after Tiananmen, Deng Xiaoping feared that the political hard-liners he had gathered around him to deal with the "bourgeois liberal" threat to party power in 1989 were also moving to throttle any further market-based reforms in the economy. They demanded to know whether the party's watchword was *socialism* or *capitalism*. In response, Deng, at the ripe old age of eighty-seven, embarked on what Chinese historians now refer to as his Southern Inspection Tour (a term once used to describe travels by the emperor to China's south). Visiting the special economic zones that were the crucibles of reform, as well as cities such as Shanghai, he declared that as long as the party was looking after the people's well-being, it was still surnamed socialist. But Deng said that no Chinese leader should remain in power unless they supported faster economic reform, opening, and development, at which point a number of conservatives were effectively removed from the ranks of the central leadership. Following his lead, General Secretary Jiang Zemin and his premier Zhu Rongji embarked on an ambitious new program to expand what they called a socialist market economy. Chinese entrepreneurs were told to build their own companies and go out beyond the country's borders. And in a supreme act of political pragmatism, they even invited those who had made it rich through entrepreneurship and the business of capitalism, both at home and abroad, to join the Communist Party itself.

Over the years, I met both Jiang and Zhu in China and in Australia. Jiang first visited our fair country while I was still a foreign ministry official (by this time I was back in Australia) and Jiang was first party secretary in Shanghai (1987–1989). He later took over from Zhao Ziyang after the latter was purged following Tiananmen. Jiang was larger than life and loved to demonstrate his understanding of the wider world and his knowledge of English. I remember him being taken to the Sydney Opera House at his request, where he asked if he could sing from the stage, albeit before an empty house. The entourage, both Australian and Chinese, dutifully applauded. Most importantly, the leader had fun in a way that we could never imagine either of his successors as party general-secretary, Hu Jintao or Xi Jinping, doing.

Zhu Rongji, like Zhao Ziyang in the past, was cut from a more conservative cloth—and as a founding dean of the school of economics and management at China's prestigious Tsinghua University, he was decidedly professorial in tone. I first met him in May 1989, when he was mayor of Shanghai. He was in the midst of a political crisis managing the pro-democratic student uprisings in his city and was determined to avoid the blood that would soon be shed in Beijing. Zhu was pale and drawn but unflappable. He still insisted on honoring his commitments to meet with our delegation, not least because we were there for the official launch of the Pudong Development District, which was then little more than a swamp on the other side of the Huangpu River across from the Bund. He took me to the window of the Peace Hotel, and as we looked across the river to the wasteland opposite, he told me this would soon rival the Manhattan skyline. I thought he was smoking something, but he proved to be right. He reminded me of this three years later when he visited my hometown of Brisbane, Australia (where, by that point, I was the state premier's chief of staff), and Zhu had risen to become vice premier of China. What animated him was what made economies tick, and Shanghai had already begun to boom.

These were still heady days in China's economic reform project, even if Tiananmen had spelled the end of meaningful political reform for a generation. Discerning these signals, the Clinton administration began a long negotiation with China, which culminated in their eventual admission to the World Trade Organization (WTO) in 2001, greatly opening up global markets to Chinese exports and fueling a further explosion in Chinese manufacturing. At the same time, as Chinese state-owned enterprises and private firms listed on domestic and foreign exchanges, American and European financial institutions started opening global capital markets to China, providing Chinese firms with the capital needed to expand quickly. These twin developments turbocharged China's economic growth, reduced poverty, and raised living standards for average Chinese families (Chinese GDP per capita, which was around $600 in 1995, nearly tripled to $1,750 in 2005). In doing so, they helped rebuild the party's economic credibility and popular legitimacy after the dark events of 1989 and the earlier ravages of the Cultural Revolution.

The net result of China's entry into the WTO and unprecedented access to global markets, coupled with its currency's deeply advantageous fixed exchange rate, was that over the next decade and a half, China became the world's leading manufacturing power, as factories relocated to the country from many advanced economies, including the US. This led to China also becoming the world's largest trading country and the world's second-largest destination for global foreign direct investment. It set the scene for the decline of American industry and the rise of populist resentment against globalization in general—and China in particular.

Throughout this process of deep economic transformation, China exhibited little interest in any form of fundamental political liberalization beyond some half-hearted experiments in localized "village democracy." From Beijing's perspective, it turned out that you could raise up a middle class and a market economy without sparking too much demand for Western-style democracy. But to make doubly sure there would be no repetitions of 1989, Jiang Zemin launched a patriotic education campaign in the early 1990s to reassert political orthodoxy and warn the next generation of Western-educated Chinese professionals of the ideological dangers posed by Western values. The campaign reminded them to never forget China's "national humiliation" by Japan and the West, and in particular the US, during a century of colonial occupation. Picking up where the 1980s campaigns against "spiritual pollution" and "bourgeois liberalization" left off, Jiang's program also specifically warned the party that unless it was careful in the domestic presentation of contemporary Chinese history, China could also fall victim to "the peaceful evolution plot of international hostile powers." In fact, the more that American political leaders emphasized the linkage between economic development and political reform in China, the more Chinese political leaders cited this as proof and pushed back in precisely the reverse direction.

In 1994, the Clinton administration explicitly decoupled human rights progress in China from an annual congressional vote on its most-favored-nation treatment of China in US trade policy (meaning it would receive the lowest tariffs the US had to offer). Several years later, Clinton also abandoned annual efforts to push through a resolution critical of China's human rights performance at the UN Human Rights Commission in

Geneva. In exchange, China agreed to sign the International Covenant on Civil and Political Rights, which guarantees citizens freedom of speech, religion, assembly, electoral rights, and due process, among other provisions. However, Beijing later refused to ratify its commitment, and the US failed to take any action as a result. The CCP's indifference to the principles of the international covenant was further underlined by the arrest in 2009 of "Charter 08" democracy activists (including future Nobel Peace Prize laureate Liu Xiaobo) who had modeled their effort on the Czech dissidents who launched the Prague Spring of 1968.

George W. Bush, 9/11, and Iraq

In its earliest years, the George W. Bush administration promised a fundamental rethink of the future of the US-China relationship. The new president identified Beijing as a significant emerging threat to American and allied interests in Asia. But Bush's stated resolve to harden America's China strategy was soon derailed by two events within the first nine months of his administration.

In April 2001, a Chinese fighter jet flying at 22,500 feet closed within ten feet of a USAF EP3 reconnaissance aircraft, resulting in a midair collision. The Chinese jet crashed, killing its pilot, while the Americans made an emergency landing at a Chinese airbase on Hainan Island, near the South China Sea. Both aircraft had been in international airspace, but Beijing exploited the spy flight incident to maximum effect, defining itself as the victim of American aggression. In exchange for releasing the plane's crew, Jiang extracted from Washington the so-called letter of the two apologies, stating that the United States was "very sorry" for the death of the Chinese pilot and "very sorry" for the American aircraft having entered Chinese airspace to land without verbal clearance. Meanwhile, the Chinese extracted a treasure trove of technological and intelligence data from the damaged aircraft.

The second, and far more significant, development was the September 11, 2001, terrorist attacks on New York and Washington, which led to the longest large-scale military operation in American history. The American and allied invasion and occupation of Afghanistan was supported by a UN Security Council resolution that was backed by both China and Russia. But when President Bush broadened his "War on Terror" to include the disastrous invasion of Iraq in 2003, Beijing was not among his supporters. What's more, the political, military, and financial costs of these wars were a strategic and foreign policy boon to China. They damaged American global prestige, sapped American strategic self-confidence, and divided American public opinion and its allies. Most importantly, they kept Bush preoccupied for the duration of his administration with the Middle East, even as China flexed its regional and global strategic muscles in a manner that had not been possible before.

Much later, as the leader of the opposition in the House of Representatives and then prime minister, I spoke to Bush about his handling of China during his presidency. Bush told me the China relationship had been difficult during his time in office but that China had been helpful in building a united front against Al Qaeda's global operations. When we had first met in Sydney during an Asia Pacific Economic Cooperation (APEC) summit, and when his best buddy, then conservative Prime Minister John Howard, was my bitter opponent in the 2007 Australian national elections, Bush had not exactly been entirely warm and friendly toward me. Howard had backed him in the Iraq War, whereas I had opposed the war from the get-go. I handed Bush a few tomes on Chinese politics and foreign policy as my "welcome to Australia" gift, which at least opened a conversation with him on China's rise—and whether it would be benign.

When I visited Washington the following year as prime minster (on an around-the-world trip that later took me to Beijing), we spent most of our time on China, after I congratulated him on his handling of a potentially dangerous period in the relationship. The Taiwanese president at the time, Chen Shui-bian, had repeatedly flirted publicly with the idea of an independent Republic of Taiwan—an act that would likely have triggered war with Beijing. Bush adjusted US policy in a manner that sent a clear message to Chen that if he continued to play with fire, the Eighty-Second

Airborne would not necessarily come running to the rescue. Chen got the message. Bush, backed by his national security advisor, Steve Hadley, had handled a difficult set of Taiwan problems well.

It was the first of many, many conversations over the years on China with US presidents, vice presidents, secretaries of state and defense, and US trade representatives throughout the Bush, Obama, and Biden White Houses. The exception was the alternative universe of Trump—although as president of the Asia Society Policy Institute in New York, I was able to strike up a good, respectful, and professional relationship with Trump's USTR, Bob Lighthizer, who was usually a voice of quiet reason in the midst of the chaos.

The Global Financial Crisis

The worldwide financial crisis of 2008–2009 and the global recession that followed had an even more profound effect on Chinese strategic thinking. For decades, China's leadership had been deeply respectful of American military, economic, and technological power. But thirty years later, as the scale of the economic carnage wrought by the structural weaknesses of America's financial system in the 2008 crisis became apparent, a less reverent perspective emerged in Beijing. Not only was there the fact that the crisis was born and incubated in the US, but also, for the first time, the world needed economic solutions that were beyond America's ability to provide alone. Instead, as a member of the G20, China was sharing the world stage as an engine of global economic recovery. When I attended the first leader-level meeting of the G20 in 2008 as Australian prime minister alongside other leaders, including Chinese president Hu Jintao, it was clear how significantly the center of global economic gravity was shifting. China had finally arrived at the top table of global affairs, recognizing the strength and size of its economy and the success of the reform program that had produced it.

However, Chinese financial and economic technocrats, who had been trained in the United States and diligently sought to apply the principles of the American model back home, were challenged by their more conservative colleagues within China over how the Americans could have allowed such a crisis to occur. As then–Vice Premier Wang Qishan famously observed to then–US Treasury Secretary Hank Paulson, "You were my teacher, but . . . look at your system, Hank. We aren't sure we should be learning from you anymore."

China had already been prepped for this reappraisal a decade earlier by the Asian Financial Crisis of 1997, in which a series of currency and credit crises devastated economies across Asia. Chinese thinking was affected by the impact of laissez-faire, free-market, antistate approaches adopted by the International Monetary Fund (IMF) under the so-called Washington Consensus on the developing countries of East and Southeast Asia (including, in Indonesia's case, triggering the toppling of the Suharto regime). In 1998, Beijing proposed what became known as the Chiang Mai Initiative (CMIM), a network of bilateral currency support agreements between the ten member states of the Association of Southeast Asian Nations (ASEAN), together with China, Japan, and South Korea. This would help them avoid the harsh budgetary austerity measures demanded by the American-driven IMF as a prerequisite for help in stabilizing their currencies and their capital accounts. At about this time, China also became more proactive in regional foreign policy initiatives when it successfully established the "ASEAN+3" (with Japan and South Korea) as a grouping that excluded the United States.

None of this meant that China was immediately abandoning the preexisting American-led order, anchored in the UN and the Bretton Woods institutions, such as the World Bank. Far from it. In fact, China played a more active role in these long-standing institutions that had been created as part of the post–World War II settlement. China, for example, already had a privileged position on the UN Security Council as one of its five permanent members armed with the power of a veto and was in no rush to surrender it. But the Chinese also looked outside this framework where opportunities arose and quietly built the elements of a more Sino-centric order within its immediate region.

The question of China's future role within the global rules-based order was brought to a head in a 2005 speech by US deputy secretary of state Robert Zoellick, which framed the question of whether China intended to become what he described as a "responsible stakeholder" in the existing international order or simply remain a free rider on an international system sustained by the United States and its principal allies. The speech infuriated hard-liners in Beijing, but it gained attention around the world for what seemed to be its conceptual clarity on the choice facing China.

The CCP's operational response to Zoellick's challenge was selective. In effect, the position they took was that China would become a more active stakeholder in the existing order where it so chose, but it would also start building the elements of a new, more China-friendly order when opportunities to do so presented themselves. This latter ambition would be reflected not only in the continuation of the Chiang Mai Initiative but also in a range of new multilateral institutions and initiatives set up by Beijing in the decades that followed. This included new regional development banks and, most spectacularly, the Belt and Road Initiative launched in 2013.

The great inflection point in this long, evolving process of China's growing international self-confidence was the Beijing Olympics of 2008. Its spectacular opening ceremony was interpreted around the world and within China itself as the People's Republic's global coming-out party. The estimated $43 billion sum the Chinese government put into hosting the games was only part of the enormous Chinese investment in projecting a positive image. Decades of effort had been made in preparing its athletes to shine on the global stage, and China's one hundred medals (forty-eight of them gold) were the country's highest total since it began competing in the Olympics—seemingly another signal of China's growing self-confidence in its ascent. I attended the opening ceremony with George W. Bush and a gaggle of global leaders. As a Sinologist, I found it fascinating: the visual collage of Chinese traditional civilization and culture, with not a single reference to Mao, the Communist Party, or the People's Republic. The intended impression for the world was civilizational continuity, with the current Communist leadership simply forming yet another dynasty of the eighty-three dynasties that had preceded it. The opening ceremony mysteriously forgot to mention that Mao, as a Leninist iconoclast, did his best on several occasions to destroy the symbols and substance of China's physical culture across multiple campaigns in a manner that no previous emperor had attempted since Qin Shi Huang in the third century BCE. The ceremony was nonetheless a stunning public relations success for the party and the country. I said as much to Premier Wen Jiabao over lunch the following day, when I was seated next to him at the Great Hall at a gathering of all visiting heads of state and government. China had formally, and with great fanfare, entered the world stage. And it was all planned as such.

Obama, the "G2," and a New Type of Great Power Relationship

It was this increasingly self-confident China that greeted the Obama administration when it came into office in 2008. Unlike Ronald Reagan, George H. W. Bush, Bill Clinton, and George W. Bush, Obama chose not to engage in bellicose rhetoric against Beijing during his election campaign. This was, in part, a reflection of his cautious intellectual temperament, but it was also because his foreign policy team had seen what happened with previously successful presidential candidates: after attacking their predecessors for being weak on China, an inevitable chill in the bilateral relationship followed, after which the winner would discover that he, too, would have to eat humble pie and justify to the American public a reopening of a line of communication with Beijing. Obama's more moderate language during his 2008 campaign also reflected a realization that the presidential election would be fought almost exclusively on economic grounds given the global financial crisis, and China's economy would be an important source of global growth that was essential for the global economic recovery. To the extent the foreign policy debate mattered at all, it was largely constrained to the American quagmire in the Middle East. As a result, Obama, by and large, left China alone in the 2008 campaign.

Once president, Obama tried to work with Beijing in areas that mattered to his administration: namely, North Korean and Iranian nuclear proliferation, G20 collaboration on the stabilization of international financial markets, restoring growth to the global economy, and multilateral action on climate change. Obama's senior China advisor, Jeffrey Bader, sought to define the administration's strategy during this period as resting on three broad principles: China should not be defined as an inevitable American adversary (although Bader conceded that could turn out to be the case) but as a potential partner in resolving critical global challenges. China's rise should be respected on the condition that it conformed with the rules, norms, and institutions of the existing international order on security, the economy, and climate. And China's rise should not threaten the security or sovereignty of US friends and allies or the stability of the wider Asia-Pacific region.

Despite expected friction over Taiwan and human rights in Tibet, by and large the relationship developed smoothly during the first few years of the Obama administration, including reasonable progress on the president's core policy priorities. Obama persuaded Hu Jintao to join multilateral action against Iran. He had much less success with the Chinese on North Korea, however. China did little to rein in Pyongyang, despite a series of highly provocative acts by the North, including a 2009 public declaration of a uranium-enrichment program, the sinking of a South Korean naval frigate, and lethal artillery bombardment of a South Korean island. China also collaborated closely with the US and its allies in implementing the full range of fiscal, monetary, and regulatory measures necessary to stabilize financial markets and the global economy following the global financial crisis, although China continued to resist American pressure on the management of its still artificially low exchange rate.

There was a reciprocal dimension to the relationship during this period as well—namely, an American preparedness to accept the political legitimacy of China's Communist Party state. This was no small matter. It was deeply important to Chinese leaders, given long-standing American and international reservations about the ultimate legitimacy of a revolutionary party that maintained power through armed force. Validation was also important domestically, where the CCP leadership faced a growing civil society movement that increasingly raised questions about how long a modernizing country should be governed by a single party with a stranglehold on all political power. International recognition of China's national achievements and, as a result, the inherent legitimacy of its political system is an enduring core interest of the Chinese party-state.

Meanwhile, in an effort to give effect to the new breadth of the strategic relationship, the Obama administration recommended, and his Chinese counterpart Hu Jintao accepted, a proposal to enhance the existing bilateral machinery of the relationship established under the G. W. Bush administration through the Strategic Economic Dialogue (SED). This was to become a twice-annual meeting to discuss economic issues and was soon expanded to become the Strategic *and* Economic Dialogue, led by the US secretaries of state and treasury and their Chinese counterparts. The inclusion of a formal political and security agenda that, for the first time, incorporated senior representation from each side's military was an important breakthrough. Though still more talk than action, the idea of a comprehensive partnership embracing all elements of the relationship, including the most contentious, was taking shape.

These changes gave rise to a public discussion among policy analysts in the United States on the desirability of developing what came to be described as a "G2" relationship between the world's two largest economies. The idea had first been conceived back in 2004–2005. Indeed, US Treasury secretary Paulson had said in 2006 that he saw the SED as "sort of like the G2." Three years later, former national security advisor Zbigniew Brzezinski, who advised Obama during the 2008 campaign, went further. In a January 2009 speech marking the thirtieth anniversary of the establishment of diplomatic relations between China and the United States, Brzezinski called for the "G2" to become the conceptual framework for US-China relations and the cornerstone of US foreign policy more generally. He described this as "a mission worthy of the two countries with the most extraordinary potential for shaping our collective future." Robert Zoellick, the president of the World Bank, chimed in, suggesting that "without a strong G2, the G20 will disappoint." In retrospect, these calls for a fundamentally new and constructive strategic framework for the relationship were remarkable.

Beijing responded negatively to the idea. Its foreign policy elite was concerned the whole concept was incompatible with Beijing's decades-long advocacy of multipolarity as the preferred form of global governance. Moreover, China's leaders felt the costs would be too high in terms of diminished foreign policy flexibility, along with domestic political and ideological complications in explaining how China was unable to run the world except as America's junior partner. Flattering as they may have found the American entreaties, in the CCP's view, it was far better to continue to grow China's economy, modernize its military, and remain selective in its international engagements in order to steadily improve China's comprehensive national power (a core analytical term in internal Chinese strategic deliberations) as measured against that of the United States. Besides, by this time, many Chinese policy analysts accepted the argument that America was in a process of national economic and military decline. Therefore, what China required, above all, was continued strategic patience. This view, in turn, conformed with many deep learnings from classical Chinese thinking about how national power was best secured (i.e., unobtrusively) and when and under what circumstances it should be actively deployed (i.e., only when powerful enough that victory was assured).

However, in the last year of Hu Jintao's leadership in 2012, Beijing proposed its vision of a "G2"-flavored world order, which it called a "new type of great power relations." Deliberately imprecise, the idea was to delay what was seen by Chinese strategists as the inevitability of renewed great power rivalry and conflict with the United States until China was fully equipped to deal with it and, if necessary, prevail. This framework explicitly ruled out the possibility of future Chinese or American military conflict, a proposal that, if taken seriously, would have fundamentally strengthened

China's strategic hand for decades to come, while Washington would endure as the dominant military power. China argued that "a new type of great power relations" was technically applicable to all "great power" relationships, carefully avoiding naming which countries were in or out of contention for that title in order to avoid offending any of them (in particular the Russians). However, the message was clear: in this vision, China and the US would coexist as explicit equals.

Chinese diplomats went into overdrive, seeking to secure American acceptance of this new framework, although Washington's level of enthusiasm for the idea of a US-China "condominium," as Henry Kissinger put it, ranged from lukewarm to ambivalent to outright hostile. China's intransigence at the Copenhagen Climate Summit in December 2009 had left a deeply negative impression on Obama as to how far China was prepared to go in cooperating with America to address the challenges of global governance. His administration was also mindful of the likely reactions at home, including by his Republican party critics, not to mention the European and Asian allies of the US, who feared the prospect of being left behind by an exclusive Washington-Beijing grand accommodation.

Nonetheless, it remains an open question as to whether in these middle years of the Obama administration, covering the latter years of Hu Jintao and the early period of Xi Jinping, it might have been possible to find at least some new level of strategic convergence between these two fundamentally different Chinese and American worldviews. Instead, it seemed as though the two sides ended up talking past each other. But however small or large those possibilities may have been for a time, the political window for reaching any such agreement closed as soon as new tensions unfolded in and around the South China Sea.

Obama's Pivot Points

In 2010, security analysts detected manifestations of a more assertive, and at times more confrontational, approach on the part of the Chinese in their response to the movement of US naval surveillance ships and aircraft in the South China Sea. China argued that it would no longer tolerate foreign naval vessels operating in international waters lying within its two-hundred-nautical-mile exclusive economic zone (an area granted by international law to waters surrounding sovereign territory, in which a country has rights to resources but no right to impede the passage of ships or aircraft) without express permission. This contravened the UN Convention on the Law of the Sea (UNCLOS), to which the PRC was an original signatory and which it ratified in 1996 (and which the US has not).

China has long laid claim to the entire South China Sea based on the so-called nine-dash line (a map that showed the whole of the sea marked as an addition to Chinese territory by enclosing it in nine hand-drawn dashes, first issued by the Nationalists back in 1947). This includes all of the land features, some currently controlled by other claimants, such as the Philippines and Vietnam, that lie within the sea—a vital waterway through which approximately one-third of global shipping passes. It appeared to the US that Beijing was effectively trying to turn the open seas into a de facto Chinese lake. ASEAN also reported increasing Chinese forcefulness when encountering fishing and naval vessels from various ASEAN member states seeking to utilize the disputed waters. China's state councilor for foreign affairs privately warned the Americans that China now saw the South China Sea as part of its "core interests."

These developments occurred at a time when the tone of China's official and semiofficial commentary on the United States also changed. Articles appeared with increasing frequency in the Chinese media highlighting America's decline as a global superpower, pointing to the destruction of its economy as a result of the self-inflicted wounds of the global financial crisis and the political, economic, and foreign policy cost of its now decade-long military engagements in the wider Middle East. A theory of American declinism took hold in large parts of China's internal foreign policy debate, and nationalist commentators predicted the end of the American century, some arguing that China's time had arrived. In June 2010, the Chinese foreign minister exploded at an ASEAN regional forum meeting following a speech by US secretary of state Hillary Clinton. He angrily warned the ASEAN states against forming an anti-Chinese cabal organized by an outside power and pointedly reminded them that "China is a big country, and other countries are small countries, and that is just a fact."

The next year, the Obama administration developed what became known as his "pivot to Asia." It had three main tenets. First, the US would deploy a majority of its naval, air force, and marine assets to the Pacific theater, moving some forces from Europe and the Middle East. This was intended as a direct response to the rapid modernization of the PLA's capabilities and to its new military doctrine of air-sea denial targeting US forces in and around China's "near seas." Second, the Obama administration would seek to strengthen its military alliances and strategic partnerships with Japan, Korea, Australia, Singapore, Vietnam, and India. Third, the military dimensions of this strategy would be reinforced by a major new pan-regional free trade initiative that, in time, came to be called the Trans-Pacific Partnership (TPP), which aimed to link twelve Asian-Pacific economies but pointedly excluded China. Since more than one-third of total global trade was with the TPP economies, Chinese leaders realized this strategy was designed to squeeze it out of these markets and impede its participation in the future development of global supply chains. It was, they concluded, an elemental threat to its national economic interests and future prosperity and power, which relied on the rapidly emerging markets of the Indo-Pacific region.

The Pivot and the TPP, and China's public hostility to them, once again transformed the US-China relationship. The US continued to engage the Chinese leadership on common questions of global governance (from economic management to climate change), but at a regional level, it drew a line in the sand. US secretary of state Hillary Clinton spent more time in Asia than any of her predecessors, carrying the message that America had no intention of leaving the region to China.

Beijing's retaliation was not limited to the US. Following Tokyo's decision to "nationalize" the disputed uninhabited islands in the East China Sea known as the Senkaku to the Japanese and the Diaoyu Dao to the Chinese, it placed its relationship with Japan in a deep freeze for the next seven years. Australia's choice to increase the size and frequency of US marine deployments in Darwin also invited a sustained political and diplomatic offensive from Beijing. Meanwhile, Singapore's decision to allow American helicopter carriers a home port resulted in a deep deterioration in the city-state's relationship with Beijing, until Prime Minister Lee Hsien-Loong negotiated a rapprochement with the Chinese leadership in 2018.

By 2012, China could no longer operate largely unhindered as a result of a distracted America saddled with a declining economy. Instead, analysts in Beijing identified a worrying hardening of political attitudes and strategic postures toward China, both in the US and across the region. It was into this context that a confident, self-assured, and instinctively assertive Xi Jinping rose to take over leadership of China. He also changed the course of China's strategic relationship with the United States forever.

The purpose of this chapter is to make plain that the current state of the US-China relationship is the product of a long, complex, and contested history. This history has created the conditions that now prevail between Beijing and Washington, including the narrowing of the balance of power between them. More importantly, it has shaped the deep perceptions, frustrated expectations, and underlying animosities of each country's political elite toward the other.

At its core, the CCP has seen the US as representing a worldview hostile to its own. Since the 1920s, the CCP has railed against the fundamental ideological divide between the two worldviews: liberal capitalism and the international order (including the human rights order) that America constructed to serve it versus Marxism-Leninism, across all its Chinese iterations since the party's founding in 1921, and the concept of a revolutionary socialist party that had no qualms about obtaining and sustaining political power through the barrel of a gun—either against counterrevolutionaries at home or imperialists (a.k.a. America) abroad. Thus it is not just a question of political and ideological preference on the CCP's part. Its hostility to the American ideal—from John Dewey's influence on the early Chinese Republic, through Tiananmen, to the crackdown on Protestant Christianity under Xi Jinping—has been grounded in the view that the American concept of freedom represents a continuing existential threat to the political legitimacy of the party within China itself. This is particularly the case now that Chinese incomes have risen so much as a result of the CCP successfully adapting the Western capitalist model over the last forty years, breathing life into an otherwise moribund Chinese economy. The CCP sees "bourgeois liberalism" as more of a threat today than at any time in its history, with the single exception of the tumultuous events of 1989. That is why ideology remains at the core of the US-China divide.

If ideology has been one major factor in defining this divide, race has been the other. With race comes the wider question of ethno-nationalism and Chinese revulsion (extending beyond the ranks of the CCP) at acts and attitudes of Western political and cultural condescension toward China over the centuries. To a large extent, this exists across much of the postwar colonial world, but in China's case, there is a view that they are now in a position to do something about it. So when Xi Jinping talks about the historical inevitability of "the rise of the East and the decline of the West," he is not just advancing the tired arguments of Marxist historical materialism and the self-destructionism inherent in a liberal-capitalist model. He is much more fundamentally making a point about Chinese culture, race, and nationalism, which is infinitely more unifying for the 1.3 billion Chinese people who are *not* members of the CCP. The Chinese people, whatever their politics, feel a collective pride about the return of China to a central place in the global order—one commensurate with its civilizational longevity, cultural depth, and sheer size.

It's for these reasons that I have described Xi's worldview as "Marxist-Nationalist," because while his appeal to the party remains ideological (not least because ideology is the backbone of Leninist discipline), his appeal to the people is assiduously nationalist. That is why Xi Jinping Thought is not, as Xi would have us believe, a new theoretical revision of the deepest precepts of Marxism-Leninism. Rather, it is a skillfully constructed primer that brings together an emotionally appealing, focus group–tested set of precepts, axioms, and anecdotes. It is an amalgam of simplified ideology and reified nationalism, which, when combined, represent an appeal to the mind and heart, respectively, with the latter aiming to bring forward the collective consciousness of an ancient people to the politics of the present. In that sense, it is potentially much more potent a nationally mobilizing force than Mao Zedong Thought was half a century ago.

Ideology and nationalism have long been powerful forces in national and global politics. But so too are economics and the basic living standards of the people. This has also been an enduring theme in the history of the US-China relationship. This will be explored in greater depth in chapters 4 and 6. But for our purposes here, it is important to understand the creative interplay among ideology, nationalism, and economic prosperity as contending, or perhaps mutually reinforcing, sources of domestic political legitimacy for the CCP. Historically, the party despised the West's economic exploitation of China and the rest of the developing world. But as a ruling party, it discovered that state socialism, as defined by Mao and the ideologists who consistently preferred class struggle over economic development, had left China impoverished and insolvent by the end of the Cultural Revolution. Deng had to turn to a capitalist model at home and liberal-capitalist order abroad to secure his country's economic salvation. This faith dimmed greatly following the global financial crisis in 2008 and then China's domestic financial crisis in 2015, after which collective faith in the Western development model eroded considerably. But it is an open question whether Xi Jinping's return to a revised form of state capitalism will continue to bring home the bacon or if what others have described as "the return of the state" and the emergence of a new "CCP Inc." under Xi's "New Development Concept," in fact, undermines economic growth and impairs rising living standards moving forward. At this stage, we don't yet know because the change in China's development model has been relatively recent. But across the three pillars of political legitimacy that have permeated the debates about the CCP's role in Chinese national politics over the last century (Marxism-Leninism, nationalism, and economic prosperity), the latter has been the most difficult of all to get right and the easiest to get wrong.

It remains to be examined, as we will in the next chapter, how these three enduring themes in the complex history of the US-China relationship continue to permeate the deeply held views, usually unstated, that each country's political elite have about the other and how these perceptions continue to shape each side's policy and behavior toward the other today.

2

★ ★ ★ ★ ★

The Problem of Distrust

Before examining more closely the defining characteristics of Xi Jinping's China and post-Trump America, it's important to look more deeply at enduring views from both sides of the ideological and cultural divide. Understanding these is no easy thing. As noted in the previous chapter, it is made more difficult because there is little, if any, shared Sino-American historiography on the evolution of their relationship. This interpretive task is made even more problematic because the CCP places absolute priority on continuing official secrecy as part of its ongoing statecraft. So while it may be impossible to conclude with confidence that Beijing thinks X or that the established consensus in Washington is Y by pointing to an official document as our definitive proof, it is nonetheless useful to probe these unstated but still potent dimensions of this most difficult of relationships.

The View from Beijing

Americans typically believe that their country's approach to China has been driven by high ideals in defense of democracy, free trade, and the integrity of the global rules-based order. But the broad Chinese view is that American strategy is nothing more than the prosecution of its core national interests. To pretend otherwise, in China's view, is political hypocrisy. Moreover, as seen from Beijing, American strategy is rarely if ever cognizant—let alone respectful—of China's national aspirations. In China's perspective, this is reflected in 150 years of US commercial efforts to penetrate China's vast domestic market—from the age of opium to the age of Apple. It sees it in the history of US national security strategy. First, handing over Chinese territory to appease Japan after World War I. Then, using the protracted Japanese occupation of China during World War II to keep the bulk of Japanese imperial forces bogged down for the duration of the Pacific War instead of prioritizing a liberation of the Chinese mainland. And finally, leveraging Beijing against Moscow as part of an ultimately successful strategy to contain the Soviet Union during the Cold War. While China sees such US policy and statecraft as a normal expression of US national interests, it objects to the American view that this somehow represents a uniquely moral approach to foreign policy. Even more ridiculous, in Beijing's view, is any claim that US policy has ever been an exercise in generosity toward China's interests. For example, the US might see its support for Chinese accession to the WTO in 2001 as an investment not only in the future of the global rules-based order but also as a moral investment in China's domestic economic and political progress. Beijing's interpretation, however, is purely pragmatic: the US and the rest of the West simply wanted more access to profitable Chinese markets—with a nefarious secondary hope of driving liberal-democratic "evolution" in China's political system.

Despite the protestations of successive US administrations (at least until Trump) that the US had no interest in overthrowing Communist Party rule, successive generations of party leaders have never believed them. Any talk in Washington of "changing China" or the moral purpose of US-China policy only heightens their suspicion. The CCP is already deeply conscious of the long-term threats it faces to its domestic political legitimacy. These include the destructive legacies of the party's own making in the Great Leap Forward, the Cultural Revolution, and Tiananmen; the rising political expectations of its middle class; growing concerns about the robustness of China's state-capitalist model, given the challenge to the party's authority from an increasingly self-confident private sector; and the spectacular rise of Buddhism and Christianity as spiritual alternatives to Marxism-Leninism. Protestant Christianity, in particular, is booming in China, growing from twenty-two million church members in 2010 to at least thirty-eight million in 2020. This number doesn't include an estimated additional twenty-two million who, following a major crackdown on churches by Xi since 2017, are thought to worship in underground churches not registered with the state. Nor does it include those who do not attend any formal services at all. In total, scholars estimate there may now be more than one hundred million Protestant believers in China—more than the entire membership of the party.

The CCP suspects the US is exacerbating these problems in several ways: by fanning expectations of political agency and governmental responsibility among China's middle class and helping to grow a troublesome civil-society movement through the work of American NGOs across the country; acting as foreign "black hands" behind the "turmoil" in Tiananmen and Hong Kong while seeking to replicate a color revolution, such as that in Ukraine in 2004–2005; and continuing the long tradition of American missionary activity by allowing Christian organizations to ship illicit bibles into China and backing other belief systems in China, such as the Falun Gong, whose leader lives in the United States. More broadly, the party is painfully aware of the more amorphously subversive but pervasive power of American cultural, educational, technological, and other soft powers, particularly among China's young people and private entrepreneurs.

There is also an equally potent, enduring, and understandable theme in Chinese perceptions about America on the question of race. Though rarely discussed in public, it is deeply felt in China's private political discourse and goes beyond the propaganda campaigns of the Communist Party. This was shaped by a century of European and Japanese colonial domination and was then sustained and amplified by the party's "national humiliation" narrative for the generations born after 1949. As a result, the underlying sensitivity on the question of racial, cultural, and national pride is that it is now central to how the CCP sees itself and the United States.

This fact is also almost always ignored by Americans in seeking to understand China. No young person could ever graduate from the Chinese school system without being exposed to the sign said to have been erected in the international concession in Shanghai in the 1920s proclaiming, "No dogs or Chinese allowed." That sign—destroyed with a flying kick by Bruce Lee in *Fist of Fury*—may have been apocryphal, but the racist attitudes in the foreign semicolonial holdings in Shanghai and elsewhere were real enough. Few in China grew up without at least a passing familiarity with America's history of anti-Chinese sentiments. Nor would they have missed the fact that before anti-immigration laws were imposed (due to American fears that too many Chinese arriving to work would ultimately undermine "white civilization" in the United States), Chinese laborers had done the backbreaking work of building America's transcontinental railways while suffering widespread abuse. Today, violence against Asian Americans and Chinese citizens in the United States—including a major surge in attacks and harassment following the outbreak of the COVID-19 pandemic—has also been widely covered in the Chinese press, furthering a sense of persistent American racial prejudice.

At the same time, China has a remarkable incapacity to reflect on its Han ethnocentrism, including its historical predisposition for racial stereotyping and the widespread view that most non-Han ethnicities are racially inferior, or *luohou* (backward), and in need of Sinicization. But our question here is not one of relative moral virtue on the part of Chinese and Americans on the question of race. It is to understand that when China identifies what it sees as American policies of containment designed to frustrate China's rise, these are interpolated through the prism of race, depicted and often seen as a last-ditch stand on the part of "white" Western civilization to prevent an Eastern civilization from supplanting it. China's view of America is that it is insufferably arrogant, condescending, and systemically incapable of treating China or its leaders with appropriate national respect, let alone as equals.

For post-1949 China, questions of national *dignitas* remain paramount, be it official respect for Chinese culture and accomplishment or smaller-scale personal interactions. In an earlier age, Confucian scholar-officials described the foundational importance of *li*, or the proper rites and ceremonies of political office. Modern Chinese leaders perceive many American government officials as routinely trampling on such basic protocols of mutual respect, either by ignorance or design. Whereas Americans would see their approach as reflecting practicality, informality, and even friendship rather than disrespect, the reflex reaction in Beijing is to see the reverse. The US is also seen as demanding that others give America "face" while routinely denying their Chinese interlocutors the same basic courtesies.

The Chinese Communist Party is also convinced that the moral dimensions of "American exceptionalism" as the self-proclaimed "city upon a hill" (originally a characteristically American Protestant notion) has meant that US foreign policy has been unable to restrain itself from interfering in the internal affairs of other states. Beijing contrasts this with its post-1978 foreign policy, which abandoned Mao's attempts to help overthrow governments for ideological reasons and now simply works with whatever government is thrown up as a result of local political circumstances—be they dictatorships or democracies, friend or foe. Such flexibility is maintained as long as they are not interfering with what Beijing considers its core interests. Beijing contrasts its approach with the *selectivity* of American interventions around the world—a selectivity that targets some countries, such as Iraq, Syria, and Libya, in the name of democratic principles but not other undemocratic states, such as Saudi Arabia, that happen to be strategic allies of the United States.

Beijing also asks, often with a level of exasperation, what the world would look like if China did act as a seriously revisionist, revanchist, or imperial power in the tradition of many other great powers in recent history. For these powers, the acquisition of far-flung colonial empires was seen as natural, normal, and even moral. China does not respond well to what it sees as the self-serving argument that the colonialist and neocolonialist obscenities of the past represent a bygone era that "civilized" nations in the postwar West have long left behind. They point to the accumulated wealth of many Western powers as having been extracted from their former colonial possessions, for which no compensation has been offered to postcolonial successor states. As for the United States in particular, which claims it has never been a classic colonial power, China points to the long and checkered history of the Monroe Doctrine and the unabashed American national self-interest alive in the very idea of the Western Hemisphere being, somehow, the unique preserve of US power. This, it notes, has been a conceit marked by the violent exclusion of all others from this American sphere of influence, including multiple armed interventions across Latin America to fashion governments to their strategic and political taste, often with cavalier disregard for fellow democracies. While America may have learned some lessons from this hypocrisy, Chinese scholars routinely ask (and not entirely rhetorically) why a similar Chinese *droit de regard* in the "Eastern Hemisphere" (i.e., wider East Asia) is now considered illegitimate.

The CCP also points to a long history of US intervention in China's domestic politics and society. They point to American missionaries' two-centuries-long endeavors to convert China's "soul" and destroy China's indigenous philosophical and religious inheritance. They also point to continuing American efforts to create a fully capitalist Chinese economy despite the party's proclamation of "socialism with Chinese characteristics" and the mixed-economy model that comes with it. The party also identifies an explicit post-Tiananmen American agenda of so-called *heping yanbian*, or peaceful transformation, whereby the United States' ultimate objective is to corrode and undermine the Chinese political system and see it replaced by an American-style democracy. Then there is the party's deep objection to the American expectation that China simply join the US-led international order without ever challenging it.

Exacerbating these Chinese frustrations is an abiding CCP recognition of the continuing potency of American military and economic power— and what it perceives to be the willingness of most US administrations to deploy that power whenever they judge it important for US national interests. The concern this power could be turned on China has endured in the minds of Chinese leaders for more than a century. The PLA has a deep institutional respect for the capacity of all branches of the US military—not just its formidable range of capabilities but also its historically proven capacity to fight and win interstate wars in multiple, complex, and often distant theaters of operation. This institutional respect has remained intact even if the American military's struggles against insurgencies have weakened its image as an "all-conquering" force. In contrast, China's leaders are aware that modern China has negligible battlefield experience in air and naval warfare. China has also seen the US leverage its geopolitical influence through its global network of military alliances, partnerships, and other bilateral arrangements, for which China, as yet, has no comparable alternative.

For decades, the party relied on rolling assessments of US and Chinese "comprehensive national power," a methodology that seeks to measure and integrate all relevant aspects of power, including political, military, diplomatic, economic, financial, technological, energy and resource access, and, more recently, cultural soft power. These formal analyses of American and Chinese objective capabilities also incorporate more fluid assessments concerning the changing nature of the international environment in which the two countries are required to operate.

All this sounds par for the course when it comes to the analysis of the international environment. But while China's understanding of modern America may be imperfect, it is more disciplined and sophisticated than what we find today among Washington political elites in their understanding of what actually makes China tick. Not only do Chinese strategists rigorously keep up-to-date with Washington's English-language policy debates (which Washington elites do not do in reverse), but they also use a consistent analytic framework to make sense of their strategic environment. In line with Marxist-Leninist dialectical analysis, Chinese leaders are trained to identify what is called thesis and antithesis, trend and countertrend, and action and reaction across politics, economics, society, technology, and international relations. This, in turn, is based on a deeper assessment of the unity of opposites, contradictions, and struggle as drivers of historical change. These formal assessments of China's international operating environment are the product of multiple inputs from across the party, government departments, and official think tanks. As good Marxists, the Chinese leadership regard their conclusions—never reached lightly over a weekend but usually over several years—as revealing long-term trends that are "scientifically and objectively true," to use the Marxist formulation. As such, once reached, such conclusions tend to guide strategy and policy for an extended period and are hard to shift. Indeed, this can create an analytical inflexibility on Beijing's part in dealing with contrary worldviews (even from within China), which are often written off by the CCP's political and analytical system as "subjective and inaccurate." As a result, foreigners whose perspectives directly conflict with the party's received wisdom are often invited to reflect on their "incorrect views" and form instead a "correct" view of history. It is much more difficult for the party to concede that its analysis might be flawed.

It is within this disciplined and, at times, rigid methodological approach that China sees the balance of world power, or "the correlation of forces," between itself and the United States moving steadily in China's direction, providing China with "a period of strategic opportunity" in which it has greater freedom of maneuver. But Chinese policy makers, at least until recently, have also concluded that China must still proceed with great caution and even greater strategic patience, given the continued strength of American military and financial power. It has been this rolling calculus of relative national power that has informed much of China's internal debate about how far and how fast to push its international interests at any given time.

The View from Washington

As of June 2021, 76 percent of Americans had an unfavorable opinion of China, according to polling by Pew Research. However, most of this ire is directed at the Chinese state, with only 15 percent expressing confidence in Xi Jinping to "do the right thing regarding world affairs." Underlying American perceptions of China, however, are by no means exclusively negative. Most Americans have a positive view of Chinese civilization, including the depth of its history and culture—and not least its remarkable cuisine, an import spread and popularized by the more than five million Americans claiming Chinese ethnicity today. America has a long experience of waves of Chinese immigration, and despite periods of outright racism, there is now a general view that Chinese Americans are hardworking and entrepreneurial citizens who make up a valuable part of the great American melting pot. At the same time, there is also widespread sympathy and admiration for anyone who lived (or still lives) under Communist rule.

Given these positive associations, it is hard for many Americans not to admire China's "rags to riches" story—seen as a combination of capitalist policy and a Chinese work ethic that has taken full advantage of the opportunities provided by the country's newly opened markets. Slowly, Americans have also learned that China today is not just a source of copying, counterfeiting, and cheaply made knock-offs but also a powerhouse of technological innovation. And among America's China-watching policy and business community, respect is extended, albeit grudgingly, to China's post-Mao leadership for their political resolve, policy pragmatism, and capacity to navigate the crises they have faced in bringing about the country's economic modernization. There is, therefore, a significant level of underlying American regard for China's national achievements, both current and historic, which Americans extend to relatively few other countries or cultures.

It is much harder, however, for Americans to understand what the Chinese Communist Party actually wants as opposed to the common, understandable human desires of the Chinese people. This difficulty in deciphering what the party wants, beyond the goals explicitly laid out in the public speeches of its leaders, is once again compounded by the purpose-built opacity of the Chinese political system. Indeed, the system is designed to keep prying foreign eyes as far away as possible from the actual core of Chinese leadership processes, including those factors that ultimately drive its political decisions. In part, this comes from the perceived need to present absolute unity of purpose at all times and a fear that if anyone discovers that the CCP's internal processes are much messier than they would have us believe, it would lead to a perception of weakness and turmoil. It is also the product of a Leninist party's long-standing predisposition to maintain secrecy at all costs, no matter the topic. This has made the party its own worst enemy in seeking to explain to the international community what China's national intentions really are. It causes other states to distrust official Chinese statements as being any real guides to what China is up to around the world. Instead, foreign governments conclude that the only reliable way to reach hard conclusions about Chinese strategic aspirations is to base their judgments on observable Chinese behaviors and US intelligence community product. This deep skepticism is reinforced by a long-running view formed over many generations among American officials that the Chinese Leninist state is not only opaque but also has zero moral compunction about actively lying to foreigners whenever its political needs so dictate—just as the state lies to its own people about critical aspects of recent party history.

As a result, the US often concludes that the best course of action is to distrust anything the CCP says. Instead, America's predisposition is to connect the dots itself, as best it can, to try to divine China's actual strategic intentions—in other words, to assume the worst and to prepare accordingly. This is understandable within the framework of the long-standing realist traditions of American foreign policy. It can, however, also be counterproductive if it discounts Chinese declaratory positions in their entirety. China's official media, while rarely providing a clear picture of Chinese political decision-making, nonetheless can be helpful in understanding the conceptual framework within which the party is operating and where changing political and policy positions may be emerging. After all, CCP leadership has to communicate its message to its ninety-five million members and to the country at large and, in doing so, cannot rely on classified party documents alone. Reading the Chinese media is sometimes like watching a movie on mute without subtitles: you have a general idea of what's going on, but other sources of information are necessary to provide a better, albeit never complete, understanding of the detailed story line. Even in the Chinese political system, the public narrative ultimately has to overlap with the internal reality. The party's need to communicate with its mass membership, therefore, provides external observers with important insights about Chinese strategic perceptions, intentions, and capabilities. This is reinforced by China's vast array of specialist journals that enable its professional elites to remain abreast of changing circumstances. When read carefully, these also provide insight into the party's internal policy debates. Thus, if American policy makers ignore the official media altogether, there is a danger that the US will trade partial insights for the construction of baseless conspiracy theories. Nonetheless, getting the balance right between what is to be believed in the official literature and what must be interpolated from Chinese strategic behavior is always difficult. To state the obvious, to do so requires a particular expertise on the part of those who, through textural experience, understand when there has been a change in the party line and the reasons for it.

The idea of systematic deception on China's part has not been the general sentiment among American political and commercial elites until relatively recently. It began in the latter years of Hu Jintao's leadership and intensified after Xi Jinping's ascension in 2012. For example, in 2012, Chinese vessels massed around a Philippine-controlled feature in the South China Sea known as Scarborough Shoal. Seemingly attempting to seize control of it, a dangerous standoff with the Philippine Navy ensued until Obama administration officials mediated a deal for both sides to withdraw. The Philippines' ships ultimately withdrew, but China's stayed. Shocked American officials learned their lesson, but Beijing was emboldened. By 2014, China was engaged in a major campaign to create "facts on the ground" in the South China Sea, with swarms of dredging ships pouring sand onto reefs and islets in order to create multiple artificial islands, some large enough to house military-style airstrips, hangars, and supply depots. Standing beside President Obama at a summit in 2015, Xi Jinping pledged that the islands would never be militarized. American officials were doubtful, scoffing at China's public protestations that its island-reclamation efforts were merely to "assist meteorological and oceanographic research." The publication of photographs by American reconnaissance aircraft of armed PLA garrisons and, later, military aircraft being deployed on the reclaimed islands quickly sunk Xi's claims.

There is only a small step between the sense of being deceived and the even deeper sense of betrayal that follows. That's because deception shatters trust, as much between states as between individuals. Indeed, as seen through American eyes, this is where we find ourselves in the continuing downward spiral of the US-China relationship. In America's current view, not only has China deceived the US for decades about its long-term strategic intentions, but it has also betrayed the explicit content and implicit spirit of the contract it agreed to with the international community back in 2001, when China was first welcomed into the WTO. From Washington's perspective, supporting China's accession to the trade body was the single most important decision made by a US administration since diplomatic normalization in 1979, the effect of which was to turbocharge China's economic rise, enabling it to become the largest trading power and second-largest economy in the world within a decade. However, China did not open its markets fully to the US and the rest of the West as promised. In the view of America and many of its allies, China continued to protect its industries (contrary to WTO rules), subsidize its exports, manipulate its currency, and steal intellectual property as a deliberate stratagem to accelerate its economic and military development. On top of this, China deployed the full resources of the state in a bold bid to overtake all its international competitors in the high-technology industries of the future. In other words, China had no interest in becoming a market economy anchored in the principles of competitive neutrality as provided for under the terms of its WTO accession. Instead, it intended to continue to use the full powers of its authoritarian capitalist model to win an undeclared economic war against the US and the West. Even worse, in the American view, China continued to run massive trade surpluses with the United States, serving to hollow out much of American industry at the same time.

The controversy surrounding Beijing's "Made in China 2025" (MIC 2025) strategy provided yet another illustration of the same problem for American eyes. Increasingly, corporate America felt that China's overall approach to trade and investment policy was becoming more nationalist, mercantilist, and protectionist. American exporters complained of a vast array of Chinese nontariff barriers, such as complex and arbitrary health-and-safety regulations on imported products, making it difficult for American goods and services to have competitive access to China's ever-growing domestic market. Now, MIC 2025 proclaimed China's intention to dominate all major global high-technology markets by 2030, listing each sector by name as well as the proportion of the global market that China intended to occupy by a given date.

This of itself was seen as ambitious but not necessarily offensive; many nation-states articulate long-term industry policy targets. But in America and in Europe, a line was crossed when China subsequently unleashed unprecedented state funding across an army of public research institutions to give effect to the strategy. China made assurances to foreign governments about competitive neutrality, but the Chinese aphorism on deception—that "above, there are policies, but below, there are counterpolicies" (*shang you zhengce, xia you duice*)—seemed to be in effect. To American exporters and investors, the driving sentiment was that whatever international economic agreements China signed up to were largely a political smoke screen, behind which the deeply nationalist and protectionist orientation of the Chinese state continued to churn.

Meanwhile, a Chinese exclusion list proscribing multiple sectors from any form of inbound investment tied the hands of American investors seeking access to the most profitable areas of the Chinese economy. Indeed, where investment was permitted, it was often on the condition of reexport of products to third-country markets rather than allowing effective access to Chinese consumers. Added to this was unlimited official funding for a foreign acquisition spree by Chinese state-owned enterprises across Europe and the United States, as China sought to buy up high-tech firms around the world. At the same time, foreign companies in the Chinese market were prevented from acquiring full or even majority ownership over the joint ventures they were required to enter into with Chinese firms.

US investors also complained of unilateral rule changing by various levels of the Chinese government and party once an investment had actually been made, by which time the investor was at the whim of local political decision makers. Corruption was also the "normal" price for doing business, particularly in the pre–Xi Jinping period, and a major problem for American corporations, given that they were subject to strict reporting and compliance requirements under the US Foreign Corrupt Practices Act. Finally, the absence of an impartial legal system for commercial dispute resolution meant that foreign businesses had a next-to-zero success rate in Chinese courts, leaving them exposed to the exploitative practices of local business partners and the various arms of the Chinese government. These problems were compounded by American business allegations of being forced to transfer technology to their Chinese joint-venture partners as a de facto requirement for doing continued business within China. Washington, therefore, concluded that Beijing was embarked on a comprehensive, state-driven strategy to dominate future global technology markets. Chinese protestations that China was still a poor, developing country in need of more time to adjust to international standards of economic competition were increasingly seen as a cynical public relations tactic by Beijing.

It became clear that Beijing seemed to have no intention of complying with the terms of its WTO accession on domestic-market access and the subsidization of Chinese exports. Large parts of corporate America, which had long been the main pro-China constituency in American politics throughout the many storms in US-China relations over many decades, lost its enthusiasm for the China market. The American public also concluded as much, figuring that China knew perfectly well what it was doing in preferencing its companies and exporters at the expense of America's.

Deception and betrayal are raw emotions. Once felt, they also give rise to a sense of righteous indignation and a resolution to adopt a radically different course of action for the future to avoid being tricked again and to punish the offending party. In this case, the offending party was China.

These are the sentiments that helped give rise to the Trump campaign's successful political position against China in the 2016 US presidential election as well as Trump's subsequent prosecution of the US-China trade war, beginning in 2018.

In Graham Allison's analysis, the peaceful transition in global leadership after World War I between the UK and the US was made possible not just because of Britain's postwar economic exhaustion. More importantly, it was because London concluded that, while it might have been undesirable to give up its global leadership role, it was not a catastrophe. America, in Britain's view, was a familiar power, steeped in similar (though not identical) values, with an understandable worldview and national ambitions. America could, thus, be trusted to accommodate British interests and concerns, even if it took the lead. This logic simply does not apply between the United States and Xi Jinping's China. The gulf between Chinese and American worldviews, communication, and trust is simply too vast to accommodate any such compromise.

Why Perceptions Are Important in Developing a Common Strategic Narrative

So where does this assessment of Chinese and American perceptions take us in our analysis of how we can avoid an unnecessary war in the future? It's often assumed that clear-minded strategic analysis can only be based on a rigorous distillation of the capabilities and intentions of other states. But if these continue to be opaque, the question of how the capabilities and intentions of one side are *perceived* by the other is of equal importance. Rarely, if ever, do US-China summits address the most fundamental elements of strategic distrust that each side harbors against the other. There have been some exceptions, such as Obama's early encounters with Xi Jinping, which, for a time, had a refreshing tabula rasa quality to them, as each leader sought to understand the worldview of the other. Much earlier, there were the raw exchanges between Nixon and Kissinger and Mao and his premier Zhou Enlai—although the deep strategic realism that characterized these early exchanges has rarely been replicated since. Perhaps this has been because, as the relationship developed, it simply became too difficult to raise these elemental questions. They were seen as too controversial or too offensive, or diplomatic practitioners from both sides simply became too weighed down by the traditional rituals of state-craft. Whatever the reason, these most deeply held perceptions now seem to be "no-go" areas between them.

Still, to ignore perceptions simply because they are imprecise or implicit is to willfully ignore a large part of strategic reality. Or, as one senior Chinese military leader once said to me, "No state is ever fully transparent with another state, particularly in the context of unfolding strategic rivalry." That much is understandable. But an understanding of each side's deep perceptions can help fill a gap in the normal channels of American and Chinese diplomacy. It may be that through a process of sustained strategic dialogue and the presentation of objective evidence through transparent means, some of these calcified perceptions and misperceptions can change over time. Given the complete collapse of strategic trust, this kind of blunt political exchange may no longer be possible.

So what can be done to improve this situation? At a minimum, policy makers need to make a genuine attempt, free of ideological bias or self-delusion, to understand the prevailing "perception environment" in each other's capitals. Pretending that reality is different to what it really is no longer works for anyone. There is simply too much accumulated information available to both sides of this relationship. Second, each side should moderate its public language for maximum clarity of communication based on understanding how it will play to the other's perceptions. Washington and Beijing's public communications are understandably often tailored to domestic political audiences, but this must always be tempered by a realization of how such messages will be read in the other capital. Third, a granular understanding of each side's "perceptions environment"—how they think about the world—should also be incorporated into its operational strategy. Finally, seeking such an understanding should lie at the heart of any agreed joint strategic framework the two countries might develop to manage their future relationship by using high-level political, diplomatic, and military channels of communication between them. This is easy to say, but hard to do. However, given the current state of the relationship, it has now become essential. The US and China need to learn from the strategic candor of the US-Soviet relationship in the 1970s and 1980s, when a mutual sense of vulnerability facilitated blunt communication of core priorities and probable lines in the sand.

In forming a better understanding of China's perceptions, some prioritization is also in order: right now, there is no greater need than to understand the outlook of China's current paramount leader, Xi Jinping. In the following chapters, I will try to look beneath the current mélange of CCP slogans, concepts, and language that so often seem impenetrable in an attempt to define Xi's core priorities. His ten priorities, which I identify, gleaned from multiple sources over many years, can best be understood as ten concentric circles of interests, starting from the most important and proximate to Xi and expanding outward. When I have shared this list and the concept that underpins it with my Chinese colleagues and friends, many of them have privately indicated that they recognize it as being "relatively objective," although this is generally seen as too uncomfortable to acknowledge. For those of us who deal regularly with both the rigors and randomness of the Chinese system, this is high praise indeed. So let us now turn to the world as seen by Xi Jinping.

3

★ ★ ★ ★ ★

Understanding Xi Jinping's Worldview: Ten Concentric Circles of Interest

To understand China's long-term strategy toward the United States and how the US might most profitably respond to it is to understand where America fits within the wider framework of the Communist Party's worldview. While Xi Jinping, given his unprecedented power within the party, has had a profound impact on how the CCP sees its and the country's future, there are also many consistencies from the past. If Xi is not China's paramount leader tomorrow, much of what is described in this chapter would remain in place. In many respects, what Xi has done is intensify and accelerate priorities and plans that have long been part of the party's strategy. Where Xi has changed China's worldview has been in the reinvigoration of the party's Marxist-Leninist foundations, the turbocharging of Chinese nationalism, and the sharpening of the country's national ambitions.

I argue that Xi Jinping's worldview is made up of ten concentric circles of interest—starting from the most important, concerning Xi's position in the party itself, and moving out to other domestic political priorities and then to his unfolding international aspirations for the country. In this schema, each layer builds on the other. For those familiar with Maslow's hierarchy of needs and its relevance to political psychology and behavior, this is an attempt to apply a similar framework to the priorities of the Communist Party as set by Xi Jinping. They are summarized as follows:

1. **The centrality of Xi and the party and the hard business of staying in power:** Core to the CCP is its overriding determination to remain in power. While radically different from the worldview of Western political parties, this deeply Leninist reality should never be forgotten. Under Xi Jinping, this fundamental interest dictates every other interest of the Chinese party and state. In that context, Xi himself is also determined to secure his position, including an enduring legacy in national and party history superior to that of Deng Xiaoping and at least equal to Mao Zedong.

2. **Maintaining and securing national unity:** Xi's second core interest is the unity and territorial integrity of the motherland. Maintaining firm control over Tibet, Xinjiang, Inner Mongolia, and Hong Kong is nonnegotiable for the CCP. Even more fundamental is the "return" of Taiwan, which remains the holy grail of party politics because it would complete the sole task left unfinished following Mao's revolution and establishment of the PRC in 1949. These internal security priorities will always remain central to the party's perception of its continuing political legitimacy, given that Chinese history has always been kind to those emperors who have held the empire together and unforgiving to those who have allowed it to fall apart.

3. **Growing the Chinese economy:** Continued economic prosperity forms a key part of the unofficial social contract between the party and the people. If growth were to falter badly, this contract would come under severe strain. That's why the party has been adamant for so long about ensuring sufficient economic growth to sustain living standards, employment, and social stability—and why it is also increasingly concerned about the problem of high economic inequality. Xi also recognizes that the basis of all national power

ultimately hangs on economic power and no longer simply "from the barrel of a gun," as Mao used to say. This includes China's ability to defend itself and assert its role in the world. But Xi is also seeking to build this power without China becoming permanently and structurally dependent on the international economy, the dollar-denominated global financial system, or foreign manufacturing and technology.

4. **Environmental sustainability:** A parallel dilemma arises from the litany of challenges posed by water, soil, and air pollution, as well as food safety. The tragedy of China's rapid economic development over the last forty years was the relegation of the environment as a secondary concern. Now, environmental sustainability has become a major problem, intricately connected to China's economic and political future. Increasingly, the Chinese public demands a clean environment and not just jobs as part of its social contract with the party. Moreover, the party has also realized that environmental devastation, including the global climate crisis, threatens the future of China's economic development, international image, and ultimately its national security.

5. **Modernizing the military:** Xi sees China's military and its technological capacity as the linchpins not only of the party's security but also of China's ability to project power throughout the region and the world. Xi also sees himself as a military man and a grand strategist and was appalled, on coming into power, by what he saw as the military's corruption and lack of "war-winning" capabilities. He has significantly transformed the leadership, institutional structure, and capabilities of the People's Liberation Army, turning it from a mass land army concerned with internal security and the defense of China's continental borders to a technologically advanced fighting force capable of rivaling any leading competitor and projecting power beyond China's shores.

6. **Managing China's neighboring states:** Neighboring states—of which China has fourteen, the largest number of contiguous borders

of any country in the world along with Russia—occupy a particular place in China's strategic memory. Historically, they've been the principal avenue through which China's national security has been threatened, resulting in successive foreign invasions. In Chinese strategic thought, this has entrenched a deeply defensive view of how to maintain China's national security. But Chinese historiography also teaches that purely defensive measures have not always succeeded. For these reasons, modern Chinese strategic thinking has explored an approach prioritizing political and economic diplomacy with which China aims to secure positive, accommodating, and—wherever possible—compliant relationships with all its neighboring states.

7. **Securing China's maritime periphery in East Asia and the west Pacific:** China may see its continental periphery as problematic, but it sees its maritime periphery as deeply hostile. Here, China perceives a region strategically allied against it—with a ring of US allies from South Korea to Japan to Taiwan to the Philippines and Australia. China's strategic response to this is clear. It seeks to fracture US alliances. It has said as much repeatedly in its declaratory statements, claiming that they are relics of the Cold War. Meanwhile, as noted above, Xi has overseen a transformation of China's military capabilities in which the army continues to shrink and its naval and air forces continue to expand, along with an arsenal of missiles and other asymmetric weapons. China's overall political-military strategy is clear: to cause sufficient doubt in the minds of American military commanders and policy makers about its ability to win any armed conflict against Chinese forces in the region, including in the defense of Taiwan, that the United States would choose not to fight. Xi's objective is to secure China's territorial claims in the East China Sea, the South China Sea, and Taiwan without ever having to fire a shot—and eventually displace the United States as the dominant military power in the Asia-Pacific.

8. **Securing China's western continental periphery:** China also seeks to establish strategic and economic depth across the vast Eurasian continent, reaching as far as Western Europe, the Middle East, and Africa. We see this in China's political, economic, and military diplomacy across its vast continental flank, including most dramatically in China's Belt and Road Initiative across (and around) Eurasia. As with its immediate neighboring states, China wants to secure a benign strategic environment, cultivating a vast landmass hospitable to Chinese interests and much less susceptible to American strategic influence than its maritime periphery to the east.

9. **Increasing Chinese leverage across the developing world:** Beyond China's immediate region, the party devotes substantial effort to building China's ties in the developing world. This has long historical roots going back to Mao and Zhou Enlai's role in the Non-Aligned Movement (a Cold War organization of developing states that were not aligned with any great power), particularly in Africa. Over the last twenty years, much of the developing world has seen their economic relationships with China become much more important than those countries' relationships with the United States—the product of large-scale public and private Chinese trade and investment across Africa, Asia, and Latin America. While China is looking to secure commodities and other resources, its ability to build close relationships by meeting the needs of developing states has proven remarkably adaptive. As a result, when China needs support for its interests in the UN or other international institutions, it enjoys the ability to pull in unprecedented political and diplomatic leverage from across the developing world.

10. **Rewriting the global rules-based order:** Finally, China aims to reshape the institutional rules and norms that govern the international order. As the victors of World War II, the United States and its closest allies constructed the underlying architecture of the postwar liberal international rules-based order and have dominated its key institutions ever since. The CCP has always argued that it was

never included in that process. But China now finds the world in a period of great change and challenge and sees the time as ripe—as it grows in economic, diplomatic, and military might—to challenge American leadership of that order and to change the nature of the order itself. China has done this through three approaches: drawing on its growing support across the developing world to secure changes to existing international norms and procedures deemed to be offensive to Chinese interests and values, installing Chinese or China-friendly candidates in the senior leadership of a growing number of existing international institutions, and creating its own network of new multilateral institutions outside the framework of the post-1945 UN and Bretton Woods system. While Xi has not described specifically what a future international order of the CCP's choosing would ultimately look like, he has made plain that he does not intend China to simply replicate the current US-led liberal international order. Rather, China will seek an order much more conducive to its political, ideological, and economic interests.

This list of ten core priorities will never be found neatly laid out in China's strategic literature. The Chinese system is more opaque than that. Rather, it is my attempt to distill Xi's principal objectives out of what I've learned from many conversations with a multitude of Chinese interlocutors and other sources over many, many years. I first met Xi in 1986, when he was vice mayor of Xiamen and I was an embassy staffer preparing then Australian prime minister Bob Hawke's visit to the embryonic Xiamen Special Economic Zone (one of only four in the country) on China's southeastern coast opposite Taiwan. Later, as prime minister myself, I hosted Xi in Australia when he was Chinese vice president in 2010 and already Hu Jintao's designated successor. During that visit, I spent a total of ten hours in conversation with Xi in six separate meetings, including about three hours around a winter fire at the prime ministerial residence in Canberra with just the two of us and our ambassadors. That meeting was almost exclusively in Chinese and covered a vast range of topics. I also talked with him by telephone after he became general secretary and president in 2013. Since I left office in Australia in late 2013, I have been in several small group meetings with Xi in Beijing as head of an American think tank (the Asia Society Policy Institute). I have found Xi to be an impressive, knowledgeable, engaging interlocutor who rarely uses notes in his dealings with either foreigners or locals. He rarely reads a speech. Like Mao, and to some extent Deng, Xi speaks his mind directly and forcefully. He is firm in his position but without thumping the table. More importantly, I have spent a lot of time with many of Xi's most senior officials, formally and informally, fleshing out the impressions I gleaned from across the Chinese system on how China views the world over many years.

What follows are my conclusions from all these conversations, observations, and readings over the decades. They are not all-encompassing, but by and large, I believe they are a reasonable representation of the strategic prism through which Xi's China observes and responds to its domestic and international circumstances. And, as we shall see, the United States is relevant to all of them, and in some cases decisively so.

4

★ ★ ★ ★ ★

The First Circle: The Politics of Staying in Power

Xi Jinping's top priority is to ensure the Communist Party remains permanently in power and that he remains its paramount leader. It is important to understand that this is the central organizing principle for everything else in Chinese domestic politics and international policy. Xi's view is that the party, having spent twenty-eight long, hard, and bloody years as an insurgency movement before eventually winning political power through armed revolution in 1949, is not about to concede that power to anyone else. On this, Xi is haunted by the demise of the Soviet Communist Party in 1991 and the ensuing collapse of the Soviet Union. He is determined this will never happen in China.

Even prior to Xi Jinping's rise, there had already been something of a tipping point in the pattern of Chinese politics. Since the Deng Xiaoping era, there were many internal debates within the party in which consideration was given to the possible long-term transformation of the CCP into a sort of social democratic party as part of a more pluralist political system. Party leaders were mindful of what happened with the collapse of the Soviet Union. They had also witnessed the many political transformations that unfolded across eastern and central Europe. Study groups were commissioned to sort out why the Soviet Union collapsed, and a series of internal discussions were held over many years on what could be learned from these tumultuous events. My Chinese contacts told me in 2001 that the party had concluded this internal debate; there would be no systemic political change. It was decided that China would continue as a one-party state. It might be a less authoritarian state than during the Maoist era, but the Leninist party would retain its place. The party's leadership had concluded that this was a necessity for their long-term survival. They also believed that China could never become a global great power in the absence of the party's strong central leadership and that in the absence of that leadership, the country would simply dissolve into the bickering camps that had so often plagued China's past.

These internal debates were concluded a decade *before* Xi's appointment as general secretary. Xi's rise, therefore, should not be interpreted simplistically as the triumph of a new form of authoritarianism over those who supported the party's long-term democratic transformation. Rather, his ascent should be seen as part of a narrower party debate about the particular form of authoritarian capitalism that China's new leadership now seeks to entrench.

In previous decades, under Deng's guidance, the role of the party shrank to a more narrowly defined form of ideological supervision, while the actual powers of policy decision-making gradually migrated to the institutions of the state bureaucracy. (Chinese politics is officially divided into a dual-track model of separate state and party institutions, although most officials hold both party and state positions simultaneously.) The state, meanwhile, devolved many of its economic powers to China's burgeoning private sector, and China's traditional state-owned enterprises were increasingly seen as financial burdens rather than assets. Xi Jinping reversed all this. He realized that if the party was taken out of the country's most important policy decision-making processes, it would lose its relevance altogether and, in time, fade away. Not being prepared to stand idly by while that happened, Xi decided to intervene decisively and reverse this trend. Under his leadership, we have seen the return of the party to the epicenter of the Chinese political and economic policy-making process.

Another feature of Xi Jinping's "new authoritarianism" has been the renewed role of political ideology over pragmatic policy. For the previous forty years, the CCP told the world (and the Chinese people) that China's governing ideology was "socialism with Chinese characteristics." As the decades rolled by, the economic reality soon became that there was much less socialism than Chinese characteristics. Indeed, *Chinese characteristics* became the accepted popular euphemism for good old capitalism. However, Xi and his colleagues knew that international political theory predicted that demands for political liberalization would quickly arise once per capita income was sufficient to create a significant middle class. They were poignantly aware of the profound "contradiction" (in Marxist dialectical terms) that existed between China's national development goal of raising average incomes on the one hand and the resulting peril of unleashing demands for political liberalization on the other. Xi's response to this dilemma has been a zealous reassertion of Marxist-Leninist ideology across the full fabric of Chinese life.

In addition to Marxist-Leninist ideology, Chinese nationalism also became a mainstay of the party's continuing claim to domestic political legitimacy. This began soon after Tiananmen in 1989 and accelerated after the 2008 Beijing Olympics. But Xi Jinping made cultivating nationalism an even stronger priority, leveraging an increasingly sophisticated propaganda apparatus that has seamlessly fused the imagery of the modern CCP with the national mythology of a proud and ancient Chinese civilization.

This has included the rehabilitation of Confucianism, once dismissed by the CCP as reactionary and anticommunist, as part of the restoration of the party's emphasis on the uniqueness of China's national political philosophy. According to the official line, a long-standing continuity of benign hierarchical governance (as represented by Confucianism) is what differentiates China from the rest of the world. The shorthand form of Xi's political narrative is simple: China's historical greatness, across its dynastic histories, always lay in strong, authoritarian, hierarchical Confucian governments. By corollary, China's historical greatness was never the product of Western liberal democracy or any Chinese variation of it. By extension,

China's future national greatness can lie only in the continued adaptation of its indigenous political legacy, derived from the hierarchical tradition of the Confucian/communist state.

Xi wants to secure a place for himself in Chinese party history that is at least equal to Mao and greater than Deng. At the Nineteenth Party Congress in 2017, Xi had his colleagues vote to amend the party constitution to include Xi Jinping Thought as one of the three fundamental doctrinal additions to the Chinese Communist Party's version of Marxism-Leninism, together with Mao Zedong Thought and Deng Xiaoping Theory on socialism with Chinese characteristics. By contrast, Xi's two immediate predecessors, Hu Jintao and Jiang Zemin, are credited with lesser intellectual contributions on individual aspects of party building or economic development—a far cry from the integrated ideological system represented by Xi Jinping Thought. While the content of this thought is an evolving canon of speeches, articles, and reflections, it seeks to cover the full gamut of political, military, economic, environmental, and international strategy. The key point is that Xi's personal reflections (past, present, and future) on these subject areas now have the status of a priori formal party ideology. This requires the Chinese system, as well as those of us seeking to analyze China from the outside, to take his words seriously.

Xi Jinping Thought includes a proliferation of new phrases seeking to define Xi's vision for the party and the country. The cornerstone of this vision is the China Dream. It is defined by two goalposts. First, by China becoming a "moderately prosperous society" (defined as doubling China's per capita income to $10,000 from where it stood in 2010) by the centenary of the party's founding. This was achieved with great fanfare in 2021. The next goal is China becoming a fully advanced economy by the centenary of the founding of the People's Republic in 2049, with average income levels to be the same as the US. To achieve these goals is to achieve what Xi describes as "the great rejuvenation of the Chinese nation," or the restoration of China to the central role in global affairs it once held for "five thousand years of continuous history" before its lamentable Century of Humiliation at the hands of foreign powers. Xi defines this great rejuvenation as meaning a "strong China—militarily, economically, politically, diplomatically. and technologically"; a "civilized China," based on the principles of "equity, fairness, morality, and cultural development"; a "harmonious China," anchored in social and ethnic concord; and a "beautiful China," with environmental sustainability at its core.

But the core of Xi Jinping's China Dream remains the economy. Unless China can sustain high levels of economic growth for the decades ahead, its national strength will falter, living standards will fall, and unemployment will rise, with potentially dire consequences for the party's legitimacy in the eyes of the people. But to continue to grow the economy requires sustained market-based reform, which is where Xi's economic objectives run headlong into his political objective of maximizing party control. Certainly, those at the center of China's economic reform team, including Vice Premier Liu He, Politburo Standing Committee member Wang Yang, and Vice President Wang Qishan, understand the imperative of further market reform. They know from China's bitter historical experience that to stand still is, in fact, to fall behind. They also understand that the only real source of employment growth in China's economy over the last thirty years has come from the private sector—not state-owned enterprises (SOEs)—although this has become increasingly ideologically contentious in Xi Jinping's China.

For China's private sector, this has not been plain sailing. First, the role of party secretaries within private firms has been enhanced. Second, there is an open debate in China as to whether the state should acquire equity within China's most successful private firms in order to secure greater political influence over these companies' future direction. Third, there is a growing concern among China's entrepreneurial class that the party may be starting to apply unofficial growth caps on how big they are prepared to allow private firms to become in order to keep these firms from acquiring power capable of challenging the authority of China's party-state. The need for private firms to walk a political tightrope makes their success much more precarious in a way American companies do not have to face. For example, in the wake of Xi's anticorruption campaign and other compliance irregularities, a number of prominent Chinese private firms found themselves in real political difficulty. In one case, Anbang Insurance

Group, we saw the temporary "assumption of state control" of the company's assets after its chairman and CEO was taken into custody, tried, and incarcerated. His case was followed by that of real estate tycoon Ren Zhiqiang, a close friend of Wang Qishan, who was also jailed.

By 2020, the party had doubled down on making its control over private firms explicit, with Xi delivering "important instructions" on "strengthening the united front work of the private economy" in September of that year. That document was clear in its aim to "better focus the wisdom" of "private businesspeople on the goal and mission" of the party and country to make sure they are "dependable and usable in key moments." It called explicitly for "strengthening party-building in private enterprises" in order to "realize the party's leadership over the private economy." All this came to a head in November 2020 with a crackdown on China's most famous entrepreneur, Jack Ma, and his companies Alibaba Group and Ant Group. Reportedly enraged by the high-flying Ma's commentary on the backwardness of Chinese financial regulators, Xi Jinping is said to have personally ordered the last-minute suspension of Ant's planned $35 billion mega-IPO on the Chinese stock market in November 2020. Ma virtually disappeared from public view (until about one year later, when he reappeared on a trip to Spain), and regulators forced a significant restructuring to split apart his business empire before unleashing a broader antitrust regulatory crackdown on China's largest technology and financial companies in 2021 (as discussed in more detail in chapter 6).

Xi's economic advisors know that the future of Chinese productivity, innovation, and employment hangs on whether there is sufficient private business confidence to make the investment decisions necessary to guarantee long-term sustainable growth. Yet Xi's closest political advisors, including Politburo Standing Committee members Li Zhanshu and Wang Huning, reinforce Xi's natural instincts to preference internal political and ideological control over all other considerations. There is real risk to China's long-term economic growth trajectory should this reassertion of party control lead to businesses forgoing capital investments or a substantial—perhaps massive and unprecedented—flight of private capital that would result in a reimposition of even tighter capital controls by the state in the future. Given China's already formidable ratio of public debt to GDP, there is a limit to how much it can continue to revert to government stimulus to augment any future economic growth gap arising from a faltering private sector. And if economic growth, private-sector business formation, and employment falter, this of itself generates the very social and political unrest that Xi Jinping's political strategy seeks to avoid.

The core political challenge for Xi, therefore, is whether a crisis of business confidence prompts him to decisively throw his lot in with his economic reform team and accept a partial loss of political control as an acceptable price to pay for the realization of his much-cherished vision of the China Dream. This will cut against his instincts to strengthen party control over the private sector, but the pressures of ongoing trade and technology disputes with the United States and its allies may have made this an easier decision for him than it otherwise would be. The evidence so far, however, points in the reverse direction. China's future, including its political future and its future influence in the world, will ultimately turn on this core decision.

In this context, it is easier to understand why the Western liberal-democratic value system, most potently championed by the United States, is anathema to Xi Jinping. America, with its simultaneous embodiment of political and religious liberty, a powerful and innovative economy, and a strong military is fundamentally problematic for party ideologists. This is because it offers a powerful countercase to the core arguments underpinning China's authoritarian-capitalist model: that state direction and ideological control are essential preconditions for both national greatness and individual prosperity.

Like most of his colleagues across the CCP leadership, Xi has long seen US support for universal human rights, democracy, and the rule of law as a fundamental challenge to the party's interests. Lest there be any doubt on this score, China's indigenous democracy movement has long been condemned by the party as one of the "five poisons" that threaten the Chinese system, together with Uyghur activists, adherents of Falun Gong, Tibetan activists, and the Taiwanese independence movement—all of which the party contends are backed by the United States.

The party's historical antagonism toward human rights, electoral democracy, and an independent legal system will, therefore, continue because these concepts strike at the very heart of the perceived legitimacy of the Chinese party-state, both at home and abroad. This explains China's continuing hostility toward any foreign government that dares challenge the moral fundamentals of the Chinese political system. In Beijing's eyes, the most potent of these critics will continue to be the United States. China remains deeply mindful of the damage that can still be done to "brand China," both around the world and within China itself, by concerted American diplomacy focused on regime legitimacy. Despite the aberrations of US human rights advocacy during the Trump presidency, Beijing knows that the US remains the country least likely to buckle to its pressure to remain silent on this existential political issue for the Chinese Communist Party.

That Xi implemented a wide-ranging crackdown against "bourgeois liberalization" in China's education system during the first six months of his term in 2013 is, therefore, unsurprising. He identified seven sensitive topics that could no longer be the subject of any form of academic discussion or debate. These were "universal values, freedom of speech, civil rights, civil society, the historical errors of the Communist Party, crony capitalism, and judicial independence." This was followed in 2017 by China's new foreign NGO law, which placed new security restrictions on the operations of any NGO attracting philanthropic funding from abroad. With the strike of a pen, this law crushed an active civil society that developed over decades, with organizations promoting everything from occupational health and safety to the schooling of migrant workers' children. Then, more recently, Xi has also moved to ban private schooling and the hiring of foreign teachers as well as the use of international textbooks and curricula.

These and other similar measures reflect Xi Jinping's long-standing anxiety about the potential potency of a "color revolution" in bringing about the end of Chinese Communist Party rule. This is unsurprising, given that just before Xi took power, similar revolutions occurred in eastern and central Europe as well as in the Arab Spring that brought down governments across the Middle East. Unsurprisingly, he shares this disquiet with

Russian president Vladimir Putin. Both have concluded that the United States was the principal instigator of these internal revolutions—not just through Washington's historical human rights advocacy but also through covert American intelligence operations aimed at undermining authoritarian political systems.

Of even greater concern in China has been the flourishing of religious belief in China and the challenge this is perceived to represent to the future of party power. Xi's 2016 address to the National Religious Work Conference outlined his new policy on the Sinicization of foreign religions with a presence in China (principally Islam and Christianity, each of which present their own distinct risks to the CCP) in order to force them to more fully conform to Chinese cultural and political norms. This was followed in 2018 by new Regulations on Religious Work as well as the consolidation of all religious policy under the party's United Front Work Department. This was designed, in particular, to tighten control over the explosion in Protestant Christianity operating outside the framework of the officially sanctioned patriotic church, which was established in the earliest years of the People's Republic. The party's response was to warn Chinese citizens of the dangers of foreign manipulation of religious practices in China designed to undermine the Chinese party-state and disrupt China's rise. The subsequent demolition of unauthorized churches across the country and arrest of church leaders was widely reported across Chinese and international media.

The party is also increasing its efforts to harness indigenous Chinese religion, philosophy, historiography, and culture to reinforce the party's ideological claim to continuing political legitimacy. In a civilization where the party claims human rights, electoral democracy, and an independent legal system have always been alien concepts within the Chinese tradition, they have sought to identify more accommodating Chinese alternatives, such as the Confucian system of mutual obligation tying citizens to rulers. This approach underlines Xi's determination to delegitimize ideological and theological challenges from abroad that in any way undermine the party's domestic political legitimacy. This, of course, ignores the inconvenient truth that Marxism and Leninism are also foreign imports, but

Xi's response would be that this is the whole point of adding Chinese characteristics to socialism—the Sinification of Marxism itself. The overall political message is clear: Western notions of democratic governance, civil liberties, and religious faith are not only ideologically unacceptable to the party but also alien to what it is to be Chinese.

Unlike the rulers of China's past, Xi's efforts to sustain an authoritarian state are aided by a vast new array of technological tools of political control beyond the imaginings of any Chinese emperor in history. If the core precept of Confucianism is "know thy place," the CCP intends to also know everyone's place at all times. A vast network of CCTV cameras with AI-enabled facial, iris, voice, and gait recognition capabilities; geospatial monitoring of individual movements through cell phone positioning data; a nearly universal cashless payment system for monitoring all financial transaction (including, as is planned for the future, through a fully government-controlled digital currency); and, most recently, a carefully crafted "social credit system" that permanently monitors and rewards or punishes people's political trustworthiness based on everything they say or do in China's omnipresent digital world. Technology like this is creating a surveillance and police state of unprecedented power. Digital technologies not only allow the state to keep track of nearly everything its common citizens do but also enable party leadership to closely monitor the political compliance of local party cadres right across the country.

All previous Chinese rulers have struggled with the almost impossible challenge of maintaining political control over the country's vast population, its formidable geography, and the power of local elites—a difficulty encapsulated by the oft-cited twelfth-century proverb, "The mountains are high, and the emperor is far away." These new digital technologies may enable the Communist Party to remain several steps ahead. In the past, absolute political control was seen as an ideal but ultimately unattainable dream for a committed Leninist party. Now, for the first time in its history, Xi and the party see such control as lying within their reach.

5

★ ★ ★ ★ ★

The Second Circle: Securing National Unity

M any Americans may not appreciate how central the Taiwan question is to the CCP's political priorities, the extent to which this has intensified under Xi Jinping's leadership, or how much Taiwan shapes how China views its overall relationship with the United States. Over the years, Taiwan has often been at the margins of most public policy debates in Washington about the future of US-China relations. The reverse applies in Beijing. It is true that Taiwan remains core business for US Indo-Pacific Command in Honolulu. But there has often been a real disconnect between this strategic awareness within the US military establishment and the way both the White House and Congress have considered Taiwan's place within the overall US-China relationship. That is now changing as tensions across the Taiwan Strait increase.

The fundamental tensions between China and the United States over Taiwan have continued since 1949, notwithstanding the signing of the three joint communiqués that established the basis for diplomatic relations between Washington and Beijing between 1972 and 1982. China never renounced the right to use armed force to return Taiwan to Chinese sovereignty if it deems it necessary. For its part, the United States, while recognizing that Taiwan is part of China, has always rejected China's right to use force to achieve its goal of national unity. No other country has the equivalent of America's Taiwan Relations Act of 1979 (TRA), which stipulated legal obligations future American presidents must observe in protecting Taiwan's political, economic, and security interests. No other country regularly resupplies Taiwan with the necessary military hardware to maintain defensive capabilities sufficient to deter Beijing from launching an armed assault. And certainly no other country offers an implied, albeit deliberately ambiguous, security guarantee to defend Taiwan with its own armed forces in the event of Chinese military action. The language of the TRA stipulates that the US will "consider any effort to determine the future of Taiwan by other than peaceful means, including by boycotts and embargoes, a threat to the peace and security of the western Pacific area, and of grave concern to the United States." The expansive regional scope of this language is often interpreted as a potential trip wire designed by Washington to help trigger wider allied participation in any future US military action over Taiwan. Therefore, in Beijing's eyes, the United States represents the paramount obstacle to the completion of its "sacred historical mission" of national unification.

There is, however, a third and more volatile dynamic at play on the Taiwan question. This is the changing attitudes of the Taiwanese government and people since the island first democratized twenty-five years ago. The Taiwanese military dictatorship that lasted from 1949 to 1987, first under Chiang Kai-shek and then his son, Chiang Ching-kuo, was always resolute in its support for a One-China policy, disagreeing only on whether the legitimate government of that China was in Beijing or Taipei. But the rise of the Taiwan independence movement and the repeated election of the pro-independence Democratic Progress Party (DPP) candidates to the presidency in Taipei have muddied the question of Taiwan's relationship to the mainland.

After the Taiwan Strait Crisis of the late 1990s, Xi Jinping's immediate predecessors changed course and sought to seduce Taiwan into political reunification through long-term economic dependency and eventual political absorption. Indeed, China's long-term strategy of absorbing Taiwan over time by gradually converging the two economies into one, including by tempting Taiwanese investment into the mainland, has produced some positive results for Beijing. There is a significant constituency within the Taiwanese business community, typically represented by the Kuomintang (KMT), that argues that closer relations with the mainland are crucial to Taiwan's fundamental interests. Nonetheless, this gradualist approach is seen in Beijing as moving far too slowly, if not thrown into reverse altogether.

This gradualist economic-absorption strategy suffered a significant setback in 2019 when, with Beijing's backing, the Hong Kong government introduced a draft extradition law that weakened Hong Kong's existing legal autonomy within the framework of "one country, two systems." Millions of protesters took to the streets, only to be eventually crushed by Hong Kong police and the enactment of the draconian Hong Kong National Security Law, which criminalized most forms of protest. To the extent that reunification under the model of "one country, two systems" ever attracted political support in Taiwan itself, that support died with the Hong Kong crisis. Even normally pro-Beijing KMT leaders in Taiwan were forced to publicly disavow "one country, two systems." The crackdown in Hong Kong offered yet more evidence that in an increasingly authoritarian China, domestic political and policy dissent would no longer be tolerated. This left Beijing with ever-declining credibility in its efforts to bring about a negotiated political compact with rambunctiously democratic Taiwan. Indeed, the Taiwanese people are now unlikely to ever yield to any form of "political deal" between its political elites and China. That being the case, Beijing is likely to conclude that political, economic, and military coercion are the only options remaining on the policy shelf.

Xi appears to have already concluded that the gradualist approach has failed. In his view, it has simply provided the pro-independence Democratic Progressive Party (DPP) with the time to cultivate a growing nationalist constituency on the island (especially among the young generation). It also allowed Taipei to permanently postpone the question of political union while imposing limits on how far economic integration was allowed to go. When the DPP's Tsai Ing-wen first won the presidency in 2016 and refused to accept the standard One-China formulation as the basis for continuing negotiations across the strait, Xi cut off all formal communications. When Tsai then secured a landslide reelection in 2020, based largely on a campaign pointing to the prodemocratic protests in Hong Kong and the impossibility of Taiwan ever accepting the "one country, two systems" model, it only served to further enrage Xi. He publicly reaffirmed China's preparedness to use all necessary means, including armed force, to bring about reunification if other measures failed and warned that Taiwanese independence would "only bring about profound disaster for the Taiwanese."

In a further signal to the United States, Xi stated that China would "brook no foreign interference" on the resolution of the Taiwan question. As we'll discuss in a later chapter, he has accelerated the PLA's military modernization and expansion program with the explicit aim of fighting and winning a war in the Taiwan Strait. The PLA has deployed more ships and aircraft in exercises and operations close to the Taiwanese coast than ever before. For the first time, Chinese forces regularly circumnavigate the island, reportedly simulating a naval blockade. And China has launched a concerted effort to further reduce Taiwan's "international political space" through a diplomatic offensive to pressure Taiwan's dwindling number of diplomatic partners in the international community to switch their official recognition to Beijing.

Furthermore, Xi has sought to tighten the screws on the Taiwanese economy, where Tsai has been more politically vulnerable. China slowed the number of mainland tourists visiting the island to a trickle, at a time when Taiwanese growth was slowing. Finally, there are growing accusations (by both the Taiwanese government and independent observers) of attempted Chinese cyberinterference in Taiwanese electoral processes and of concerted disinformation and influence-buying operations being waged in its media.

A key question is how much of this new approach is driven by a new internal political timetable for reunification. Following the centenary celebration of the establishment of the Chinese Communist Party in 2021, the second major official centenary in the coming decades—that of the founding of the People's Republic itself in 2049—looms much larger on the political calendar. Xi may plan to be in power for the long term, but given that he turns sixty-nine in 2022, time is running out for him to achieve his dream of returning Taiwan to the warm embrace of the motherland. To become the CCP leader who finally achieves national unity by bringing Taiwan into the fold would be to achieve a level of political immortality in the eyes of the party and country that rivals Mao's. It would also be an accomplishment that would permanently solidify his political legitimacy against any other internal criticism. Against this logic, it seems increasingly likely that Xi will want to secure Taiwan during his political lifetime. Xi is a man in a hurry when it comes to Taiwan.

This timeline realistically takes us out to the mid-2030s, by which time Xi would be in his early eighties. If this analysis holds true and Beijing's military advantage across the Taiwan Strait becomes even stronger, the trajectory for Beijing's Taiwan policy is likely to become more hard-line throughout the 2020s (a projection bolstered by Xi's order at the end of 2020 for the military to accelerate its modernization process to completion by 2027 instead of a previous goal of 2035). This is unlikely to change even if there is a return to a more politically accommodating KMT administration in Taipei.

While the "return" of Taiwan remains the holy grail of Communist Party politics, Tibet, Xinjiang, and Inner Mongolia are also seen as belonging to a core set of Chinese national security interests. Each represents a confluence of external and internal security factors. Tibet, once the source of much internal unrest, has today been largely "harmonized" by a mix of heavy-handed security measures, surveillance technologies, internal Han migration, and cultural assimilation policies among Tibetans that have now been exported to other "problem" regions of China—namely, Xinjiang. Concerns about ethnic unity run very deep in the CCP, and Beijing still keeps a wary eye on Tibet. Tibet also plays a central dynamic in China's strategic relationship with India, given that India has long played host to the exiled Dalai Lama and considering the two countries' continuing Himalayan border disputes.

Meanwhile, Inner Mongolia, despite the resolution of China's common border with Russia decades ago, also represents a continuing source of strategic anxiety between China and Russia. The two powers have competed for influence in greater Mongolia (encompassing the Inner Mongolian autonomous region in the PRC and the independent nation of Mongolia) for centuries. Despite its vast economic and population advantage, for Beijing, the political distinctiveness of ethnic Mongolians living along China's border has become a growing concern. This has led to new measures to impose Chinese language and culture programs across Inner Mongolia in order to contain what is perceived in Beijing to be an emerging separatist threat.

However, in recent years, it is the Xinjiang Uyghur Autonomous Region that has been the object of the most severe security paranoia in Beijing—and the growing attention of the outside world. Xinjiang, which literally translates as "new frontier" in Mandarin, represents China's western gateway to what it perceives to be the increasingly hostile Islamic world of central Asia, South Asia, and the Middle East. This sense of the region being a dangerous frontier is reinforced by concerns about the threat from China's homegrown Islamic separatist movement within Xinjiang itself, which has long sought independence from China. This has included acts of terrorism against Han Chinese in other parts of China, as well as in Xinjiang (including one when Xi was physically present in the region), which have infuriated Xi and the CCP.

After ethnic riots between Han settlers and Uyghurs broke out in Xinjiang in 2009, Beijing appointed a new party secretary, Zhang Chunxian, to the region, who embarked on a strategy of economic development as a means of preventing unrest. However, the riots triggered an internal argument within the party, with China's leading counterterrorism expert, Hu Lianhe, issuing a call in 2011 for a "second generation of ethnic policies" that would move to forge a more cohesive and unified "state-race" (*guozu*). Previously, adapting the Soviet model, the PRC officially recognized fifty-five *minzu* (ethnic minorities) as equal to the Han majority and granted them a certain amount of limited autonomy, such as the freedom to pass on their language and customs. Many Chinese scholars warned that changing this policy would likely lead to an escalation of resentment, violence, and chaos.

But after a Uyghur terrorist rammed a vehicle into a crowd at the Gate of Heavenly Peace in Beijing and killed two people, Xi Jinping announced at a December 2013 politburo meeting that China would follow a new strategic plan for Xinjiang. This would include "a major altering of the region's strategy," in which the party would strike hard at the presumed root causes of social instability: the three "evil forces" of splittism, extremism, and terrorism. Then, in March 2014, Xinjiang-linked terrorists armed with knives attacked a Kunming railway station, killing 31 and injuring more than 140. Enraged by what was quickly described as "China's 9/11," Xi called for an all-out "struggle against terrorism, infiltration, and separatism" using the "organs of dictatorship" that would show "absolutely no mercy."

Soon village-based work teams were ordered to begin a "people's war against terrorism" and were instructed to visit each household in their respective jurisdictions to identify any radical elements and then to begin "educational transformation" work. They concluded that up to 30 percent of the people of Xinjiang were infected with extremist thought, urgently requiring what the party described as "concentrated and forceful educational dredging work." In 2016, hard-line Tibet-security veteran Chen Quanguo was sent to replace the softer Zhang Chunxian. He quickly implemented a "grid-style social management" policy that he trialed in Tibet, placing police and paramilitary troops at checkpoints every few hundred feet in the capital Urumqi; establishing thousands of "convenience police stations"; and deploying advanced digital tools, such as facial recognition software, to surveil the local Uyghur population. By 2017, a directive had gone out to use "concentrated educational transformation centers" to manage "key groups" in Xinjiang society.

This policy led to what Western journalists, researchers, and academics reported as the mass involuntary detention and "brainwashing" of up to one million ethnic Uyghurs in Xinjiang. By the summer of 2020, reports also emerged claiming that large-scale "population control" measures were being enforced in Xinjiang, including forced abortions and the involuntary sterilization of Uyghur women. These reports led the US in January

2021 to become the first country to define what was happening in Xinjiang as "genocide" and a "crime against humanity." The Biden administration upheld this declaration when it entered office weeks later. Other countries, including Canada, the UK, and the Netherlands, soon followed suit—along with a growing international activist movement that called for a boycott of goods made in Xinjiang and of the 2022 Winter Olympic Games in Beijing.

Xinjiang has, therefore, become not only an internal concern for Beijing but a defining international challenge as well. So far, Xi Jinping has shown no signs of moderating what he described in 2014 as his determination to "unflinchingly walk the correct road of China's unique solution to the ethnic question." In 2020, Xi declared that the party's Xinjiang policy was a "totally correct" success that "must be adhered to for the long term."

Taken together, from Beijing's perspective, Tibet, Inner Mongolia, Xinjiang, Hong Kong, and Taiwan have long been seen as major challenges to national unity. The difference today is that Xi Jinping has adopted a much harder line than any recent Chinese leader. Xi, unlike his recent predecessors, has been indifferent to international reaction. He believes that the national security imperatives of "complete security" are more important than any foreign policy or wider reputational cost to the regime. Xi also believes that the rest of the world now depends on the Chinese economy so much that international political reactions to Chinese measures will, in the main, be superficial, symbolic, and temporary. The Chinese leadership has a long memory and can remember how international political and economic sanctions against China after Tiananmen in 1989 quickly faded away once there was money to be made. They concluded that the international reaction to the 2019–2020 crackdown on Hong Kong's freedoms would be similarly muted. And from Beijing's perspective, they were largely right.

6

★ ★ ★ ★ ★

The Third Circle: Ensuring Economic Prosperity

Xi Jinping's third priority is ensuring economic prosperity and the political stability that he believes it fundamentally provides. The CCP's mission is to eliminate poverty, raise national living standards to developed-country levels, and grow government revenues to cover increasing social welfare outlays in education, health, and aged care. The CCP also harbors ambitions for China to become a leading global power in science and technology. Funding the ever-growing demands of a modernizing Chinese military is not cheap either. Sustained long-term economic growth in the vicinity of 5 to 6 percent annually is, therefore, essential for achieving these core objectives.

Increasing living standards and improving the quality of life for the Chinese people is a core part of Xi's effort to build the party's political legitimacy in the post-Mao era. This is the unspoken social contract between party and people: that the public will continue to tolerate an authoritarian political system under the party so long as the people's material livelihood continues to improve. While Xi is no economist and appears to have surprisingly limited feel for how market economies actually function (he is much more comfortable in the classical political domains of ideology, security, and international relations), he understands the axial link between continued public prosperity and the security of his long-term leadership.

Indeed, popular resentment about a failing economy has generally been seen by his detractors as the one factor that could bring him down. One of the recurring patterns of internal Chinese politics is that someone in authority must always take the blame if something goes radically wrong that the party elites judge to have been a preventable disaster. An economic recession would be a case in point, given that China has not experienced one since the Cultural Revolution. Even a lesser economic failing, such as a rapid decline in growth that wiped out many small and medium businesses, would also ultimately demand a political price. It is for these reasons that the economy still looms as the political Achilles' heel for the party's—and Xi's—future.

Xi finds himself wrestling with five major interconnected, and in some cases conflicting, challenges in China's unfolding political economy: (1) to maintain economic growth to provide employment and rising living standards; (2) to do so while maintaining an optimal internal balance between the state and the market without ceding the party's political control to a new generation of entrepreneurs; (3) to ensure that growth is better distributed than in the past so that economic inequality is reduced; (4) to impose new carbon constraints on China's previous economic development model to deal with the now accepted reality of climate change; and (5) to manage the external economic pressures now being applied by the United States on trade, investment, and technology.

The First Three Phases of Xi's Evolving Economic Strategy

In dealing with these various challenges and opportunities, China's political economy has undergone three separate transitions under Xi Jinping—before now entering the early stages of a potentially revolutionary fourth phase. The first phase, from 2013 to 2015, began with the party adopting what became known as "the Decision." China's previous economic model was characterized by labor-intensive, low-wage manufacturing for export; high levels of state investment in national infrastructure; a significant role for state-owned enterprises (SOEs); and scant regard for environmental consequences. After a ferocious internal debate once Xi took office in 2013, the party, for the first time, explicitly declared that it would let market force play "a decisive role" in the economy. This new model sought to make a rapidly expanding private sector, particularly the services, financial, and technology sectors, the new engine of economic growth. There was, however, to be a significant continuing role for SOEs, concentrated in a defined list of critical industries, given Xi's ongoing concern that ultimate state ownership of the economy be maintained and never ceded to China's burgeoning private sector. Finally, all this would be tempered by new principles of environmental sustainability. The 2013 "Decision on Several Major Questions About Deepening Reform" was accompanied by a detailed blueprint of sixty specific reform agenda items (the "Sixty Decisions") that were seen as Xi Jinping's answer to catching up from what had come to be called ten wasted years of economic reform under his two immediate predecessors, General Secretary Hu Jintao and Premier Wen Jiabao—and escape the CCP's long-standing fear of being caught in the middle-income trap.

All this changed, however, with the Chinese financial crisis of 2015. The event marked the beginning of the second transition in political and economic policy during the Xi Jinping period. That summer, Chinese authorities struggled to manage a stock market bubble driven by excessive liquidity and financially illiterate investors. The proliferation of margin-lending practices by individuals and corporations borrowing heavily from financial institutions to make investments in dubious asset classes (in what was assumed to be a permanently booming economy) soon turned into a disaster on Chinese equities markets. Once the asset bubble burst, state and private institutions were quickly directed by the government, as part of what became known as a national team, to invest heavily in equities to try to steady the market. This failed comprehensively, investors interpreting this radical intervention as a sign that it was time to jump ship, resulting in even more spectacular losses. The Shanghai Composite Index (China's equivalent of the Dow Jones Industrial Average) collapsed 32 percent in less than three weeks in July 2015. At its 2015 high, its market capitalization was $10 trillion; by September 2018, it was at $5.7 trillion. Markets were finally stabilized at much lower prices by early 2016, but the damage had been done; they would take until 2020 to eventually recover. To Xi, it was more than a matter of financial management; it was a political fiasco. Tens of millions of average citizens had lost their savings, and they blamed the party and government. As a result, Xi's intuitive skepticism toward what he soon described as the reckless expansion of capital was intensified—just as his political appetite for further broad-based market reforms, and not just those in finance, eroded.

The 2013 economic blueprint became the casualty as the pace of reform ground to a virtual halt. Tight capital controls were implemented in 2015–2016 to prevent capital flight, but this made it more difficult for Chinese private firms to expand abroad and, in many cases, even sustain their existing international operations. Meanwhile, concern over China's debt-to-GDP ratio spiked, driven by a largely unregulated shadow banking sector and ballooning local government debt. The strong regulatory clampdown on shadow lenders that followed, as part of a general deleveraging campaign, also had a suffocating effect on China's private firms. The administrative allocation of credit through China's official banks favored SOEs at the expense of the private sector. This was despite the fact that by 2016, private firms had become the crucial—indeed almost exclusive—driver of overall economic growth. As a result of the credit squeeze, many troubled firms were bought up by the state sector, in part or in whole, in what became known as China's new mixed-economy model. Other firms simply went to the wall.

The third phase of Xi's evolving economic policy emerged in late 2018, after the party realized that, over the course of that year, growth was radically slowing. This slowdown was driven by faltering confidence in the private sector and declining fixed-capital investment growth, although the unfolding trade war with Trump's America also played a role. The reasons went beyond the blunt and brutal impact of the post-2015 deleveraging campaign. They included the party's public equivocation on how big major

private firms should be allowed to grow, the increased status of party secretaries within the management of private firms, and the ongoing vagaries
of China's legal system. Taken together with the party's far-reaching anticorruption campaign, which often targeted executives as well as officials,
all these measures generated growing angst among Chinese entrepreneurs
about their personal and financial futures.

Prompted by this emerging crisis of private-sector confidence, the
party launched a multilayered policy response from November 2018. First,
Xi once again talked about the need for "institutional economic reform,"
suggesting at least a partial return to the 2013 blueprint. The following
year, both Xi and his principal economic policy lieutenant, Vice Premier
Liu He, convened high-level gatherings of China's leading private entrepreneurs, reiterating the centrality of the private sector to China's future.
Liu reminded the nation in a speech that "the private sector was responsible
for 90 percent of new employment growth, 80 percent of urban development, 70 percent of technological innovation, and 50 percent of the country's taxation." This put party officials and China's powerful SOE sector on
notice that China could not grow at the pace it needed to in the absence
of a strong, resilient, competitive private sector. Then, as a third step, both
Liu He and Central Bank governor Yi Gang accelerated the release of a
series of financial-sector reforms aimed at opening China's banking, insurance, equities, debt, and credit rating markets to much greater international competition. This was intended to both improve the effectiveness of
China's woefully inefficient credit-allocation system for private firms and
to prepare the country for a greater dependency on future foreign-capital
inflows to deal with what the country's monetary authorities then believed
would be China's emerging current-account deficit. Simultaneously, China
"internationalized" a number of trade, investment, and intellectual property protection standards that it had agreed to during the course of its 2019
bilateral negotiations with the United States to try to resolve the trade war.
By extending these selected policy liberalizations across the board to all
China's economic partners, it made them appear less as political concessions to Washington and more about China's ongoing financial reforms.

Finally, never wanting to take unnecessary political risks with the country's overall economic growth rate, Xi also authorized stimulus measures to prop up growth, reinforced by repeated public assurances from China's Central Bank governor that Beijing still had significant headroom in its fiscal- and monetary-policy settings to sustain economic growth in the vicinity of the politically sensitive 6 percent threshold. This figure reflected the party's internal calculus of what was necessary to sustain employment for the growing supply of new graduates each year, improve living standards, and maintain overall social stability.

All these domestically induced economic problems predated the US-China trade war of 2018–2019, the COVID-19 crisis of 2020, and the broader debate that erupted in both countries on the possibility of a more general decoupling of the US and Chinese economies. But these combined internal and external factors, which together brought unprecedented pressures to bear on Chinese policy makers in what has already been one of the most challenging periods in China's remarkable economic growth story, also made clear China's continuing vulnerability to the United States. Xi Jinping concluded that US economic pressure could become lethal if China's domestic economic engine continued to falter, crushing the growth rate altogether. This presented hard policy questions for Xi Jinping and his advisors, all core dilemmas on the future resilience and direction of the Chinese economy.

The most difficult challenge for Xi Jinping in the 2018–2019 period became how to maintain acceptable growth levels into the future while also dealing with the combined pressures of a rising Chinese middle class demanding a better life, a disgruntled but increasingly powerful private sector at home, and an increasingly angry America abroad. Concern about the United States is not just about China's vulnerability to contacting American export markets. More fundamentally, it is about the implications for China of a fundamental rupture in the relationship arising from growing restrictions on exports and investments in technology and from the extent to which international capital markets will remain open to China's domestic policy needs. This includes the risk of greater weaponization of the US dollar against China as well as the possibility of further financial sanctions arising from Chinese policies on Taiwan, Hong Kong, and Xinjiang. These specific challenges, the differences between them, and the risks of US-China economic decoupling will be explored in the last section of this chapter. Collectively, these constitute the terrain for the next phase of economic warfare between Washington and Beijing. They have also deeply shaped Xi Jinping's ever-hardening economic worldview—a view that has led him to make them the major focus of his latest major pivot in the evolution of China's macropolicy settings since 2013.

The Fourth Phase: Xi's Populist-Socialist Economy

Xi Jinping is now implementing a fourth major pivot to restructure China's economy, this time far larger in scope than anything since the 2013 Decision and reflecting his core priorities to protect China and the CCP against countervailing forces, both internal and external. Since 2020–2021, Xi has been implementing a new comprehensive economic strategy—now called the New Development Concept—to prioritize security, political stability, and economic equality over rapid individual wealth accumulation; societal cohesion over economic efficiency; and national self-sufficiency over the benefits of open international exchange. This new economic era also reflects a deeply waning commitment to the continuation in the future of the market reforms of the past.

This shift in policy first exploded into public awareness with the state's suspension of the highly anticipated IPO of Jack Ma's Ant Financial Group, followed by a furious regulatory investigation launched into Chinese ride-hailing giant Didi Chuxing in July 2021 after its $4.4 billion IPO on the New York Stock Exchange, which regulators had explicitly warned the company not to pursue. New data-security rules were quickly implemented, restricting IPOs by Chinese companies abroad. That wasn't all. China's cyber regulator accused 105 apps—including job-recruitment and short-video apps such as ByteDance—of illegal collection of personal data and demanded immediate rectification. The Chinese government quietly took a 1 percent ownership stake and a board seat in the domestic Chinese subsidiaries of ByteDance (the owner of TikTok) and Chinese micro-blogging platform Weibo. Discussion of an antimonopoly crackdown on China's tech giants reached a fever pitch. Finally, in late July of that year, Beijing published new regulations banning for-profit tutoring and private education companies, effectively killing overnight a thriving sector attracting billions in investment. Chinese stocks plunged, as it dawned on executives and investors, both in China and around the world, that a new policy reality had crept up on them, that the policy assumptions they had made in the past, based on decades of experience, were changing rapidly, and that this was just the start of what Xi had planned.

However, the ideological seeds of this new era were planted by Xi far earlier. At the Nineteenth Party Congress, held in the fall of 2017, he announced that the principal contradiction facing the party had changed. Due to its arcane phrasing in the old-school theoretical language of Marxist dialectical materialism, the significance of this was largely missed in the international community—not only in the West but even in China itself. In dialectical analysis, the principal contradiction of the hidden dynamic opposing forces driving economic and social change is what defines the whole shape and direction of China's political economy within the party's underlying Marxist theoretical framework. Correctly identifying and solving the principal contradiction in a changing internal and external environment is the top political job of the ruling party and its leadership. Failing to do so would inevitably lead—as Marx predicted—to revolution. Therefore, for Xi to define such a profound ideological change, for the first time in thirty-five years of reform and opening, meant that he had identified something he considers to be of existential importance.

The principal contradiction the party had identified and worked to resolve since 1981 had been "the ever-growing material and cultural needs of the people versus backward social production" (a contradiction solved by the reform and opening-driven "central task" of doing whatever was necessary to generate rapid GDP growth). But the principal contradiction, according to Xi, became "the contradiction between unbalanced and inadequate development and the people's ever-growing needs for a better life." This meant that, to resolve this contradiction, the "central task" of the party's economic and social strategy would again have to shift to create what is described as "more balanced, better-quality development across regions and sectors" and provide more equitably for the people's needs. After all, state media noted at the time, "common prosperity is the hallmark of socialism."

Still, it took time for the party's cadres—let alone business executives and the broader public—to grasp what this ideological change would mean in reality. Xi himself may not have immediately settled on how to address this critical shift in the principal contradiction in the aftermath of the 2017 Party Congress. Threads of a more statist approach to economic policy emerged during the course of 2018–2019. But it was not until the second half of 2020 that Xi's new economic thinking took a comprehensive form, as it congealed into a strikingly populist return to the party's socialist roots, becoming the core of what is now officially dubbed Xi Jinping Economic Thought for the New Era.

Xi's New Development Concept

In 2020, Xi's new economic approach consolidated into what he calls the New Development Concept (NDC). In essence, the NDC is intended to serve as the economic strategy with which he will guide China through an increasingly dangerous world, including what he describes as "changes unseen in a century." Ultimately, as Xi told a meeting of China's top policy makers in July 2021, the NDC is meant "to ensure our survival" through both "foreseeable and unforeseeable storms." This makes one thing quite clear: Xi's political narrative is that the only way to do this is to have a strong party, a strong "core leader," and a clear strategy to navigate China through the years of domestic and international "struggle" that lie ahead. Indeed, "struggle," once Mao's catchcry during the Cultural Revolution, has become Xi's leitmotif for his eponymous "new era." At the core of that strategy lies Xi's NDC, which is designed to replace Deng Xiaoping's old era of reform and opening that followed the Mao era and ran from 1978 to approximately 2017. Welcome to the brand-new era of Xi Jinping.

So what does the NDC actually mean for Chinese economic policy? Although it first appeared in 2015 (when it was brought up by Xi at the Second Plenary Session of the Eighteenth Central Committee), for the next few years, the term *New Development Concept* was of secondary significance in the party's official discourse, left vague enough to encapsulate whatever Xi's take on economic policy happened to be at the time. Its intended significance was then underscored by Xi's decision to have it formally incorporated into the Chinese state constitution in March 2018. Over the years that followed, Xi gradually imbued the concept with more meaning, and by 2020, the NDC came to embody the confluence of three key priorities: nationalist self-reliance, his protectionist concept of a dual-circulation economy, and his new redistributive doctrine of common prosperity.

The first pillar of the NDC is the concept, already touched on previously in this account, of self-reliance (*zili gengsheng*), which literally means "to rejuvenate through one's own strength." This is a revival of the Mao-era obsession with eliminating China's vulnerabilities to any pressure from the outside world. But where Mao sought to boost grain yields and steel production, Xi seeks a China capable of producing its advanced semiconductors, software operating systems, and cloud-computing infrastructure—in short, leading on the cutting edge of critical strategic technologies through China's indigenous innovation effort, notwithstanding any restrictions that might be imposed by a future US administration.

In Xi's worldview, the key to China achieving self-reliance is in increasing its ability to marshal national capital to advance its research and development sector, though also securing foreign collaboration wherever possible. For example, Vice Premier Liu He has been appointed to lead a key $1 trillion initiative to help Chinese semiconductor manufacturers overcome US-led restrictions. But, crucially, while in Xi's vision self-reliance extends to everything from heavy manufacturing to genetically modified seeds for agriculture, a key new area has also recently emerged in the official discourse:

financial self-reliance, or the necessity to build systems capable of resisting pressure from a US dollar–dominated global financial system.

The second pillar of Xi's NDC is his vision for a dual-circulation economy. Introduced in the fall of 2020 as part of China's latest five-year plan for 2021–2025, dual circulation, in essence, calls for a much greater contribution to aggregate economic growth from China's massive domestic market by ramping up consumer demand from a large, strong, and emerging middle-income class (i.e., internal circulation). Simultaneously, it would focus on rebalancing China's global economic engagement from a model anchored in labor-intensive manufacturing for mass export to a model prioritizing both imports and high-value chain exports (external circulation). It is, in part, a conscious reversal of the "great international circulation" strategy adopted by Deng Xiaoping in the 1990s to power China's rise under the general strategic direction of reform and opening.

Xi's dual-circulation strategy is fundamentally a bid to make China's economy more resilient to external shocks brought on by geostrategic turmoil, global supply chain disruption, punitive tariffs, and a contraction in global trade. It therefore goes hand in hand with self-reliance as a means of reducing China's overall vulnerability to outside forces. Together, both emphasize state support for key strategic industries, including greater support for China's state-owned enterprises. Moreover, with a dual-circulation economy, China's vast internal market can, in Xi's vision, not only drive self-sufficient economic growth but also become what he has called a "huge gravitational field attracting international commodity and factor resources" that forces the rest of the world to engage with China on Beijing's terms or risk falling behind commercially. Or as Xi himself stated in the party's theoretical journal in April 2020, "We must sustain and enhance our superiority across the entire production chain . . . and we must tighten international production chains' dependence on China, forming a powerful countermeasure and deterrent capability against foreigners who would artificially cut off supply [to China]."

However, the third pillar of Xi's New Development Concept is focused exclusively internally—on fundamentally resolving the new principal contradiction identified by Xi in 2017. This is Xi's operationalization of his long-standing concept of common prosperity (*gongtong fuyu*). Common prosperity, according to Xi's goals defined in the party's fourteenth five-year plan, means that "all people shall make more tangible progress in substance over the next five years." This is notably a direct modification of Deng Xiaoping's guidance that it was okay to "let some people and some regions get rich first"—although (and this is often forgotten) Deng also said that this was meant only as "a shortcut to accelerate development and achieve common prosperity," which remained the "general principle." Therefore, in framing his economic campaign as prioritizing "common prosperity for all," Xi is portraying himself as completing what Deng was unable to finish during the forty-year-long period of reform and opening.

In truth, common prosperity reflects Xi's concern that income inequality had gotten radically out of hand in China, to the extent that it was threatening the party's popular legitimacy. Xi has made this point directly, warning his colleagues in January 2021 that "achieving common prosperity is not only an economic issue, but also a major political issue related to the party's governing foundation." With nominally communist China having one of the most unequal income distributions in the world, in which the top fifth of households have a disposable income more than ten times as high as those in the bottom fifth and the top 1 percent own approximately 30 percent of the wealth (compared with around 35 percent in America), Xi said, "We must not allow the gap between rich and poor to get wider."

This message was echoed by the Central Financial and Economic Affairs Commission meeting held in August 2021, which pledged to narrow the gulf between the rich and poor and reform income allocation by adjusting "excessively high incomes," encouraging high-income groups and enterprises to "give back more to society," and cracking down on "illegal gains." The party will encourage "getting rich through hard work and innovation" as opposed to speculation. The goal, according to Xi, is to create an "olive-shaped distribution," where the middle class of society is large and the two ends (rich and poor) are small. Common prosperity, thus, also aims to feed directly into dual circulation by boosting middle-class consumptive power. The bottom line, Xi said at the meeting, was that common prosperity was an "essential requirement of socialism"—so essential, apparently, that by August 2021 Xi had already used the phrase more than sixty-five times in his speeches.

Tangibly, common prosperity is reflected in a prioritization of maximum employment, increasing consumer purchasing power, and breaking monopolies to (theoretically) promote competition by smaller businesses and allow innovative new entrepreneurial start-ups to emerge and prosper. Also crucial to common prosperity is breaking the Chinese working and middle classes' growing sense that they are being exploited by a system of ruthless capitalism, in which entrenched corporate interests have cornered markets, devalued labor, and made it increasingly hard to get ahead in life.

All institutional stakeholders are expected to participate. For example, the People's Bank of China declared in August 2021, "We must make promoting common prosperity the starting point and the focus of all financial work." Under common prosperity, as defined by Xi, there is no escape for private firms. Or as Xi put it, "We should guide companies to obey the party leadership and serve the big picture of social and economic development."

The panicked sell-offs in large Chinese private-sector companies' equities following this wave of statements were sufficient to force Liu He's deputy, Han Wenxiu, to release a statement in August 2021 that attempted to clarify that while the plan was to "encourage getting rich through hard work and innovation. . . . We will not 'kill the rich to help the poor.'" Instead, the rich will merely be "encouraged" to give back more through what is labeled as a "tertiary distribution of wealth"—coming after the "primary distribution" of wealth through market wages and the "secondary distribution" of state spending. Calling on the rich to participate in charitable causes or otherwise assuming wider social responsibilities, "tertiary distribution" is, in essence, forced philanthropy. Politically literate companies, such as e-commerce platform Pinduoduo, quickly got the message—in that case, pledging to donate its entire second-quarter profit in 2021, or as much as $1.5 billion, to rural agricultural development. Meanwhile, online technology giants Tencent and Alibaba each pledged to donate more than $15 billion for common prosperity funds.

But common prosperity is not just about easing income inequality. It also has a significant social and cultural component. This appears to have been motivated, in part, by growing frustrations among Chinese youth, who have complained of poor postcollege employment prospects, a harsh 996 work schedule (9:00 a.m. to 9:00 p.m., six days a week) required by tech companies (since made illegal), and an exploitative gig labor sector commonly used by online tech platform companies to keep labor costs to a bare minimum. This practice has recently attracted growing public and therefore party scrutiny and discontent over poor pay and working conditions. A culture of nihilistic despair has appeared among Chinese netizens, commonly aired on social media in the form of popular slang terms such as *neijuan*, or involution, which describes a turning inward by individuals or society due to what one social media post described as a "prevalent sense of being stuck in a draining rat race where everyone loses." This despair also manifested itself in a movement known as *tangping*, or lying flat, in which people resolve to do the absolute bare minimum of work in life, relying instead on the generosity of the state.

While concerned about citizens' sense of economic injustice, Xi has little patience for the *tangping*. Hence, common prosperity measures have also gone hand in hand with a cultural crackdown on everything from video games (labeled "spiritual opium" by state media, with minors banned from playing them for more than three hours per week) to entertainment industry celebrities (where internet regulators have promised to censor "vulgar" displays of wealth and "resolve the problem of chaos" in online fan culture) to education ministry plans to "cultivate masculinity" in school-boys. As one nationalist blogger wrote recently in a post shared widely by state media, the goal is that "the cultural market will no longer be a paradise for sissy stars, and news and public opinion will no longer be in a position of worshipping Western culture." Applying copious doses of paternalistic, Confucian, and Leninist morality, Xi apparently doesn't want China's youth to lose their nationalistic virility and become apathetic slackers who do not make patriotic, productive citizens.

But nor, in Xi's eyes, does China have enough children. Another closely connected reason for Xi's common prosperity push is China's demographic crisis. China's 2021 census found that the Chinese population grew by only seventy-two million in 2020, representing a massive 18 percent drop in the number of newborns from 2019 and putting China's fertility rate at a record low of only 1.3 births per woman. Analysts predict China's population could peak as early as 2022, a full decade earlier than previously predicted. And with the portion of working-aged Chinese (fifteen to fifty-nine) relative to the entire population already standing at only 63 percent in 2020 (down from 70 percent in 2010), the demographic challenge to future economic growth appears acute. This has caused anxious planners in Beijing to lift China's one-child policy restrictions and allow up to three children per family (with all limits likely to soon be scrapped) but to little effect. Frustrated Chinese young people say the costs of having even one child are already outrageous. According to one study, the average Chinese family spends around $115,000 per child from birth to seventeen, before college costs. One survey found that 90 percent of respondents said they simply "would not consider" having three children. Hence, expensive private tutoring services (which grew at an average annual pace of 30 percent between 2017 and 2019) were among Xi's first targets in a blunt-edged effort to address this problem.

All three components of the New Development Concept are also grounded in Xi's fondness for what he regularly calls the "real economy," including sectors such as manufacturing, agriculture, merchandise trade, or consumer-oriented services that benefit the middle-income classes. This is in stark contrast with his apparent disgust with those speculative, "fictitious economy" sectors that, in his Marxist view, produce nothing of material value while extracting wealth from the middle-income class in the form of rent-seeking, "walled garden" monopolism, price collusion, financial speculation, the peddling of addictive or socially corrosive products, property speculators, online technology companies, and the "reckless" capital of the financial firms that enable them. As Xi warned in 2019, while the digital economy is important for GDP, "we must recognize the fundamental importance of the real economy . . . and never deindustrialize."

This merges with Xi's other strategic goals as well: to prevail in global strategic competition, he apparently does *not* believe that Chinese urbanites have a critical need to be provided with pricey ride-hailing services financed by Western investors, that Tencent provide increasingly addictive video games, or that globally oriented financial services firms vacuum up more of China's top university graduates as securities analysts. Rather, it seems that in Xi's worldview, it *is* critical that those graduates become patriotic engineers capable of helping China produce world-class semiconductors, for China to retain its world-leading manufacturing capabilities, and for middle-class consumers to be able to afford homes, raise and educate multiple children, and so power the dual-circulation economy.

When viewed through the lens of Xi Jinping's ideological and economic worldview, these otherwise seemingly scattershot policies and announcements from Beijing's regulatory crackdown on the private sector become parts of a coordinated strategic shift on how China's economy is intended to function, and for whom. For Xi, politics always comes first. And it certainly comes above simply economic efficiency and total factor productivity. As has been amply demonstrated since November 2020, Xi no longer cares what the Chinese billionaire class thinks is the best direction for China. He no longer cares if they (let alone some Wall Street investors) lose money as he pursues his core national strategic priorities. And he no longer cares if his policies are not, as the superwealthy would point out, the most efficient way to grow China's national GDP. Instead, Xi is laser-focused on a different, much larger constituency, "the people"—or, as he would define them, China's vast working-class and lower middle-class masses. It is their support—gained through addressing income inequality, cost of living, lack of good jobs, lack of equal opportunity, urban-rural divides, and their sense of social malaise—that Xi cares about now.

It should not be surprising that Xi's regulatory crackdown on what he defines as the monopolistic private-sector behavior of China's massive digital firms—the "trusts" of China's version of the American Gilded Age—is, so far, immensely popular with the Chinese middle class. Xi, always a keen politician, is clear-eyed about what is at stake here. He has harnessed a form of Chinese economic populism with a view to grafting it on to socialism with Chinese characteristics for his "new era."

In an April 2019 article published in the party journal *Qiushi*, Xi made an underreported declaration: "In recent years, some public opinions at home and abroad have raised questions about whether China is currently still socialist. Some people say it is 'capital socialist,' while others simply say it is 'state capitalist.' . . . These are all completely wrong!" Rather, he said, "socialism with Chinese characteristics is socialism," and "only socialism can save China, and only socialism with Chinese characteristics can develop China. This is the conclusion of history and the people's choice." Xi made clear that he would put socialism back at the forefront of economic policy.

All this has been enshrined as Xi Jinping Economic Thought in official party ideology—an ideology that, like the New Development Concept, has been enshrined in the text of the Chinese constitution. Both Xi Jinping Thought and New Development Concept are elastic concepts, capable of being expanded and contracted over time to suit prevailing political and economic circumstances. But they also contain within them what others have called a "band of meaning" that is radically different from the ideational bandwidth of the age of reform and opening. For the political economy, that means a significant shift to the left—between party and state, between market and state, between state-owned enterprises and the private sector, and from Deng's most famous aphorism that "to get rich is glorious" to Xi's new age of "common prosperity." These changes are real, and they are consistent with Xi's overarching worldview, anchored in the centrality of the party and his pan-ideological mission of Chinese nationalism.

This then has become the North Star of China's emerging political economy for the decade ahead. Xi believes that his New Development Concept, made up of this combination of self-reliance, dual circulation, and common prosperity, will be sufficient to transform China into a superpower strong enough to prevail in its unfolding strategic competition with the United States. As he put it to his comrades in January 2021, "As long as we can stand on our own and be self-reliant and maintain a vibrant flow of goods and services domestically, then we will be invincible no matter how the storm changes internationally. We will survive and continue to develop, and nobody can beat us or choke us to death."

The most important question for the period ahead is whether the truth is more likely to be the opposite: that these top-down solutions, or what Xi likes to call top-level design, and his general obsession with political control will be a hurdle, not a boon, for future economic growth. Or if they will, in fact, strangle the goose that laid the golden egg altogether. After all, China's largest private-sector players, once hailed as the country's national champions for driving the Chinese economic miracle—including, as Liu He admitted, nearly all productivity increases, wealth creation, technological progress, and a significant proportion of new employment—are increasingly being crushed by the clenched fist of the Chinese party and state.

The Relationship Between Xi's Worldview and China's Economic Decoupling with the United States

Xi Jinping's economic worldview has not evolved in a vacuum. As we've seen already, it has been influenced not only by his ideological beliefs but also by the real-world financial implosions on Chinese stock markets in 2015–2016, the ongoing challenges of deleveraging in order to manage systemic financial risk, and the enduring challenge of securing a sustainable growth strategy that delivers the economy from the middle-income trap that Chinese planners have long feared. It has also been deeply shaped by the changing international economic circumstances in which China found itself in the aftermath of the global financial crisis. But in this, as with everything else, the US-China economic relationship has loomed as the largest influence of all.

The previous section of this chapter sought to examine the impact of the trade war of 2018–2019 in causing Xi to become even more skeptical of China charting a future course based on a further wave of market reforms at home and integration with increasingly fractious markets abroad. Indeed, Xi's ideological predisposition to prefer the state over the market was reinforced by the major market disruptions that unfolded as a consequence of the trade war—from supply chains to technology markets to financial markets. The early signs of economic decoupling between the US and China in each of these areas had a profound effect on Xi. While economic nationalism had long been part of Xi's political personality, the growing fear that unilateral American action could undermine China's continued growth strategy has propelled him in a mercantilist, protectionist, and state-interventionist direction more rapidly than would otherwise have been the case. This has been particularly so with semiconductors, where China remains chronically dependent on critical suppliers from the US and its allies—and where major restrictions on Chinese access to the most advanced chips have been put in place. For these reasons, it is important to understand in greater detail the dynamics of the overall "decoupling" debate across trade, foreign direct investment, technology, and capital markets and the critical question of the future relationship between the US dollar and the Chinese yuan.

As we shall see in the next section, the answer in each of these five domains on the state of decoupling is different, although the overall trend line is decisively negative. Its impact on Xi Jinping's worldview has also been significant. China's leadership is on hyperalert to externally generated economic risk and any associated internal instability. This means that the future of decoupling writ large will not simply be a discretionary *American* policy option. It has also become a *Chinese* policy option and, in some cases, is already a preference. It is also sharpening Xi's preexisting economic worldview in a much more ideological, conservative, and nationalist direction—one where worst-case scenario planning has become the norm and where it may become a self-fulfilling prophecy.

US-China Trade

At this stage of its economic development, China's vulnerability to the United States restricting its markets to Chinese goods and services remains significant. The US has long been China's largest export market, and by a massive margin. By contrast, China is less significant to overall US exports. Whereas the US, on average, over the last decade represented 19 percent of Chinese exports, China represented only 8 percent of total US exports—consistently coming in as America's third-largest market after Canada and Mexico. Furthermore, China's economy in the aggregate is more trade exposed than that of the United States. As of 2020, China's exports and imports combined were equivalent to 34 percent of total Chinese GDP. By contrast, the traded sector of the US economy in the same year was 24 percent of US GDP. The US market, as of 2020—notwithstanding the trade war—still represented 17 percent of total Chinese exports, thereby still contributing significantly to China's overall economic growth. Therefore, while trade remains important to both economies, it is much more important to China. For these reasons, China's leadership in framing its overall policy response to the US is acutely aware that the US can still inflict more economic damage on China through trade than China can inflict on the US. America—for the time being at least—remains a key component of China's economic future.

However, because of the declining role of Chinese exports to GDP over the previous decade, China is less vulnerable now than it was on the eve of the global financial crisis. In 2006, Chinese exports to GDP had risen to 36 percent, whereas by 2020, they had halved to 18 percent. Second, Chinese household domestic consumption has been steadily increasing, replacing exports as the principal driver of economic growth. Boosting household consumption will continue to be an even more important part of Xi Jinping's strategy to reduce his country's overall vulnerability to international economic forces. China is also acutely aware that the United States is China-dependent for a range of consumer goods that cannot be readily replaced in the near term without producing an American consumer revolt. For example, 2018 data from the US Census Bureau showed that 82 percent of mobile phones and 94 percent of laptop computers imported to the US were from China. In other words, America does not hold all the cards in this game, and China knows it.

Xi is also likely to expand Chinese export opportunities in third-country markets in Europe, Japan, Korea, India, Southeast Asia, and BRI countries across Eurasia in order to reduce export dependency on the US over time. This may be implemented in tandem with a new diplomatic offensive in these states, as China seeks to widen its penetration of global markets. In the meantime, China achieved a major political and economic milestone with the signing of the long-negotiated Regional Comprehensive Economic Partnership (RCEP) multilateral trade agreement in November 2020. RCEP has been heralded as the largest free-trade agreement in the world. While it is not a "high-quality" agreement in terms of high-level and immediate market access across the participating economies, it has introduced major new changes to existing rules-of-origin arrangements that will have a significant effect in enhancing overall intraregional trade flows. Similarly, in September 2021 China formally applied to become a member of the Comprehensive Progressive Trans-Pacific Partnership (CPTPP), an attempt by eleven regional economies to salvage the TPP after the US withdrew from it in 2017. The move by Beijing presented the TPP-11, led by US allies Japan and Australia, with a major dilemma, particularly as China was not seeking to renegotiate standards in order to gain access to this higher-quality trade agreement (and all the more so because Taiwan also swiftly applied to join the agreement only six days later). Were China to successfully join, it would represent a final inversion of the Obama administration's original vision of using the CPTPP to reduce regional dependence on trade with China. Beijing is also likely to use its widening political influence in the WTO to prevent any US-led multilateral action led by the Biden administration against China's global economic and trading practices.

In summary, Xi Jinping recognizes the significant tactical threat to the economy from the US-China trade war for the coming years. His short-term strategy is to manage the trade war down by offering sufficient concessions to prevent further escalation while not compromising on what he regards as core national interests—both economic and political. In the longer term, Xi has a far more ambitious plan to protect China's economy, which we will discuss soon.

Foreign Direct Investment

Foreign direct investment (FDI) flows between China and the United States represent a relatively recent development in the overall bilateral economic relationship, only registering significant numbers over the last twenty years—and, in the case of Chinese investment in the US, only the last ten. Indeed, it was for these reasons that both sides negotiated a draft bilateral investment treaty (BIT) in 2009 to enhance the overall investment relationship to deal with China's historically restrictive approach to investment in multiple sectors of its economy that it deemed to be too sensitive. But amid the continuing travails of the trade war, these negotiations stalled. As of 2020, the total stock of US FDI in China had reached $284.9 billion, with annual flows dropping to $8.7 billion in 2020. The figure marks a fall of roughly a third from 2019 and is also the lowest since 2004. Meanwhile, Chinese FDI in the US reached an accumulated stock of $175.52 billion, with completed Chinese FDI in the US reaching $7.2 billion in 2020. The 2020 total is a slight uptick from $6.3 billion in 2019. In total, FDI between the US and China fell to $15.9 billion in 2020 amid pandemic-related disruptions and rising tensions in the US-China relationship. This represents the lowest level for two-way flows since 2009.

To put this into a wider context, total US-China bilateral FDI flows in 2018 represented approximately 1.4 percent of the total global FDI flows. As for total foreign investment coming to the United States, Chinese FDI in 2018 represented 1.4 percent of the stock of overall global investment into America and 2 percent of total 2018 flows. US FDI made up just over 9 percent of global FDI 2018 flow to China. Therefore, unlike trade, where US-China exchange is a significant portion of global trade in goods and services and represents a major component of each country's total trade, the same does not apply to the US-China FDI relationship.

Nonetheless, from China's perspective, foreign direct investment has been an important means of securing access to advanced technology. This applies to China's domestic FDI strategy as well as to the types of firms it has sought to acquire or invest in abroad, including in the United States. However, in the last several years, China encountered new and significant resistance to its approach to US investments. Washington has tightened Committee of Foreign Investment Regulations in the United States (CFIUS) procedures, introduced the Foreign Investment Risk Review Modernization Act (FIRRMA), and reactivated the Export Control Reform Act (ECRA), all of which imposed new levels of scrutiny and control on inbound Chinese investments and on what US firms may be allowed to collaborate on with Chinese partners abroad. These new measures have the potential to reduce not just foreign direct investment between the US and China but also portfolio investments, including venture capital activity, between the two countries. This is particularly significant given that, as of 2019, pre–COVID-19 crisis, venture capital (VC) investments in both countries had not been affected by the general downturn in bilateral FDI. That has changed. In 2020, two-way VC investments declined slightly in terms of both total value and number of funding rounds. Chinese VC in the US increased slightly and exceeded flows in the other direction for the first time ever, but only marginally so. In contrast, US VC in China dropped to the lowest level in five years.

For these reasons, from China's perspective, the investment door to the United States is closing, just as Beijing anticipates that US technology firms will face increasing resistance from Washington regulators in collaborating with Chinese companies and institutions in the future. Furthermore, any limited expectations Xi Jinping may have had about the restrictions put in place under the Trump administration being substantially reduced under Biden will have evaporated. The Biden administration has not only maintained most of the Trump-era restrictions but has also imposed new ones. As with trade, China is seeking to improve its foreign investment environment for other potential investors from third countries, along with improving reciprocal arrangements for Chinese investors abroad. This includes the introduction of China's new Foreign Investment Law with new provisions for intellectual property protection and the rendering of forced technology transfer illegal in China. China has also removed foreign equity caps for investors in the Chinese finance and insurance sectors.

In 2020, Beijing relaxed its requirements for entry into its financial sector. Subsequently, a number of foreign firms, including Goldman Sachs and JPMorgan Chase, acquired licenses and entered China's financial market, acting on the belief that Beijing's long-term commitment to further opening of its capital markets remains unchanged. Certainly, Beijing's lifting of all foreign ownership restrictions on mutual fund companies in April seemed to mark a significant demonstration of its intent to prop open China's doors for continued foreign capital. Since then, a number of Western mutual fund firms, including JPMorgan, Morgan Stanley, and Fidelity International, immediately applied for approval. And by December of that year, Goldman Sachs announced that it had reached an agreement to buy out its Chinese joint-venture partner, Beijing Gao Hua (Beijing granted full approval for the deal in 2021). As of January 2021, foreign companies have been able to obtain full ownership of companies in both the futures and insurance industries on the mainland. And by June 2021, BlackRock became the first global asset manager licensed to start a wholly owned onshore mutual fund business in China. In short, the securities, futures, and insurance sectors have all benefitted from Beijing's opening up.

However, the takeaway message for investors is that capital must be directed to industries Beijing wishes to develop. Internet platform companies are off-limits because foreigners holding such data would threaten the state. On the other hand, wealth management has been given the green light because Beijing needs foreign expertise to guide and develop a sector where investible assets are projected to surpass $70 trillion by 2030. That is a crucial need for a country with a fast-growing middle-income class and accumulated savings. Doing so does not conflict with Beijing's sensitivity to foreign capital leaving China; rather it doubles down on Beijing's belief that the weight of China's economic gravitational force will continue to attract more foreign capital.

Therefore, it is important to maintain perspective. Beijing is allowing more foreign participation in domestic financial markets but only within tightly controlled parameters, and it maintains heavy controls on capital outflows. Moreover, allowing foreign investors into sectors where Beijing has carefully weighted the risks and carefully selected while still maintaining significant control will allow Xi to argue to the crowd at Davos that recent regulatory actions are not meant to sever ties with the external world. Indeed, they were meant to reassure nervous investors about China's commitment to further opening. At the same time, as the overall global geopolitical climate continues to deteriorate, China is seeking to advance its overall investment relationships with Japan, India, and Europe in an effort to offset the prospective loss of American FDI, venture capital, and possibly the full range of portfolio investment opportunities. The actions it has taken so far to open its markets generally, along with hoped-for (but not yet completed) investment treaties such as the China-Europe Comprehensive Agreement on Investment, may help in that effort, but all three countries are also increasingly wary of the geopolitical risks.

Technological Self-Reliance

For Xi Jinping, achieving national self-reliance, particularly in indigenous technology and innovation, has become a key strategic priority, particularly following US efforts to constrict important technology exports to China, such as of advanced semiconductors. Xi's ambition is for China to achieve national autonomy in all critical technology categories in the decade ahead and—where possible—to achieve technological dominance over its economic and geostrategic competitors. In particular, this applies to the principal drivers of the artificial intelligence revolution; next-generation mobile, information, and telecommunications (ICT) technologies; and quantum computing. These ambitions are made clear in the "Made in China 2025" strategy of April 2015, which identified ten core technologies where China would need to prevail. The list is led by ICT but includes other major strategic technology categories as well, such as industrial robotics and new-energy vehicles. The strategy sets targets for China to be 70 percent nationally self-sufficient by 2025 and then globally dominant in all sectors by midcentury.

Made in China 2025 was supplemented in July 2017 with the state council's "New Generation Artificial Intelligence Development Plan," which explicitly states that AI is a major area of international economic and strategic competition, where China has a "major strategic opportunity" and where Beijing could achieve significant "first mover advantage." China's leadership believes that, collectively, these not only represent the principal next-generation technologies that will determine China's future global competitiveness but also represent the engine room of a much broader fourth industrial revolution. Following earlier revolutions driven by paradigm-shifting technologies in fossil fuel combustion, electricity generation, and, most recently, digital electronics, this fourth revolution—driven by profoundly disruptive technologies clustered around new breakthroughs in artificial intelligence, the convergence of human and machine capabilities, and its multiple potential applications through the internet of things—is seen by Chinese leaders as the process of transforming the fundamental structure of the global economy and determining the future distribution of global economic power. It is also seen as deeply instrumental in the ongoing "informationization" of warfare, including the deployment of new forms of autonomous offensive and defensive weaponry in remotely controlled battle spaces. China views embracing the fourth industrial revolution as pivotal to its pursuit of national self-reliance.

Given the revolutionary, game-changing nature of these emerging technologies, Beijing sees a combination of threat, opportunity, and urgency. China, having badly lagged behind the West in the first three industrial revolutions, is determined not to do so again. Indeed, Beijing sees an opportunity to dominate and deploy these technologies to leapfrog the US and the rest of the West economically and—if possible—militarily. China has also concluded that the US and its allies are embarked on a strategy to deny it access to these technologies in the future. From Beijing's perspective, this leaves them with little alternative than to achieve national self-reliance as quickly as possible. China has therefore embarked on a centrally coordinated strategy embracing an unprecedented national scientific research effort, the large-scale acquisition of targeted foreign firms, technology transfer from foreign joint ventures in China, the rapid development of national and global product champions, and, according to the US authorities, large-scale technology theft. In this rapidly unfolding technology war, the stakes have become very high indeed, dwarfing the traditional domains of trade, investment, foreign policy, and even classical security policy in its overall significance. In many respects, it has become the new central terrain of the relationship.

Artificial intelligence lies at the epicenter of this struggle for technological supremacy. AI has many definitions, but fundamentally it describes systems that interpret large quantities of digital information, make algorithmic decisions based on that information, and adapt and learn from the outcome of previous decisions. In recent years, advances in artificial intelligence have accelerated with the ability to process big data through improvements in semiconductors and computing power. China sees itself as being in a highly competitive race with the United States across the full spectrum of artificial intelligence technologies. Within this field, China has a range of strengths and weaknesses. It begins with the availability of pure data itself. China—at least at this stage—has great advantages over the collective West, given the vast size of its population; the volume of collectable data from the existing Chinese network of digital communication, economic, and social transactions; and other personal information where there are few privacy restrictions inhibiting effective access by the state for national purposes. Because this access to data represents a major potential first-mover advantage over competitors, China has limited the cross-border flow of its data banks to other countries. Under its cybersecurity law, it has mandated that foreign firms such as Apple must build data-storage facilities within China itself rather than using any offshore facilities. Nonetheless, there is a real debate as to whether China's current data advantage will be permanent, as digital governance regimes in the US, the UK, and Europe become more settled and greater access to individual data becomes more feasible at scale. However, for the time being, China's raw data advantage is real.

In the race to produce the most effective and efficient semiconductors and computer chips, a significant advantage is still held by the US and a number of other non-Chinese firms. In terms of semiconductors, as of 2018, China was only manufacturing 5 percent of total global supply. By contrast, the US provided 45 percent of the total global supply, primarily through its major corporate leader in the field, Intel. The other two global leaders in semiconductor technology are the Taiwan Semiconductor Manufacturing Company (China's largest supplier) and Korea's Samsung. Indeed, as of 2019, the US semiconductor industry represented about 50 percent of total US exports to China. China's vulnerability to US domination of the field was demonstrated by the 2018 decision by the Trump administration to ban all US semiconductor sales to the Chinese national champion ZTE (subsequently temporarily lifted), which came close to killing ZTE altogether (discussed in greater depth in chapter 14). This followed a 2017 decision by the administration to block the purchase of a US semiconductor firm by a Chinese SOE on CFIUS grounds (Taiwanese law entirely prevents Chinese ownership of semiconductor firms, and Korea has similar limitations). As a result, the US semiconductor industry believes that as of 2019, China was at least five years behind the most recent advances in global semiconductor technology. This is an assessment that has been reinforced by some Chinese industry analysts, who argue the gap to be even greater. While Chinese efforts to close this critical gap will continue, the degree of difficulty should not be underestimated.

As for the technology that integrates semiconductors into a single computer chip, a more complex and competitive picture is emerging. China has made more rapid progress in the development of specialist chips, particularly focusing on 3D images, voice, and text recognition. This is in contrast to more generic chips targeted at the general computing market, but which are then repurposed for AI-algorithmic purposes. This type of chip has been the long-standing strength of the American industry.

China's significant indigenous AI state research and development effort has focused on high-powered specialist chips, where the gap with the US and the rest is narrower than for generalized chips.

What China is seeking to do is to overcome its natural deficiencies in specific AI technologies and systems by directing a massive state research effort across the industry at large. For example, as of 2019, 48 percent of all AI start-ups globally were listed as Chinese, while 38 percent were American. It remains to be seen the extent to which these Chinese start-ups represent genuinely new, freestanding technologies or whether their numbers have been inflated because many are dealing with almost identical patents. The truth is that from a near-zero base only a decade ago, Chinese firms have become significant big-data and AI innovators by global standards. They have also become the leading adopters of emerging technologies developed elsewhere (for example, in digital payments systems), thereby providing massive cash flow for reinvestment back into primary research. Indeed, in the commercial adaption of AI technologies, China, on an economy-wide basis, leads the US in many fields.

Therefore, the reality is that a significant degree of technological decoupling between the United States and China is already underway. Of course, in reality, this began nearly two decades ago, when China embarked on internet sovereignty to restrict the free flow of information to its citizens. It is likely to occur with 5G because of US and allied national security concerns. And on AI, a combination of US national security requirements and China's preexisting strategy of achieving national self-reliance also places this sector on a decoupling trajectory. This does not mean that future sales of American semiconductors and chips to China are likely to be totally banned. But it does mean that the regulatory restrictions on trade will become greater. While US-China collaboration in other fields of emerging technology may continue—for example, in biotechnology and pharmaceuticals—new restrictions are also likely to emerge. Decoupling will also have a profound impact on future global industry standards, regulation, and governance arrangements as a range of unilateral, plurilateral, or multilateral regulatory worlds emerge. All of this serves to underline the urgency with which Xi's China is motivated to achieve national self-reliance so that it can better shield vulnerabilities from Washington's economic and technological sanctions while spurring economic resilience and technological dominance.

Continued Codependence in Capital Markets

However, the prospects for decoupling US and Chinese capital markets presents a different and more complex picture than we find elsewhere in the US-China economic relationship. The reason is that the current scale, interdependency, and mutual exposure of Chinese and American financial interests are simply too great. As of 2021, the US-China bilateral financial relationship stood at just over $5 trillion. This includes Chinese listings on US stock exchanges ($1.9 trillion), $1.5 trillion in Chinese stocks and bond holdings on Chinese and Hong Kong exchanges intermediated by US firms, $200 billion in Chinese holdings of US corporate stocks and bonds, $100 billion in US cross-border lending to Chinese firms, $1.1 trillion in Chinese official holdings of US Treasuries, and a further $200 billion in other US government bond holdings. The bottom line is that these are very large numbers indeed.

By and large, whatever strategic difficulties these two governments may have with each other, at this stage, it is still in each country's interests to maintain these arrangements. From China's perspective, there is no immediate alternative to the diversity, depth, and liquidity of US capital markets. Furthermore, China, for the first time in a quarter of a century, has been projecting that it will soon need to fund a modest current account deficit. This is consistent with other countries' experiences at this point in their economic history. As a result, if China faces a net financing requirement, it will need continued access to global capital markets to balance its current account. Of course, China could look to European or other financial markets to meet its external financing needs. Indeed, China has contingency plans for such scenarios, should the decoupling contagion infect capital markets. But at present, because of the large-scale mutual interests at stake in keeping capital markets open, the prospects of that happening at this stage seem limited.

That said, during 2020, a number of proposals were put before the US Congress with the potential to change this equation. The Holding Foreign Companies Accountable Act, signed into law by President Trump at the tail end of his term, requires that foreign companies listed on US stock exchanges must comply with auditing by the Public Company Accounting Oversight Board or be delisted. Many Chinese listings are state-owned enterprises that have routinely failed to comply with full accounting standards, and around 281 Chinese firms currently listed on US exchanges would be subject to such delisting. While many assumed that under the Biden administration, this law would be not be as zealously enforced as it might otherwise have been, this was proven false in March 2021, when the US Securities and Exchange Commission, under the direction of the new administration, announced that it would police compliance. SEC chair Gary Gensler in August 2021 doubled down on his stance to cast further scrutiny on Chinese firms, noting, "The path is clear. . . . The clock is ticking." In September 2021, he stated that Chinese firms would have until 2024 to comply with new auditing requirements or be forced off American exchanges. Therefore, at present, Washington's message appears to be set: Chinese companies must choose between submitting to more scrutiny and getting out.

A second 2020 legislative proposal, introduced by both Republican and Democratic lawmakers, sought to restrict US public pension funds, particularly the Federal Retirement Thrift Investment Board (FRTIB), from investing in Chinese stock indexes. Additional versions of this legislation were then proposed for debate in 2021. Notably, the Biden administration also signaled support in principle for investment restrictions by declining to reverse a Trump administration order banning investment in a list of dozens of companies with alleged ties to the Chinese military, including aerospace company AviChina Industry & Technology, surveillance company Hikvision, and telecom company China Mobile. To give a sense of the magnitude of impact should the broader legislative restrictions become law, the FRTIB currently manages a total fund of $600 billion.

Full application of the standard would thus have a tremendous effect on the investment decisions of other US portfolio managers. It would also generate an inevitable Chinese reaction.

While US legislators have been developing such restrictions, China has largely been moving in the reverse direction by further opening up its capital markets. In September 2019, China removed all quotas on qualified foreign institutional investors to purchase domestic RMB-denominated shares on the Shanghai and Shenzhen exchanges. At present, foreigners only hold about 2 percent of Chinese equities. This is likely to rise to 10 percent by later this decade, as institutional investors seek to increase their China exposure as part of a balanced global portfolio. These developments have been enhanced by recent decisions to include Chinese equities in both the popular Morgan Stanley Capital International (MSCI) and Barclay's indexes. Similar liberalizations and correspondingly increasing purchases are occurring in Chinese bond markets, where, at present, foreigners hold only about 8 percent of total bonds issued by Chinese firms. Changes allowing fully owned foreign companies to become majority participants in the Chinese domestic insurance, brokerage, and other financial service industries also point in a liberalizing direction. Therefore, despite restrictive legislative proposals being advanced in the US Congress, the actual prospects of passage for this and similar measures remain unclear. This is because of the continuing opposition of the US financial services industry, coupled with the very scale of the mutual economic interests at stake linking US and Chinese capital markets. Combined with China's domestically driven decision to internationalize its domestic financial services sector to help service its long-term current account deficit, the prospects, therefore, of any significant decoupling of the two countries' capital markets still appears to be a long way off.

Currency Markets and the Continued Dominance of the Dollar

As for the future of currency markets, three sets of issues arise. The first is the long-standing debate between the US and China on the proper valuation of the yuan. The second concerns the yuan's role as a future global reserve currency. And the third is China's recently announced determination to launch its international digital currency, in part to reduce its future exposure to the risk of the full weaponization of the dollar against Beijing if the bilateral political relationship collapses altogether.

On the first of these, despite episodic rhetorical fusillades between the two countries—including President Trump's temporary declaration that China was a currency manipulator—China is likely to maintain its current "managed float," whereby the yuan is allowed to move within a defined band each trading day. If the trade war were to continue or deteriorate further, economic decoupling to gather pace, and the political relationship to collapse, then a further round of exchange rate wars would be possible. China might be attracted to using the exchange rate to mitigate against the impact of future tariff increases or other market-driven, upward movements in the yuan exchange rate in order to sustain China's competitive position in global export markets.

The problem remains that this could result in an exchange rate war between China and all its trading partners, generating political frictions on every front. However, as of mid-2021, China had not depreciated its currency. Having fallen to a low of nearly 7.2 against the USD during the height of the trade war in 2019, the yuan saw an almost unprecedented surge to around 6.5 against the USD in October of 2020 before strengthening even further to 6.45 to the USD in mid-2021. Some analysts, such as Goldman Sachs, predict the currency will continue to strengthen over the longer term. This surge appears to have been driven by a number of factors, including the opening of China's financial services market to full foreign ownership, China's strong economic recovery from the COVID-19 pandemic, and Chinese government bonds that provided better rates of return than other options as the developed world rushed to print money to fund massive fiscal stimulus. However, what was most noticeable was that Beijing took little action to limit the rise of the yuan. Many analysts noted that China—already confident in its export machine—appeared to have calculated that a stronger currency would help strengthen the global purchasing power of its domestic market and advance the long-term internationalization of the yuan.

The internationalization of the yuan has long been a project for the People's Bank of China. Yet China's political leadership, mindful of the lessons of the Asian financial crisis of the 1990s, has long resisted floating the currency and opening the country's capital account. China's long-standing fear has been its potential exposure to international hedge funds and the possible political manipulation of currency markets to destabilize China's political system. These decisions (both on the yuan and the Chinese capital account) have long constrained China's ability to turn its currency into a significant international reserve currency, thereby lessening China's dependency on the dollar intermediation of its global financial transactions. But China has succeeded in having the yuan accepted as part of the IMF's special drawing rights reserve basket of currencies. It has initiated some thirty-six separate bilateral currency swaps with its trading partners, although the proportion of global trade settlements concluded outside the dollar-denominated system remains small. With Russia, China has also launched an alternative to SWIFT—the dollar-based international financial settlement system. But as of 2019, the dollar remained dominant. And the yuan was still, at best, a marginal player in the international currency system, with 62 percent of global reserves held in US dollars, 20 percent in Euro, 5 percent in Japanese yen, and 4 percent in pounds sterling, whereas less than 2 percent were in yuan—about the same as global reserve holdings of the Australian dollar. Furthermore, as of 2019, the US dollar was still used in 88 percent of all foreign exchange transactions, compared with 4 percent for the yuan. Because of the long-standing depth, liquidity, and reliability of US global debt markets, in contrast to China's continued reluctance to open its capital accounts and float its currency, China has so far limited its options for reducing its global dollar dependency. This is despite growing paranoia in Beijing that China could become the victim of dollar-denominated financial sanctions, as it has witnessed with other US geopolitical adversaries, including Russia, Venezuela, and Iran.

However, China also examined and experimented with more unconventional approaches to dealing with its continuing strategic concern over the country's dollar exposure—as well as expanding its global financial footprint. Chinese commercial platforms Alipay and WeChat Pay are already two of the world's largest digital payment platforms. By way of example, in the first quarter of 2019 alone, they generated some $8.4 trillion in payment transactions. China wants to build on this strength by developing its international digital currency. It also wants to prevent other potential international competitors, such as Facebook's Diem, from securing serious first-mover advantage in the international marketplace. Indeed, Mark Zuckerberg warned Congress in 2019 testimony that unless the US backed commercial efforts like Diem (then called Libra), the US risked ceding the global ground to China in this new, rapidly unfolding global domain. China does not want its international digital customers becoming tethered to a digitized currency that is still within the regulatory control of the United States. China's new cryptography law, which came into effect at the start of 2020, will support the release of the new digital RMB, and pilot programs began in several Chinese cities and in various foreign countries. The digital RMB has the potential to challenge the dollar over the long term, as the global payments system becomes progressively digitized.

These are still early days, and the precise impact of the digital RMB on the dollar remains uncertain. But China clearly senses a serious opportunity to reduce its global dollar dependency by leapfrogging the United States as an early adopter of international digital currency innovation. Its immediate objective is for the digital RMB to supplant the dollar as the preferred reserve currency for the developing world—including both BRI and non-BRI countries. This would have a profound impact in itself on American geofinancial and geopolitical power. It would also precede decisions likely to be made later this decade on a full float of the RMB, the removal of capital controls, and the liberalization of China's capital account. China's 2019 financial market liberalization measures, together with the launch of the digital RMB, are the likely precursors to this decision. The Chinese leadership are also likely to be more confident about making this decision as the current decade progresses—particularly as China's ability to withstand any external manipulation of its currency markets becomes more robust as China's GDP approaches parity with that of the US and then becomes the undisputed largest economy in the world. By that time, the size of Chinese capital markets is also likely to rival those of the United States, further enhancing the leadership's self-confidence in its ability to finally slay the dollar dragon. This would become an époque-ending development in the history of the modern international financial system. If China succeeds in this strategy, it would remove two of the four pillars of American global power—the two remaining pillars then being the US military and its continued lead in most, but not all, categories of advanced technology.

Conclusion

While the economy is not everything, it is *nearly* everything when it comes to our efforts to understand the underlying dynamics of US-China relations. Its impact on politics, social stability, the environment, international relations, and the military is profound. Therefore, given the nature of the Chinese political system, where the policy leanings of the leader are fundamental to all major national decision-making, it is critical that we understand the complex contours of Xi Jinping's economic worldview. Xi, by instinct, is what I call a "Marxist nationalist." His analytical framework is deeply Marxist-Leninist, and it shapes how he sees and interprets the world. His political economy is equally Marxist-Leninist—both in terms of his belief in socialist values (albeit with some traditional Chinese overlay) and in the paramount importance of the power of the party and the state. He is, as a consequence, not a natural believer in markets. At best, he sees them as a necessary evil—of instrumental importance in increasing living standards and enhancing national economic power, but they are not a natural part of his deepest ideological beliefs. For these reasons, if there is a conflict between the power of the market and the future power of the party, Xi will instinctively side with the party, which marks a radical difference between his worldview and Deng's.

Xi's political economy is also nationalist. In this sense, his ideological conservatism on the domestic economic front reinforces his instinctive distrust of the type of international interdependence delivered through global markets—particularly if this interdependence were to render the party vulnerable to the policies and prejudices of "hostile foreign forces." Xi's view is that international markets can be readily manipulated by other states, placing China at risk. In this case, blind to China's manipulation of market principles when it has suited Beijing in the past, Xi would point to the United States as engaging in politically driven interventions in free market arrangements (for example, over semiconductors) in crude pursuit of America's national interests. Once again, Xi's instincts, therefore, trend toward national self-reliance rather than markets, just as, once again, the power of the Chinese party-state and its ability to intervene forcefully in defense of Chinese national economic interests remains paramount.

For these reasons, the political machinery of the CCP and the Chinese state occupy the centerpiece of Xi Jinping's economic worldview. Markets, both foreign and domestic, occupy a subsidiary position. The evolution of Xi's economic strategy in the years since he first assumed office in 2013 provide proof positive of this trend. We see further proof in Xi's growing determination to rewrite the rules of the current liberal international economic order (for example, on global digital governance) in a manner more compatible with China's domestic economic model. The question for China, the US, and the world, however, is whether Xi's bold new economic policy experiment works—or if Chinese economic growth will falter.

7

★★★★★

The Fourth Circle: Making Economic Development Environmentally Sustainable

Environmental sustainability in China, as in most countries around the world, has steadily edged its way up the ladder of political priorities as people become increasingly aware of the impact of environmental degradation on their daily lives. The tragedy of China's rapid economic development over the last thirty-five years is that the CCP subordinated environmental concerns to economic growth. This led to serious and health-threatening levels of air and water pollution as well as desertification, significant loss of biodiversity, and water scarcity. As a result, China has been paying the price. Despite the risks of protesting in China, there have been frequent and angry demonstrations against endemic pollution and the lack of government oversight in towns and villages across the country. Air and water pollution levels across China have been so high in places as to have given rise to a new range of respiratory diseases and other medical conditions, including localities with rates of cancer so high they have been dubbed "cancer villages." There has also been growing public anger over food-quality scandals by producers sacrificing safety and quality to save costs—as in the case of the 2008 contaminated milk scandal that sickened and killed a number of children, prompting mass outrage.

These politically charged environmental challenges make the leadership's economic development task much more complex than before. It has forced the party to make environmental sustainability a critical new component of its efforts to consolidate its political legitimacy in the eyes of the Chinese people. In other words, a clean environment is a new part of the unofficial social contract between party and people—in addition to the economy, employment, and rising living standards.

Prior to 2013, China's development model marginalized environmental constraints in favor of economic growth rates, which were made an absolute priority, with local political leaders rewarded or punished accordingly. But in that year, shortly after assuming the presidency, Xi convened a key politburo meeting on combatting pollution, where he declared that moving forward, China would "not sacrifice the environment for temporary economic growth." Environmental sustainability—or what Beijing intriguingly describes as the need to build an "ecological civilization"—was then formally injected into China's new economic model as part of the thirteenth five-year plan in 2015. While there is limited evidence of progress so far on improving overall water, soil, and air quality, performance reviews for state and party officials have changed under Xi Jinping. Meeting performance benchmarks on protecting the environment are officially rated as of equal importance to driving economic growth. In the past, the blunt instrument of economic stimulus could simply be applied to catalyze economic growth without any real political or career cost arising from the environmental consequences. That is no longer the case, although the environment is still likely to come second to economic priorities such as unemployment, which is still seen by the party as the most dangerous cause of social unrest.

Nonetheless, the existential questions of clean water, useable land, uncontaminated fish stocks, clean air to breathe, and uncontaminated food have been genuinely added to continued job growth, increased living standards, an aging population, and other daunting issues as among the day-to-day challenges that keep the CCP leadership up at night.

Of course, these are not just domestic concerns; the impact of China's greenhouse gas (GHG) emissions on climate change is a decisive factor for the future of the planet. China is the world's largest greenhouse gas emitter, and its actions, both at home and abroad, are of unparalleled global significance. China has increased its carbon dioxide emissions by an average of 1.5 percent a year since 2011, and in 2019, its total national emissions outstripped those of the developed world combined for the first time.

In 2020, China contributed 28 percent of the world's annual GHGs, a share projected to peak much higher in the late 2020s as other developing countries' emissions—most notably India's—continue to rise and the developed world accelerates its decarbonization. By contrast, the United States will halve its 2005 emissions by the end of the decade—even if America's per-capita carbon emissions are still more than twice those of China. By 2050, China will also reach parity with the United States in terms of its historical emissions of greenhouse gases—bringing into sharp focus Beijing's much-vaunted mantra of developed versus developing country responsibilities.

However, the party's focus on staying in power has meant that its primary commitment to environmental and climate action has often, in reality, failed to extend beyond its borders. China's first round of commitments under the 2015 Paris Agreement were to have its carbon emissions peak around 2030, to have 20 percent renewable energy by that date, to reduce its carbon intensity as a portion of GDP by 60–65 percent compared to 2005 levels, and to increase its forest stock volume. In the lead-up to COP26 in Glasgow in November 2021, these were revised marginally to align with China's latest projections. However, according to Climate Action Tracker, China's commitments are still not ambitious enough to limit global warming to below 2°C, let alone to 1.5°C, unless other countries make much deeper reductions than China.

This is unsurprising to anyone who has followed the international climate policy debate. While the Obama administration lobbied hard to induce China into a more forward-leaning commitment on GHG reductions, China only agreed in Paris in 2015 to what was its likely trajectory at that time. This was, nevertheless, a big turnaround from the 2009 Copenhagen era for which many of us—myself included—still bear the scar tissue. There, I had to personally lean on Premier Wen Jiabao to even join me and other world leaders in discussions. In an attempt to save face, he insisted it was a "breach of protocol" that there was not a formal invitation for such a meeting, thus leaving it to his negotiators to hold a firm line. China's biggest concern then was the idea of the developing world having to commit to make cuts in their emissions while believing they had the same right to industrialize their economies on the back of coal as had the West. This argument has some moral salience. But it does not hold up to any real mathematical or scientific scrutiny if we are to avoid a full-blown climate crisis. Nor did it stack up with the technological advances we were already seeing back then, especially in solar power. The idea also of a globally agreed temperature limit—an idea that the Maldives' Mohamed Nasheed and I first proposed—was also deemed objectionable, until we both organized for one developing country after another to weigh in with their support for it. At one stage, I convinced Vice Minister He Yafei—an outstanding professional diplomat—to sign on to what ultimately became known as the Copenhagen Accord during an all-night session, only for this to later be walked back. Premier Wen Jiabao then had him demoted for agreeing to sign.

Against this history, it is unsurprising that under the first commitment period of the Paris Agreement, China only agreed to national targets for 2030 that could easily be met. This helped avoid any risk of international embarrassment while also providing Beijing room to increase its national commitments later on, if it chose to do so. This inbuilt Chinese hesitancy was accelerated when Donald Trump was elected and declared that the United States would withdraw from the Paris Agreement altogether. Suddenly, China was no longer under sustained US pressure, as it was prior to 2017, to continue to expand on its Paris commitments. However, the world owes China a debt of gratitude for not similarly walking away altogether. The Paris Agreement would have collapsed if Xi had followed in Trump's footsteps. It is not coincidental that China's annual carbon emissions increased from 2017 throughout the Trump years, having leveled off over the previous four years. This appeared to reflect a Chinese conclusion that US recalcitrance on climate meant that China was no lon-ger under as much international scrutiny and that it could get away with doing little more than showing up at international climate conferences to look good compared with the United States' absence from the field alto-gether. Beijing's decision to take its foot off the pedal on its GHG reduc-tions also reflected the domestic economic pressures in China arising from the US-China trade war in 2018–2019, the missteps in China's domestic economic policy settings since 2015, and the COVID-induced economic downturn in 2020. All of these hit home, with climate action falling by the wayside as a result. This backward step was reflected, for example, in a progressive whittling down of the scope of China's domestic emissions trading scheme (which was reduced to the power sector alone) and the fresh commissioning of a massive new fleet of coal-fired power stations, despite having already successfully peaked its emissions from coal.

However, Beijing's calculus appears to have changed again in 2020. A surprise announcement during his speech to the UN General Assembly in September demonstrated climate action had crossed the geopolitical Rubicon for China. Xi pledged the country would reach carbon neutrality before 2060, for the first time establishing a timeline to decarbonize the world's soon to be largest economy. This goal was then included in Chi-na's fourteenth five-year plan, with specific carbon intensity targets and renewable energy goals integrated into the final plan, a national carbon trading market established, and specific industry-compliance plans drawn up—even if it is not yet matched by a credible plan to make the necessary reductions in the immediate term.

What prompted this significant change in political course? Likely Chi-na's leadership perceived several overlapping opportunities. First, Beijing concluded that it could potentially accomplish two victories at once: res-pond positively to the growing environmental consciousness of its people and seize an opportunity to demonstrate global leadership in the eyes of an increasingly anxious world. These were the final months of the Trump administration, when Washington was notably absent from the world stage, allowing China to position itself as a responsible global partner that took its international obligations on climate seriously. This pleased the Europeans in particular, reflecting Beijing's overall strategy toward Brussels to drive a long-term wedge in the transatlantic relationship on trade, investment, technology, capital, and now climate.

Additionally, China's new carbon commitments dovetailed with Xi's economic, industrial, and technological goals. It provided an opportunity to channel extensive state investment into transforming China's energy and transport infrastructure while also making China a world leader in high-demand emerging technologies—such as renewable energy, electric vehicles, high-efficiency smart cities, advanced energy storage, and carbon capture. In other words, beyond meeting its domestic political needs, and now its international policy obligations, China's renewable energy revolution has become a core part of its state-driven industrial policy, parallel to the other elements of its wider "fourth industrial revolution."

Finally, Xi calculated that there could be benefits vis-à-vis the US-China relationship. He knew the Biden administration was likely to call on China to do more on climate and aimed to preempt that pressure by turning the tables on Washington and putting Beijing in a stronger negotiating position. Xi also saw climate as a potential mechanism to restabilize US-China relations after four years of strategic competition and partial decoupling under Trump. However, it remains an open question to what extent Washington's interest in climate collaboration with Beijing is able to leverage a broader improvement in the bilateral relationship. At this stage, the odds appear to be against it.

Achieving China's new carbon-neutrality pledge will not be easy or cheap. Independent analyses have placed the total amount of investment necessary at between $5 and $15 trillion over the next three decades. Also required will be substantial structural changes in the Chinese economy. In particular, China remains heavily reliant on coal power but will need to phase this out entirely by 2040 to achieve Xi's carbon-neutrality pledge (and begin immediately restricting its reliance on coal rather than simply waiting until later in this decade). That is a tall order, given China consumed more coal in 2019 than the rest of the world combined. Some 20 percent of the entire world's carbon emissions stemmed from Chinese coal-fired power stations alone. Indeed, electricity generated from coal still accounts for more than half of China's total energy consumption (albeit down from 62 percent in 2016 to 57.7 percent in 2019). By contrast, around a quarter comes from renewables (mostly hydropower, but also wind and solar) and only around 5 percent from nuclear. As noted above, following the lifting of a previous construction ban in 2018, China planned to build a new fleet of coal-fired power plants, with new approvals going into overdrive at the start of 2020, when COVID-19 threatened its economy most acutely. The result is that there are more coal-fired plants under construction in China today than the entire installed capacity in the United States. This decision sent a shiver down the spine of climate scientists, negotiators, and NGOs around the world, especially as it came just months after Xi's carbon-neutrality pledge, which many had hoped represented a turning point. It didn't—at least, not yet.

The Chinese government's fondness for coal power is not just a problem in China. It has become an international problem, given large Chinese investments in coal-fired capacity in countries across the developing world as part of the Belt and Road Initiative. Of all coal plants under construction outside of China, roughly one-quarter—or over one hundred gigawatts of generating capacity—have either secured funding from Chinese financial institutions and firms or benefitted from the use of Chinese equipment or labor. This is effectively double Germany's total installed coal-fired power capacity. Much of this construction of BRI coal projects is done by Chinese SOEs, who then recycle Chinese soft finance back into the Chinese economy. Furthermore, the use of Chinese labor has also helped offset the pre-2020 downturn in the construction of coal-fired power plants domestically. Other international finance for coal projects has primarily come from Japan and Korea, and after both countries bowed to domestic and international pressure to stop this practice, China also did so in September 2021. However, whether Xi's official decision to halt China's overseas financing of coal-fired power stations will similarly impact private and state-owned capital flows out of China or affect those plants already under construction or about to be—and whether China will seek to simply replace its support for coal with other high-emission alternatives such as gas—remains to be seen. So too does whether the large amount of Chinese labor involved in the construction of coal-fired power stations around the world will continue. These will also be key tests as to whether China can fundamentally reengineer the BRI into a "green BRI," which it has been eager to do but has always been worried about doing so simply at the behest of outside pressure. What was clear to Xi by 2021, though, was that it was time for change: not only were BRI countries themselves eschewing Beijing's thirst for supporting coal-fired projects, but the Biden administration was ramping up the alternative (and clean) energy finance available to many of these countries where China had a foothold. And if Xi had not acted, BRI countries would have accounted for more than half of global emissions by the middle of the century, bringing the futility of anything China did at home into stark relief.

Ultimately, however, both China and the world will need to confront the underlying scientific reality that the planet doesn't lie, whatever individual governments may say or do. GHGs will either be stabilized and rapidly reduced to the levels necessary to give the planet a reasonable shot at keeping temperature increases this century within 1.5 degrees Celsius, or they won't. And China, the US, and Europe (and later India) will, between them, be responsible for most of the core decisions that determine our planet's future.

The harsh political reality for China is that it is, therefore, increasingly judged on the same playing field as the United States on climate change. This is compounded by the fact that so many nations in the developing world (China's fellow members of what is called the G-77 political bloc) are among the most vulnerable to the impacts of climate change. This means that the emerging world expects China to lead by action, not just by political rhetoric. In addition to halting support for the overseas financing of coal-fired plants, another key test in the next few years will be whether China can peak its carbon emissions as soon as 2025, as opposed to 2030. If it cannot, then not only will China have failed to deliver meaningfully on its broader commitment to the Paris Agreement's temperature goals, but also the government will have demonstrated it is not prepared to take the necessary action to reach Xi's stated vision of carbon neutrality by 2060, thereby undermining his credibility in the process.

Climate policy is, therefore, set to become an even sharper priority within Xi Jinping's overall strategy. This is likely to be driven by three overriding party interests: (1) the impact of sustained environmental degradation on the party's and his personal political legitimacy, especially over the next decade and a half, when he wants to remain in power and when climate impacts on the Chinese people will become progressively worse; (2) the political and economic impact on China of intensifying and more frequent droughts, floods, storms, and other extreme weather events if climate change impacts continue unabated; and (3) the potential for failure—that China's emissions do not come down, along with those of a "brown" BRI, and that this derails Xi's efforts to use climate change as a means of legitimizing China as a model global citizen or even global leader, just as the international community ponders what sort of leadership China would provide for the world in the future.

8

★ ★ ★ ★ ★

The Fifth Circle:
Modernizing the Military

From the beginning, Xi's definition of the China Dream has incorporated the military: "The Chinese Dream is to make the country strong. China's military take their dream of making the military strong as part of the Chinese Dream. Without a strong military, the country can neither be safe nor strong." Xi sees China's military strength as the ultimate linchpin of China's future power in relation to its neighbors, the region, and the world.

Xi also sees himself as a grand strategist. Before coming to power, he was contemptuous of the lack of real war-fighting and war-winning capabilities by the People's Liberation Army (PLA)—whereas since 2012, he has sought to transform its leadership, structure, and capabilities from, in his view, an antiquated Mao-era people's army, concerned mainly with the defense of China's interior and its continental borders, to a high-tech force capable of projecting air and naval power beyond China's shores. While Deng Xiaoping issued guidance on the modernization of China's defense as part of the "four modernizations" and shifted the PLA from a force devoted to Maoist guerrilla and human-wave tactics into a more conventional military, Xi has launched a much more fundamental series of reforms. He has also unleashed an anticorruption campaign within the PLA officer corps to professionalize its leadership, restore discipline, and enforce absolute obedience to the party's political leadership—especially himself as commander in chief. This campaign has removed thousands of senior personnel whose personal loyalty to Xi was judged to be less than absolute.

For its part, the US military has gone from seeing Beijing as a regional strategic adversary in the 1950s and 1960s, to a strategic collaborator against the Soviet Union in the 1970s and 1980s, to becoming an emerging strategic competitor in the early 2000s, and now—once again—an adversary. The formal US assessment of the Chinese military today is that it is already a "peer competitor" in East Asia and a "long-term strategic competitor" around the world. The focus of that military competition with China today is over Taiwan, the South China Sea, the East China Sea, and a growing array of new security threats, including AI, space, and cyberspace.

Although Beijing sees the overall correlation of forces between China and the United States moving steadily in its favor, the Chinese leadership still sees many dangers lying ahead. These include sophisticated American countermeasures developed to meet China's rapidly evolving military capabilities and the unpredictable variable of American intervention to prevent the forced return of Taiwan to Chinese sovereignty. There is also the problem of America building or reviving alliances and partnerships across the Indo-Pacific (such as the Quadrilateral Security Dialogue or "Quad" with Australia, Japan, and India) and now in Europe in common cause against Beijing.

Xi Jinping's Dream of a Strong PLA

Xi Jinping's emphasis on modernizing the People's Liberation Army is driven in large part by his personality. Xi is a strategic realist who believes that, as important as economic prosperity is, it is military power that ultimately lies at the heart of state power. The lessons of modern Chinese history, most notably China's repeated defeats at the hands of more advanced Western and Japanese militaries during the country's Century of

Humiliation, have fostered in Xi a deep resolve, shared by the party and the nation more broadly, to never allow this to happen again.

Xi's attitudes are also shaped by his military service from 1979 to 1982 at the beginning of his professional career and by his father's time as a senior military commander during the revolutionary war. He has a healthy appreciation of the military traditions of the PLA and, unlike his recent predecessors, has chosen to wear combat fatigues on major ceremonial occasions. His military service, albeit at a junior level, also makes Xi aware of the operational limitations of the PLA, including its complete lack of field experience since China's border war with Vietnam in 1979, where the PLA fared badly. Even worse for China, the PLA Navy has not experienced any major naval engagement since its founding along with the People's Republic in 1949.

There is also a resolute determination on Xi's part that the military remains the ultimate instrument of political control against any *internal* challenges to the party's power. This is reflected in the PLA remaining under the direct political control of the party (through the Central Military Commission) rather than through the administrative apparatus of the Chinese state. One of the reasons Xi is so determined to assert absolute control over the military lies in his openly contemptuous remarks on the failure of the Soviet Union's Communist Party to deploy the Red Army to reassert control amid the anticommunist revolts of 1991 that led to the collapse of the USSR. Xi is determined that no such hesitancy will ever be permitted within the PLA, where every senior PLA commander is made to swear unswerving loyalty to both the party and to Xi himself. Xi has already dismantled several powerful military bureaucracies that he believed were resistant to his overall reform drive, simultaneously consolidating his personal control over the PLA's command structure and removing any future sources of political resistance to his leadership.

Since its founding, the PLA has been provided with nine sets of formal strategic guidance by the party leadership. The first five were developed prior to 1980 and dealt with how China would counter either an American or Soviet invasion. The four since then—adopted in 1980, 1993,

2004, and 2014—have addressed new contingencies concerned with local wars over Taiwan, China's maritime claims in the East and South China Seas, and the Korean Peninsula. In all of these, China's principal potential adversary is the United States. Chinese military contingencies also deal with the country's long-standing border dispute with India.

For these reasons, Chinese leaders, including Xi, have paid the closest attention possible to the historical evolution of the US Armed Forces and its vast array of state-of-the-art capabilities. China's military commanders were riveted by the lethality of modern American firepower deployed in the First Gulf War, the Balkans conflict, and the 2003 invasion of Iraq. In particular, they were challenged by the "revolution in military affairs" (or RMA), as real-time strategic and tactical information provided by satellite and electronic sources was integrated with joint air and land forces and weapons systems on the battlefield. Over time, the RMA in the US Armed Forces triggered major reforms in the Communist Party's formal strategic guidance to the PLA.

China's military and political leaders have also studied Alfred Thayer Mahan's classic work on the relationship between sea power and national greatness and cite it frequently, along with historical examples of British and American naval power during the nineteenth and twentieth centuries. In this view, sea power has an axiomatic relationship with global great power status, including the power that subjugated imperial China during the Century of Humiliation. They, therefore, see this as an important strategic lesson for China in the twenty-first century. As a result, China has concluded that the PLA's maritime power must be expanded, not only to defend China's shores but also to offer an important means of asserting Chinese power, influence, and prestige into the wider Indo-Pacific region and perhaps, in time, other theaters beyond.

The party's official guidance documents to the PLA have dealt with four essential questions: With whom will China fight? Where will China fight? What is the character of the war China will fight? And how will China fight? While the answers to these core questions have changed over the course of the decades, of all the external contingencies that the

PLA has to deal with, Taiwan remains, by far, the most important of all. Ultimately, the power of the military, together with the strength and reach of the Chinese economy and its unfolding indigenous technological success, is seen by Xi Jinping as the essential means by which Taiwan can ultimately be coerced into a form of national reunification with the mainland.

Xi Jinping's Approach to Chinese Military Modernization

Xi's most recent guidelines for the PLA were issued in 2014 (a public version was published as "China's Military Strategy" in 2015) and was implemented in a massive structural reform program beginning in 2016. The 2015 document, drafted two years into Xi's first term, is the first to bear his personal, authoritative stamp on the military. There are four major new elements in the strategy: an unequivocal declaration of the importance of what military strategists call informationized warfare (integrating the use of digital data and intelligence with fighting forces) across all military domains; a doubling-down on integrated joint operations (bringing air, land, sea, and other forces together in unified battlefield operations); a new doctrine on the centrality of the navy and the maritime domain in China's overall strategy; and a new definition of the PLA's maritime domain of operations as extending beyond China's "near seas" to a wider area of open seas and even far seas—all as part of what some analysts have described as a move toward a new Chinese military strategy of *forward defense*.

Informationized Warfare

The 2015 document placed the military's deployment of information technology platforms at its center. This included long-range, smart, stealthy, unmanned weapons and equipment and the emergence of cyberspace as "the commanding heights in strategic competition." While previously China had seen informationized warfare as *one* of the conditions for the successful prosecution of modern warfare, it has now become *the* fundamental condition for doing so. In an earlier 2013 speech, Xi expressed dissatisfaction that the need for the integration of all functional systems of the PLA (e.g., intelligence, electronic warfare, and logistics) "had not been fundamentally resolved." To address this, he moved to create new joint service structures at both the central and regional levels and stressed the creation of what both American and Chinese military literature refers to as a "system of systems," or an information-based joint operational approach.

A New Priority of Sea Power over Land Power

While the expansion and modernization of the PLA Navy (PLAN) had been underway for a decade and a half prior to the 2015 reform, this most recent doctrinal shift is of fundamental importance to the US and its allies. It represents the next step in the evolution of the PLA away from its historical preoccupation with internal security and China's continental defense to an emerging doctrine of deploying military power beyond China's shores. Specifically, the new strategy states that "the traditional mentality that land outweighs sea must be abandoned." Instead, it calls for "highlighting maritime military struggle" and "preparations for maritime military struggle."

As a logical extension of this new official emphasis on the primacy of sea power, the 2015 document codifies what the strategy refers to as China's "open seas protection" mission. It extends China's proposed military reach out to the mid-Pacific in order to better secure its territorial claims in Taiwan, the East China Sea, and the South China Sea through a strategy of antiaccess/area denial (A2/AD) against US forces operating in the western Pacific. It also aims to make China's emerging global naval and maritime power capable of independently securing its sea line of communication that brings critical trade and resources to China by sea as well as protecting its nationals abroad in times of crisis and cementing the global projection of Chinese national prestige. These are significant changes in Chinese naval doctrine, and although they are not inconsistent with the PLA's strategic guidance since 1994, they represent a substantial acceleration of China's intentions to build a navy that is a peer competitor of the United States. China's second aircraft carrier, and the first to be domestically built (the *Shandong*), was commissioned in December 2019. A further four carriers are reportedly to be built by 2035—beginning with a larger carrier roughly equivalent to American models, the Type 003, to be launched in 2022. Chinese surface, submarine, and amphibious-lift capabilities also continue to develop at pace. The PLA's naval forces, weaponry, and organizational sophistication are beginning to rival that of the United States within the western Pacific theater.

Chinese naval forces semiroutinely circumnavigate Taiwan, simulating possible future naval blockades of the island and testing likely Taiwanese and American naval reactions to any such scenario. This has been described by Admiral Lee Hsi-min, Taiwan's chief of general staff from 2017 to 2019, as "incremental military provocations below the threshold of armed conflict, with the objective of compressing the space in which Taiwan's military can operate while intimidating its people." China's coast guard and large maritime militia (composed of fleets of hundreds of networked, and often armed, fishing vessels) have similarly been enhanced and deployed in order to assert China's offshore territorial claims.

Beyond China's mainstream naval forces, China also continued to develop other capabilities to enhance the country's overall strategic posture. In the South China Sea, East China Sea, and around Taiwan, China routinely engages in what military strategists refer to as gray-zone activities. Under this approach, Beijing seeks to gradually shift strategic circumstances in its favor by deploying assets that are technically nonmilitary (such as its coast guard and maritime militia) to physically press its territorial claims without triggering a full-blown military reaction from the US or its allies. By doing so, China aims to achieve its de jure objectives by de facto means, or what China's strategic literature describes as "winning without fighting." That such deployments are frequently in violation of established international law does not seem to bother China. In fact, Beijing has only intensified the practice since 2016, when the dispute resolution panel of the United Nations Convention of the Law of the Sea rejected the legal validity of any of China's South China Sea claims made under the "nine-dash line."

Modernization of Air and Ground Forces

As for the PLA Air Force (PLAAF), China produced fifth-generation stealth fighters and is developing long-range bombers, along with airborne early-warning and control aircraft, aerial refueling tankers, and strategic lift capabilities to deal with a full range of contingencies. Meanwhile, under Xi's reorganization, PLA ground forces appear to have three principal functions: being ready to lead an amphibious assault on Taiwan; dealing with threats in China's western theater, including along the border with India; and dealing with perceived terrorist threats both from within Xinjiang and from beyond the western border, including from Afghanistan and Pakistan. But in a move reflecting Xi's appraisal of where future conflicts are likely to erupt and how they will be fought, he has ordered a reduction of the ground forces' troop numbers by 300,000, leaving the army with a historically low standing force of 850,000 at the same time that the personnel and budget of the navy and air force have increased.

A New PLA Rocket Force

As part of the reorganization of China's military command structures, Xi also created a new PLA Rocket Force (PLARF) to become a separate force on equal footing with the army, navy, and air force. The PLARF integrates both China's nuclear and conventional rocket forces. Its conventional capabilities, including China's latest missiles, have become central to the PLA's asymmetric A2/AD strategy that aims to hold at bay US naval and air operations out to the second island chain in the Pacific. The rapid expansion of China's rocket forces, with a full array of medium-range land-attack missiles targeted at Taiwan, anti-ship missiles (including so-called carrier-killers) that can target any approaching US aircraft-carrier battle groups, long-range land-attack missiles (including the so-called Guam-killer), and missiles designed to destroy American satellites in space, are all central to China's overall A2/AD strategy.

A New Regional Command Structure Focused on Maritime Theaters

Xi also established a PLA Strategic Support Force (PLASSF) to bring together and integrate all of China's space, cyber, reconnaissance, and electronic warfare capabilities in support of informationatized joint operations across all branches of China's military services. To reinforce the PLA's new strategic structure, command, and focus, China's seven regional military commands, which prioritized defending China's interior, were collapsed into five active theater commands to emphasize integrated, battle-ready joint operations—of which three are maritime commands along China's eastern and southern coasts, facing the US, Taiwan, and its allies.

Xi's Vision for a World-Class Military

Just as Xi Jinping set new benchmarks for 2035 as a midpoint on the way toward achieving the full realization of China's dream of advanced economy status by 2049, he also initially advanced 2035 as the date for the completion of the modernization of the Chinese military. However, during the finalization of the CCP's fourteenth five-year plan (covering the period 2021–2025) in the fall of 2020, this date was suddenly brought forward to 2027. There is much speculation as to why Xi did so. It's conceivable that the main reason is simply that a nearer-term objective could motivate ambitious military commanders to prove their worth by speeding up reforms. It's also conceivable that Xi, intending to remain in power into the 2030s, wants to be in a position to be able to act militarily to secure Taiwan from as early as the late 2020s should he choose—or at least to have a sufficient military edge against the US by that time to cause Taipei to seek political terms.

A PLA capable of achieving Xi's Taiwan objectives may be sufficient to satisfy the party's goal of being a world-class military, first set out in Xi's address to the Nineteenth Party Congress in 2017. As Taylor Fravel, the acknowledged international authority on PLA doctrinal evolution, has noted, the term *world-class* has been used relatively widely across China's other modernization tasks, including universities, scientific research, and China's ambitions for various sectors of the economy. However, in Chinese strategic literature, a world-class military is specifically defined as one that can compete effectively with any world-class adversary *overall*, possessing a "strength and deterrent capacity to match them." Indeed, Chinese Academy of Military Sciences analysts have written that world-class militaries should possess, inter alia, "transregional and transcontinental force delivery capabilities."

In 2021, China completed construction of a naval base in Djibouti and is seeking to develop additional such bases adjacent to the Indian Ocean, including on the east African coast. Potential locations, where China has already invested in or signed leases for large-scale civilian port infrastructure include Cambodia, Myanmar, Pakistan, and Sri Lanka (where China signed a ninety-nine-year lease on Hambantota in exchange for forgiving large Sri Lankan debts). Chinese naval visits to Indian Ocean ports—including by nuclear submarines—have also been increasing steadily.

At the same time, an extensive Chinese workforce is distributed across Africa and the Middle East, many working on BRI projects and others running their own businesses. This has led the PLA to argue that it needs the capability to deploy with global reach in order to protect Chinese nationals and their assets abroad in the case of natural disasters or major local political unrest—a scenario often vividly portrayed in popular Chinese films, such as *Wolf Warrior 2* and *Operation Red Sea*. As noted above, China also argues that it should be in a position to defend its sea line of communication transiting the India Ocean, particularly given China's chronic dependence on unimpeded access to the Persian Gulf for its energy needs.

Despite this, the pattern of China's military operations outside the western Pacific theater do not yet reflect a comprehensive strategy to regularly deploy forces so far abroad. It's still not clear from China's naval operations that it intends to become a global, as opposed to just regional, peer competitor with the US military. Nonetheless, China's naval operations to date do demonstrate a determination to establish a global political and logistical network that could be adapted for such purposes in the future.

The Cyberrealm

In cyberwarfare, the technological advantage still lies overwhelmingly with the attacker rather than the defender. Given the potential rewards it yields for the relatively modest investment made, it is also a remarkably cost-effective form of asymmetric warfare. And it is a form of warfare that flatters long-standing Chinese strategic instincts about "winning without fighting." Nonetheless, it is also deeply destabilizing and dangerous, presenting real risks to the future integrity and security of critical social and economic infrastructure—from hospitals to transportation and communication systems to power supply. It risks "blinding" military command, communication, control, and intelligence systems in times of tension or crisis, undermining the normally conservative national security decision-making processes of a country under cyberattack. Such countries would likely fear, legitimately or otherwise, that they had been deliberately blinded by an adversary to conceal an imminent military, or even nuclear, attack. Under these circumstances, the case for immediate retaliation could become irresistible.

A further danger is that cyberattackers can often initially hide who they are or where they are based. Rogue actions by state actors, such as Russia or North Korea, or malicious individuals operating from anywhere in the world, have the potential to trigger retaliation, military or otherwise, directed at the wrong target, especially during periods of tension and crisis. Both China and the US are potentially vulnerable in this regard, not just as targets but in terms of being falsely identified as being behind an attack.

Xi Jinping has rapidly accelerated the development of China's offensive and defensive cyber capabilities. Like AI, cyber is seen as one of a number of new technology platforms that could turbocharge Beijing's existing military capabilities and enable China to leapfrog the United States. China already sees great strategic advantages by surreptitiously accessing critical US military data and deploying that information to design its offensive weapons systems, including the ability to disable American command, communication, and control systems. However, at the same time, China recognizes its vulnerability to cyberattack—not just in the military and economic domains but also in the civil sphere, where China's adversaries could obtain and release sensitive political information that might delegitimize and destabilize China's political leadership. This is part of why China has one of the strictest censorship regimes and tightest internet controls in the world, with severe penalties for such crimes as "spreading rumors" online. (*Rumors* can encompass real-time citizen reports on anything from industrial accidents to environmental disasters to the story of how the COVID-19 pandemic unfolded in Wuhan.) Given that protecting the CCP's political position is Xi Jinping's core priority, along with cementing his leadership, it's understandable that Xi had himself appointed as head of the Central Leading Group for Cyberspace Affairs in 2014, barely a year into his leadership.

China's cyberwarfare establishment consists of three agencies that generally target the US, the West, and other significant adversaries. The first, run by the PLA, focuses on military network warfare; the second is run by the Ministry of State Security (China's external intelligence agency) and focuses on stealing information of all sorts; and the third, run by the Ministry of Public Security, focuses on domestic targets. All three arms are able to deploy non-state agencies to execute their missions, according to independent cybersecurity analysts, sometimes using Chinese public and private corporations as fronts and conduits for data collection and transmission or often simply hiring Chinese cybercriminals to work secretly for the state. Meanwhile, China's cyber defense operations are centered in the Central Cyberspace Administration Commission (CCAC), which, per Xi, is required to "adhere to the principles of defense, self-defense, and retaliatory strike" in dealing with cyberattacks, including taking the stance that "we will not attack unless we are attacked, but we will surely counterattack if attacked."This has been reflected in a raft of new Chinese laws aimed at protecting the state from any such attack. These laws effectively compel all data-holding firms operating in China—both foreign and domestic—to surrender their data to the authorities if so requested. Indeed, one of these—the National Intelligence Law—mandates access to data operations held by Chinese firms both inside *and* outside China, thereby potentially covering data held offshore.

The scope and intensity of China's recent legal and administrative innovations in the cyber domain is symptomatic of the growing incidence of China-linked cyberattacks abroad. According to a running tally by the Center for Strategic and International Studies in Washington, China is the most frequent source of "significant cyber events" recorded around the world and has been for some time. In most years since at least 2018, the top five national initiators of cyberattacks against state and nonstate targets were, in order: China, Russia, Iran, North Korea, and India. The United States comes in sixth. By contrast, the top targets of cyberattacks were the US, India, South Korea, and China itself. The CSIS report lists, for example, more than fifty-five attacks between 2020 and 2021, on top of twenty major attacks by China on US government and corporate targets over a ten-year period up to 2019 (along with hundreds of other smaller attacks). This included the most spectacular of all: the 2014 attack on the US Office of Personnel Management, accessing confidential personal employment data for millions of US federal employees—including highly sensitive information obtained during security clearance investigations and interviews, potentially usable by China in the identification of American intelligence agents.

Whereas Beijing and Moscow may challenge the objectivity of a report by Washington-based think tanks such as CSIS, its conclusions are not vastly different from the trends identified in other technical papers tracking global cyberactivity by state actors. In 2018, then US deputy attorney general Rod Rosenstein stated that "more than 90 percent of the department's cases alleging economic espionage over the past seven years involve China." There has been no reported Chinese response to that claim. US behavior is not exactly saintly on this score, as the CSIS and other reports also indicate. Washington has launched attacks against Chinese targets, although the US government claims that it avoids attacks on civilian or corporate targets, focusing exclusively on conducting normal intelligence gathering on Chinese party, state, and military assets instead. For its part, Beijing regularly denies that it carries out any kind of offensive cyberwarfare and stresses that hacking is illegal under Chinese law—though it has not disputed that it has such extensive capabilities.

The United States has deployed an extensive array of defensive measures to deal with this growing Chinese attack on civilian and military targets, among them its flurry of legislative, regulatory, and institutional initiatives, including the establishment of the Cybersecurity and Infrastructure Security Agency (CISA), the Cybersecurity Enhancement Act of 2014, the continued strengthening of US Cyber Command (CYBERCOM), and the National Cybersecurity and Communications Integration Center (NCCIC).

In an effort to de-escalate growing cyber tensions, in 2015, the Obama administration pressed Xi to limit cyberattacks on private intellectual property, and an agreement was reached. This was temporarily effective: CrowdStrike, an American company monitoring cyberattacks, reported a 90 percent drop in cyberattacks originating from China in the months following the deal. But by early in the Trump administration, previous patterns of activity resumed—and then matched the overall downward spiral of the bilateral relationship from 2017 onward. Indeed, before it published its 2018 National Cyber Strategy, the Trump administration made clear that bilateral cooperative agreements on cyber were no longer part of official US policy. Various other bilateral and multilateral approaches have since been explored to identify and potentially enforce rules of the road in this deeply destabilizing domain. But none have been agreed upon, let alone implemented.

It would be foolish to assume, as with other recent advances in Chinese military-related technologies and capabilities, that China is and always will be dominant in the cyberwarfare domain. The capacity of the United States remains significant. China's vulnerabilities to a sophisticated and sustained cybercampaign waged against it are particularly high, given its one-party state and its highly centralized political, economic, and military decision-making systems. It remains to be seen whether China's national vulnerabilities to all-out cyberattack caution China's recent enthusiasm for cyberwarfare—or whether they, in fact, intensify it further.

Space

Xi has made clear that for China, "becoming an aerospace power has always been the dream we have been striving for." He also invokes China's space ambition as a further reason for China to strive for national self-reliance in technical innovation. China is committed to becoming a "major global space player by around 2030" and the "global leader in space equipment and technology by 2045." This is about more than being the first to land a spacecraft on the dark side of the moon, as the Chinese did in 2019, or landing men on the moon to scope out prospects for construction of a moon base, as China is planning for later in the decade. China has concluded that America's domination of space has been central to the effective deployment of US military force "beyond the line of sight" in all global theaters and across the full range of strategic scenarios. China has concluded that it must do the same—both to deter and to counter any future US military operations against it. The PLA is acutely aware that satellites represent the eyes and ears of fully integrated military operations for the foreseeable future. As the US Defense Intelligence Agency has recognized publicly, "The PLA views space superiority, the ability to control the information sphere, and denying adversaries the same, as the key components for conducting modern, informationized warfare."

Following Xi's directives, China is dedicating significant financial resources to developing a wide array of space capabilities currently possessed by the United States. This includes advanced rocket technologies associated with space launch vehicles for all altitudes; a full range of intelligence, surveillance, and reconnaissance satellite capabilities to monitor and assess relevant weather conditions, enemy signals intelligence, enemy military deployments, and battlefield damage in real time; specialized satellites to provide global coverage for precise positioning, navigation, and timing data; and command-and-control systems for military forces to detect any preparation of ballistic missile activity or provide early warning of any hostile missile launches and coordinate offensive and/or defensive measures in response. All these space missions lie at the nerve center of the modern Chinese military machine.

China is also working on developing its offensive "counterspace" capabilities. These include a combination of ground- and space-based systems (radars, lasers, signals, and optics) to track enemy satellites; electronic systems designed to interfere with the integrity of communications between ground-based transmitters, satellites, and receivers; kinetic energy weapons (usually ground-based antisatellite missiles) aimed at destroying enemy satellites; and directed energy weapons using laser, microwave, or other radio frequency waves, either from the ground or from space, to blind or disable enemy satellites.

While China's military space program falls under the direct control of the Central Military Commission headed by Xi, the operational deployment of space-based systems for military purposes has been given to the newly established Strategic Support Force (SSF), which, according to the US Defense Intelligence Agency, "integrates cyber, space and electronic warfare capabilities into joint military operations across the entire PLA." At the same time, the State Administration for Science, Technology and Industry for National Defense (SASTIND) is charged with the allocation of budgets for the entire space program, including research, systems development, and the military acquisition program. Both SSF and SAS-TIND have received robust budget support from the central government, and although there is limited transparency as to the precise amounts they are given, they are undoubtedly large. Just as important—and maybe more so—is that, in contrast to the US, the Chinese space program is also wired to the center of the country's political and military leadership, whereas in America this relationship is much more diffuse.

As of 2021, some 3,372 active satellites were orbiting Earth. Of these, 1,897 were American (including at least 300 owned by the US military) compared with 412 Chinese (including at least 80 of which—and likely more—are known to be operated by the PLA). However, China is catching up in the total number of new satellite launches—with 35 in 2020, compared with 40 for the US and 17 for Russia. China's space-based intelligence, surveillance, and reconnaissance systems are only second in scope and sophistication to the US—with more than 120 separate space assets, half of which are operated by the PLA. This has given China a genuinely global intelligence reach for the first time.

Meanwhile, in the civilian-military domain, China has launched thirty-five satellites that have allowed it to become a major provider of global navigation satellite systems (GNSS) through its BeiDou satellite network—potentially to become a real global rival to GPS, the long-established American system. China is already hoping to extend this feature of the "space silk road" by negotiating contracts with Belt and Road Initiative countries, the Shanghai Cooperation Organization members, and the BRICS countries (Brazil, Russia, India, China, and South Africa) to offer these services to participating states. The fact that BeiDou's two-way communication system can track the location of ground-based receivers has raised some concerns about privacy. Yet by 2021, Vietnam, Thailand, and Cambodia had signed up, and more countries are likely to do so.

Therefore, by most measures, China is fast closing the gaps in space technology between itself and the US. There are still difficulties, including those China has experienced in developing the reliable, high-altitude, heavy-lift rockets necessary to support China's manned spacecraft ambitions for the future. But it is catching up faster than any external analyst anticipated a decade ago.

Nuclear Weapons

China has been a nuclear weapons state since 1964. Since then, China has developed and maintained a modest-sized arsenal, spread across land-, sea-, and air-based delivery systems, where its stated objective has been to avoid nuclear blackmail at the hands of Russia (during the Sino-Soviet split) and, now, the United States. Beijing has defined its nuclear doctrine as one of "minimum deterrence." This is anchored in a declaratory policy of no first use, underpinned by a sufficiently hardened nuclear force capable of surviving an initial strike from an adversary and then being able to launch a credible retaliatory strike. This doctrine has enabled the bulk of China's military modernization efforts to be concentrated to date on its conventional capabilities, as most recently reflected in Xi Jinping's 2015 Military Strategy discussed earlier.

However, given the recent structural deterioration of the US-China relationship, there are indications that China is in the process of reexamining its previous nuclear assumptions. In doing so, Chinese military leaders have examined a number of questions. First, to what extent has the long-standing stability of Chinese and American nuclear doctrine been challenged by new technological developments in areas such as ballistic missile defense, hypersonic missiles, and various forms of algorithmically driven warfare, as well as the type of offensive cyber and space capabilities referred to previously? Second, to what extent will the nuclear efforts of third countries—such as Russia, North Korea, and Iran—impact the future of US-China nuclear doctrine? And third, perhaps most critically, to what extent do US and Chinese nuclear capabilities, operational doctrine, and declaratory policy reduce the real risk of conventional conflict? Or are they beginning to have the reverse effect: that the nuclear factor is seen as so irrelevant to the risk of conventional conflict over Taiwan, the South China Sea, and the East China Sea that this perceived "minimal risk" of nuclear escalation actually serves to exacerbate the risk of conventional conflict? These are all critical considerations for the future. Too often in the US-China debate, they are pushed to one side because they are too complex, too unknowable, or too remote. I would argue the risk of nuclear escalation between the US and China must be considered afresh.

Beijing, for one, seems to have landed on some unsettling answers. While it was estimated in 2020 that China has a nuclear arsenal of some

290 warheads spread across a full nuclear triad of some ninety ICBMs, six nuclear submarines, and strategic bombers, China appears to have embarked on a major nuclear expansion. In 2021, satellite imagery revealed that China began construction of more than two hundred new missile silos in its northern deserts. Some of these silos are likely to be empty decoys. But even if only some of them are filled, this would represent a large increase in China's active nuclear arsenal. Additionally, in August 2021, China reportedly tested a nuclear-capable hypersonic glide vehicle that successfully circled the earth in space before maneuvering to its target. The test of the vehicle, which would have the capability of evading US missile defenses, reportedly astounded US intelligence officials with the speed of China's modernization. "We have no idea how they did this," one told the *Financial Times*. Combined with this are persistent and growing indications that China's leadership is considering switching from a strategy of no first use or second strike (only launching nuclear weapons after surviving a nuclear attack) to a strategy of launch on warning (launching as soon as a likely attack is detected). All this suggests that Xi and China's military leadership feel that a far more hostile external environment and, in particular, the prospect of prolonged struggle with the United States have necessitated a significant buildup in its strategic nuclear deterrence capabilities.

In recent years, China also sharpened its existing capabilities with improved range, accuracy, and survivability, including developing new road-mobile missiles and deploying other advanced ballistic missiles, such as the DF-41, with multiple warheads designed to better evade missile defenses. China is also scheduled to deploy a new generation of Type 096 strategic nuclear submarines in the 2020s, which will carry a new J-3 missile with a nine-thousand-kilometer range. Still, these capabilities remain dwarfed by those of the United States. By contrast, the US currently has some six thousand nuclear warheads spread across some four hundred ICBM installations, a fleet of fourteen ballistic missile submarines, and sixty-six strategic bombers with nuclear-launch capabilities. Each of these legs of the US strategic triad is also the subject of rolling modernization and replacement programs. Therefore, even if Chinese military planners have shifted their strategy, it will take quite some time before the nuclear balance could be brought closer to equilibrium.

US nuclear doctrine also differs considerably from that of China and is usually expressed in terms of four pillars: first, to deter any conventional or nuclear attack on the United States; second, to do the same on behalf of US allies over whom the American "nuclear umbrella" is extended, obviating their need to develop their own nuclear capabilities; third, to prevail against an adversary in the event of deterrence failing; and fourth, to hedge against any future developments in military technology, conventional or nuclear, that might threaten US national security. These pillars were reaffirmed in the most recent 2018 US Nuclear Posture Review (NPR). Importantly, the NPR explicitly named both China and Russia as threatening the US nuclear posture and the future effectiveness of US deterrence. The NPR also rejected a no-first-use doctrine in order to maintain strategic ambiguity in the eyes of American adversaries about the circumstances in which Washington would consider a nuclear response. As the NPR noted, "Our tailored strategy for China is designed to prevent Beijing from mistakenly concluding that it could secure an advantage through the limited use of its theater nuclear capabilities or that any use of nuclear weapons, however limited, is acceptable. . . . The United States is prepared to respond decisively to Chinese nonnuclear or nuclear aggression. US exercises in the Asia-Pacific region, among other objectives, demonstrate this preparedness, as will increasing the range of graduated nuclear response options available to the president." In other words, the US has made clear that any use of conventional, tactical, or theater-level nuclear attacks in East Asia could potentially trigger a menu of nuclear options in response. It is, of course, a separate question as to whether Chinese political and military leaders regard such statements as credible. PLA commanders, for example, have regularly questioned whether US counterparts really believe that a future American president would sacrifice San Francisco to nuclear attack as the price of defending Taipei. Nevertheless, this represents a large—and potentially fatal—leap of faith on the part of the PLA concerning American strategic intentions.

The US deployment of Terminal High Altitude Area Defense (THAAD) systems in South Korea in 2016 to counter the growing nuclear and ballistic missile threat from North Korea highlighted how the installation of space-based monitoring systems can endanger nuclear deterrence. From the perspective of the Chinese military, THAAD—which is designed to shoot down ballistic missiles descending from space in their terminal phase by drawing both land-based radar and satellite-based early warning, tracking, and targeting systems—is particularly problematic. THAAD would cause trouble for the PLA in situations where it aimed to deploy missiles in future Taiwan-related contingencies, including against US carriers and bases, in the event of military conflict. These concerns extend to the deployment of other American sea-based technologies (e.g., the Aegis Ballistic Missile Defense System), which, in China's view, would have a similar effect. Unsurprisingly, China protested against the THAAD deployment in South Korea, having concluded that its installation would undermine the integrity of China's second-strike nuclear capability that has long been central to China's overall deterrence strategy against the US. China has also been deeply concerned by the significance of the United States' conventional prompt global strike plan, which seeks to develop a new capability to take out any target anywhere on the globe within an hour of a command being given. This presents another threat to China's second-strike nuclear capability and, therefore, the integrity of its entire doctrine of minimal deterrence. Such developments may have played a role in China's decision to expand its nuclear arsenal.

These developments have also resulted in a range of other Chinese countermeasures. China's decision to deploy a new hypersonic missile (the DF-ZF), designed to evade any ballistic missile defense system with its extreme speed and maneuverability, adds a further dimension to an unfolding US-China nuclear arms race. Persistent concerns have also spurred China's development of its ballistic missile defense systems. This, in turn, will have a further escalatory effect on US calculations on the adequacy of its arsenal, each side constantly seeking to secure temporary advantage over the other.

Despite the possibility of a new nuclear arms race, China continues to spurn US invitations to engage in either bilateral nuclear arms control negotiations or trilateral negotiations with Russia. It appears that China, fearing the vulnerability of its relatively small force, may have concluded that its only option for the future is to radically increase the size and sophistication of its arsenal. Overt nuclear competition between Beijing and Washington, once almost exclusively the preserve of the US-Russia relationship, may become the new norm.

The Overall US-China Military Balance

So where does this leave the regional balance of power as of 2021? As various studies have emphasized in recent years, the military balance cannot be calculated purely on the basis of some mechanical, quantitative comparison of the Chinese and American order of battle—that is, the crude numbers of troops, ships, submarines, planes, rockets, and so on. Rather, the list of difficult-to-measure factors is a long one, including

- the relative sophistication and survivability of military platforms, systems, and weapons;
- the effectiveness of battlefield experience and training;
- the robustness of command, control, communications, and intelligence systems for integrating and sustaining effective joint operations;
- the sustainability of military budgets over time;
- the continuing political will in Washington, Beijing, and relevant allied capitals to support and sustain the deployment of military forces in given strategic situations;
- the capacity to harness the nonmilitary dimensions of overall state power (e.g., diplomatic, economic, financial, and technological resources, together with the ability to shape global public opinion) in the prosecution of a military campaign;
- the impact of nuclear deterrence on the scope, intensity, and duration of any conventional conflict; and

- most critically, the application of all these variables, both quantitative and qualitative, by individual leaders to individual crises in different locations as they arise.

For example, the answer to the military balance equation will differ depending on whether we are applying it to particular scenarios in the Taiwan Strait, the South China Sea, the East China Sea, or the Korean Peninsula, let alone in potential operational theaters in the Indian Ocean or even further afield, where China's power projection capabilities beyond the western Pacific become increasingly stretched.

Nonetheless, a number of clear trends are becoming apparent. First, the capabilities gap is narrowing in virtually all categories and more rapidly in some categories (e.g., cyber) than US military strategists had anticipated. Second, in desktop military war games conducted by Washington, Beijing, and Tokyo across a range of Taiwan scenarios, the United States has reportedly lost repeatedly (according to some reports, this includes on as many as nineteen successive occasions—and, in some cases, even when fighting with a range of its strongest regional allies). Third, where Japan and the United States respond together to military crises in the East China Sea close to Japan, however, war-gaming produces more favorable results, reflecting the supreme importance of geography. Fourth, the same does not, however, apply in the South China Sea, where China is largely pushing on an open door. This partially explains why Beijing has been more cautious in prosecuting its territorial claims in the East China Sea around the Senkaku / Diaoyu Dao Islands than in the Spratly and the Paracel island groups in the South China Sea. In the South China Sea, the US has no specific treaty obligations at stake beyond the Philippines. Consistent with this, the US did not respond militarily to China's program of island reclamation in the South China Sea over 2014 and 2015. This caused Beijing to become increasingly confident of its overall military position in the theater. Fifth, China's overall net military advantage over the US, however, dissipates the greater the geographical distance from China's shores. This will change over time, as China's long-range strike, blue-water navy, force protection, and sustainment capabilities improve, but it appears in no hurry to significantly scatter its resources until it becomes absolutely confident of its strategic position closer to home—most particularly regarding Taiwan. Finally, Washington should be aware that the Chinese state's capacity to marshal the full resources of the Chinese economy in any given conflict is greater than the United States', given the radically different nature of the two countries' political and economic systems.

All that said, Xi continues to face many problems with his military modernization program, not least how to pay for it. The Stockholm International Peace Research Institute estimates that the Chinese defense budget grew approximately 233 percent from 2008 to 2020—from $108 billion to $252 billion. As of 2020, it represented close to 10 percent of the total Chinese government budget. Xi will be aware of the headwinds confronting China's political-economic model, including a potential decline in China's future private-sector-driven growth rates and the implications this will have for future Chinese budgets. Xi is also aware that the underfunding of China's domestic policy needs increasingly demanded by the public, particularly in health, aged care, and retirement income to support a rapidly aging population, risk making substantial military outlays a risky political proposition.

Furthermore, Xi has awoken the American bear from its long strategic hibernation. Since 2017, the US defense budget once again grew at an average of more than 5 percent per year, following a post–Iraq War slump. While Biden's first annual defense budget request totaled $715 billion—an increase of only 1.6 percent—the budget deliberately shifted significant spending to focus on systems designed to deter China. This included more than $5 billion designated for a newly created Pacific Deterrence Initiative, an effort to develop and deploy advanced long-range strike weapons to the region (in a version of China's A2/AD strategy, which has proven so problematic for American naval planners). Japan and Australia, as two of America's three principal allies in East Asia, have also both signaled that they intend to significantly increase their military budgets. Indeed, I signaled the same back when we prepared the 2009 Australian defense white paper, including doubling the Australian submarine fleet and increasing the surface fleet by one-third. As Beijing has become aware, it may not have been the best idea to be so loud and proud about China's growing military prowess. Indeed, since 2018, there has been a dramatic decline in public references to Xi's world-class military in Chinese state media. This seems to parallel the decision to remove all reference to China's 2025 high-technology strategy for fear of generating further international reaction.

In the end, theoretical war gaming aside, it remains unclear whether Xi's military reform and expansion program will work in delivering a PLA capable of "fighting and winning wars." As of 2020, the PLA was still in a process of major internal upheaval; any near-term regional crisis would, therefore, have to be dealt with by a military apparatus still in the throes of a profound institutional transition. Military reform is also deeply politically sensitive in China itself. The demobilization of three hundred thousand soldiers has resulted in a large number of public protests by veterans unhappy with the financial terms of their forced retirement. Meanwhile, other senior commanders have been purged, detained, or imprisoned for a combination of corruption and disloyalty—whether real or confected. This has included several once-powerful generals, leaving gaps in experience and potentially dangerous levels of resentment in the force. Sacked military commanders are also a powerful source of potential dissent across the Chinese political system. And on top of all this, Xi has waged a relentless campaign to reconsolidate the party's authority over the PLA, including his decision to bring China's formidable paramilitary apparatus (the People's Armed Police) under direct party control, removing it from the supervision of the state council altogether.

While there is unlikely to be any fundamental objections to these changes from his politburo colleagues, there will be professional and political disquiet if more political and military power is concentrated in Xi's hands. It contributes further to Xi's existing reputation within the Chinese political system of being the "chairman of everything." There is a danger this adds to any political "antibodies" already accumulating within the party. But so far, Xi has demonstrated himself to be a master at eliminating potential opponents—and doing so well before any of them could effectively organize and move against him.

Despite these not inconsiderable difficulties, as noted previously, Xi Jinping sees the overall regional balance of military power moving steadily in China's direction. Xi would take some pride in the fact that the United States Department of Defense formally refers to China as "a peer competitor." This was not the case before 2018. Based on its analytical models, China believes the "objective" balance of forces is moving in its favor over time. This is reinforced by its internal calculus of the overall "correlation of forces" between the US and China, incorporating its models for calculating each country's comprehensive national power, which takes into account the full range of military and nonmilitary capabilities in a carefully constructed international league table. Until 2009, China published these tables. Now it doesn't. This reflects the same sort of internal political sensibilities that prompted China to reduce its official public media reporting of anything that smacks of China's growing capabilities, grand ambitions, or public triumphalism. However, on the underlying reality of Chinese military power, China's internal calculus finds a steady shift in the regional balance in its favor.

Senior Chinese military leaders, however, are aware that, despite the closing of the capability gap between China and the US and its closest allies, they still face formidable adversaries in the US and Japan in particular. I attended a well-lubricated dinner with a number of Chinese two- and three-star generals at the National Defence University after I became a senior fellow at the Harvard Kennedy School following my second term as prime minister in Australia. I was at the university to deliver a public lecture on US-China relations in the presence of the notoriously hard-line General Liu Yafei, the university president. It was a torrid session, one of a number I attended with the Chinese military over recent years. But over dinner and much maotai later that evening, the conversation turned to concrete military scenarios. Relations with Japan at that time had hit rock bottom over Tokyo's "nationalization" of the disputed islands of Senkaku / Diaoyu Dao, and naval and air assets from both countries were becoming increasingly engaged. I remember vividly the high degree of military caution from my Chinese colleagues on what it would be like to actually fight a major engagement in the East China Sea against the Japanese alone—quite apart from whether the Japanese were also joined by US naval and air assets. The Chinese military are acutely conscious of their lack of direct field experience. They are not lacking in courage. Far from it. But their level of professional prudence was striking.

For Xi Jinping, the political loyalty and the effective modernization of all branches of the Chinese military are central parts of his overall strategy. The PLA is directly relevant to his future hold on power. It is fundamental to securing and maintaining national unity, most acutely in relation to Taiwan. But it is undeniably a major drain on the budget: effectively funding it over the long term makes it imperative that China's future economic development model is a success, or else China will face even harsher budgetary choices than it does now. But as we will see in the chapters that follow on Beijing's growing role in the region and the world, China's military power is becoming as fundamental to China's international policy ambitions as its economic power has been for a considerable time already.

9

★ ★ ★ ★ ★

The Sixth Circle: Managing China's Neighborhood

So far, we have looked at those core elements of China's official world-view that are largely focused inward on China's domestic challenges—although the Chinese military, of course, is both a domestic *and* external actor. The remaining five circles of interest extend outward, covering Xi's ambitions in the world beyond China's shores. There is both a conventional and classical Chinese logic to this sequence: strength at home is fundamental to whatever ambitions Xi may pursue abroad.

The sixth circle concerns China's fourteen neighboring states, with whom China has the largest number of contiguous borders of any country in the world except for Russia, which has the same number. Throughout most of Chinese dynastic history, threats to national security have typically emerged from its vast frontier. This was in the form of successive foreign invasions by steppe nomads, such as the Xiongnu during the Han dynasty, the Mongols in the twelfth century, and the Manchurians in the mid-seventeenth. The traditional Chinese concern with protecting the country's land borders that resulted is, of course, best symbolized by the Great Wall of China.

Later, new threats came from across the sea, including Western and Japanese imperialist powers in the nineteenth and twentieth centuries—threats for which China was not prepared. However, China's land borders remain a fundamental strategic concern for Beijing, not least because of the four border wars it has fought since 1949 (with the US in Korea in 1950, India in 1962, the Soviet Union in 1969, and Vietnam in 1979). All of these were brought about, at least in part, by unresolved border disputes or by broader Chinese concerns about territorial integrity and political sovereignty.

History has taught China that purely defensive measures have not always succeeded in dealing with threats posed by neighboring states. Therefore, modern Chinese strategic thinking has adopted a range of approaches. Foremost among these is military preparedness. But they have also included political and economic diplomacy, through which China aims to secure positive, accommodating, and—wherever possible—compliant relationships with all its neighbors.

China's core interest today is to reduce—and eventually eliminate—any significant threats along its borders. This includes the continued strategic presence and influence of the United States among its neighbors. This applies to China's fourteen land neighbors (North Korea, Russia, Mongolia, Kazakhstan, Kyrgyzstan, Tajikistan, Afghanistan, Pakistan, India, Nepal, Bhutan, Myanmar, Laos, and Vietnam). It also applies particularly to those with whom China has contested maritime boundaries, including South Korea, Japan, the Philippines, Indonesia, Malaysia, and, again, Vietnam. As a strategic rule, China would much rather solve any dispute by dealing with these states bilaterally rather than allowing them to gain additional political and diplomatic leverage by elevating disagreements to multilateral mechanisms, let alone to formal international arbitral forums—or, worse still, bringing in the United States.

China's strategic approach has also been influenced by having carefully studied the history of America's Monroe Doctrine. Beijing observed Washington's ruthless determination under this doctrine and how it sought, over nearly two hundred years, to secure its wider strategic environment by denying access to the "American" hemisphere to any other great power. By extension, the US repeatedly acted to ensure that its regional neighbors across the Americas complied with Washington's political and strategic interests. This was codified by the 1904 Roosevelt Corollary to the Monroe Doctrine, which asserted the United States' right to intervene in the internal economic affairs of Central American and Caribbean states if they were unable to pay their international debts. This policy led to political cartoons of President Teddy Roosevelt patrolling America's "Caribbean Lake," threatening small countries with his big stick.

Beijing reasons that if this were a moral and strategic course of action for a rising United States, then there is no reason China can't apply it to East Asia as well. In other words, if America can have its Western Hemisphere, then why can't China have an Eastern Hemisphere of its strategic making? This doesn't necessarily mean a Chinese Monroe Doctrine is likely to be prosecuted by military means. It does mean that the notion of great powers having the right to establish spheres of influence—while publicly rejected as being a part of official Chinese policy—lies well within the parameters of contemporary Chinese strategic thinking.

However, since the late 1980s, China has sought to moderate its policies toward its neighbors for the sake of prioritizing economic growth, culminating in the adoption of its Good Neighbor Policy of 2003. While not resiling from its position on major territorial disputes, China sought, wherever possible, to deploy the full force of its economic power and political diplomacy to maximize its leverage and influence. Still, China has not shied away from using so-called gray-zone pressure by its military and paramilitary forces to advance its territorial claims—quite the reverse. Indeed, in many cases, the intensity of these operations has increased significantly over time. But they have been carefully conducted in a manner to avoid the risk of full-scale armed conflict with neighboring states (especially those with formal alliance relationships with the United States), usually backing off if enough resistance is encountered and before any particular confrontation gets too hot. Instead, China's overall strategy with its neighbors is to *economically* overwhelm them and make them so dependent on continued access to Chinese trade, investment, and capital markets that any remaining foreign and security policy objections to Beijing's territorial claims are rendered politically futile and economically debilitating. The same principle has been applied to China's wider efforts to secure a growing role in the global order, where it aims to cause others to conclude that resisting China's global rise is futile, given its sheer economic size, momentum, and determination—particularly when measured against the cracks they may perceive are already appearing in the facade of American power.

Russia

From the earliest days of his leadership, Xi has been more committed than any of his predecessors to improving Beijing's strategic relationship with Moscow. Indeed, no other leader since Mao has placed such a priority on China's relationship with Russia. While Mao's relations with Moscow were fractious (including a bout of actual border warfare during the extended Sino-Soviet split of 1959–1989), Xi has found a growing degree of strategic comfort in his engagement with Russian president Vladimir Putin, which is unique for China's Communist Party leadership. Indeed, Xi has publicly described Putin as "his best friend," shared birthday phone calls with him, and publicly declared that the two of them "have similar personalities." It is unusual for a Chinese leader to express personal feelings about a relationship with a foreign counterpart. It is doubly remarkable given the troubled four-hundred-year-long history of Sino-Russian relations, ever since the Russian czars first pushed east to the Pacific in the seventeenth century and progressively seized large swathes of Chinese territory from the Qing. Thanks to this close personal relationship and to their common strategic interests, Xi and Putin have transformed what had been a bitter rivalry into a de facto political, economic, and strategic alliance—notwithstanding frequent official protestations to the contrary.

Xi is the beneficiary of recent historical developments that helped create the benign circumstances of today's China-Russia relationship. Deng Xiaoping's 1989 meeting with Gorbachev led to the resolution of the long-standing border dispute between the two countries. Moscow then ceased to be a serious strategic threat to China following the collapse of the Soviet Union in 1991. Moreover, Russia's relative economic decline during the 1990s, at a time when the Chinese economy was growing rapidly, further reduced Chinese perceptions of its vast common border with Russia being a threat. These changes fundamentally altered the dynamic between the two countries. It also caused a reluctant Moscow to accept, over time, its newfound junior status in the relationship. This was not an easy pill for the Russians to swallow, especially given their sense of vulnerability arising from the small Russian population in the Far East—in contrast to the vast Chinese population lying to their immediate south. There have also been ongoing concerns about the security of the Russian border against unauthorized Chinese crossings. These have been compounded by persistent racist attitudes toward "Asiatics" among the broader Russian population. Nonetheless, despite these reservations, the transformation of the bilateral relationship since 2013–2014 has been remarkable.

Xi has skillfully surmounted Russian concerns by flattering Russian pride and prestige, respectfully inferring that Beijing and Moscow still see each other as political and strategic equals, even though this is clearly no longer the case. Both leaders share common political concerns over the ever-present threat of liberal values and Western-backed "color revolutions" to their respective regimes. However, the greatest glue in the new relationship between Moscow and Beijing is economic. When the West imposed sanctions against the Russian state and individual Russian leaders, beginning with the passage of the 2012 Magnitsky Act in the United States, followed by further measures after Russia's invasion of Crimea in 2014, Moscow looked to Beijing with greater urgency than ever before. As economic sanctions began to bite and were compounded by sliding oil and gas prices, Putin recognized that Russia had nowhere else to turn for economic relief other than China. Policy collaboration between Moscow and Beijing intensified as the two countries increasingly pursued common cause against their collective strategic adversary—the United States—and, together, sought to shape a more "multipolar," less liberal, and less US-centric global order.

This growing strategic and diplomatic collaboration between Moscow and Beijing could be seen not only bilaterally but also in multilateral organizations such as the G20, the UN, the Shanghai Cooperation Organization, the Conference on Interaction and Confidence-Building Measures in Asia (CICA), and the BRICS. Meanwhile, the level of security coordination between the two increased across the board, represented by the growing frequency and scale of joint military exercises and naval maneuvers conducted in the Pacific; the Atlantic; and even the Mediterranean, Black, and Baltic Seas.

Thus, over the past thirty years, Russia has gone from being China's strategic opponent to an increasingly useful strategic asset. Over time, Russia's supply of oil and gas will reduce China's chronic dependency on imports from the Gulf, alleviating China's vulnerability to the interruption of these critical energy imports through the Strait of Hormuz and the Strait of Malacca—two strategic choke points that have long preoccupied Chinese military strategists. Russia has also long been adept at deploying a range of disruptive behaviors that distract and preoccupy American and European strategic attention in a manner beyond what Beijing's more cautious strategic culture would allow. Syria is a classic case in point. This has also left China with more uncontested geopolitical space to pursue its strategic goals in the Pacific over much of the last decade.

While Xi Jinping sees Russia as a declining economic power with limited global reach beyond its impressive military capabilities, he nonetheless recognizes great value in Moscow being prepared to act far more adventurously than China itself. Moscow has always been prepared to push back, both militarily and in foreign policy, against the Americans and Europeans much more aggressively than Beijing. This suits Xi well, as Russia's international reputation as a potential global "spoiler" has enabled China to project an image of being a more conservative, consultative, and responsible actor in the eyes of the wider international community—characteristics that, in Beijing's eyes, are seen as more befitting of the world's next superpower. All this has made the Sino-Russian relationship of great value to China's overall strategic interests.

India

By contrast, India has become an increasingly problematic neighbor for Xi Jinping. The strategic prism through which Beijing and Delhi view each other is fundamentally shaped by the unresolved 3,488-kilometer border between them, the territorial dispute between India and Pakistan over Kashmir, and China's long-standing alliance with Pakistan. Beijing has long seen Delhi as a strategic partner of China's principal adversaries—first the Soviet Union during the long years of the Sino-Soviet split, followed more recently by the United States. India has also been a long-standing rival of China's for the affections and support of the wider developing world. While at the dawn of the current century, India and China were seen as having comparable economic potential, twenty years later, China became five times the size of India. This has created an emerging sense of strategic vulnerability in Delhi. Combined with continuing frictions across the border and China's growing naval presence in the Indian Ocean— including access to port facilities in India's neighbors, such as Sri Lanka and Pakistan—Delhi, in the last decade, expanded its bilateral military ties with Washington and initiated trilateral naval exercises with the US and Japan. Still, despite these changes, India seemed determined to maintain its long-standing tradition of a neutral foreign policy.

After a three-day summit between Xi and India's prime minister Narendra Modi in Wuhan in 2018, a new political determination emerged in both capitals to improve their bilateral relationship. This was driven by a desire in Delhi to stabilize the border and attract greater Chinese investment as well as a growing domestic skepticism about the long-term strategic and economic reliability of the United States, particularly given the inherent volatility of the Trump administration at the time. For Xi Jinping, India was seen as being diplomatically "in play" in a way that it had not been since the border war of 1962. Moreover, Chinese companies were eager to expand into the large Indian developing market before their US rivals. Overall, Beijing could see many advantages to having a friendly relationship with India instead of having yet another significant strategic adversary on its maritime and continental peripheries.

However, this budding relationship deteriorated rapidly when long-running border frictions exploded in June 2020. A high-altitude face-off near the disputed Pangong Lake in the Himalayan Ladakh region descended into a bloody hand-to-hand melee in which twenty Indian soldiers and at least four Chinese soldiers were killed. This was followed by mass nationalist demonstrations in India at which protesters burned Chinese goods, Xi's portrait, and the PRC's flag and called for countrywide boycotts of Chinese goods. Indian prime minister Modi promised a firm response, saying Indians could be "proud that our soldiers died fighting the Chinese." Diplomatically insensitive wolf warriors in the Chinese media, who blamed India for the clash while simultaneously mocking the Indian military's losses, helped fan the flames before Beijing finally brought them under control. While an escalation in the military conflict was averted, by September, the import of dozens of categories of Chinese products had been blocked by Delhi and more than 250 Chinese software apps (including TikTok and WeChat) were banned from India. This was a significant setback for China's technology companies, who had viewed the Indian market as the cornerstone for future global expansion. Tensions with Delhi were amplified further by the impact of the COVID-19 pandemic, particularly given the origins of the virus in Wuhan and the disastrous human and economic toll in India.

On the strategic front, Delhi quickly doubled down on its security relationship with the United States, immediately expanding naval exercises with the US Navy, signing a number of defense and intelligence cooperation agreements, and, for the first time, deploying an Indian warship to the South China Sea. India also moved beyond its trilateral military cooperation with Washington and Tokyo to finally embrace the Quadrilateral Security Dialogue, or Quad, grouping of the US, Japan, Australia, and India, promoted afresh by the Trump administration, inviting Australia, for the first time, to participate in quadrilateral maritime exercises. Subrahmanyam Jaishankar, India's foreign minister, explained that, from India's perspective, the Quad had a "larger resonance" following the border clashes and that there were much greater "comfort levels" in Delhi and Washington on a need "to engage much more intensively on matters of national security." This new level of multilateral security cooperation has significantly complicated China's strategic maritime environment. This is discussed in greater depth in the following chapter.

Taken together, these developments in 2020 represented a major strategic setback in Xi's two-year-long effort to improve relations with India. Xi had no desire to find himself with strategic adversaries on every front. With India moving more decisively into the US strategic orbit at the same time as tensions across the Taiwan Strait, in the South China Sea, and with Japan in the East China Sea were also growing, Xi was in precisely the predicament he had sought to avoid.

In the second half of 2020, Beijing diligently sought to defuse the Indian border crisis with a minimum of drama. China largely kept silent when a PLA soldier was captured by Indian troops—somewhat implausibly claiming he accidentally chased a herdsman's lost yak across the line of control—while Beijing sought to quietly negotiate his release. Simultaneous offers of COVID-related support and assistance were made by China, though Delhi rejected most of them. And an initial deal to mutually withdraw troops from the contested area and revert back to the status quo was—according to the Indian side—not adhered to by Chinese forces. After more than a year, in which more than a dozen rounds of talks were held between military commanders, a new tentative agreement was reached in the summer of 2021, but the situation remains both tense and tenuous. In a sign of continuing heightened tension, India has moved fifty thousand troops from the border with its archrival Pakistan and redeployed them to the border with China, while the PLA has enhanced its forces along the border with new long-range artillery and additional winter-warfare equipment. Meanwhile, Xi Jinping pointedly made a surprise visit to the border in July 2021—becoming the first Chinese leader to do so since Jiang Zemin in 1990—conspicuously riding a new high-speed rail line designed to quickly move troops and supplies to the Himalayan plateau in Tibet.

Both sides, therefore, appear to have dug in for a protracted standoff along their border, and it is difficult to predict the extent to which relations between Beijing and Delhi can recover. Nevertheless, just as Deng normalized the relationship with Russia by resolving that border dispute back in 1989, we should never rule out the possibility of Xi doing the same with

India. If China did so, it would fundamentally alter the strategic triangle between Beijing, Washington, and Delhi.

Japan

China's relationship with Japan has developed in fits and starts under the long shadow of World War II. The brutality of the Japanese occupation during that time saw up to twenty million Chinese civilian and military deaths, including the wholesale massacre of Chinese civilians, widespread sex slavery, and germ warfare experiments on Chinese POWs. The lack of contrition and atonement for these war crimes on the part of some of Japan's postwar leaders has (in an environment of state-supported anti-Japanese nationalism) periodically led to explosions of mass outrage in China. This includes riots in which Japanese businesses and even people merely driving Japanese cars have been attacked.

In a deeply provocative move, just before Xi assumed the party leadership in 2012, the Japanese government effectively "nationalized" the disputed Senkaku / Diaoyu Dao Islands by purchasing them from a private landholder. (This was actually meant to preempt an even more provocative bid to buy them by Tokyo's ultranationalist governor, Shintaro Ishihara, but Beijing did not accept this as a justification.) Washington regarded the Senkaku Islands as Japanese territory for the purposes of the US-Japan security treaty of 1954, and the islands have been administered by the Japanese government since the war. China feels otherwise. Almost immediately, the bilateral political relationship with Tokyo deteriorated as significant naval, air, and other paramilitary assets were deployed by both sides to areas surrounding the islands. Japanese prime minister Shinzo Abe intensified these tensions further when he decided to visit the Yasukuni Shrine in Tokyo, a memorial to Japan's war dead that includes the remains of fourteen Class-A war criminals—a highly politically incendiary act for China. Japan also refused to support Chinese regional development initiatives such as the Asian Infrastructure Investment Bank and the Belt and Road Initiative, stating that these measures subverted the post-1945 global rules-based order by challenging institutions promoting good governance. Meanwhile, China added further fuel to the fire in November 2013 with the unilateral declaration of an air defense identification zone (ADIZ) across the East China Sea, requiring all foreign aircraft to notify Chinese civil aviation authorities of proposed flight movements in advance, in a bid to demonstrate its sovereignty over the territory. Japan and the United States immediately flew military aircraft through the zone to challenge that premise.

To some extent, however, this icy state of relations began to thaw in late 2018. At that time, Xi and Abe took tentative steps to normalize the relationship through a mutual exchange of high-level visits. Abe, like Modi, appeared to have begun a process of long-term strategic hedging between Washington and Beijing, not wishing to be left as the "last man standing" in the event of any strategic drift toward isolationism on the part of the United States during or after the Trump era. Abe was particularly alarmed by the Trump administration's overall attitude to its traditional allies, its chaotic handling of North Korean policy, and the threatened imposition of tariffs against both Japan and South Korea. Abe, therefore, made the first move to improve relations with Beijing in September 2017 by dropping in for a surprise appearance at an event marking China's National Day at the Chinese Embassy in Tokyo—the first time a Japanese prime minister had done so in fifteen years. There, Abe made his first reference to the possibility of Xi visiting Japan. In November of that year, Xi made a point of meeting with Abe on the sidelines of the APEC leaders' meeting in Vietnam. Abe came away enthused, reporting that the meeting was "very friendly and relaxed" and that the two men had had a "frank and open exchange of views on international affairs, including the North Korea issue." He urged a Japan-China-South Korea trilateral summit meeting on North Korea be held "as soon as possible." For his part, Xi pressed for Japanese economic cooperation under the framework of the Belt and Road Initiative, including the funding of regional infrastructure projects, and said the meeting "represented a new start for Japan-China relations."

In April 2018, the two countries resumed a high-level bilateral economic dialogue after an eight-year hiatus following the crisis over Senkaku / Diaoyu Dao. And in May, Abe hosted Chinese premier Li Keqiang and South Korean president Moon Jae-in to Tokyo for a trilateral summit, at which Abe and Li agreed to implement a new maritime and aerial crisis communication mechanism for the East China Sea. In September 2018, Abe and Xi met again in Vladivostok, holding "intensive discussions on the North Korean issue" that left Abe pleased with China's commitment to maintaining sanctions against the North. By the time the two met again in Beijing ahead of another trilateral summit in December 2019, relations had warmed considerably. Abe spoke of a "new stage of relations" and drafting a "fifth political document" to add to the four diplomatic agreements that formed the foundation of postwar Sino-Japanese ties, this time to be based on future global cooperation. He invited Xi to visit Japan in spring 2020, saying it would be "a good chance to show the common responsibility which Japan and China" shared in their approach toward the world.

However, the 2020 closure of borders due to the pandemic, increasing tensions with China over the origins of COVID-19, and escalating global outcry over Chinese crackdowns in Hong Kong and Xinjiang succeeded in putting the visit by Xi to Japan on ice. Furthermore, over the course of that year, there was an operational intensification of Chinese naval, coast guard, and paramilitary deployments around Senkaku / Diaoyu Dao. Japan's military collaboration with the US, India, and Australia also intensified—both bilaterally and through the Quad—and, in 2021, Tokyo announced it would significantly increase its expenditure on security, taking the historic step of abandoning its long-standing cap of 1 percent of GDP on annual defense spending. Japanese defense minister Nobuo Kishi explained to the Japanese people that, despite Japan's pacifist constitution, "the security environment surrounding Japan is changing rapidly with heightened uncertainty," and Tokyo had to "properly allocate the funding we need to protect our nation," including by developing "new areas such as space, cyber, and electromagnetic warfare." The time had come, he said, when "we have to wake up, and we have to prepare."

Perhaps most significantly, in 2021, Tokyo spoke out publicly for the first time on Taiwan, reflecting the conclusions of a Defense Ministry white paper that concluded that the regional balance of power was shifting dangerously in China's favor. Kishi declared that Japan had an obligation "to protect Taiwan as a democratic country," while Japan's deputy prime minister Taro Aso warned that an attack on Taiwan, or "various situations, such as not being able to pass through the Taiwan Strait," would pose "an existential threat" to Japan, which would "need to think hard that Okinawa could be next." He noted that "if that is the case, Japan and the US must defend Taiwan together." In August 2021, Tokyo and Taipei held their first bilateral security talks. This has represented a fundamental shift in Tokyo's diplomatic and strategic approach, which has traditionally always been extremely careful to moderate its rhetoric and its image as a regional security actor, even as it has deepened cooperation with the United States. Beijing, for its part, immediately threatened that Japan would "dig its own grave" if it joined the US in intervening in a conflict over Taiwan.

When Abe's politically short-lived successor as prime minister, Yoshihide Suga, resigned and was replaced by the more left-leaning Fumio Kishida in September 2021, the new administration began to make policy tweaks, including a shift away from Abe's signature "Abenomics" economic policy. The trajectory of Tokyo's approach to China notably did not change, however, with Kishida quickly creating a post to oversee economic and security risks related to Japan's reliance on the Chinese market and committing to a plan to eventually double defense spending.

Tokyo, therefore, appears to be in the process of reevaluating its overall strategic stance on relations with China and may continue to try to bolster its military capabilities (along with the US) to deter what it perceives to be Chinese aggression in the region. Nonetheless, Japan's overall strategic calculus regarding the long-term trajectory of the US-China balance of power on the one hand and the possibility of America's continued drift toward isolationism on the other is unlikely to have substantially changed. How Tokyo will continue to balance its approach, therefore, bears careful and detailed scrutiny.

As for Xi, despite continued attempts to affirm Chinese "administration" over the disputed islands in the East China Sea with regular maritime patrols, his overall interest appears to lie in reducing strategic tensions on both his Japanese and—if possible—his Indian flanks. Given the abrupt shift in bipartisan political sentiment in the United States toward China, he would much prefer to face the US alone if at all possible. Xi also sees Japan (which remains the world's third-largest economy) through the lens of China's global trade, technology, and investment interests, especially if the US continues to move in the direction of greater economic decoupling with China.

The Korean Peninsula

The Korean Peninsula represents a conundrum for China. China and Korea share not only geographical proximity, long historical links, and a deep cultural affinity but also the enduring legacy of the deployment of more than a million Chinese troops to the peninsula in 1950 to roll back America's advance during the Korean War. That war holds special significance in Chinese political psychology because it symbolizes the ability of the Chinese Communist state (even in its infancy) to inflict military defeat—or at least stalemate—on the all-powerful US military. Yet despite this shared history, Xi's relationship with North Korean leader Kim Jong-un was—at least until 2018—undoubtedly the worst between the leaders of the two countries in nearly two-thirds of a century. The reason was North Korea's accelerating nuclear weapons and ballistic missile development programs, culminating in a series of nuclear and long-range missile tests between 2006 and 2018, that violated multiple UN Security Council resolutions. To Pyongyang's chagrin, China had supported these resolutions, including the economic sanctions that came with them. Given that his actions were raising tensions with the South and the US to unprecedented levels, threatening the disastrous possibility of direct American intervention once again on the peninsula, Kim was much more of a strategic problem for Xi than a valuable ally.

But to Xi's relief, Trump's unilateral decision to engage in direct summit diplomacy with Kim in Singapore, Vietnam, and South Korea in 2018 and 2019 enabled Xi to unfreeze his political relationship with Kim. North Korea had become China's problem child, in that continuing political support for Pyongyang was undermining China's efforts to build its global reputation as a responsible emerging superpower. Now, an American president, of all people, had come to the rescue. Xi offered superficial assistance to Trump in his dealings with Kim on the nuclear question. This was based on China's calculation that Kim would never surrender his nuclear arsenal, and that it was not in China's interests to undermine its strategic relationship with the North by trying to force Kim to do so, but that political and diplomatic benefits could be found by helping Trump in his futile, quixotic quest. Xi concluded that Trump would come and go, but China's North Korean neighbor would always be there.

No matter Xi's personal difficulties with Kim, he does not want to see the North Korean regime collapse. He would then have to deal with the wave of refugees that would flow into China from the North. It is also unclear what a post-Kim government would look like. In a worst-case scenario, it could risk the reunification of Korea by Seoul and the creation of a strong, united pro-American state on China's immediate borders. Still, Xi believes the US is unlikely to take military action against the North even if Pyongyang makes no substantive disarmament commitments. Moreover, Beijing's view is that any North Korean nuclear capability, while problematic for China, is likely to be targeted only at the US and its Asian allies, including South Korea and Japan, not China. In fact, a North Korean nuclear capacity is likely to complicate US strategic planning in East Asia and the western Pacific far more than China's. It would also arguably improve China's overall strategic circumstances, given that the US (and Japan) would need to deal with significant regional security threats from *both* China and North Korea rather than China alone.

As for South Korea, despite periods of tension—such as over the deployment of THAAD discussed in the previous chapter—Xi remains sanguine that long-term strategic, economic, and cultural factors will continue to draw Seoul into Beijing's political orbit. The policies of the Trump administration, both on the US-Korea Free Trade Agreement—which Trump demanded be renegotiated—and the demands for the Korean government to pay considerably more for the retention of US troops, undermined much popular goodwill for the United States in South Korea. The pull of China's economy, growing anti-Japanese sentiment, and more recognition that China does not support armed reunification by the North have improved Korean political sentiment toward Beijing. The continued fracturing of Japan-Korea relations and the failure of the United States to effectively arbitrate between the two, as it has done in the past, also represents a further advance in China's relative position vis-à-vis Seoul. Furthermore, there is an emerging view in Seoul that China may offer a better long-term guarantee for the South against any resumption of hostility by the North than the US is able to provide. All this points toward a growing rapprochement between Seoul and Beijing, despite continued cordial relations with Washington.

The continued political disarray of the political right in South Korean politics enhances China's confidence, including Chinese perceptions that generational change in the South is weakening the older generation's political and emotional attachment to the US. Indeed, at its most confident, Beijing believes it may eventually be able to peel Seoul away from America's military embrace, thereby removing US troops from their current proximity to the Chinese mainland and returning Korea to its proper historical place—in China's worldview—within China's sphere of influence. Regardless, the less China has to worry about Korea and its other neighbors, the more it can start to look beyond its most immediate neighborhood in Northeast Asia.

Southeast Asia

Apart from Korea, continental and archipelagic Southeast Asia is the region where imperial China developed its network of tributary state relationships most intensively over the centuries—receiving envoys who formally acknowledged the superior status of the Chinese emperor, brought gifts as tribute, and received gifts in return as a form of useful, ritualized trade. It is also the region that attracted the greatest levels of Chinese migration over the last several hundred years. Even today, around half of China's outward migration in recent years has been to Southeast Asia, typically in search of business opportunities. It is estimated that about two-thirds of the total number of people with ethnic Chinese ancestry living abroad are settled in Southeast Asia.

For these reasons, it is of little surprise that Beijing has worked strenuously to cultivate close ties with the region, aiming to create Southeast Asian client states through a combination of diplomacy, loans, investment, and trade. Despite China's island and maritime claims in the South China Sea continuing to challenge its relationships with at least five ASEAN states, from Beijing's perspective, China's relationships with continental Southeast Asia are proceeding well. Laos and Cambodia have increasingly become Chinese satrapies, with Cambodia acting as a de facto Chinese proxy in internal ASEAN deliberations. Thailand—despite technically still being an American ally—has been under a range of US sanctions since the military takeover of Bangkok in 2014 and is moving gradually in China's direction. As for Myanmar, China had invested heavily in its relationship with Aung San Suu Kyi's administration in order to overcome whatever setbacks it faced with her in 2015. The coup by Myanmar's military in February 2021 that seized control of the country was initially viewed as a frustrating setback in China. However, Beijing adapted quickly to the circumstances, adopting an increasingly firm policy of support for the military regime. In Southeast Asia, as elsewhere, China's diplomatic relations today are guided by pragmatic self-interest; political ideology and the type of government with which they are dealing are of little concern.

China's relations with Vietnam, unsurprisingly, are more complex, given that they go back a thousand years and have often been adversarial. During the Vietnam War, China aided the winning Viet Cong against their American allies in South Vietnam. However, soon after, in 1979, the two countries fought a bitter border war. Relations warmed slowly during the 1980s, but despite elaborate official celebrations in 2020 to mark seventy years since the normalization of diplomatic ties between the two socialist states, relations are more tense today than they have been in decades. Still, even Vietnam, which had opened an embryonic security-cooperation relationship with the United States after 2010 (following Beijing's escalation of the South China Sea dispute), is hedging its strategic bets by continuing to calibrate its relations between the US and China. Beijing has some cause for hope that, despite the adversarial history, Hanoi is not yet a lost geopolitical cause.

As for Malaysia, despite Prime Minister Mahathir Mohamed's anti-Chinese rhetoric in the 2018 elections that brought him back to power, China renegotiated its more controversial debt-laden BRI projects in Malaysia to the satisfaction of the new government in Kuala Lumpur. Indeed, even amid the continuing turmoil of Malaysian politics, which then saw Mahathir fall to Muhyiddin Yassin only for Muhyiddin to fall to Ismail Sabri Yaakob in 2021, China-Malaysia relations appear to have effectively renormalized. Meanwhile, Singapore (a military partner rather than a formal ally of the United States) incurred China's wrath by deciding in 2015 to allow the home porting of US warships in the city. But since a formal "reset" in its relationship with Beijing in 2018, Singapore has undertaken to be more sensitive to Beijing's interests, especially given its immense and growing economic relationship with China. After entering office, the Biden administration made a point of quickly dispatching multiple senior officials to Singapore, including Vice President Kamala Harris and Secretary of Defense Lloyd Austin, to bolster relations with the city-state (as well as Southeast Asia more broadly). Nevertheless, it remains to be seen what Singapore's strategic trajectory will be for the long term.

The most dramatic shift in the regional US-China competition for strategic influence has been in the Philippines under the administration of populist president Rodrigo Duterte. The Philippines is—like Thailand—a formal US treaty ally. But under Duterte, Manila has radically changed course in its relationship with Beijing—especially in its approach to its historical dispute with China over competing claims in the South China Sea. Duterte's erratic attempts to balance the Philippines' traditional closeness to Washington with greater outreach to Beijing saw Manila abandon a landmark 2016 UN Permanent Court of Arbitration decision on a case brought by the previous Philippines government against the legitimacy of Chinese claims in the South China Sea—despite the fact the court had ruled decisively in the Philippines' favor. Duterte, whose presidential term began the month before the ruling, called it "just a piece of paper" and said he'd "throw it in the wastebasket" to improve relations with Beijing. His attempts to reap the economic benefits of a close relationship with Beijing while managing the Philippines' traditional closeness to Washington has seen roller-coaster decision-making. But in July 2021, he again tilted back toward the United States by re-signing a pact—which he had threatened to abandon in 2020—allowing US forces to operate in the country. Overall, Duterte's China strategy divided the country, with his opponents claiming he has relegated Philippines to the effective status of a Chinese province, prompting his backtracking. Ultimately, the country's next presidential election, in May 2022, will likely determine whether the Philippines grows closer still to Beijing or refocuses on Washington.

However, of all the Southeast Asian states, arguably the most important exercise in great power rivalry is unfolding in Indonesia, where China is locked in active competition with the US, Japan, and Australia for strategic influence. The stakes are high: with a young, growing, tech-savvy population of 273 million people in 2020, Indonesia is Southeast Asia's largest emerging market and is destined to be a key battleground for global economic competition between Chinese and Western firms. Moreover, Indonesia occupies critical strategic geography; located across the vital Malacca and Lombok Straits, it is in a decisive position to influence access to and control over the South China Sea. While Indonesia has historically always maintained a strictly neutral foreign policy, both the US and China know Jakarta has the potential to become *the* critical swing state in the "great game" for strategic influence in the broader Asia-Pacific region. Today, the legacy of 1966—when the Chinese Communist Party actively sought to intervene in Indonesia by supplying arms in support of an attempted communist coup—no longer shapes the decision-making processes of the Indonesian government as it once did, with the imperatives of economic development now taking precedence. This means the potential economic benefits of China loom large for Jakarta, which also found in Beijing an eager source of vaccines and medical assistance during the COVID-19 pandemic. From Xi's perspective, therefore, Indonesia is very much in play, with active consideration being given to offering to include Indonesia in the BRICS grouping in an effort to further induce Jakarta into China's strategic orbit.

Across all of Southeast Asia, three big developments are unfolding that give Xi confidence that the region is moving steadily in China's direction. The first is the sheer size of China's regional economic footprint relative to that of the United States. Southeast Asia is China's second-largest trading partner, while China is ASEAN's largest. By contrast, Southeast Asia is America's fourth-largest trading partner while the US is ASEAN's second largest. Meanwhile, Japan is ASEAN's fourth-largest trade partner, while ASEAN is Japan's second largest. In terms of foreign direct investment (FDI) to Southeast Asia, the picture is more complex: Japan is the top source of external FDI in ASEAN, followed by China and the United States. Nonetheless, the centrifugal force of the Chinese economy is proving to be increasingly irresistible for the states of the region and is shaping long-term political and diplomatic trends in China's favor.

Second, under Xi, China has modified its strategy toward its South China Sea claims vis-à-vis its ASEAN neighbors. Until 2016, China pursued an aggressive strategy with other claimant states, whereas over the last several years, we have generally seen China pursuing a more effective diplomacy in the region. Beijing, having summarily rejected the UN Permanent Court of Arbitration ruling that China's expansive maritime claims in the region were illegal under international law, now seeks to put conflicting claims to one side while advancing potential joint-development partnerships with the other claimant states as an alternative—tempting them to abandon their strict sovereignty claims in favor of more immediate economic benefits. Meanwhile, Beijing continues to herald the possibility of reaching a negotiated agreement on a South China Sea Code of Conduct with the ASEAN nations. Since 2017, China has not reclaimed additional "islands" in the South China Sea, although it has continued to militarize the seven that it has already built. The one recent exception has been the deployment of a mass fleet of nearly three hundred armed Chinese paramilitary "fishing" vessels to occupy waters near the Philippines-claimed Whitsun Reef—an act intended to pressure Manila into not reversing its foreign policy course by improving relations with the new Biden administration. While this and other Chinese actions (such as increasingly common incursions by Chinese ships and planes into waters near Malaysia) continue to generate political turbulence across the region, open conflict with regional states has generally been less intense than it was in the previous decade.

Third, the common refrain across Southeast Asia is that the US, after the heyday of Obama's pivot to the region, has in recent years been increasingly missing in action—militarily, economically, and politically. Even though the Trump administration increased the pace of freedom-of-navigation operations challenging Chinese maritime claims and, in 2019, warned that hostile behavior by Chinese coast guard and maritime militia vessels would not be treated any differently by the US Navy under its rules of engagement than similar acts by a foreign navy, neither step has deterred—let alone dislodged—China's assertive presence in the South China Sea. Meanwhile, Trump's decision to abandon the Trans-Pacific Partnership free trade agreement and refusal to engage in the Regional Comprehensive Economic Partnership with ASEAN and five other regional states were universally interpreted across the region as tantamount to wholesale American economic withdrawal. Diplomatically, the Trump administration could not even be bothered to turn up at presidential-level major regional summits, including APEC and the East Asian Summit, over several years. This has left a lasting negative legacy in the region that the Biden administration has yet to turn around—especially given its hesitancy toward multilateral free trade agreements.

It would be wrong to say that Trump's retreat from Southeast Asia has made China popular in the region, but it has certainly become more competitive. Xi Jinping's China is once again playing the long game, drawing on its economic power, persevering despite periodic setbacks, and confident that the United States is an increasingly spent force in Southeast Asia.

Reviewing the Strategic Map

When Xi reviews the map of China's immediate neighborhood from a strategic perspective, he is likely pleased with most of the trends that have emerged. From Beijing's perspective, Russia is almost completely on side. Japan is hedging but may not be able to escape its economic reliance on China. India has regressed but is still not a lost cause. Korea is trending positively and Southeast Asia even more so. China's position has been abetted by a complacent American approach that wrongly assumed Beijing's more assertive behavior would, of itself, generate sufficient anti-Chinese reaction across the region to alleviate the need for much further effort by Washington offering an alternative. This has simply not been the case. There have certainly been ebbs and flows in the advancement of China's overall interests across its immediate region, but due to China's major economic advantage and the seeming political inability of the United States to offer anything comparable in trade, investment, and potentially technology (Huawei's 5G, for example), from Beijing's perspective the trend remains positive. Nonetheless, it is not a uniformly positive picture for China. One particular success by Washington is worth noting: rallying pan-regional opposition to China through the Quad by building out from the current framework. This is causing significant alarm in Beijing. And it forms a large part of the focus of the next chapter.

10

★ ★ ★ ★ ★

The Seventh Circle: Securing China's Maritime Periphery— the Western Pacific, the Indo-Pacific, and the Quad

Over the last 180 years, all the biggest threats to China's security have come from the sea. It was from the sea that Britain and France successfully attacked China's maritime defenses during the First and Second Opium Wars. It was from the sea that Japan launched a series of successful military campaigns against China between 1895 and 1945. And it is the sea—and the American naval forces that have dominated it for decades— that has so far prevented Communist China from reclaiming Taiwan. It is, therefore, unsurprising that China has long seen its maritime periphery to the east as particularly hostile.

Securing China's maritime periphery and maximizing the country's strategic depth into the Pacific, including by pushing US forces all the way back to the Second Island Chain (running from the Japanese archipelago in the north, through Guam, to Papua New Guinea and Australia in the south) remains a critical component of Xi Jinping's overall strategy. This is seen as essential for a number of reasons. First, to force US reconnaissance aircraft and ships back from their decades-long practice of conducting regular operations just off the Chinese coast. Second, to assist China in its outstanding territorial claims over Taiwan, the South China Sea, and in the East China Sea. And third, to finally "break through the thistles"—as Chinese naval strategists put it—of the constricting geography that currently keeps China's naval forces effectively bottled up behind the First Island Chain (Japan, Okinawa, Taiwan, the Philippines, and the Indonesian archipelago), allowing China to become a truly blue-water maritime power.

The American Factor

China rightly sees the forward deployments of US armed forces across East Asia as indispensable to the projection and sustainment of American power in the region. China understands that these deployments are anchored in the long-standing US base on Guam and its array of military, naval, marine, and intelligence facilities scattered across the territories of US allies Japan, Korea, and Australia and the freely associated states in the North Pacific and supported to a lesser extent by Singapore, Thailand, and the Philippines. Under the direction of Indo-Pacific Command in Honolulu, the US military's capabilities across the region are formidable in their own right. But their ability to forward deploy across the vast expanse of the Indo-Pacific is profoundly enhanced by the strategic real estate offered by these allies and other strategic partners. That is why China has a long-standing strategic objective of fracturing US alliances if at all possible. China's strategic logic is clear: America, without its alliances, would be considerably weakened, if not pushed out all together from the Indo-Pacific. Whereas China currently lacks strategic reach into the Pacific, America's allies afford the United States an extraordinary advantage. This is a state of affairs that Xi Jinping wants to reverse.

The key element of China's strategy for securing its wider maritime periphery is military—the rapid expansion of Chinese air and naval capabilities, reinforced by land-based missiles and cybersystems, which would aim to overwhelm US and allied combatants. They would achieve this by sheer force of numbers and by controlling the informationized battle space. But China's military strategy is greatly reinforced by its economic strategy, leveraging the magnitude of the Chinese market with each of America's critical allies in an effort to peel them away from Washington over the long term—gradually increasing the economic costs of standing against China and so reducing over time their sense of loyalty, commitment, and obligation to the US. In addition, China has sought to wield its political and diplomatic muscles, along with its economic power, against individual allies that have proven to be particularly recalcitrant in their insensitivity to Chinese national interests. The intention here is to make punitive examples of such states by limiting their access to the Chinese market (or, in extreme cases, interfering with their assets or even arbitrarily detaining their citizens in China), thereby warning others of the price to be paid for thumbing their nose at Beijing's political demands. The corollary, of course, is to reward those countries (for example, the Philippines in Asia or Greece in Europe) that increasingly reject political cooperation with America. All three parts of this strategy are designed to weaken the solidarity of US alliances over time. China had considerable success on this score during the years of the Trump administration—both as a product of its strategic efforts and because of the negative impact of the Trump phenomenon itself on the resilience and cohesion of American alliance relationships.

The Entrance of the Quad

A critical new development in the Indo-Pacific region's alliance structures has been the rebirth since 2019 of the Quadrilateral Security Dialogue between the United States, Japan, India, and Australia—otherwise known as the Quad. The Quad, although falling far short of a formal alliance structure with mutual defense obligations (India not being a treaty ally of the US or Quad member states), nonetheless appears to be rapidly evolving as the most significant direct regional response to date to Beijing's increasingly assertive strategic posture. Xi's response to this important new challenge is evolving as well.

When Japan's Shinzo Abe invited diplomats from the United States, Australia, and India to gather for a working-level meeting on the sidelines of the November 2017 Association of Southeast Asian Nations (ASEAN) Summit in Manila to discuss significantly deepening their cooperation, Beijing dismissed it as of little concern to its strategic interests. The Quad, said Chinese foreign minister Wang Yi after the meeting, was only ever a "headline-grabbing idea. . . . They are like the seafoam in the Pacific or Indian Ocean: they may get some attention but will soon dissipate." Beijing's strategic community at this time viewed the countries of the Quad as simply too divergent in their national interests to come together with any coherence. Beijing had some good reasons to think so at the time.

The Quad had, after all, been tried once before, a decade earlier, in the mid-2000s. At that time, it never progressed beyond informal breakfast talks among officials, having been rejected categorically by the Australian government of my predecessor as prime minister, John Howard. Abe's original vision for the Quad emerged in the aftermath of the 2004 tsunami that devastated much of South and Southeast Asia, killing more than 227,000 people across fourteen countries. At the time, Japan, the United States, India, and Australia coordinated a joint—if somewhat haphazard—natural disaster response. Abe envisioned building up the four countries' capacity to work together in the region to meet shared challenges, including regional security.

In the other capitals, the response was tentative at best. In Washington, Vice President Dick Cheney was a supporter, but President George W. Bush was lukewarm from the start. He worried that the appearance of intensifying security cooperation between the four countries would alienate the Chinese support he sought in helping with nuclear proliferation in both North Korea and Iran. By December 2008, the Bush administration was privately assuring regional governments that the Quad would never coalesce—as evidenced in diplomatic cables subsequently published by another Australian, founder of WikiLeaks Julian Assange. In Delhi, Prime Minister Manmohan Singh openly ruled out any real security cooperation with the Quad, also categorizing ties with Beijing as his "imperative necessity." Indeed, before my government said anything about the Quad, Singh had publicly declared that it "never got going" and consigned it to history. Meanwhile, in Canberra, Howard's conservative government was also eager to maintain strong, economically beneficial ties with China. He adamantly opposed expanding existing trilateral strategic cooperation with the US and Japan by adding India to the mix. His government signaled its withdrawal from the Quad at a meeting of the US-Japan-Australia trilateral dialogue held in Washington in July 2007—also documented in a WikiLeaks diplomatic cable—and announced the decision in Beijing soon after. So when Abe, as the driving force behind the Quad, then unexpectedly resigned in September 2007, it delivered the death knell to Quad version 1.0. His successor Yasuo Fukuda then consigned the Quad to history. By the end of 2007, when my government entered office, all engagement within the Quad framework had already been dead in the water for months. Taking the temperature in other capitals, we found no interest in attempting to revive it.

The Emergence of Quad 2.0

However, a decade later when Abe—back in office once more—set out to get the band back together, the region's strategic circumstances had fundamentally changed. By 2017, the US-China relationship was adrift, and each of the Quad capitals was reevaluating its strategic calculus toward China. But Beijing was not yet paying serious attention to these developments.

At its first 2017 meeting in Manila, the Quad countries seemed to demonstrate their previous level of internal disarray by failing to issue a unified communiqué outlining any common strategic purpose. Instead, they each released their uncoordinated statements, serving mostly to highlight divergences on key concerns. Japan left off American and Australian language on "connectivity" efforts in the Indo-Pacific (meant to offer an alternative to China's BRI), while Tokyo considered whether to cooperate with the BRI. Meanwhile, India left off all references to maritime security, freedom of navigation, and international law included by the others. The only thing the four countries did agree on was to meet once a year on a regular schedule.

It was not until September 2019 that the Quad's four foreign ministers finally met in New York for their first ministerial-level meeting. However, this time they agreed in principle to work together on what would become the Quad's mantra: to "advance a free and open Indo-Pacific." Even still, Beijing remained largely indifferent. By the time the Quad foreign ministers met again in October 2020 in Tokyo, Beijing began to pay attention. Seven months earlier, the first round of what became known as the Quad-Plus talks had also been held, with South Korea, New Zealand, and Vietnam joining the Quad countries to discuss cooperation on trade, technology, and supply chains—a development Beijing eyed with growing concern. Then in June 2020, Chinese and Indian forces clashed along their shared border in what would prove to be the most significant and catalytic event in the development of the Quad. As discussed at length in the previous chapter, that clash caused Delhi to fundamentally reassess its defense priorities, and India—heretofore the most reluctant of the four partners—suddenly became eager to deepen its participation in a more formal security framework that could serve as a potential strategic balance against China. For example, that fall, India, for the first time in thirteen years, invited Australia to join the annual Malabar joint naval exercises held with the US and Japan. This was especially notable because despite growing closer to the rest of the Quad since 2017, India had refused to allow Australian participation in the Malabar exercises in 2018 and 2019, fearing it would unnecessarily antagonize China by portraying the Quad as a militarily focused partnership. But after the June 2020 border clash, all remaining political hesitation in Delhi was gone.

So when the Quad met in Tokyo that October, the geopolitical *wei qi* board, from Beijing's perspective, already looked far more problematic. Then US secretary of state Mike Pompeo bluntly declared that Washington's goal was ultimately to "institutionalize" the Quad, "build out a true security framework," and even expand the grouping at "the appropriate time" to "counter the challenge that the Chinese Communist Party presents to all of us." To Beijing, it suddenly seemed as though the Quad was not only alive and well but that it might also expand.

Changing Chinese Reactions to the Quad

Watching all these events unfold over the course of 2019 and 2020, China's strategic community had been undergoing a significant shift in its conceptualization of the Quad as a potential threat to Chinese national security interests. Tellingly, two scholars at the influential Central Party School warned of the Quad's "increasing institutionalization." Another, at the Chinese Academy of Social Sciences, noted that trends were demonstrating the Quad's transition from an "informal framework of cooperation" to a "formal regional organization." The October 2020 Quad ministerial meeting seemed to confirm these concerns.

But all such analysis appeared to point to a relatively straightforward solution: China could still use a combination of sticks and carrots to drive a wedge between the Quad countries where possible by accentuating their conflicting national interests. In particular, the overwhelming economic reliance of each of the Asian Quad partners on the Chinese market seemed like a key weakness ready for exploitation. The simple idea was to break the Quad apart.

Beijing implemented this strategy almost immediately following the October 2020 Quad meeting. Chinese foreign minister Wang Yi dropped all nonchalant references to seafoam and changed his tone dramatically. Instead, he slammed the effort to build an "Indo-Pacific NATO" and said the Quad's Indo-Pacific strategy was "itself a big underlying security risk" to the region. China then quickly selected a target on which to use its stick. A classical Chinese axiom advises to "kill one to warn a hundred" (*shayi jingbai*), but in this case, the goal was to kill one (Australia) to warn two (Japan and India).

Beijing previously seemed intent on improving relations with Canberra. But without specific explanation, it suddenly imposed restrictions on imports of Australian coal—and then meat, cotton, wool, barley, wheat, timber, copper, sugar, lobster, and wine. At the same time, Chinese state media unleashed a blitz of messaging, accusing Canberra of having used the Quad meeting to "promote its own global status," asking, "How much strength does Australia own with its limited economy and population?" It warned that "if Canberra is bent on infuriating China, Australia will only face dire consequences." One analyst in China's unofficial *Global Times*, which is authorized to deliver hard-line messages to foreign countries that the government and the party won't, declared simply, "Being a mouthpiece for US aggression against China will cost Australian jobs." Then, at a press conference in Beijing, Chinese foreign ministry spokesperson Wang Wenbin urged Australians to "reflect upon their deeds" if they wanted any chance of restoring trade relations. While there were other elements at play in the Australia-China relationship beyond the Quad, the timing and content of the message from Beijing was unmistakable.

The campaign of economic retaliation against Australia continued to escalate, with China regularly using the Australian example elsewhere around the world as a warning that countries who "let themselves be led by the nose" by Washington risked being cut off from China's huge domestic market. Beijing clearly estimated that Australia was the least likely of the Quad countries to actually break with the United States; the most vulnerable to economic coercion (as the smallest of the four Quad states); and the least threatening to Chinese interests (being more distant from China's borders than Japan, India, or the long arm of American power).

The second part of China's strategy was to try to simultaneously repair relations with Japan and India—efforts also discussed at some length in the previous chapter but that are worth summarizing again briefly here. Beijing had already been engaged in an effort to thaw relations with Japan since 2018, when Chinese premier Li Keqiang traveled to Tokyo for a trilateral summit along with South Korean president Moon Jae-in. There, Abe and Li agreed to implement a new maritime and aerial crisis communication mechanism to handle encounters in the disputed East China Sea. After a series of meetings between Abe and Xi on the sidelines of various multilateral fora, relations briefly appeared to be on the upswing, and a major visit by Xi to Japan was planned for the spring of 2020—only to be delayed by the COVID-19 pandemic.

After the October 2020 Quad meeting, Beijing stepped up its attempts to finalize the visit by Xi to meet with Abe's new successor as prime minister, Yoshihide Suga. Chinese foreign minister Wang Yi embarked on a visit to Tokyo in November 2020 in an attempt to reenergize the diplomatic thaw, only to be met with a frosty reception. Crowds of demonstrators, angry about human rights abuses in Xinjiang, Tibet, and Inner Mongolia, gathered outside Suga's residence to protest Wang's visit, while legislators from Suga's governing Liberal Democratic Party drafted a resolution calling for an official cancellation of the summit with Xi. Meanwhile, Suga's chief cabinet secretary, Katsunobu Kato, conveyed Tokyo's "concerns about the activities of the Chinese government ships around the [Senkaku] islands," reporting that the situation was "extremely serious." By early 2021, the proposed visit to Tokyo by Xi was officially off—fatally undermined by escalating Chinese incursions into Japanese-claimed waters in the East China Sea and growing Japanese public and official concerns over human rights.

At the same time, Beijing was trying to de-escalate tensions with Delhi by seeking to defuse the border crisis and entice India with offers of economic and COVID-19 vaccine aid. But in the end, Beijing met with little success in slowing India's embrace of the Quad. While the immediate standoff on the border may have been resolved, wariness of China had been deeply implanted in Delhi's psyche.

As the Quad continued to solidify and the scope of its activities expanded, entering into a series of new bilateral and multilateral security agreements and exercises, Beijing's confidence that the Quad could be split apart waned. China seemed not to have fully comprehended the impact of their actions in accelerating overall Quad solidarity. Moreover, China's ability to execute a coherent strategy of simultaneous targeted escalation with Australia and de-escalation with Japan and India was badly undermined by the lack of discipline of its ultranationalistic wolf warrior diplomats, who succeeded in regularly offending countries across the globe. For example, a Communist Party social media post mocking India's death toll when combatting COVID-19 incited fury and disgust not only in India and the West but also from many social media users in China itself.

Finally, the election of President Biden and his focus on allied, regional, and multilateral engagement changed the dynamic. China lost the relative freedom of diplomatic international maneuver it had during the "America First" days of the Trump administration. The new administration was willing to quickly resolve Trump-era trade and military-basing disputes with US allies such as Japan and South Korea, stabilizing relations. Whereas during the Trump period, Beijing largely pushed on an open door in its efforts to bolster its influence with other countries in the region, it suddenly faced a much more united front from Washington and its allies and partners.

Quad Alarm

Beijing's thinking on what to do about the Quad shifted again, coming to a head in March 2021, when the four countries held their first leader-level summit. The pivotal meeting saw the group release its first unified joint communiqué. Titled the "Spirit of the Quad," the statement agreed to "strive for a region that is free, open, inclusive, healthy, anchored by democratic values, and unconstrained by coercion" and to "facilitate collaboration, including in maritime security, to meet challenges to the rules-based maritime order in the East and South China Seas."

The Quad leaders also launched a joint vaccine distribution initiative in the Indo-Pacific, challenging China's "vaccine diplomacy" efforts by agreeing to cooperate to produce and distribute one billion vaccines for the region. They also set up a vaccine expert working group, a climate change working group, and a "critical and emerging technologies" working group on securing technology supply chains, all aiming to strengthen cooperation in meeting these challenges in the region. Indian prime minister Narendra Modi spoke to what may have been Beijing's worst fears when he declared, "Today's summit meeting shows that the Quad has come of age. It will now remain an important pillar of stability in the region."

To Beijing, the summit seemed to confirm the worst: that the Quad would—by providing an alternative multilateral source of infrastructure development funding, trade initiatives, and other public goods, along with diversified regional supply chains—soon expand its competitive challenge to Chinese influence from the security realm to the economic. Moreover, Beijing appeared to worry that the Quad would soon coordinate more closely with the Five Eyes intelligence grouping, the G7, and NATO to isolate China—a concern that turned out to be well-founded.

China's Full-Scale Attack on the Quad

After the March 2021 summit, China quickly made a third pivot in its strategy to try to deal with the Quad: full-scale political attack. There was soon an explosion in Chinese official condemnations of the Quad as a "small clique" (*Xiao Quanzi*) of countries. As Xi Jinping put it in a speech in May 2021, in Beijing's eyes, they were using "multilateralism as a pretext to . . . stir up ideological confrontation." Their collective goal, Beijing claimed, was nothing less than to "start a new Cold War." In contrast, China increasingly portrayed itself as the true champion of a "genuine multilateralism" that was "inseparable from the UN system" as well as being the leading defender and reformer of that system and of global governance in general. References by Xi and others to "great power responsibility" (*daguo dandang*) and China being a responsible international leader became pronounced.

Beijing's strategy transitioned to diplomatically isolate and marginalize the Quad by outflanking it internationally. As one Central Party School scholar argued, China should "deepen strategic interactions" and increase maritime security cooperation with ASEAN as a "type of counterweight" to the Quad. Another Chinese scholar wrote that strengthening pan-Asian economic cooperation through the RCEP and CPTPP trade agreements would "cushion" the Quad "and its negative impact on the regional order." In essence, the strategy aims for China to "go bigger" than the four-member Quad grouping in order to contain its influence on the regional and global stage.

Yet such denunciations have so far done little to stall the Quad's progress in galvanizing multilateral resistance to China. In June 2021, President Biden made an extended trip to Europe, including a G7 summit in the UK that was joined by Australia and India, among others. Biden then met with both EU officials and NATO. In every case, relations with China became the top subject of discussion. Moreover, when South Korea's President Moon traveled to meet with Biden in Washington in May that year, the United States pressed Seoul to join the Quad's three new working groups and to make a statement supporting the Quad. Although Moon has been reluctant to take sides overtly with the US in any wider strategic contest with China, in this case, Washington succeeded, and the two countries' joint statement agreed that they "acknowledged the importance of open, transparent, and inclusive regional multilateralism including the Quad"—and "the importance of preserving peace and stability in the Taiwan Strait." And in September 2021, the leaders of the Quad met in person for the first time at a summit in Washington, agreeing to expand cooperation on vaccines, climate change, infrastructure financing, and supply chains for critical and emerging technologies such as semiconductors and 5G as well as cybersecurity.

All this has reinforced Beijing's worst fear: that not only could the Quad expand—for example, by taking in South Korea to become "the Quint"—but also that it could become the multilateral building block for a broader anti-China coalition of North American, European, and Asian liberal-democratic states. An example of this growing concern manifested itself in May 2021, when China's ambassador to Bangladesh delivered a strongly worded warning to Dhaka that it would "substantially damage" its ties with China if it joined or coordinated its actions with the Quad. The warning was striking because Bangladesh (which called the remarks "aggressive" and "very unfortunate") has retained a strenuously neutral foreign policy and had given no previous indication at all that it was planning to work with the Quad. The incident, therefore, seemed to demonstrate a level of worry bordering on paranoia that seems to have taken hold in Beijing regarding the potential expansion of the Quad and its activities.

Australia and the Quad's South Pacific Flank

China's relations with Australia, New Zealand, and the fourteen independent island nations of the Pacific have also come under strain under Xi. Beijing has long seen Australia as an important—albeit middle-ranking—trade and investment partner and is still highly dependent on Australian iron ore and natural gas. Australia had also become the second-largest destination worldwide for Chinese students studying abroad, after the US.

Yet the Chinese leadership has long attacked Australia's strong military alliance with the United States, claiming it to be a "relic of the Cold War" and part of a wider containment strategy against China. Even before the revival of the Quad, the relationship was deteriorating rapidly following the introduction by the Turnbull government in 2017 of new foreign interference transparency laws to reduce foreign (universally understood as Chinese) influence in Australian politics—and within the Chinese-Australian diaspora. This triggered a series of other measures taken by Australia to tighten controls over Chinese engagement with Australian state and other subnational governments and public entities, as well as Chinese foreign investment activity, with almost immediate consequences for inbound investment flows.

As a result of the subsequent unprecedented retaliatory trade measures against Canberra described earlier, the Australia-China relationship was, by late 2020, in its worst state since diplomatic normalization in 1972. By 2021, Beijing had written off Australia as an unthinking proxy of American strategic interests that had to be punished lest others follow suit. The Australian government, meanwhile, continued to double down on strengthening ties with Washington, Tokyo, and Delhi, as well as London, Berlin, Brussels, and Ottawa.

China had correctly seen New Zealand as less pro-American than Australia. In the 1980s, Wellington decided to sever its formal, postwar tripartite alliance with Washington and Canberra—a decision upheld by both sides of New Zealand politics ever since. China's first free trade agreement with a developed economy anywhere in the world was notably with New Zealand. Beijing has seen New Zealand as the soft underbelly of US influence in the southwest Pacific ever since.

However, the eruption of strategic tensions between China and Australia has greatly complicated Wellington's efforts to remain below the radar in the growing great power conflict between China and the United States. New Zealand—driven by the depth of historical ties, long-standing bilateral security relations, and shared values with Australia—has reluctantly joined the cause in opposing Beijing's punitive economic measures against Canberra. This is despite the fact that China has surpassed Australia as New Zealand's largest overseas market. This unity between Wellington with Canberra against Beijing's retaliation against Australia has created new challenges for China in its efforts to peel New Zealand away from Australia and its other "Five Eyes" security and intelligence partners (the US, UK, and Canada). Still, New Zealand's 2019 defense white paper, which referred to the country's "increased defense cooperation with China" and—contrary to the Australian position—argued that "China was now deeply enmeshed in the international rules-based order," highlighted the depth of Wellington's conflicting economic and political priorities. The differences in Australia's and New Zealand's approach are also reflected in the radically different nature of the political debates in each country around China's overseas influence operations, with Wellington often more relaxed than Canberra.

China's economic pressure has been applied much more acutely to the fourteen Pacific island nations, many of which are microstates. Between them, they have a combined population of only ten million people and a collective GDP of only $35 billion but an overall exclusive economic zone of some twenty-seven million square kilometers of water—equivalent to three times the total land area of China. Beijing's interests in the Pacific states are driven by multiple factors, the first of which is their relations with Taiwan. Until recently, six of these states were among Taipei's dwindling group of external diplomatic partners, but a concerted campaign by Beijing to buy influence by offering infrastructure funding and other carrots has successfully reduced that to four, peeling off both Kiribati and the Solomon Islands.

Beijing is also interested in the vast mineral and energy reserves of Papua New Guinea as well as the wider region's fisheries. China has already exhausted most of the fisheries in waters near to the Chinese mainland, and marine pollution has led to concerns about the quality of the remaining catch. There is growing Chinese interest in using the wider South Pacific to satisfy the Chinese domestic market's massive demand for seafood. This, of course, raises concerns on the part of the island states—especially for those whose fisheries are their only significant source of external income—about their own food security and the sovereignty and security of their exclusive economic zones, especially given proven cases of Chinese fishing fleets' illegal fishing.

China also has a growing array of intelligence, security, and communications interests across the Pacific. For example, China is deploying a network of undersea sensors and submerged buoys along the southern flank of the second island chain extending southward from Palau. These are capable of monitoring undersea activity, including that of submarines approaching the South China Sea. Chinese military academics have also argued the advantages of developing military bases among the island states, particularly in Papua New Guinea, Fiji, and Vanuatu, among other locations. This would allow China to secure strategic proximity to the Bismarck Sea and the Vitiaz Strait, through which three of Australia's five major sea trade routes pass, including those supporting the supply of 60–70 percent of Japan's total imported coal and iron ore needs. Furthermore, access to secure locations within the region would give China an anchor in the Southern Hemisphere to secure truly global coverage for its BeiDou satellite navigation system. This may explain China's recent negotiation of a long-term lease on the entire island of Tulagi (located in the Solomon

Islands archipelago), where China could construct a ground station to complement and complete its Southern Hemisphere satellite coverage.

Finally, China is actively competing for contracts to construct undersea telecommunications cables in parts of the region. While Australia has so far successfully made counteroffers to regional governments (including beating out a Chinese company in a recent bid to build a fiber-optic cable to Palau in cooperation with the US and Japan), competition for the future construction and control of the region's critical infrastructure is likely to become increasingly acute. The next stage in this process will be Huawei's efforts to build the region's 5G network.

As elsewhere, trade, investment, and loans-based aid lead Chinese strategy across the Pacific islands. China is already the biggest trading partner of the Pacific island states, having increased trade volumes twelvefold in the period from 2000 to 2017, supplanting Australia in 2014. China has also become the dominant player in foreign direct investment. A similar pattern is emerging with development aid, although Australia remains the region's biggest donor by some stretch. From 2011 to 2017, total Australian aid delivered to the region stood at $6.3 billion, while Chinese aid was $1.2 billion, coming in third after New Zealand. But China's forward commitments into the 2020s are closing in on those of Australia, despite the Australian government's decision to restore the large cuts it made to regional aid after 2013. Australia has also launched a new $1 billion export credit facility to support regional trade and a new $1.4 billion Pacific Island Infrastructure Fund. Such funding is part of what the current Australian government has called its Pacific Step-Up, initiated as a direct response to the intensification of Chinese activism across the Pacific island region under Xi Jinping. This was made clear in the 2017 Australian Foreign Policy white paper, in which Canberra portrayed itself as in direct strategic competition against China for influence in a region that Prime Minister Scott Morrison has described as "our patch."

However, Australia's more assertive posture in relation to China's growing regional presence in the Pacific islands region has been compromised by the Australian government's lack of serious interest in addressing climate change. For many Pacific island states, the risk from climate-induced sea-level rise is existential. This led the Pacific island leaders to issue the landmark Majuro Declaration on Climate Change in 2013, which labeled climate change "the greatest threat to the livelihoods, security, and well-being of the Pacific people"—and which marked a turning point in their passionate advocacy on climate action. The commander in chief of the Fijian Armed Forces put it like this: "The South Pacific faces the impact of three major powers: the United States, China, and climate change." The conservative Australian government has repeatedly acted to undermine the strength of Pacific Island Forum communiqués on climate action, refused to adopt more ambitious national targets for carbon reduction, and impeded international action on climate change—all seriously undermining Australia's historically strong standing across the region.

This has created valuable new political opportunities for Beijing, given China's supportive role in the 2015 Paris Agreement on climate change and its self-proclaimed status as champion of the "global south." After the 2019 Pacific Island Forum meeting in Tuvalu (one of the most climate-exposed islands in the region), China accused Australia—which insisted on watering down the wording of the meeting's communiqué on the climate crisis—of acting like the "condescending master" of the Pacific island states and suggested that Australia "reflect" on the state of its relationship with the region. A similar sentiment was echoed in angry pronouncements by Pacific islanders themselves. One regional prime minister at the time said he was "stunned" by the "un-Pacific tenor and manner" of the Morrison government, whose attitude he described as "take the money and shut up" about climate change. Although the Pacific islands region may not be central to China's long-term strategic interests, it is, nonetheless, important. And, thanks to the persuasive power of China's economy and foot-dragging on climate change by the Australian government, Beijing is making progress in the region.

Although traditionally the United States has effectively entrusted regional security in the South Pacific to Australia, Washington is becoming more directly diplomatically and militarily engaged in the region. This is in direct response to the intensification of China's strategic push into the region, which had hitherto been seen as a quiet and relatively secure strategic backwater.

The Coming Indo-Pacific Arms Race

It was in this context that the surprise trilateral security partnership between Australia, the UK, and the US known as AUKUS landed with a splash in September 2021, just ahead of the first in-person summit of the Quad's leadership. Negotiated in secret between Morrison, Biden, and UK prime minister Boris Johnson, the pact was billed as addressing regional security concerns that the leaders said had "grown significantly"—that is, from China. To begin with, the core of the agreement is a deal for the US and UK to share nuclear submarine propulsion technology with Australia, which intends to build at least eight nuclear-powered attack subs in Adelaide. But the pact also features broader security cooperation measures, including an agreement for Australia to explore hosting US bombers on its territory, the acquisition by Australia of long-range precision strike missiles, and joint cooperation on "cyber capabilities, artificial intelligence, quantum technologies and additional undersea capabilities." Beijing predictably reacted with alarm, calling the agreement "extremely irresponsible" and a move that "seriously undermines regional peace and stability and intensifies the arms race." Given Australia's strategic geography and the relative weakness of China's anti-submarine capabilities, this is unsurprising from a security perspective.

Overall, Xi Jinping has therefore achieved mixed success in securing China's maritime flank. China has had a number of strategic diplomatic successes, but the rise of the Quad has crystallized geopolitical resistance to the sustained weight of China's economic and foreign policy assertiveness into a focused institutional response. If the Quad—or a Quad-Plus—was in the future to attract both Korea and (a more remote prospect) Indonesia, this would add considerably to the grouping's overall strategic heft and present a serious challenge to China's ambitions. Even if the Quad does not increase its membership, it may, of its own accord, prompt other regional states—particularly in Southeast Asia—to be bolder in asserting their autonomy when dealing with Beijing. The Quad provides a classic example of the kind of strategic coalition building aimed at balancing against an emerging great power that international relations theorists predict—possibly arresting the bandwagoning effect among other smaller states that gained momentum during the Trump years. Even if these states publicly object to the Quad's polarizing effect across the wider region, they may privately enjoy the additional leverage that its existence affords them. These are not necessarily incompatible possibilities.

Xi Jinping's strategic response to the Quad (as well as AUKUS) is likely to focus afresh on Seoul, Jakarta, Tokyo, and Delhi, redoubling China's efforts to fracture and limit the grouping's long-term strategic solidarity expansion and effect. In addition, China is also likely to continue its current strategy of discrediting the Quad in international institutions. But Xi's more fundamental response to the emergence of the Quad is likely to be both economic and military: to make China the indispensable economic power across the wider region and to double down on China's current military expansion program in an effort to cause the wider region to conclude that China will outspend and outbuild any of its strategic competitors in the decades ahead, including the combined militaries of the Quad. The emergence of the Quad, and China's response to it, is likely to accelerate the regional arms race that is already underway.

11

★ ★ ★ ★ ★

The Eighth Circle: Going West—the Belt and Road Initiative

B eyond China's immediate neighborhood, Xi's next circle of priorities lies in projecting strategic, diplomatic, and economic power
westward across the vast Eurasian continent and the Indian Ocean to
reach the Middle East, Africa, and then Europe. To make this possible,
Beijing has made use of many institutional tools, such as the Shanghai
Cooperation Organization (SCO) and the Conference on Interaction
and Confidence-Building Measures in Asia (CICA). But the core of
this effort is China's Belt and Road Initiative (BRI), which includes the
Transeurasian Silk Road Economic Belt and the Maritime Silk Road that
charts a course across the Indian Ocean, through the Red Sea, and into
the Mediterranean. The BRI aims to accomplish a number of goals at
once. These include enhancing economic exchange with Europe and the
Middle East, securing a more benign strategic environment for China
itself, and stabilizing Islamic central and South Asia—and all this across a
vast continental landmass less susceptible to American strategic influence
than maritime East Asia. China also hopes to build up new markets to
help mitigate the consequences of being excluded from future economic
opportunities in the United States and its closest allies.

The Belt and Road Initiative

Much of the official American commentary on the BRI has focused on poorly constructed projects, the exploitation of local labor, poor environmental standards, the absence of transparency, and hidden "debt traps" with partner countries. The general assumption has been that these failings—of which there are many—will be sufficient to eventually destroy the BRI over time through a self-inflicted "death by a thousand cuts." But so far, that has not been the case, nor is it likely to be for the decade ahead. While the BRI may be regularly criticized in the West, it has often been welcomed—with some reservations—in many places in the developing world. The BRI and its associated institutions are often the only infrastructure funding facility available to many countries—a fact that they appreciate no matter how flawed China's loan programs may be. So while the BRI may be attacked as a gargantuan, ill-coordinated, multi-trillion-dollar Chinese geopolitical project, the cold hard reality is that the only counterprogram launched by the US during the Trump years was a single $100 billion loan program called the Build Act. The BRI, by contrast, had by 2021 funded some 2,600 projects across one hundred countries at a cost of $3.7 trillion.

Biden came into office declaring that "America cannot afford to be absent any longer on the world stage" and quickly suggested to British prime minister Boris Johnson that the democratic world should come up with an infrastructure building plan that could rival the BRI. When Biden and Johnson met with leaders of the G7 in June 2021, the group agreed to cooperate on what was widely seen as an alternative initiative to the BRI. It is called Build Back Better World (B3W). The plan hopes to mobilize $100 billion in private-sector capital annually into four areas—green energy and climate adaptation, health, digital connectivity, and gender equality—through development finance funding to be provided by G7 member states. The plan calls for investments to be based on "high standards," including "good governance," and to be "values-driven" and "sustainable." One senior Biden administration official told the press that B3W was intended to be more than "just an alternative to the BRI. . . . We believe [it] will beat the BRI by offering a higher-quality choice." However, it remains to be seen how well the G7 group can fill out the plan's organizational details and successfully get it off the ground, as well as how much capital can actually be mobilized and how quickly. It is also true that the governments of many developing countries have tended to lean toward Chinese finance in the past precisely because it comes with limited compliance standards—an attitude that may challenge the democracies from funding such projects. For their part, Chinese state media was quick to savage the plan, with one outlet stating, "The B3W project is not an alternative. . . . It is better described as a talk shop that pledges no funding, wishcasts the private sector to fulfill the work, and has no serious organization, cohesion, or unified means whatsoever." Meanwhile, Beijing has continued with its BRI work, seeking to make adjustments where its strategy has gone awry, but is still confident it will remain an important tool to win influence around the world.

The BRI in Central Asia

The Belt and Road Initiative is of particular significance to the states of central Asia, the first landing point for the BRI beyond China's western borders. Security is high on the list of China's interests in central Asia. Xinjiang—with its Muslim Uyghur population, which the CCP has risked international condemnation to suppress and control—borders five majority-Muslim central Asian republics. Their peoples, in some cases, also share ethnic ties to the Uyghur communities of Xinjiang. US withdrawal from Afghanistan and the possible resurgence of Islamist terrorist activity in the broader region has also accentuated these concerns. China believes that maximizing its political, economic, and security relationships with these nations will help minimize material and popular support for the Uyghur cause, both inside China and on the international stage. China therefore sees the economic development of the wider region as the most effective long-term antidote against religious extremism, terrorism, and cross-national, pan-Muslim solidarity.

It was in Nur-Sultan (then Astana), the capital of Kazakhstan, that Xi first launched the BRI in 2013. Since then, the Kazak government has described their country as the "buckle on the belt" of what Xi describes as the "project of the century." Central Asia is a significant source of energy and raw materials for China—hence the decision to fund and construct a twenty-five-hundred-kilometer oil pipeline from the Kazak oilfields on the Caspian Sea to Xinjiang. As with many other parts of the BRI, China sees central Asia as a useful new market for the Chinese construction industry as demand within China itself slows over time.

Becoming central Asia's largest economic partner, however, has also created new diplomatic and security challenges for China. Some central Asian leaders increasingly express fears that BRI loans and reliance on the China market could turn their countries into Chinese dependencies in the decades ahead. Moscow is concerned about this as well, being ever mindful that all five republics were formally part of the Soviet Union not that long ago. Russia today continues to see central Asia as a region of primary strategic interest—hence its 2014 decision to establish the Eurasian Economic Union (EAU) together with Belarus and Kazakhstan, building on earlier forms of regional economic collaboration between the former Soviet republics. China has been careful to ensure that its BRI program did not disrupt the EAU, and in 2015, Xi and Putin agreed to a protocol that established a dispute resolution mechanism between their two governments. While this may serve as interim modus vivendi for Moscow and Beijing, China's long-term economic dominance of the wider region could generate security implications for the Chinese leadership beyond their current preoccupation with controlling their Muslim minorities. For these reasons, there remains some potential for strategic tensions to reemerge between China and Russia over their respective spheres of influence in central Asia. Chinese diplomacy to date has been adept at accommodating Moscow's sensibilities—another reason American strategic analysts would be wise not to become too excited at the prospects of a new Sino-Russian split over central Asia. Besides, there is still one vital interest that continues to bind Russia and China together in central Asia: preventing the long-term Islamization of the wider region, which both countries see as a major threat to their national security.

The BRI in South Asia

China's all-weather ally, Pakistan, is pivotal to the overall strategic architecture of the BRI. China's interests in this neighboring country of 222 million people are grounded in the need to prevent the country—one of its only long-term allies—from becoming a failed state in the face of systemic economic decline and political instability. China is deeply concerned about the long-term Islamization of Pakistani politics and the security consequences of the rise of radical Islamist terror groups within the country, including their ability to threaten China's many major BRI investments there.

It is through Pakistan that the Continental and Maritime Silk Roads are to intersect via the $70 billion China-Pakistan Economic Corridor (CPEC). The corridor includes multiple energy, road, port, industrial, and telecommunications projects and is the single largest of all China's BRI initiatives. The CPEC was launched in 2014 as a three-phase, fifteen-year plan through to 2030. It aims to radically improve Pakistan's domestic power supply and transport infrastructure, followed from 2020 onward by a period of rapid industrialization. In its final phase, it would aim to deliver a direct and seamless connection for trade between the Chinese and Pakistan economies. Should Pakistan's economic modernization—driven by rapid infrastructure development—succeed, it could also become yet another significant new market for Chinese goods and services.

The geographical end point of the CPEC is the port of Gwadar on Pakistan's southwest coast, close to the Iran-Pakistan border. In 2017, China took over a forty-year lease for the construction of a deepwater port, a three-hundred-megawatt coal-fired power plant, and an associated special economic zone. The Gwadar port—together with Pakistan's existing ports of Karachi and Bin Qasim—are all likely to become dual use, serving both the Chinese navy and commercial purposes. Other port developments that are underway as part of the Maritime Silk Road—extending from the South China Sea across the Indian Ocean to the Gulf, the Red Sea, and Suez—could similarly become dual use in the future.

However, the whole CPEC project is facing persistent security challenges. To reach Gwadar, the CPEC runs through the province of Balochistan—the site of an active insurgent separatist movement that has explicitly condemned the project as a colonial occupation meant to exploit the province's resources. Various militants have conducted an escalating series of attacks on Chinese-backed projects in the region in recent years, including a 2018 attack on the Chinese consulate in Karachi; a suicide bombing on the hotel housing China's ambassador in April 2021; and a July 2021 car-bomb attack on a convoy carrying engineers to a hydropower dam that killed thirteen people, including nine Chinese nationals. The inability of Pakistan to sufficiently protect the CPEC from such attacks led to years of growing frustration in Beijing, which has long pressed Islamabad to dedicate additional military forces to guard the project but to little effect.

The situation is even more complex for China in neighboring Afghanistan. Despite playing a negligible security role in the country to date, China has become Afghanistan's single largest foreign investor, focusing on the country's estimated $1 trillion in untapped mineral reserves. China also envisioned playing a wider strategic role in Afghanistan, partly aligned with Pakistan's interests and against those of India and the United States. However, the chaotic American withdrawal from Afghanistan and the rapid takeover of the country by the Taliban in August 2021 dramatically complicated the strategic situation facing China.

When Kabul fell to the Taliban that month—in less than a week rather than the eighteen months the Biden administration had initially said was a possibility—and the world's airwaves were flooded by dramatic footage of Afghans who had previously worked with NATO forces desperately trying to flee the country on departing US planes, Beijing immediately sensed strategic advantage. Chinese state media was quick to describe the defeat as a massive blow to US reliability and staying power in the eyes of its allies worldwide, with *Xinhua* declaring it "the collapse of the international image and credibility of the US" and the "death knell of US hegemony." The nationalist *Global Times* was even more direct: "Once a war breaks out in the Taiwan Strait, the island's defenses will collapse in hours, and the US military won't come to help."

Harder heads in the national security apparatus in Beijing, however, will, unlike the wolf warrior propaganda class, have a more sober view of this. Whatever global reputational damage the US suffers, two major questions arise. First, if the US has indeed suffered in domestic political and alliance credibility terms, it is more likely that Washington will respond more sharply to any China-related incident in the Indo-Pacific than would have previously been the case. Second, with America gone as a security provider and stabilizer in Afghanistan, China is the only remaining adjacent great power, but with neither the military experience nor a detailed road map to restabilize the country.

The problem for China is that (despite any schadenfreude in seeing America's twenty-year effort in the country brought to naught) it actually has a critical national security interest in seeing stability in Afghanistan. Beijing had already launched its diplomatic initiatives to lay the groundwork for a working relationship with the Taliban. It attempted to bring about a peace settlement between them and the government in Kabul. Drawing on China's relationships with both sides and on the Taliban's connections with Pakistan's intelligence service (the ISI), China also hosted talks with the Taliban in Beijing. Nonetheless, following the Taliban's victory, China was forced to temporarily evacuate many of its citizens from the country while it began new direct negotiations with the Taliban leadership. In line with its policy of "respecting the sovereignty" of any governing authority, China's foreign ministry indicated to them that it would continue to prioritize "cooperation with Afghanistan and play a constructive role in the peace and reconstruction of the country," regardless of the Taliban's takeover—as long as they abided by their promise, made a month earlier to Chinese foreign minister Wang Yi in Beijing, to "never allow any force to use Afghan territory to engage in acts detrimental to China." That redline makes clear Beijing's most burning concern: that Afghanistan could become a home base for Xinjiang separatist movements, such as the Eastern Turkestan Islamic Movement (ETIM) and the East Turkestan Liberation Organization (ETLO), and could also degenerate into a general hotbed for terrorism and the narcotics trade on China's border.

As it so often does, China is likely to reinforce this political arrangement with Kabul with economic incentives. For example, the door is open to extending the CPEC to Afghanistan if the Taliban abides by Beijing's rules. But in reality, Beijing is deeply wary of what the real future is likely to hold. After all, China is aware that a Pakistani branch of the Taliban claimed responsibility for the deadly July attack (mentioned above) that killed nine Chinese citizens. The unstable situation in Kabul may cause Beijing to conclude that it has little choice other than to play a greater political, economic, and security role in Afghanistan and the broader region, given the strategic vacuum that was created by America's retreat. This was a probability highlighted by a virtual meeting between Xi and Russia's Putin in September 2021, at which the two leaders pledged to join forces in working to maintain stability in Afghanistan and the wider region, including by sharing intelligence and holding regular security dialogues. As a result, it is possible that over the decade ahead, Afghanistan will increasingly fall within China's strategic and economic orbit—although China's foreign and security policy establishment is undecided on just how far Beijing should wade into this tar pit of great power ambitions. Direct military engagement in the internal affairs of another state, particularly one as politically volatile as Afghanistan, is not something China has recent operational experience with.

The BRI and the Indian Ocean

China's national security strategy is, in part, aimed at minimizing China's vulnerability to the interdiction of its oil supplies in the event of a global or regional crisis—including the possibility of armed conflict with the United States. About 80 percent of all Chinese oil imports pass through the strategic choke points of the Strait of Hormuz between the Persian Gulf and the Gulf of Oman, and the Strait of Malacca between the Indian Ocean and the South China Sea. China's continuing interest in securing land-based oil and gas pipelines from central Asia, Russia, and possibly Iran is driven by the desire to reduce these vulnerabilities in energy supply. But its continued reliance on maritime energy imports—and the fact that 80 percent of total global sea trade crosses the Indian Ocean—explains China's deep interest in developing its military capacity to protect its sea line of communication linking the Gulf to China's eastern seaboard through the Indian Ocean.

To do this, the PLA has been developing a series of ports (often referred to by American analysts as China's "string of pearls") across the Indian Ocean region to support the long-term projection of Chinese naval power. This is consistent with the evolution of Chinese naval doctrine under Xi to "protect China's overseas interests"—not just in its near seas but in its "far seas" as well. At the time of writing, large-scale Chinese port development projects were underway in Cambodia (Koh Kong); Bangla-desh (Chittagong); Myanmar (the $10 billion Kyaukpyu port, special eco-nomic zone, and oil pipeline); and Sri Lanka (the ninety-nine-year lease on Hambantota port, which Beijing secured after the country was unable to pay its huge debts to China, along with a separate deal on the port of Colombo), as well as the naval base in Djibouti and port projects in Paki-stan. Added to these could be new port facilities on the east African coast, potentially in Tanzania. Some of these arrangements give China exclusive control. Others offer open facilities for other nations' vessels to use as well. However, the long-term leasing arrangements in Koh Kong, Hambantota, Gwadar, and Djibouti suggest that the Chinese navy will likely construct dedicated resupply, repair, and maintenance facilities to sustain a larger Chinese Indian Ocean naval presence into the future. The economic util-ity of each of these investments appears marginal, given the relative size of the Cambodian, Sri Lankan, and Pakistani economies and the modest cargo throughput for each. In other words, commercial opportunity alone does not justify the level of investments that have been made. Of greater strategic significance over the longer term will be the future use of adjacent airports (for example, at Koh Kong) by the Chinese military, potentially projecting Chinese air and missile power deeper into the region—a much more attractive option than using Chinese carrier battle groups for Indian Ocean deployment, given the vulnerability of carriers to missile attack.

If some of this sounds familiar, it should: China seems to be emulating the American historical playbook in rolling out its global network of port facilities and airfields capable of sustaining a blue-water navy. And so far, China appears to be pushing on relatively open doors with the countries of the region. Regional reactions have been generally supportive. Changes in governments in Pakistan, Sri Lanka, and Myanmar have been accommodated without any significant interruption to Chinese plans. Meanwhile, despite the importance to Washington of the US Fifth Fleet homeported in Bahrain, these Chinese port projects have so far generated surprisingly little tangible response on the part of the United States.

The BRI and the Middle East

Over the last decade, China's growing engagement across the Middle East is challenging—and in some areas supplanting—the United States as the region's most important external power. As in other regions, the sheer weight of China's expanding economic presence in trade, investment, infrastructure, technology, and innovation, driven in large part by the BRI, has led the way. This economic diplomacy has been accompanied by China's rapidly expanding political and foreign policy engagement and influence across the region. This has been combined with a steady growth in China's military visibility, from weapons sales to active deployments. Beijing has justified this growing military presence by citing the need to protect the growing number of Chinese civilians and corporations based in these countries in addition to its critical energy supply routes through the Gulf.

This expanding strategic presence across the Middle East has been rapid and remarkable. Once again, China's ability to execute this strategy with minimal public fanfare has been based on its formidable economic leverage in each major regional capital—and its ability to minimize the risks of being caught in the complex web of intraregional tensions. By not taking sides, China has established, developed, and maintained friendships with all the region's belligerents, carefully balancing its relationships with Iran, the Arab states, and Israel while always ready to use economic inducements to offset any offense that might be caused when binary foreign policy choices have to be made. China, at this stage, has no interest in replacing the United States as the principal external provider of regional security. Beijing fully recognizes the financial and political costs accrued to the US from the last thirty years of sustained American military interventions in the Middle East. Indeed, Beijing has concluded that the region's disputes are largely intractable; that US interventions have, in large part, been folly; and that America's long history of embroilment in the Middle Eastern discord has only contributed greatly to the steady erosion of America's financial capacity and political will.

China has no interest in repeating what it sees as America's central strategic mistake of the last several decades. Instead, it distances itself from disputes in which it feels it might be sucked into the interminable vortex of Middle Eastern politics and military action. At the same time, China is happy to see the continuing decline in American influence, always alert to tactical opportunities as they arise, and keeping an open mind as to what longer-term strategic role Beijing might come to play in the future. China's central strategic mission for the period ahead remains in East Asia and the west Pacific, but in systematically advancing its economic interests in the Middle East, it is accumulating political capital that might be useful in the future.

The foremost dynamic driving China's evolving perception of the region's importance is long-term energy security. The Middle East represents 47 percent of China's imported oil and about 12 percent of its natural gas needs, a dependence that is only expected to continue to grow. At the same time, the United States, in large part because of its hydraulic-fracturing revolution over the last decade, has grown much less dependent on the Middle East for its energy needs. The Gulf states are acutely aware of this shift, as the share of their sales going to China continues to grow.

By 2020, China represented around 23 percent of total Saudi oil sales, 22 percent of Iraqi sales, 28 percent of Iranian sales, 9.4 percent of United Arab Emirates sales, and 14 percent of total Qatari LNG sales. It is also the largest export market for all these countries, whereas less than a decade ago, that position was unambiguously held by the United States. Today, overall Chinese trade with the Arab world alone stands at more than $245 billion, a roughly 700 percent increase since 2004.

The region also represents a major opportunity for China as other foreign investment markets around the world become more restrictive. Chinese foreign direct investment in the Middle East has grown exponentially over the same period, making China the single largest source of FDI worldwide for the region since 2016. China represents a staggering one-third of FDI inflows across the Middle East, most of it focused on both upstream and downstream projects in the hydrocarbon sector, including joint investments between Chinese SOEs and Gulf national oil corporations in exploration, extraction, and refining. China is also investing heavily in transport, telecommunications, and special trade zone infrastructure across the region, including long-term operating leases for the port of Haifa, Israel; the Omani port of Duqm; and a new Suez Canal Economic Zone in Egypt. Huawei is laying out new 5G mobile telecommunications infrastructure throughout the Middle East, having secured operating licenses in all Gulf Cooperation Council states (Saudi Arabia, Bahrain, Oman, Kuwait, Qatar, and the United Arab Emirates). China is active in owning and operating a growing number of the region's undersea cables. The Middle East is also becoming a growing market for China's new BeiDou satellite navigation system.

Meanwhile, in 2017, China initiated a unique comprehensive innovation partnership with the Israeli government in what then prime minister Benjamin Netanyahu described as a marriage made in heaven. Total Chinese FDI in Israel increased from a mere $21.9 million in 2010 to $4.6 billion in 2018, making China the second-largest foreign investor in the country. China has relentlessly targeted Israel's high-technology sector, including cutting-edge surveillance systems, exploiting the close links between Israeli innovation, the Israeli military, and the United States, allowing a "back door" through which China has sought access to a number of sensitive, dual-use technologies. This resulted in a belated backlash from the United States' national security establishment against Israel's behavior with China, including movement by the Committee on Foreign Investment in the United States (CFIUS) to review the related national security implications of Israeli FDI in American companies.

China has also become a major financial player across the Middle East more generally, launching joint investment facilities with many of the region's sovereign wealth funds. Many of the latter invest extensively in China itself and in third countries in partnership with Chinese sovereign funds. In summary, by the early 2020s, China was on its way to becoming the Middle East's indispensable economic partner.

So far, China's management of its political, foreign, and security policy interests across the region has been remarkably deft. China's longest-standing significant relationship in the region has been with Iran, despite the fact that Iran, and its support for terrorist organizations, is seen as toxic in Israel, the Gulf monarchies, and much of the rest of the Arab world. Since the dawn of the Iranian Revolution in 1979, China has become a major exporter of weapons systems to Tehran and a major importer of Iranian oil. The relationship is, both politically and economically, close at multiple levels. This was reflected in the March 2021 signing of a major agreement for China to invest $400 billion in Iran over twenty-five years— not only in energy projects but also in diverse fields, including banking, telecommunications, ports, railways, health care, and information technology, in exchange for heavily discounted Iranian oil. The two countries also pledged deeper military cooperation, including intelligence sharing and joint exercises.

Remarkably, the relationship has not only survived but prospered, despite Beijing's recent economic and political openings to the Arab world—including Iran's nemesis, the Kingdom of Saudi Arabia—and China's participation in negotiations with the West to constrain Iranian nuclear proliferation. To be sure, Beijing remains deeply anxious over

Iranian threats to the overall stability of Gulf energy supplies, including Iran's attacks on Aramco facilities in Saudi Arabia. Nonetheless, China has navigated these concerns while simultaneously enhancing its relationships with both Tehran and Riyadh. Beijing has been similarly adroit in its approach to Syria. Together with Russia and Iran, China has maintained its long-term support for the Assad regime in Damascus despite sustained opposition to this policy on the part of the Gulf states and Egypt. As for the Israel-Palestine conflict, China has once again remained mostly above the fray despite its deepening relationship with Israel, seeking to balance this by launching its Middle East peace process in an effort to maintain an acceptable level of solidarity with Ramallah. Ultimately, when it comes to staying on everyone's good side, Chinese money speaks loudly.

Militarily, China's regional presence is becoming more prominent. It has been participating for more than a decade in antipiracy operations in the Gulf of Aden and regular port visits across the region; it also has naval facilities in Djibouti. But since 2011, when the PLA was forced to evacuate nearly thirty-six Chinese nationals from Libya, and again in 2015, when it had to rapidly evacuate another six hundred from Yemen on a PLAN frigate, China has been steadily increasing the active presence of its military assets and participating in joint exercises with regional states. China is also becoming a new and significant arms supplier to the region, including of armed drones and precision-strike missiles, which the Arab states have often been unable to secure from the US, the UK, and France because of a range of political restrictions on the exports of such technology. (China has no such limitations, not being a member of the Missile Technology Control Regime or other similar arrangements supported by the US and its allies.) Indeed, the Stockholm International Peace Research Institute calculates that two-thirds of China's foreign arms sales go to the Middle East.

This complex web of security and economic interests has been held together with a sophisticated Chinese diplomacy, anchored in a growing corps of professional Arabists and Persianists, a designated special envoy to the Middle East at the vice-ministerial level (who acts as Xi's personal envoy), and a well-coordinated series of high-level visits between Beijing and the region. These visits have, for several years, exceeded those between the Middle East and the United States in regularity, intensity, and seniority. This enabled China to call on diplomatic support from across the Arab and wider Muslim world whenever China's foreign and security policy interests have been attacked—including (in a sign of how deep these pragmatic relationships run) over its treatment of Muslim minorities in Xinjiang and elsewhere. Beijing, of course, has reciprocated by refusing to join attacks by Western governments and international human rights organizations on the domestic practices of the Arab states, Iran, and—from time to time—Israel.

For all these reasons, for the better part of the last decade, Xi has successfully outflanked the United States at virtually every turn in its wider diplomacy across the Middle East. The stakes may not have been as high for Beijing as for Washington, but China has moved to rapidly fill a number of political, economic, and security vacuums left by distracted American administrations wherever these gaps emerged. This has included making available large quantities of China's domestically produced COVID-19 vaccine for widespread use in Saudi Arabia, the Emirates, and Bahrain (all long-standing US allies) at a time when America focused almost exclusively domestically on its vaccine needs.

It remains to be seen whether China's success in balancing its outreach across the region's various warring parties will continue in the future. As China emerges as a global great power during the coming decade, it will be forced to take an increasing number of explicit policy positions on the binary political dilemmas that continue to divide the region. So far, China has generally managed to avoid such decisions, always preferring to be the friend of all and the enemy of none—a strategically adept, albeit ethically neutral, position. However, geopolitical reality will not allow such strategic ambiguity for much longer. Beijing's hope can only be that when that time comes, the entire region will have become so economically dependent on China that any significant political fallout will be manageable.

Future Prospects for the BRI

As Chinese BRI projects continue to roll out, the major obstacle to the initiative appears to be not the eagerness of other states to participate but China's domestic financial constraints. Concerns have also mounted in Beijing over the large number of defaults emerging from loans on BRI projects. Asset confiscation has been China's preferred response, as evidenced by the Sri Lankan port of Hambantota, which was surrendered to China on a ninety-nine-year lease. But in other cases, such as in Venezuela, China has suffered significant financial losses. In the meantime, the Paris Club of OECD creditor countries has been pressuring China to reschedule its debt portfolio so as not to trigger any sovereign debt crises in the postpandemic world. Therefore, there have been internal debates within the CCP on the wisdom of proceeding with the BRI at its current pace and scale of expansion. There are some indications that Beijing is potentially moderating some of its original ambitions, likely taking the form of a pivot to emphasize the (less costly) digital, green, and health aspects of the BRI rather than physical infrastructure. However, broad-based retrenchment on the BRI is simply not a political option. It began as a personal project of Xi Jinping, and in the Chinese political system, the current leader can never be wrong.

It is also important to understand that China's engagement with its wide western periphery is not limited to the BRI. The BRI is a major geopolitical and economic vehicle for that engagement. But it has not represented the totality of China's past across central Asia, South Asia, the Middle East, and the Indian Ocean. Nor will it represent the totality of its future. China pursues a multiplicity of economic projects and diplomatic and military initiatives on a bilateral and regional basis beyond the formal BRI framework. That will continue as China continues its efforts to turn Eurasia into a robust market, reliable investment destination, and benign strategic environment to enhance China's security and economic interests and strengthen its emerging great power status.

12

★ ★ ★ ★ ★

The Ninth Circle: Increasing Chinese Leverage Across Europe, Africa, and Latin America and Gaining an Arctic Foothold

China's grand strategy is not only regional but also global in its scope. This aspect of Xi Jinping's worldview is reflected in his statements, the pattern of his international travel, and the intensity of China's allocation of diplomatic and economic resources around the world. While Xi obviously attaches priority to China's great power relationships with the US, Russia, Japan, and India as well as its neighboring states across East, Southeast, and central Asia, China's interests are truly global in every respect.

In the past, some analysts argued that while China has both security and economic ambitions in the Asia-Pacific (or what we have come to call more recently the Indo-Pacific), its ambitions for the rest of the world were almost exclusively economic. Europeans, in particular, found this a useful analysis and argument to resist Washington's efforts to co-opt the EU or NATO into a wider alliance to respond to China's rise. But if that may have been the case in the past, it is considerably less so today.

China's global strategy is to increase its economic, foreign, and security policy influence across all regions. Europe, Africa, and Latin America are all seen as important markets for Chinese goods, especially to mitigate any reduced access to the US market. Europe is also seen as a major source of inbound foreign direct investment and capital flows into China as well as a potential source of new technologies. Finally, all three regions are critical to China's diplomatic efforts to maximize support for Chinese policy positions and candidatures and minimize criticism of its human rights practices within international organizations and forums.

China's Strategy Toward Europe

China has long seen Europe through a deeply practical lens of economic opportunity and engagement. This is an approach that Beijing has doubled down on since the beginnings of its strategic rift with the US in 2017. Recognizing with great political clarity that the continent has many different points of view and that some are likely to be more accommodating to Chinese interests than others, Beijing has focused on smaller European states, where its relative influence is greater. It has then leveraged these relationships to try to fracture EU and NATO solidarity on core questions of concern to the Chinese state. Beijing nonetheless recognizes the priority of the "big three" European states—Germany, France, and the UK—not just because of their individual global influence but also because Berlin, Paris, and—until recently—London have had a major role in shaping final positions adopted by Brussels. Of these, Germany remains the key in Beijing's eyes thanks to the strength of its economy, relative political stability, and influence across Europe—as reflected in former German defense minister Ursula von der Leyen's appointment as president of the European Commission in 2020.

As mentioned above, China's Europe strategy has been anchored in the economy—particularly trade, investment in critical infrastructure and high technology, and access to capital markets. China sees Europe as the only other global economic entity with comparable critical mass and technological sophistication to the United States. But whereas Beijing concluded the American doors had slammed shut, Europe has not shown the same sense of urgency to withdraw the welcome mat. Europe is also the final destination of the BRI. Consistent with its approach elsewhere in the world, China has sought to use its economic leverage for wider foreign policy purposes. In part, this has been made easier by a weakening in traditional European solidarity with the United States because of the foreign policy, trade policy, and political excesses of the Trump adminis-tration. However, much more significantly, Beijing has also been forensic in exploiting fault lines within Europe itself, where it has sought to break down a traditional European consensus long critical of China's human rights abuses.

While Trump never allowed human rights considerations to cloud his decision-making in dealing with Beijing, China correctly identifies univer-sal principles of human rights as being central to the European identity. Notwithstanding the election of the Biden administration, China still sees Europe as remaining the greatest defender of global human rights norms. Unsurprisingly, this role has made Europe deeply problematic for Beijing in challenging the CCP's domestic and international political legitimacy. Quieting Europe's criticisms on human rights would represent a major victory in the party's historical ideological struggle against political liber-alism, which reaches back more than a century to the earliest days of the party's founding. To extinguish Western confidence in the Western liberal-democratic tradition within its political homeland is an enormously appealing prospect for CCP ideologues. This has been a long-term objec-tive of the party, given it would provide a definitive answer to domestic and international critics who argue that liberal democracy is the inevitable political destination of all humankind.

For these reasons, after the United States and Asia, Europe represents a core Chinese strategic priority for the future. For Beijing, a more sup-portive Europe, or even a more neutral Europe, would be a great strategic prize—not only an ideological triumph in its own right but also as a deci-sive factor in the wider global geopolitical and economic contest being fought against the United States. But for a range of economic, cyber, and human rights reasons, Europe remains a hard nut for Beijing to crack.

In aggregate economic terms, trade is China's strength in Europe rather than foreign direct investment and capital markets. Still, some fissures have recently widened in trade, including Beijing's reluctance to allow European economies reciprocal access to Chinese markets. The EU became China's largest trading partner in 2019. Europe had previously been China's second-largest export market after the US, but with the impact of the 2019 trade war, America slipped to become second at $419 billion, compared with Europe at $429 billion. Meanwhile, combined annual two-way trade between China and the EU stood at $705 billion. China's total trade surplus in goods and services with Europe stood at $175 billion that year, having grown by about 10 percent annually since China's accession to the WTO, in large part because of Chinese market restrictions on European services exports. However, for Europe, the United States remains its most important trade partner. Annual US-EU trade in 2019 stood at $1.18 trillion, with Europe boasting a $162 billion surplus, not least because of the strength of European exports to a relatively open American market. The contrast is even more stark in foreign direct investment. Investment between Europe and China is minuscule compared with that between Europe and America: total stock of US FDI in Europe was $2.36 trillion in 2019, and European investment in the US was $2.55 trillion, while the total stock of European FDI in China stood at $235 billion and Chinese investment in Europe only $82 billion.

Chinese and European capital markets have also been limited in size and scope compared to those that operate between the United States and Europe. Combined US and European investments in each other's debt, equity, and other capital market instruments stood at about $7 trillion in 2017, whereas the comparable number for Chinese and European capital markets was only $330 billion. This relatively modest performance reflects a variety of factors, including significant restrictions on China's overall capital account transactions, the large number of sectors of China's economy closed to foreign direct and portfolio investment, and the emergence of growing European restrictions on Chinese investment based on concerns over China's state-driven approach to the acquisition of sensitive technology industries.

This reinforces a long list of European concerns about the fairness of Chinese trade and investment policies and practices over many years, despite China's WTO affirmations. Here, Europe's objections have, by and large, paralleled those of the United States, so much so that the EU—led by Germany—instituted a more restrictive regime against Chinese state-owned, state-subsidized, or state-supported corporations investing in Europe. This sea change in European political and policy sentiment toward Chinese economic behavior first unfolded after 2017, culminating in a March 2019 decision by the European Council to screen all future Chinese investments. It recommended new restrictions on member states for investments in "critical infrastructure," "critical, dual-use technologies," "critical inputs," access to personal data, and protections for media independence and political pluralism. These guidelines mark a significant turning point in Europe's overall economic relationship with China.

Economic concerns have become intertwined with Europe's wider political, foreign policy, and security policy relations with Beijing. After the Norwegian Nobel Committee awarded the Nobel Peace Prize to imprisoned Chinese prodemocratic dissident Liu Xiaobo, Beijing canceled all high-level bilateral meetings, including a proposed trade agreement and artistic and scientific exchanges, before imposing sanctions on Norwegian salmon. It took six years and a statement by the Norwegian government saying Norway "fully respects China's sovereignty and territorial integrity, attaches high importance to China's core interests and major concerns, will not support actions that undermine them, and will do its best to avoid any future damage to bilateral relations," before Beijing was willing to unfreeze relations.

Meanwhile, China's relationship with Sweden quickly deteriorated following official Swedish protests over the kidnapping and arrest of Hong Kong book publisher and Swedish citizen Michael Gui for selling books deemed offensive to the Chinese leadership. He was sentenced to ten years' imprisonment in 2020. The incident, paired with Beijing's outrage at Sweden's subsequent decision that year to ban Huawei from operating its 5G network, has cast a deep chill over bilateral relations.

These cases serve as examples to other countries not to "interfere in China's internal affairs," most particularly Xinjiang and Hong Kong. China's attempts to use its economic leverage with countries such as Greece and Hungary to veto or otherwise undermine internal EU consensus on China's human rights record have only increased European reservations. Brussels has also become increasingly aggravated by what it sees as China's efforts to divide Europe through its annual "16+1" summit mechanism with the former Eastern European states—previously the "17+1" until Lithuania quit the body in May 2021, citing Beijing's failure to fulfill its promises of improved market access, human rights concerns, and China's growing relationship with Russia.

The future of global digital governance is another area of contention. Europe has pushed strongly for systems that prioritize citizens' privacy, as reflected in Brussels' General Data Protection Regulation (GDPR) policy. In 2021, China passed its Personal Information Protection Law (PIPL), which closely resembles the GDPR, setting extensive data privacy restrictions on businesses' handling of user data and including provisions to prevent the personal data of Chinese nationals from being transferred to countries with lower standards of data security (likely including US companies, should Beijing choose). Unlike in Europe, however, the Chinese state will retain full access to personal data, China having put the interests of state sovereignty, state control, and state access at the center of its approach. The American model of digital governance, meanwhile, has prioritized corporate access to data, which—while also at variance with the European model—from Brussels's perspective may still be less problematic than Beijing's approach.

European national governments have also been at the epicenter of a fundamental strategic divide between China and the US on the future of 5G mobile telecommunications—in particular the role of Chinese telecom giant Huawei. Across the continent, the debate has pitted economic ministries of state, who have argued that there are few, if any, affordable alternatives to using Huawei technology in their telecommunications grids, against foreign policy, as security and intelligence communities are convinced that going with Huawei would compromise national security. The latter argue that using Huawei 5G systems would also undermine Europe's intelligence relationships with Washington, including—in the UK's case—the Five Eyes intelligence alliance. While many European countries have ruled out using Huawei systems, it is still unclear how the 5G debate will finally be resolved. If enough European nations choose Huawei, it will represent a significant schism between the US and its NATO partners, to both China's and Russia's strategic advantage.

The growing evidence of strategic condominium between Beijing and Moscow is also heightening European concerns about China as a future global actor beyond Asia. In 2017, joint Russian and Chinese naval exercises in both the Mediterranean and the Baltic were justified in the Chinese official media as reflecting China's "sincerity" toward Russia—repaying Moscow's solidarity with Beijing during the latter's 2016 naval exercises in the South China Sea. The Chinese statement added that "by sending our most advanced guided missile destroyers . . . we were sending a strong signal to others who might provoke us." In Europe, this has been seen as part of a disturbing pattern of across-the-board security collaboration between Beijing and Moscow, including exercises, training, and increased military equipment sales between the two countries. Taken together with China's growing capabilities in dual-use artificial intelligence, cyber, and space, European governments have concluded that Beijing sees itself as having a global security role, and—by cooperating so closely with Russia—it represents a growing challenge to European and global security.

In 2019, the European Commission, for the first time, designated China as a "systemic rival," concluding that "the balance of risks and opportunities" had shifted considerably since 2016. It outlined a ten-point strategy for dealing more proactively with Beijing. Also, for the first time, the NATO Council in 2019 listed China as both "an opportunity and a challenge that NATO needed to address together as an alliance." This represented a significant change in NATO's official language: in the past, China did not figure in NATO communiqués at all, with only Russia being considered a strategic focus. Moreover, NATO secretary-general Jens Stoltenberg has said that the alliance will include a substantial focus on "the rise of China" in its next Strategic Concept document, to be adopted in the summer of 2022. The previous Strategic Concept, adopted in 2010, included no reference to China. The new president of the European Commission, Ursula von der Leyen, has also publicly called for Europe to become an effective geopolitical actor on the global stage instead of simply focusing myopically on only domestic prosperity and liberal values.

All this came to a head in March 2021, when the EU (in coordination with the US, UK, and Canada) unveiled human rights sanctions against China—for the first time since 1989—in response to growing evidence of large-scale human rights abuses in Xinjiang. After the sanctions were imposed, Beijing hit back immediately with seemingly little understanding of the likely consequences. It imposed sanctions on a wide array of European policy think tanks, individual academics researching Xinjiang, and—most significantly—multiple EU committees and members of the European Parliament.

European lawmakers were outraged. The moment marked another significant shift in their attitude and approach toward China. The European Parliament defied the European Commission by voting to freeze ratification of the EU-China Comprehensive Agreement on Investment (CAI), a landmark deal the commission had just signed with Beijing. They vowed that parliament would not budge until Chinese sanctions were lifted. The German chair of the Parliament's Delegation on Relations with China, Reinhard Bütikofer, portrayed the incident as a major strategic blunder by Beijing, saying "they had finally achieved one of their main goals of driving a wedge between the European Union and the US" by achieving a deal on the CAI, when "China miscalculated and shot themselves in the foot" with its reckless sanctions. Other parliamentarians expressed similar sentiments and emphasized that the door to Washington was open to work more closely with Europe to constrain China on multiple fronts.

Despite this, the powerful European Commission, under the leadership of Europe's largest countries, Germany and France—both large export economies that stand to gain the most from closer economic relations with China—has emphasized that it still intends to see the CAI through, one way or another. Both countries, like others in the bloc, remain deeply wary of drawing too close to Washington in what they fear risks becoming a new Cold War that would fundamentally threaten their economies. In fact, the cross-party divisions of political sentiment across Europe toward China have become clearer.

One group, represented by French president Emmanuel Macron's guiding concept of "strategic autonomy," believes that Europe should remain generally neutral in Washington's global and regional struggle for ascendancy against Beijing, maximize Europe's economic opportunities, and promote Europe's strength and independence. For Washington, this group's equivocations are frustratingly detrimental to its efforts to unite more countries behind its multilateral coalition. This tension exploded into view in September 2021 with the AUKUS agreement. With Australia moving to acquire nuclear submarines under the pact, it scrapped an existing $90 billion deal to buy diesel-powered boats from France without any consultation with Paris. Paris was predictably outraged, with French foreign minister Jean-Yves Le Drian describing Australia's actions as a "stab in the back" and something similar to "what Mr. Trump used to do." Labeling the allegedly secret negotiation of the deal between the Anglosphere countries as behavior "unacceptable between allies and partners," Macron took the dramatic step of temporarily recalling France's ambassadors to Australia and the United States (the first time France had ever done so). For Macron and those of similar mind in continental Europe, the incident only reinforced the perception—rightly or wrongly—that the US could not be relied upon. Both he and EU foreign policy chief Josep Borrell declared that it reinforced the need to achieve European "strategic autonomy."

Meanwhile, a second group, deeply troubled by a combination of China-Russia cooperation, cybersecurity, market access, and human rights concerns, believes that the dividing line between China and the liberal-democratic West is crystal-clear and that Europe and the United States should present a united front. Finally, a third group of populist and nationalist far-right European parties, epitomized by Victor Orbán's Hungary, see nothing problematic about China's illiberal political and economic development model at all, believing that Europe could, in fact, learn something from it and favoring closer relations with Beijing. At present, the second of these groups is ascendant—often led by some of Europe's surprisingly bold smaller states, such as Lithuania, which, in 2021, risked Beijing's wrath by opening diplomatic relations with Taipei. However, China still regards Europe as very much in play as part of its wider geopolitical great game with the United States.

China's Relationship with the Developing World

China's relationship with the developing world and the emerging countries of Africa, Asia, and Latin America has long historical roots going back to the 1950s and Mao's and Zhou Enlai's leading role in the Non-aligned Movement. At the time, Mao saw what was then called the third world— most of Latin America; Africa; and the rest of Asia, except Japan—as an intermediate zone between the superpowers of the US and USSR and potential allies in the struggle against those superpowers' "hegemony," imperialism, and colonialism. The CCP also organized aid and investment in the third world, including interest-free or low-interest loans, which China claimed were based on principles of international solidarity, in contrast to the exploitive practices of the West. Between 1953 and 1985, despite its domestic economic difficulties and crises, China was the world's second-largest donor of international aid after the OPEC states. But its dealings were always highly strategic—as they are now—with much talk of "win-win" relationships.

Over the last twenty years, Beijing's economic relationship with much of the developing world has become more important to many of them than their relationship with the United States—a fact that policy makers in the United States have missed or dismissed. By contrast, the United States has been largely missing from the field. China's outreach has consisted of large-scale public and private trade and investment across Africa, Asia, and Latin America, intensified and coordinated in recent years under the aegis of the Belt and Road Initiative. Many of these projects have generated local controversies, including over debt, environmental, or labor standards. The impressive thing about China's strategy in the developing world has been its persistence and its ability to adapt and adjust over time. Multiple field studies have been conducted by Western academics on Chinese investment projects in the developing world. Some of these projects have gone sour, but what is remarkable is how many positive stories have also emerged, as China has constantly learned from its mistakes.

China's long history of "South-South" cooperation has helped it maintain and strengthen a roster of traditional friendships in the developing world that have been key to amplifying Chinese influence in international institutions, such as the United Nations. But increasingly, Beijing also sees opportunities even in regions traditionally dominated by American influence, including Latin America and the Middle East. The countries of these regions have the potential to increasingly function as "swing states" in a new global "great game" for international influence with the United States. As with Asia, the critical factors underpinning Chinese success have been the growing global footprint of the Chinese economy, together with the relative decline in American power, reinforced by American complacency and lack of attention to the importance of its traditional friends and partners around the world.

The Importance of Africa

African nations have been among China's principal supporters on the world stage for more than half a century. Unlike other regions of the developing world, Africa has never fallen neatly within an American sphere of influence. Instead, it has always been contested strategic space—initially among the European colonial and postcolonial powers, then between the US and Soviet Union during the Cold War, and now between the West and a rising China.

Under Xi, Beijing's efforts to cement strong ties in Africa have been redoubled across trade, infrastructure investment, development aid, and security collaboration. By contrast, Africa largely slipped off the radar as an American priority under the Trump administration. As a result, African states have become China's most reliable supporters in the international community. This has been aided by the fact that the African states are removed from the security impact of China's expanding sphere of geopolitical influence across Asia; are eager for economic aid, trade, and investment; and are detached from the long historical shadow of American influence across Latin America and the Middle East.

As is the case elsewhere in the world, China's interests in Africa today begin with the economy. Beijing sees the continent as a long-term, reliable supplier of energy and raw materials and rising African economies as providing a new, billion-strong consumer market for Chinese goods and services exports. Applying the logic of its development model, China has poured large-scale funding into basic economic infrastructure—including hundreds of road, rail, port, telecommunications, and power projects—across the continent. For example, despite the debates raging elsewhere, Huawei has already become the top provider of 4G telecom services across Africa, having built more than 70 percent of the continent's 4G network. Meanwhile, Chinese budget smartphone brand TECNO is Africa's most popular, enabling Chinese mobile-based payment systems to gain a significant foothold on the continent. Combined, Chinese companies hold a dominant 53 percent market share of the smartphone market in Africa; South Korea's Samsung trails next with a distant 15 percent.

As China's new aid and investment drive across Africa has unfolded, Chinese officials have attacked the credibility of traditional Western-aid models, which they argue have delivered little by way of measurable poverty reduction. China has also argued that the north-south development gap between Africa and the West has been retained as a deliberate Western, neocolonial stratagem. They note that Western nations have typically applied political and policy conditions, such as adopting free market or democratic reforms, to the delivery of development assistance, forcing recipient states to transform into Western-style liberal democracies. By contrast, China's model applies no such conditions, leaving local governments to choose their political models to suit their circumstances. According to Beijing, all China wants from its development assistance is a win-win outcome that delivers tangible economic benefits to both sides.

As such, by declaring an intention to "welcome African countries aboard the express train of China's development," as Xi Jinping did in 2018, Beijing aims to use Africa as a showcase to demonstrate the superiority of its national economic development model, even in circumstances vastly different to China's. Success in Africa and elsewhere in the developing world would also contribute to China's global ideological ambition of delegitimizing liberal-democratic capitalism—and boost the CCP's ideological legitimacy, both at home and abroad. Africa has, therefore, become part of a much wider political strategy in the CCP's continuing quest for long-term ideological legitimacy.

However, China's more immediate political interests focus on consolidating the foreign policy support and voting strength from its African friends in international institutions. Africa generally provides China with a reliable bloc of approximately fifty votes in any multilateral forum, whatever the subject and whenever Chinese interests are at stake. This ranges from human rights to the future of digital governance to China-specific priorities, such as incorporating the Belt and Road into the normative language of UN resolutions on development goals. In exchange, African states are assured that China also possesses a veto in the UN Security Council that can always be deployed in support of a state (or even an individual political leader) facing the threat of censure or external intervention in times of crisis.

China has also become a more active security partner with individual African states and with the fifty-five-member African Union. In 2019, China and its African partner states established the China-Africa Peace and Security Forum, under which China embarked on a high-level expansion of defense ties with the region. Beijing has already become a supplier of arms, military equipment, and surveillance technologies to a number of states on the continent. China is also aware that, with the expanding size of the Chinese diaspora across Africa, it will need the capacity to offer physical protection to its nationals in the event of future security crises. An expanding security presence in Africa, both as a part of UN peacekeeping missions and in support of independent security missions of the African Union, provides the PLA with invaluable experience in international field operations, just as counterpiracy operations in the Gulf of Aden have done for the PLA Navy.

Evidence of Beijing's expanding security agenda in Africa can be found wherever China has a presence on the continent. Yet despite some local controversies and unfavorable press coverage, it appears to have generated little negative official reaction from African states. Indeed, quite the opposite. In 2018, at the Forum on China-Africa Cooperation, Xi announced that China would set up a new China-Africa peace and security initiative, provide further military aid to the African Union, and launch more than fifty separate security assistance programs on the continent. He pledged to African leaders that "China champions a new vision of security [in Africa] featuring common, comprehensive, cooperative and sustainable security."

Despite this increasing intensity of the political, foreign, and security policy relationship, it's important to recognize that the economic data of the emerging China-Africa relationship still tells a mixed story. It is true that China replaced America as Africa's largest trading partner a decade ago—it now represents $200 billion of Africa's total global trade of $700 billion, four times the size of the total African trade with the US. But despite the dramatic public reporting of high-profile Chinese infrastructure projects, China's foreign direct investment in 2018 still came in fifth in the overall stock of African FDI, after the Netherlands, France, the UK, and the US. Indeed, these countries represented a total of $220 billion in FDI, or more than five times China's total of $46 billion. This represents the long head start European and North American investors have had in Africa. Furthermore, Chinese FDI tended to be concentrated in a smaller number of countries (e.g., Angola, Nigeria, Ethiopia, Zimbabwe, and Uganda) rather than spread more evenly across the continent.

Similarly, great attention has been paid to China's overall development assistance effort across Africa, with $60 billion in Chinese development funds disbursed from 2015 to 2018 and Xi pledging another $60 billion from 2018 to 2021. However, only $5 billion of this came in the form of *non-loan* aid. In other words, the vast bulk of Chinese aid to Africa is by way of repayable loans, not the grants offered by the West and Japan as the majority of their official development assistance. As we know from historical experience, debt dependency generates a political reaction over time, particularly if it results in the surrender of national assets, as has happened most spectacularly in the Sri Lankan case of Hambantota. Locals can quickly become convinced that this has resulted from deliberate "debt trap diplomacy," sparking anger at perceived colonial intentions.

There are, of course, methodological problems associated with any accurate calculation of total Chinese aid flows, given that China is not bound by the transparency and categorization guidelines that govern OECD member states. So the broader development figure may be higher. And if current trend lines continue, with Western aid to Africa remaining static and Chinese aid continuing to increase by about 10 percent annually, then, by the end of the decade, even the amount of Chinese loan-free aid heading to the continent may surpass that from the West.

Whatever the absolute number, it is important not to underestimate the potential impact of Chinese loan programs underpinning so many infrastructure investment projects currently underway across Africa. It is increasingly common in the US to describe Chinese aid as "rogue aid" because it doesn't conform with OECD guidelines or assumptions. But that doesn't mean that Chinese aid is unwelcome in Africa or that it is ineffective in delivering economic results. Indeed, African analysts have also sharply critiqued Western aid in terms of its lack of effectiveness over the decades, its strings-attached agendas, how it can create a passive dependency on Western charity, and its fickle unpredictability in times of economic stress. Moreover, the West has, by and large, refused to fund economic infrastructure in Africa—preferring health, education, and "good governance" projects instead—whereas China does the reverse. Many African states welcome this decision by China, given that the balance sheets of multilateral lending institutions such as the African Development Bank have been wholly insufficient to fund project finance needs. Furthermore, the accusation that Chinese loans in Africa have increased the likelihood of default is not yet borne out by the data. In only two countries does Chinese debt figure prominently, and even there, it is matched with what is owed to a number of Western private financial institutions.

Nevertheless, China's Africa strategy is a work in progress. It has encountered problems with faulty project engineering, poor financial feasibility studies, and local antipathy to an initial large-scale use of Chinese labor, which produced ethnic tensions in a number of countries. But China has learned from the mistakes it made on the ground and consistently sought to improve its performance over time. It would be wrong to assume—as many in America do—that when projects have struggled or when local anti-Chinese sentiment has surfaced, this has resulted in some sort of tidal wave of political and popular reaction against China's Africa strategy. The evidence of that to date appears to be limited. A 2019 pan-African Afrobarometer survey showed that while more Africans still preferred the US developmental model over China's (32–23 percent), the majority considered Chinese influence on the continent to be largely positive, even if they worried about debt. This had not yet taken into account the continent's overall reaction to COVID-19. While the Chinese origin of the virus may have initially hit public opinion, by 2020, China's medical and vaccine diplomacy was hard at work across Africa, months before the G7's vaccine strategy even got off the ground, helping to solidify positive sentiment toward China on the continent.

Finally, China's presence provides Africa with leverage, for the first time, to use against its other development partners. Previously, African states simply had to accept the terms handed to them by the West, meaning that China's arrival has had significant strategic and economic impact for them. Xi's Africa strategy is a patient and agile one, and his partners in Africa—by and large—appear to appreciate it.

China's Arrival in Latin America

Unlike in Africa, China's strategic and economic interests in Latin America have only taken shape over the last twenty years—so much so that the first Chinese presidential visit to the region was not until 2001. Prior to that, Central America, South America, and the Caribbean had been a diplomatic redoubt for Taipei rather than Beijing. China had been mindful of the strategic significance of the Western Hemisphere to Washington, going back to the earliest days of the Monroe Doctrine. Earlier generations of Chinese leaders intuitively understood that they had to tread carefully in this continent, which was of primary geostrategic importance to the United States and farthest from Beijing of all the regions of the world. And while Xi has abandoned this traditional Chinese caution, some of China's increased emphasis on the region first became evident under his immediate predecessor, Hu Jintao. Xi has visited Latin America and the Caribbean five times. By contrast, President Trump only traveled to the region once during his entire presidency—and that was to participate in a G20 Summit in Buenos Aires.

The institutional machinery of the China–Latin America relationship has been formalized through Beijing's rigorous participation in multilateral gatherings in the region. In 2014, Xi attended the inaugural annual meeting of the China-CELAC (Community of Latin American and Caribbean States) Summit in Brasilia. All thirty-three states of Latin America and the Caribbean are members of the forum, which is designed to facilitate cooperation between China and CELAC in everything from trade, investment, and finance to energy and resource management, education, science and technology, agriculture, sports, aerospace and aviation, poverty eradication, health, and disaster risk management. Then, in 2018, Beijing attended the Summit of the Americas for the first time as an observer—the triennial meeting of all heads of government from North and South America. In a display not lost on Latin America, Trump failed to show up. Fundamentally, what China has identified in the region is a distracted America no longer actively committed to the Western Hemisphere. It is moving to fill that opening.

Foremost among China's immediate regional interests is the diplomatic isolation of Taiwan. Since the victory of Taiwan's antireunification Democratic Progress Party in the Taiwanese presidential elections in 2016 (and landslide reelection in 2020), Xi has taken off the gloves. He is using every ounce of China's political and economic muscle to prize these remaining diplomatic partners away from Taipei. By 2020, a further three countries had changed sides—the Dominican Republic, El Salvador, and Panama. The latter was a particularly important diplomatic success for Beijing, given its control of the Panama Canal. All three have been offered new Chinese investment, including Chinese plans to develop a new special economic zone along the canal, just as it is already doing in Egypt along the Suez. Beijing's courtship of Taipei's remaining allies in the region accelerated significantly in 2020 with the onset of the COVID-19 pandemic, with China quickly leveraging cheap, fast access to vaccines in order to tempt them to switch their allegiance. It was an effective pitch. Only a crash medical-aid package by Taiwan and a last-minute call by new US secretary of state Antony Blinken narrowly prevented Paraguay from switching sides. Then Carlos Alberto Madero Erazo, Honduras's chief cabinet coordinator (who is akin to a prime minister), publicly warned in May 2021 that the lack of Western assistance in what was the Taiwan ally's desperate moment "puts us in a very difficult situation." During the pandemic "the Honduran people start[ed] to see that China is helping its allies, and we start to ask ourselves why ours are not helping us," he said, noting that this could "definitely lead to changes in foreign policy." The Biden administration rushed vaccine aid to Latin

America as a response, averting a diplomatic coup by China—for the time being.

Apart from Taiwan, China's main interests across Latin America, as in Africa, are economic. Here, too, Beijing sees vast consumer potential for Chinese exports and investment over time. In the space of less than twenty years, China has risen to become Latin America's second-largest trading partner, with two-way trade totaling $315 billion in 2020, up from less than $18 billion in 2002. The United States remains the region's largest trading partner, with $756 billion in 2020. While that is still a significant balance in America's favor, on current trajectories, Beijing is estimated to supplant Washington as the region's top partner around 2035, according to the World Economic Forum.

As with other regions, the same pattern doesn't yet hold with foreign direct investment. The total stock of Chinese investment stood at approximately $200 billion in 2017, but that represented only about 8 percent of all the stock of FDI invested in Latin America. As for official loans to Latin American and Caribbean governments, China is by far the region's biggest financier. As of 2020, total Chinese sovereign credit to the region totaled some $150 billion, concentrated in Venezuela ($62 billion), Brazil ($42 billion), Argentina ($18 billion), and Ecuador ($17 billion). Of these, Venezuela has already technically defaulted on its loans, and China has so far exhibited zero interest in any form of debt moratorium, insisting instead that Venezuela pay off its debt by providing China with up to one-third of the country's total oil exports. While Brazil's and Argentina's debt burdens to Chinese creditors are, at this stage, still manageable, in the case of Ecuador, they represent one-third of total sovereign debt. In terms of relative scale, China's official loan book across the continent is larger than that of both the World Bank and the Inter-American Development Bank combined.

As has been the case elsewhere in the developing world, the pattern of China's trade, FDI, and official credit flows to Latin America reflects Beijing's global emphasis on energy security, raw materials, and infrastructure investment. The vast bulk of China's imports focuses on just four commodities: oil, iron ore, copper, and soya beans. About 90 percent of Chinese FDI is directed to energy, mining, and particularly infrastructure; as of 2020, some eighty-three major engineering projects—roads, rail, ports, airports, bridges, canals, dredging, and urban transport—were underway across most countries in the region. China is also investing in telecommunications infrastructure—in part to underpin the rollout of Huawei's global 5G network, which it hopes will support a Chinese-led e-commerce revolution across the wider region. While there has been some souring in Beijing over China's significant loan exposure in Latin America—particularly given the magnitude of the Venezuelan default—on his recent visits to the continent, Xi announced bold new targets for the renewed expansion of China's trade and FDI links to the region. This has included committing to expand the trading relationship to $500 billion by 2025 and increasing the stock of Chinese investment to $250 billion.

But as noted above, the Venezuelan default has generated political criticism about overseas investment within China itself. Academic articles have emerged publicly challenging the sustainability of China's recent loans strategy, and across the Chinese blogosphere, there have been calls for giving greater priority to problems at home rather than large-scale loans and investments across Africa, Latin America, and Eurasia. Tellingly, a 2019 visit to Beijing by Venezuela's beleaguered president Nicolás Maduro was—unusually—greeted with a virtual domestic media blackout in China, highlighting the level of political sensitivity in Beijing to criticism of China's Venezuelan adventure.

In some respects, China has applied the Pakistan template to Venezuela, attempting to turn the country into China's "all-weather ally" in Latin America. But this has come at a cost, as Maduro's government became increasingly unsustainable through a combination of acute domestic instability, serious accusations of human rights abuses, and chronic economic mismanagement. This, in turn, has generated negative political reactions across democratic Latin America against China's support for his government. Despite the determination of many major regional governments (including China's BRICS partner Brazil) to see Maduro gone, China has been seen to be indifferent to the needs of Venezuela's neighboring states, despite the outflow of millions of Venezuelan refugees across their borders. Moreover, China has been attacked for deliberately propping up Latin America's left-wing governments financially, assisting them to retain political power against any right-wing challengers.

Yet China already has a well-developed political and diplomatic playbook for dealing with unstable regimes. Its priority—as with Pakistan and Myanmar in Asia—has always been to preserve relations with the state, not necessarily the government of the day, in order to preserve and maximize China's long-term strategic interests. In the case of Venezuela, China has opened its line of communications with the Venezuelan opposition in order to hedge its bets in the event of a change of government.

In Latin America, this balancing strategy has been most spectacularly on display in China's relationship with its most important regional partner, Brazil. Jair Bolsonaro was elected Brazilian president in 2018 on a platform of open hostility to Beijing. The right-wing leader took the extraordinary step of visiting Taiwan as an opposition presidential candidate and repeatedly attacking what he described as China's predatory strategy across Latin America, stating, "China is not buying from Brazil. China is buying Brazil." This struck a deep, populist chord across the country and helped secure his landslide election. But within twelve months of taking office, the power of Chinese political and economic diplomacy was on full display when Bolsonaro undertook a state visit to Beijing and exclaimed that the two economies were in fact "born to walk together." In 2019, he then welcomed Xi with open arms on a return visit as part of the BRICS Summit in Brasilia. Bolsonaro had been mugged by economic reality, given China's status as the country's largest trading partner and a not-insubstantial holder of Brazilian public debt. It therefore took China less than a year to turn diplomatic adversity into political opportunity.

In managing Bolsonaro, China displayed great dexterity, electing not to respond to any of his political attacks on China during the presidential election campaign, thereby keeping the line of communication open and providing him with the political space to change direction. Meanwhile, despite public triumphalism by the Trump administration following Bolsonaro's election, heralding a new strategic partnership with "Brazil's Trump," the US had no answer to China's emerging economic influence in Brazil or in Latin America more broadly. In fact, Trump's response was to offer nothing other than gratuitous geopolitical warnings before embracing a new era of American protectionism. He berated American industry for manufacturing in Mexico and threatened to scrap (before he ultimately rewrote) the rules of the North America Free Trade Agreement. Notably, Mexico has traditionally been one of the weakest links in China's ties with the region, receiving less than 2 percent of total Chinese FDI in Latin America and selling only 1.6 percent of its exports to China in 2019. But as the result of factors such as China's deft "vaccine diplomacy" during the pandemic—with China supplying Mexico, which was badly hit, with tens of millions of doses—in January 2021, Mexico's secretary of foreign affairs Marcelo Ebrard promised to expand on a bilateral "strategic partnership" with Beijing. Also recognizing a tectonic shift in regional influence, Argentina and a number of Caribbean states are turning to China for the supply of military equipment, including, in Argentina's case, seeking a billion-dollar purchase of Chinese fighter jets for its air force.

As in Africa, China has faced some setbacks in Latin America. Beyond its debt problems in Venezuela, these include angry reactions to the environmental and human consequences of high-profile Chinese projects, such as the Hidroituango hydroelectric project in Colombia. The dam saw the displacement of twenty-five thousand people from their homes and suffered serious construction problems, including a tunnel collapse that threatened an environmental and social disaster, and a cost blowout, sparking a major popular movement. Other controversies include China's large-scale use of imported Chinese labor in such projects and the fact that where locals have been employed, it has often been in violation of national labor standards. On top of this, there have been many dramatic public announcements of new Chinese megaprojects (such as plans for a second canal across Central America to rival Panama's and the $50 billion Inter-Oceanic Railway linking Brazil to the Pacific coast through Peru) followed by long silences when a more sober assessment of the financial cost by Beijing resulted in little being done on the ground. However, none of this has, so far, impeded Latin America's appetite for wider Chinese engagement. As of 2019, nineteen of the thirty-two members of CELAC had signed up to China's Belt and Road Initiative, notwithstanding the irony that, historically, China's land and maritime silk roads never came within ten thousand kilometers of the Latin American continent.

Washington is nervous about how readily Chinese engagement with the region has survived transitions between left- and right-wing governments with apparent ease. The US has warned Latin Americans of the predations of this "new imperial power" to little effect. In 2018, then secretary of state Rex Tillerson even publicly invoked the "success" of the Monroe Doctrine in warding off other great powers from the Western Hemisphere when warning of Chinese "imperial" ambitions, articulating an even more tone deaf than usual American response to China's arrival. The 2017 US National Security Strategy—and, separately, the US Southern Command—have also publicly warned of China's expanding presence in "the hemisphere," pointing to China's growing ownership and control of critical economic infrastructure, including ports. Nonetheless, for all this American huffing and puffing, Xi must be pleased with China's strategic gains across the continent over the last decade.

China's Polar Ambitions

China has long shown an intense interest in establishing a role in the Arctic, despite its geographic separation from the polar ice caps. This attention dates to at least 2008, when Beijing began a campaign of careful diplomatic courtship to convince the states of the Arctic Council (Canada, Denmark, Sweden, Finland, Iceland, Norway, Russia, and the United States) to grant China permanent observer status on the council. China finally succeeded in this in 2013, soon after which Xi declared in a 2014 speech that becoming a "polar great power" was "an important component of China's process of becoming a maritime great power." Five years later—in its first official Arctic Strategy white paper—China declared itself a "near-Arctic state" and pledged new cooperation and joint development in the polar regions.

China's strategic interest in the Arctic—and its connection to maritime power—is explained primarily by two factors. First, the Arctic contains significant untapped energy and mineral reserves, including what is estimated to be more than 30 percent of the world's undiscovered natural gas reserves and 13 percent of its undiscovered oil reserves. As global climate change continues to rapidly warm the world's poles—with the Arctic predicted to be completely free of summer sea ice by as soon as 2030—these previously inaccessible resources will soon become obtainable. This has led to a scramble by Arctic states to locate and claim such resources before rivals do. Second, and even more important for China, the rapidly retreating Arctic Sea ice means that the centuries-long dream of a maritime shipping route connecting Atlantic and Pacific through the Arctic is becoming a reality. (A Maersk vessel in 2018 became the first large container ship to deliver cargo from East Asia to Europe through the Northeast Passage along Russia and Norway's coast.) Commercially, the Northeast Passage route is more than eight thousand kilometers shorter than transit through the Suez Canal, cutting transport times from Asia to Europe by up to fifteen days, presenting significant cost advantages for both China and Russia. Strategically, the route could become an even greater game changer, allowing Chinese maritime traffic to bypass Middle Eastern and Indian Ocean waters—including maritime choke points such as the Strait of Malacca—that are dangerously susceptible to American and allied naval power. As long as Sino-Russian relations continue to deepen, a northeastern sea route could become a more secure alternative for China in an increasingly geopolitically unstable world.

For these reasons, China has poured resources into jointly developing the route with Russia, dubbing it the Arctic Silk Road. Investing more than $90 billion between 2012 and 2017 to construct ports; overland connections; coast guard hubs; and research stations in Russia, Finland, and

Norway, China is trying to build the infrastructure necessary to service and maintain such a trade route in weather conditions that are likely to remain harsh. Since 2019, China has been building and deploying a growing number of icebreaker ships to the region while constructing new research posts in Iceland, Greenland, and other critical locations in the high north. This has provoked alarm in Washington, with then secretary of state Pompeo warning in 2019 that the Arctic had "become an arena of global power and competition" and risked being "transform[ed] into a new South China Sea." However, once again, Washington has been slow to respond beyond its copious supply of political rhetoric, with the United States continuing to field only two aging icebreakers, one of which nearly sank on a summer mission to Antarctica in 2017.

Compared to the Arctic, China's ambitions in Antarctica are much less dramatic. Like other nations, China has appeared to focus primarily on scientific activities at the globe's southern pole. However, China's rapid emergence as a scientific power in Antarctica—from having no presence there before 1985 to today having constructed a fifth research base and spending more than any other government on the continent—generated wariness among other long-standing Antarctic Treaty states. Under international law, Antarctica is supposed to belong to no one and, as a global environmental preserve, be free from mining. However, the language used in Chinese scientific and government reports—including China's first Antarctic white paper in 2017—have raised concerns that Beijing has no intention of leaving these potentially resource-rich lands and waters alone. The Polar Research Institute of China has long described Antarctica as a "global treasure house of resources" potentially critical to China's economic growth. Xi did not allay international concerns when visiting Australia in 2014; standing beside then prime minister Tony Abbott, he declared that China was ready to "better understand, protect, and *exploit* the Antarctic" (emphasis added). Chinese state media later dutifully changed the official translation of the remarks to replace *exploit* with *explore*, but the message was out. Other powers have continued to watch China's Antarctic activities with suspicion. In 2017, the Australian Strategic Policy Institute

262 | THE AVOIDABLE WAR

(an independent think tank that advises government) accused China of engaging in undeclared military and mineral exploration activities on the continent in breach of international law. Beijing has ignored such protests, reasserting its scientific intentions.

Conclusion

Overall, despite pressure on China by Washington, China perceives its global influence—especially its economic influence—as only continuing to increase. While the COVID-19 pandemic began as a public relations nightmare for China, the relative success of China's domestic response, including its highly visible "vaccine diplomacy" in the developing world (and the relative slowness of America's), has supported this rising influence. Europe still presents problems for China. But Beijing's foreign policy is nothing if not agile, and it is likely to continue to adjust course in order to advance its interests. In Africa, China continues to improve its ties on a continent where America continues to be largely absent. And in Latin America, if China can replicate over the next fifteen years the same type of progress as the last fifteen, America's proprietary role within the much-vaunted Western Hemisphere may be about to change. Similarly, China's polar strategy is enhanced by its tight strategic relationship with Moscow and growing outreach to other Arctic states. The global score card, especially in the developing world, therefore appears to be moving in China's favor, aided by the Trump administration's widespread withdrawal from multilateral and other international institutions. With China rushing to fill the ensuing vacuum and occupy a "position closer to center stage in the world" (as Xi put it in his formal address to the Party Congress in 2017), Chinese leadership sees not only the "general trend toward multipolarity" it has long predicted coming to fruition but also what Xi frequently describes as a "world undergoing profound changes unseen in a century." This is code language for the decline of the United States and its replacement by a rising China.

In essence, China's leadership sees a continuing "period of strategic opportunity" internationally, despite its regular complaints about US "containment" amid a period of "protracted struggle" with Washington. In this environment, Beijing believes it will be able to convince or coerce countries around the world into concluding that they have little choice but to jump on the bandwagon with China or be left behind. For many countries, this increasingly presents a binary challenge in which they must choose sides between China (often already their largest economic partner) and the United States (often their only hope for security against Chinese coercion). And while they resent this choice, they are inexorably pulled into it, especially when the US during the Trump era withdrew from and then disempowered the very international system that was designed to provide an alternative way forward from the world of hard power spheres of influence. The question remains whether President Biden will sufficiently revive these institutions and reassert US moral authority to frustrate China's aims to remake the rules-based international system in a manner amenable to its power, interests, and values—just as it claims the United States did after 1945.

13

★ ★ ★ ★ ★

The Tenth Circle: Changing the Global Rules-Based Order

The final circle of Xi's ambitions for China concerns the future of the global order itself. The United States and its allies—as the victors of World War II—constructed the underlying architecture of the postwar liberal international rules-based order. This architecture was laid out at the 1944 Bretton Woods Conference, from which emerged the International Monetary Fund (IMF), the World Bank, and the General Agreement on Tariffs and Trade (which later became the World Trade Organization). While the Republic of China under Chiang Kai-shek was present, Mao's Communists obviously were not. Meanwhile, the Soviet Union refused to ratify these arrangements, calling them "branches of Wall Street." Then, in 1945, following the San Francisco Conference, the United Nations was established, with both the Soviet Union and the Republic of China as inaugural members, both gaining permanent seats on the exclusive, veto-wielding UN Security Council. Then came the Universal Declaration of Human Rights in 1948, again drafted by a group that included representatives from India and the Republic of China. The United States led the way in the creation of all these institutions and then sought to defend the order it had created with a global network of alliances: the North Atlantic Treaty Organization (NATO) in Europe and bilateral and multilateral security alliances across East Asia. Throughout the postwar period and then through the Cold War and beyond, the United States remained the world's dominant superpower politically, economically, and militarily.

The People's Republic of China is challenging the political legitimacy and policy effectiveness of the Western liberal-democratic model that was inherent to the norms and rules of the order that had been created. The values espoused by these democracies and the international institutions and rules that have been built on them continue to represent a political and normative obstacle for Beijing. To combat this, China is creating its new multilateral institutions outside the framework of the postwar settlement, which China has consistently seen as an order created and imposed by the victorious Western colonial powers. This is despite the fact that China under the then nationalist government participated in the construction of this very order.

Nevertheless, the desirability of having some form of rules-based global system, rather than chaos, is also fixed deep within Chinese political consciousness. Ancient Chinese philosophers warned that the only alternative to order was chaos—a truth that Chinese who lived through the turmoil of war, Mao, and the Cultural Revolution have very much taken to heart. But it is important to remember that the order China has in mind is different to an American-made order, or for that matter a liberal international order. Instead, China's expectations for the future global order are for it to change as necessary to better accommodate China's national interests and values. At this stage, while China's political aspirations are becoming clear, it is less clear how much China actually wants to change things, at what pace, or whether the rest of the international community will agree to these changes.

What is clear is that China's growing influence will have implications for current international norms on human rights anchored in the three major international covenants and the Human Rights Council in Geneva. It will also have implications for the future international economic order, including the structure and operation of the WTO, particularly in the aftermath of the trade war with the United States. As for the future international security order—anchored in the UN Security Council, where

China continues to enjoy the privileged position of being a permanent member with the full power of veto over any collective security action—we find ourselves in uncertain terrain.

China as an Outsider

Until 2014, China exhibited little interest in playing a greater role in shaping the future of the global rules-based order and the institutions that underpin it. China's attitude to the United Nations and the plethora of its specialized agencies dealing with peace and security, economic development, and human rights—together with the Bretton Woods institutions—was largely defensive. China's aims were to use its membership in these institutions to enhance its domestic political legitimacy in the eyes of the Chinese people, entrench its international legitimacy, keep Taiwan isolated, and block any actions taken by international institutions that might harm China's core national interests. Until recently, that was because Beijing saw itself as having limited leverage either to challenge the system or to change it. The PRC therefore decided to work within the grain of the system it had inherited from the Republic of China after the West switched its recognition from Taipei to Beijing. Deng Xiaoping also realized that some multilateral institutions might be able to support his objective of rapidly developing China's economy, lifting its people out of poverty, and laying the foundations of a strong Chinese state. This applied, in particular, to China's early collaboration with the World Bank and the IMF during the first decades of Deng's reform and opening policy. It was also evident in China's accession to the WTO in 2001. Indeed, as noted in earlier chapters, for China, WTO accession was a game-changing opportunity to enter the global market.

All this changed, however, in 2014. The Communist Party Central Work Conference on Foreign Affairs convened in November that year by Xi Jinping represented a political watershed—launching a new era of Chinese multilateral activism. Such conferences are normally held every four to five years to set the party's and the country's overall foreign policy course for the period ahead. They are attended by the country's entire foreign, security, and international economic policy establishment. At this pivotal meeting, Xi laid down an entirely new approach. He formally dispensed with Deng's decades-long strategy of "hide your strength; bide your time; never take the lead" and replaced it with a new activist strategy of international policy. Specifically, Xi pointed to a new unfolding "struggle" for the future of the global order and declared that China must "strive for achievement" in that order. Or as he told another party meeting three years later, "[This] will be an era that sees China moving closer to the center stage and making greater contributions to mankind."

His instructions reflected a view that China should shape the future form of the international system rather than passively accepting the structure of the system as it was. China, instead, saw an opportunity to proactively use multilateral institutions to articulate and advance Chinese interests and values within the international system. Those attending the meeting believed that China's diplomats had, at last, been let off the leash to carve out a much larger international space for China in the multilateral world as befit—in their view—an emerging global great power.

The CCP had also been concerned that China's historical approach of general support for the UN system had the effect of legitimizing the liberal-democratic assumptions of the UN's Universal Declaration of Human Rights—and, as a consequence, delegitimizing China's domestic political order. After 2014, however, Beijing used various multilateral alliances to redefine core concepts of democracy, human rights, and the rule of law in a manner more compatible with China's domestic practice. In doing do, China was able to draw on assiduously cultivated support from across the Middle East, Africa, Asia, and parts of Latin America, where support for liberal human rights norms was also fraying. The result was that when China acted, it did so with an impressive international chorus of support from both left- and right-wing authoritarian states across the world.

China had already launched a number of global and regional initiatives *outside* the UN and Bretton Woods framework before the seminal 2014 party work conference. These included the Asian Infrastructure Investment

Bank (AIIB), the New Development Bank (established with the BRICS countries), and the BRI discussed earlier. But after 2014, the pace and scope of China's new assertive and more critical approach *within* the existing multilateral system gathered pace. Xi was further emboldened by the Trump administration's wholesale assault on the multilateral system, its defunding of the UN, and its effective withdrawal from a number of UN bodies and Bretton Woods institutions. This included a reduction in annual US funding for the UN, including a whopping $1.05 billion that the US continued to owe in unpaid dues. Meanwhile, the US withdrew or began the process of withdrawing from multiple UN agencies and initiatives, including the UN Human Rights Council (UNHRC); the UN Education, Scientific, and Cultural Organization (UNESCO); and the Paris Agreement under the UN Framework Convention on Climate Change. It also crippled the World Trade Organization's dispute-resolution machinery through its refusal to appoint new members of the WTO's appellate body. China's leaders probably couldn't believe their luck that the US had willingly—indeed willfully—created a political, diplomatic, and financial vacuum in the very system that America itself created back in 1944–1945. And China was more than happy to occupy the ensuing institutional space with minimal public fanfare.

Under Xi, China's new multilateral strategy has had two arms. The first has been to rapidly expand Beijing's influence across the existing institutions of global governance through a combination of enhanced funding for the system, the appointment of Chinese nationals to lead (or be part of the senior leadership team of) major multilateral bodies, and the launching of a series of proactive diplomatic initiatives across the UN system that went beyond China's largely defensive posture that we had seen in the past. For example, between 2010 and 2020, China's combined annual contribution to the UN and Bretton Woods institutions increased by $30 billion. China also took a more active role within the UN, securing the leadership of the UN Food and Agriculture Organization, the UN's Department of Economic and Social Affairs, the UN Industrial Development Organization, the International Civil Aviation Organization, the International Telecommunications Union, and INTERPOL.

Within the UN Security Council, China—as opposed to Russia—routinely takes the lead on non-European and non–Middle Eastern matters when US, British, or French positions are to be challenged. Meanwhile, in the General Assembly, China's capacity to marshal large-scale support from member states across all geographic regions to defeat Western resolutions is clear for all to see, including anything challenging China's position on human rights in Xinjiang. Similarly, China has harnessed significant support—both from UN member states and the secretary-general—in advancing particular Chinese diplomatic initiatives, ranging from the BRI to Xi's long-term, deliberately ill-defined proposal for a "community of common destiny" to issue-specific proposals where Beijing decided to take the lead. Beijing also remained committed to the UN Paris Agreement on climate change despite Washington's decision to withdraw in June 2017 (although it would not take formal effect until November 2020)—a choice that would likely have led to the demise of the entire agreement if Beijing had followed suit. And in 2020, Xi used the UN to make his announcement that China aimed to peak carbon emissions by 2030 and reach carbon neutrality before 2060, thereby seeking to assert China's future claim to global leadership on sustained climate action. Meanwhile, China—a major contributor to UN peacekeeping operations—enhanced its contribution in 2015 by establishing a $1 billion fund to support a standing force of eight thousand dedicated Chinese UN peacekeeping troops and equipment for rapid deployment around the world.

Beyond the UN, China nearly doubled its World Bank shareholding from less than 3 percent before 2010 to a bit more than 5 percent in 2019 and secured the positions of deputy head, managing director, and treasurer of the bank's $62 billion portfolio. As for the IMF, China's quota (its contributions, access to financing, and voting power) also increased by almost 3 percent between 2010 and 2019, although this continues to represent a disproportionately small voting right within the Fund relative to the actual size of China's economy. Beijing is the second-largest contributor to the WTO's research secretariat, where China is exercising its influence over the organization's overall policy agenda. And within the current WTO reform process, China—like the US—also seems determined to emasculate the institution's critical dispute-resolution processes in order to lessen its national vulnerabilities to any adverse determinations on matters where Chinese interests might be at stake. In summary, China's advances across the current multilateral system over the space of the last five years have been as remarkable as the disappearing presence of the United States.

The second arm of Xi's post-2014 strategy to increase China's influence over the multilateral system has been to build a new set of institutions altogether—ones where China, not the US, is the central organizing power. The BRI was launched in 2013 and, at the time of writing, had attracted 139 participating states that have accepted projects or endorsed the idea, including a number of OECD economies, such as Italy, Switzerland, and much of eastern Europe. In 2014, China also launched a Silk Road Fund for infrastructure development across Eurasia. This was followed in 2015 with the New Development Bank funded by BRICS member states, although China is by far the major shareholder and controlling vote. Then, in 2016, China launched the Asian Infrastructure Investment Bank, which competes for funding with the Asian Development Bank (which it already rivals in terms of the size of its balance sheet) and the World Bank. As of the end of 2020, the AIIB already had 103 member states, compared to the ADB's 68.

The concerns raised by many states across the international community on the proliferation of these Beijing-controlled institutions are straightforward: the diminution of previously existing multilateral institutions established under international treaty law; weaknesses in the internal governance structures of some of the new institutions (but not the AIIB), including their lack of transparency; their tenuous commitment to low carbon and sustainable development principles; their capacity to create new debt traps for poorer developing countries; and an undeclared geopolitical agenda to further entrench China's global political and security interests.

China's initiatives in international financial reform outside the formal institutional structures of the IMF predate Xi Jinping's most recent efforts.

272 | THE AVOIDABLE WAR

In fact, China's decision after the Asian Financial Crisis in 1997 to establish the Chiang Mai Initiative (CMI) was China's first step in breaking away from the preexisting multilateral order. It is possible that the CMI might evolve into an Asian Monetary Fund (AMF), which would be even more China-heavy than the CMI's current arrangements. This would be deeply damaging to the standing of the IMF itself, just as the creation of the AIIB challenged the preexisting international standing of both the ADB and the World Bank. However, the jury is still out as to whether China would go this far. The vast bulk of the funding for any AMF would need to come from Chinese capital allocations. More importantly, under these circumstances, China—rather than the IMF—would then need to impose its own conditions for those drawing on the AMF facility in the future. This would, in turn, impact China's financial and reputational interests, particularly in light of its experiences in relation to bad debts in both Sri Lanka and Venezuela. Beyond these multilateral financial initiatives, Beijing has also unleashed a range of region-specific investment funds for Africa, Latin America, and Eastern and central Europe as well as with the individual Gulf states. These are not small in scope. They are also designed to provide an alternative to private Western capital markets, principally the US.

Xi's institutional innovations beyond the existing UN and Bretton Woods machinery has not been limited to the economy. On a number of security-related challenges, Beijing has also stepped outside the arrangements established under the preexisting multilateral system. Xi has championed the Shanghai Cooperation Organization and the Conference on Interaction and Confidence-Building Measures in Asia (CICA) and has gradually evolved a common security agenda for BRI member countries. All these institutional arrangements are designed to underline the concept of Chinese centrality, exclude the United States, and include Russia where necessary. As with the UN and Bretton Woods institutions, China's new era of multilateral activism beyond the structures of the current international system has been impressive. And, once again, it has been largely accommodated by an America missing in action.

Determining the Global Technology Standards of the Future

Parallel to this geopolitical game within the wider international order is another ongoing form of competition that is deeply representative of shifting global influence between China and the United States. That is the struggle over the future of the digital world, including the next generation of mobile telecommunications technologies, the internet, and digital payment systems. This also involves competing national, international, and multilateral standard-setting and techno-regulatory frameworks for the major technology systems of the future.

The first of these arenas is fifth-generation (or 5G) telecom. The 5G data networks can transmit data at twenty times the speed of current 4G networks, drawing on the combination of mid-band and high-band radio frequencies used by those networks. The macrosignificance of 5G is that it is set to become a major new enabling platform for the deployment of AI systems globally, such as self-driving vehicles. China has become the undisputed leader in 5G technologies, infrastructure, and systems. The Chinese state is estimated to have invested some $180 billion since 2014 in the development of 5G technologies. This was based on a specific 2013 state plan aimed at making China a global 5G leader—including the generous allocation of high-band spectrum, the building of 350,000 mobile towers across the country, and direct state support of national champions such as Chinese telecom giant Huawei.

Now China has taken this advantage into the international arena, launching its global 5G network in 2019, an ambition that has greatly disturbed the United States, given the strategic and security implications. As the US Defense Innovation Board stated, "China is on track to repeat in 5G what the United States did with 4G." China's subsidy of its domestic 5G program extends offshore, through the rolling out of the Digital Silk Road across a growing number of Belt and Road participating states. These 5G networks—including mobile telephone, internet, and other digital services—are also likely to be vehicles for Chinese digital-governance frameworks, including the potential accessibility of local data holdings to China's security and intelligence services.

China has argued credibly that neither the United States nor its allies have developed an alternative to Huawei's 5G technology. Nor does the West have the intention or the capability of laying out a global system of undersea cables and mobile terrestrial towers necessary for supporting such a network. China, however, has a less convincing response to the American counterargument that Beijing, for similar national security reasons, has never allowed foreign providers into the Chinese domestic telecommunications market. Similarly, China is unable to provide assurances that US military, security, or intelligence communications around the world would remain sacrosanct as a result of China owning, operating, and regulating a 5G network that relied on a Chinese system, particularly at a time of crisis.

Washington's decision in May 2019 to formally list Huawei as an entity whose activities are contrary to US national security interests meant that, in the absence of specific case-by-case approvals by the commerce secretary, US firms were banned from selling microprocessors to Huawei that were essential for the further rollout of its global network. Other Chinese entities have also been listed. This has complicated China's ability to set the global industry standard for 5G, despite the fact that Huawei is the market leader in what remains a limited field of only two Chinese, two Nordic, and zero American firms. In many respects, the May 2019 Entity List represented the formal commencement of hostilities between China and the United States in a new global technology war.

Then, at a September 2019 meeting of the UN's International Telecommunication Union (ITU), a team of Chinese engineers representing Huawei, China Telecom, China Unicom, and China's Ministry of Industry and Information Technology (MIIT) jointly proposed a dramatic new idea to the global governing body: that the core structure of the internet be replaced by a new standard network architecture called New IP (meaning internet protocol). While the current Transmission Control Protocol/Internet Protocol (TCP/IP) technical standard that developed organically in the West into today's internet serves as an open and neutral conveyer of information without regard to borders, New IP would be radically different. With its centralized top-to-bottom design, it would give state-controlled internet service providers fine-grained control over what individual users could connect to on the internet. This would include what Huawei engineers described as a "shut-up command," allowing the central network to cut off communication between individual devices or the entire network. Moreover, tracking features that would be built into the network would allow easy sharing of data on individuals and their network activity as well as between firms and governments. Delegates from countries including Russia, Iran, and Saudi Arabia reportedly expressed strong support for the proposed new standard, which Huawei said was already under construction.

Were the ITU—headed since 2014 by China's Zhao Houlin—to legitimize New IP as a standard, it would allow state internet operators to choose between an open Western World Wide Web and a state-controlled network spearheaded by Beijing and built by Chinese telecom companies. Under this Chinese internet governance model, every government would have the technical ability to more easily define the boundaries and rules of its national internet. This represents a competing normative ideal for the future of the internet that China has promoted as cyber sovereignty. As one UK delegate to the ITU told the *Financial Times* after the meeting, "Below the surface, there is a huge battle going on over what the internet will look like. . . . You've got these two competing visions: one which is very free and open and . . . one which is much more controlled and regulated by governments." This battle could help accelerate a broader decoupling of China and the West into separate technologies, information ecosystems, and governance systems—in many ways mirroring the ongoing geopolitical struggle over the future of the international order.

New IP is only one high-profile example of what Beijing has come to see as an important component of China's efforts to enhance its global power. More broadly, the CCP wants to leverage China's huge market power and potential and its growing technological prowess to set standards that will come to underlie key emerging technologies, including artificial intelligence, 5G, the internet of things, and genomic biotechnology. As China's 2017 New Generation Artificial Intelligence Development Plan put it, "to build China's first-mover advantage in the development of AI," it is vital for Chinese "AI enterprises to participate in or lead the development of international standards," including "a technical standard approach to promote AI products and services in overseas applications" by going out into the world. Meanwhile, as discussed in chapter 12, China has moved decisively to implement data governance standards that, while distinctly their own, also align much more closely with Europe, leaving the United States the odd one out.

While international standards and norms may seem intangible, China's experience of being absent from the creation of most of the standards that, up until now, have quietly governed critical aspects of the liberal world order—whether for the internet or the law of the sea—means that China understands the enduring power of determining new standards when new technology fields emerge. It recognizes that shaping the new generation of technology standards that will govern the twenty-first century is powerful indeed. And it sees this as foundational for an era of long-term Chinese global influence and, if possible, dominance—as the collective West has done in the past.

The United States—long the country that set international standards in the modern era—also understands the importance of this reality. That's why Washington has pushed back strongly against Huawei's expansion beyond China. The behind-the-scenes clash over standards is therefore likely to continue as a key battleground for US-China strategic competition over the global order for the foreseeable future. Unfortunately for Washington, the battlefield on which this battle will be fought will be the same multilateral institutions that the United States has come to neglect in recent years.

An International Order with Chinese Characteristics?

Is there a detailed blueprint of what a China-led international system would finally look like in the inner recesses of the Chinese leadership?

At this stage, I doubt it. As discussed in earlier chapters, that is not the way China has approached large-scale policy projects in the past—either at home or abroad. China's preferred approach is more iterative. Beijing tends to announce an all-embracing concept and then throw it to its think tanks for further analysis before beginning a series of trials in the real world. In the domestic context, the CCP typically trials its policies in various localities, monitoring reactions and learning from mistakes— sometimes for years—before introducing them nationally. We have seen that approach with the Belt and Road Initiative, which lacked definition when it was first launched in 2013. At that stage, it was just an idea. But by 2016, it was being incorporated into UN resolutions with the new UN secretary-general, António Guterres, waxing lyrical on the BRI's potential virtues. Then, gradually, through an evolving process of trial and error, the testing of international reactions to various Chinese initiatives launched under the rubric of the BRI, and learning from what the Chinese system happily acknowledges as mistakes in the implementation process, a more refined institutional shape gradually emerged—and will continue to emerge—from the clay.

On the broader question of what type of international system Beijing wishes to build for the future, Xi's opaque response since 2013 has been that China is in the process of building a "community of common destiny for all mankind." To Western ears, this sounds like a classically high-minded Chinese concept of limited practical utility. But for China, this is the beginning of the rollout of yet another big idea—or at least a central organizing principle—around which its future efforts to craft an international system more to its choosing can be aggregated. In fact, the common destiny concept was formally incorporated into the Chinese constitution in 2018 and is finding its way into various UN resolutions and a plethora of international conferences in order to enhance its normative standing.

China has, nonetheless, been careful at this stage not to articulate with any greater specificity what exactly will be incorporated into this community of common destiny. Indeed, as with the BRI, inarticulateness in the early stages of the evolution of the concept appears to be deliberate, not accidental. China's foreign policy establishment is once again pushing and probing to see how far they can get and what international reactions are likely to be forthcoming before speaking more definitively. China's diplomatic efforts at this stage of the development of the proposal are aimed at taking the commanding heights of the debate by deploying the full normative language of the UN system to legitimize the concept across the international community—well before defining what it will actually mean in the more brutal world of policy praxis. Therefore, for the foreseeable future, this community of common destiny is likely to remain little more than a hazy, hybrid amalgam of traditional Chinese cosmology that conceptualizes a broader multinational realm of "all under heaven," blended with a superficial form of Kantian idealism from the West that emphasizes cooperation, collaboration, and converging communitarian interests but with a spine of Leninist power politics lying at the center.

Indeed, we should not be surprised if, following the Twentieth Party Congress, we see Xi's community of common destiny assume a more Marxist framework of analysis. Xi spends a lot of time on ideology. Therefore, locating this new concept within a Marxist frame of reference, as part of a new set of international progressive forces engaged in a new form of dialectical struggle against the failing structures of the Western powers of the past, could become part of Xi Jinping's brave new world. Certainly, his Marxist think tanks are working on this. But how their work will be expressed publicly, when, and with what level of explicit political authority remains to be seen.

One concrete idea that gives form and shape to the type of new international order that Beijing has in mind is China's advocacy of its development model for the world at large. This has been gathering in momentum since Xi first floated the idea at the Nineteenth Party Congress in 2017, when he said that China would not only "take an active part in reforming and developing the global governance system" but also offer "Chinese wisdom and a Chinese approach to solving the problems facing mankind," including by "blazing a new trail for other developing countries to achieve modernization." As noted previously, this was the first occasion on which

Xi advocated China's authoritarian capitalist system as an alternative development theory to that offered by the liberal-democratic world. Since then, Xi's language has become progressively more expansive on the accumulated wisdom that China has to share from its experience—as well as the new contribution to global Marxism that Xi's "socialism with Chinese characteristics" has to offer. Therefore, whether the West cares to recognize it or not, in Xi's worldview, there is a new, unfolding ideological struggle underway between state socialism and democratic capitalism, which China is determined to win. It will also inform the final content of Xi's vision for a new global order.

For the time being, however, we are left to speculate as to what form a Chinese-led international order might ultimately take—were China to eventually prevail in the face of a prevaricating America, a divided Europe, and an increasingly accommodating developing world. But at its heart, Beijing's call is for a multipolar world, appealing to decades of international political resentment over American unilateralism—most dramatically demonstrated by the folly of the second Iraq War and more recent forms of Trumpian exceptionalism. In China's internal discourse, multipolarity is a simple proposition: a dilution of American power and the increase of its own in the deliberative processes of the current multilateral system. Once again, China, to its great surprise, has found itself pushing on an open door.

But in Beijing's view, multipolarity—as with America's rendition of the same—will not mean subjecting its core interests and values to the political abstractions of a UN or WTO process. Indeed, based on its behavior to date, Beijing is likely to be as selective in its acceptance of multilateral deliberative processes in the future as—it must be said—Washington has been in the past. China's previously mentioned outright rejection of the UN Permanent Court of Arbitration's decision rejecting its nine-dash line claims on the South China Sea is the most recent and perhaps most graphic case in point. Similarly, while enthusiastically welcoming the WTO's policies on free trade, China has ignored its obligations when these have conflicted with its core economic interests. For example, China has never declared the extent of its state subsidies for Chinese commercial firms operating in the global marketplace. China is not the first country to adhere to the rules it likes and ignore those it doesn't. But for China—as the self-described architect of a new global order—not abiding by existing international standards challenges its political legitimacy as the author of any replacement system.

Conclusion

At this point, we can safely say that China is likely to support a future order that is more accommodating of authoritarian political systems, with negligible intrusion from human rights bodies in the internal affairs of member states. Instead, it will increasingly champion its version of human rights, including prioritizing the right to development, by drawing on its success in poverty alleviation and on the G-77's dissatisfaction with progress in the implementation of the sustainable development goals. Beijing would also be unlikely to authorize any future intrusion in the internal affairs of member states on the grounds of "international humanitarian intervention." The future purview of institutions such as the International Criminal Court would become even more circumscribed. As for arms control and disarmament, China is unlikely to be any more forward leaning than America and Russia have been in recent years, although Beijing is likely to share Washington's and Moscow's concerns that the nuclear club doesn't get any bigger, despite likely viewing the North Korean program as too advanced to stop and not too problematic from the perspective of China's core national security interests, given that Pyongyang is unlikely to ever target Beijing.

On the global economic front, we will see China continue to champion its position on international digital governance, preferencing its state-sovereignty model over the European and American versions, as it rolls out its internet, telecommunications, and digital payments systems across BRI countries and beyond. Finally, on climate, China may part ways with its traditional BRICS partners in Russia, Brazil, India, and South

Africa by advancing the need for greater climate action—not least because China fears the extreme economic and environmental consequences for its national future if the emissions of global greenhouse gases are not significantly reduced. Therefore, with the singular exception of climate change, a new international order with Chinese characteristics, or an illiberal international order, is likely to be significantly different to the one to which we have grown accustomed over the last seventy years.

As we see the contours of Xi's plans for the future of the international rules-based order, America's response to this challenge, in many ways, remains amorphous. While this has meant inconsistency and weakness, it also allows for flexibility. And over the past several years, America's response to China's ambitions for the future of the global order is emerging, cohering, and gradually gathering momentum.

14

★ ★ ★ ★ ★

America's Emerging Strategic Response to Xi Jinping's China

The history of the twentieth century tells us that once awakened, American power, fully harnessed, can be as formidable as any great power in ages past. This is the lesson of America's decisive entry into the two World Wars in both 1917 and 1941, its decision to establish the postwar international order in 1945, and its successful prosecution and conclusion of the Cold War between 1948 and 1991. We also saw this manifest in America's response to the Soviet Union's 1957 launch of Sputnik, the world's first satellite. And with John F. Kennedy's declaration that the United States would land a man on the moon by 1970—an audacious oath that America then spectacularly fulfilled. Finally, we also saw it in Ronald Reagan's determination to crush the Soviet Union economically through a massive arms race barely a decade after America's ignominious defeat in Vietnam. The key question today is whether the United States is sufficiently conscious of the dimensions of China's rise and whether it is still possessed of sufficient political resolve and strategic acumen to deal with this formidable challenge to American regional and global power. On this, the jury is still out. But it would be foolish for China to assume that America will remain distracted and its strategy unfocused or that its relative decline is inevitable and irreversible. In fact, following the dramatic changes in Chinese strategy under Xi Jinping, the evidence points in a different direction: America has begun to stir.

America Awakens from Its Strategic Slumber

Politicians taking a hard line on China today can count on the broad support of the American people. Public opinion polls in recent years reflect a rapid sharpening of American sentiment toward China right across the political divide, with 76 percent of Americans holding an unfavorable view of China in 2021—a historic high, up from 60 percent in 2019, 47 percent in 2017, and 40 percent in 2012. A bipartisan 63 percent of Americans polled identify China's power and influence as a critical threat to the vital interests of the United States, up from 46 percent in 2019. Moreover, the number of Americans who label China the United States' greatest enemy *doubled* in a single year: from 22 to 45 percent from 2020 to 2021. The numbers clearly reflect a hardening of public sentiment as a result of the impact of the COVID-19 pandemic on American lives, families, and the economy. But the number of Americans saying they feel China has done a "good job" in containing the pandemic has actually improved over time—to 42 percent in 2021—even as the sense of threat from China has continued to grow. It appears that the broader strategic challenge has penetrated the American psyche: that China does represent a strategic challenge to the United States and that Chinese capabilities are not to be underestimated. But will this hardening of popular opinion across America translate into sufficient and sustainable political will across the American political class to galvanize the body politic into a Sputnik moment on China? Possibly, but it is certainly not guaranteed. In the absence of war—or at least the acute threat of war—it is no easy thing to harness the level of national resolve required to mobilize America for a new national mission of this order of magnitude. This is particularly the case in a vast, lumbering democracy like the United States, which—unlike China—prides itself on divided government, the separation of powers, and a fissiparous federation of states.

China's leadership has long been careful to avoid bringing its relation-ship with the US to the absolute boil. In doing so, China has been mindful of the need to avoid generating such a unified reaction—particularly while the balance of power still remained in America's favor. Nonetheless, despite the limited attention span of much of the American political class, Xi's China appears to have crossed a line in the collective mind of the Ameri-can public and the wider political establishment. Previous Chinese leaders were generally given the benefit of the doubt despite periodic crises in the US-China relationship under previous US administrations. But that is no longer the case. Democrats and Republicans are united in their perception of the threat posed by China, even if they remain divided on what exactly to do about it. This chapter traces this awakening in Washington, includ-ing how it manifested itself over the four years of the Trump administra-tion and how it continued into the Biden administration. It examines the evolving fault lines that have emerged within the sharpening US internal debate on the future shape of American strategy for dealing with Xi Jin-ping's China. It also seeks to distill the political and policy parameters of the "China debate" that the Biden administration has inherited from its predecessors as it settles its strategic course.

Act I: The Great China Reckoning

In 2018, *Foreign Affairs* magazine ran a high-profile debate featuring some of the world's most prominent China strategists on the question of whether America got China wrong. The debate was launched by an article titled "The China Reckoning," published by Kurt Campbell, US assistant secretary of state for East Asian and Pacific Affairs from 2009 to 2013 (and, more recently, White House coordinator for the Indo-Pacific in the Biden administration's National Security Council), and Ely Ratner, deputy national security advisor to then vice president Joe Biden from 2015 to 2017 (and more recently assistant secretary of Defense for Indo-Pacific Security Affairs under Biden). In their article, Campbell and Ratner traced a growing disillusionment with America's previous strategy of engagement with Beijing over the course of the Obama administration. The administration watched as Xi's centralization of power dashed initial (if always illusory) American hopes of political liberalization; how the BRI and China's state financial institutions challenged the liberal consensus on development; how Chinese hackers launched a series of major cyberattacks on American targets, including federal government agencies; and how China steadily dredged, built up, and then militarized a total of seven artificial islands in the South China Sea, culminating in Beijing's brutal dismissal of the landmark summer 2016 ruling by the UN Permanent Court of Arbitration that China's expansive maritime claims in the region were illegal. Americans concluded that three decades of strategic engagement with Beijing had ended in failure.

As Campbell and Ratner captured in their article, the zeitgeist in Washington had reached a moment of profound shift, with a shattering of the consensus in the US foreign policy and national security establishment on the value of engagement as a strategy for managing relations with China. From this point on, Washington pivoted to a new, harder approach. This paralleled a remarkable convergence in American public sentiment on the overall China question: between left and right, business and labor, hawks and human rights advocates, all of whom were united in their collective disillusionment with the results of three decades of America's engagement with Beijing. As Xi tightened control over the political environment in China and backtracked on expected economic reforms after 2013, America's business community became increasingly disenchanted with China's failure to open its markets and allow for genuine foreign competition. With the loss of strong support from the business community—historically the most vocal advocate in Washington for strong US-China engagement—the relationship lost its traditional ballast. Meanwhile, popular anger produced by American factory closures, shuttered by cheaper Chinese imports, was reaching fever pitch. That anger contributed to a populist wave on both left and right: first lifting the democratic socialist candidate Bernie Sanders's challenge to establishment candidate Hillary Clinton in the 2016 Democratic Party primaries and then ultimately helping deliver a shocking win in the presidential race for Donald Trump, who had made criticism of the weakness of America's China policy a signature of his campaign.

By the end of Trump's first year in office, this had all coalesced into a new strategic consensus in Washington on how to approach China. That view was encapsulated by three key strategic documents produced by the Trump administration and issued within several months of each other: the US National Security Strategy (NSS), issued in December 2017 by the Trump White House; the US National Defense Strategy (NDS), issued in January 2018 by the Department of Defense; and a special January 2018 report by the US Trade Representative (or USTR, which negotiates and works to enforce America's trade agreements) to Congress on China's WTO compliance. Echoing the new mood in Washington, the NSS noted that "for decades, US policy was rooted in the belief that support for China's rise and for its integration into the postwar international order would liberalize China" but that this assumption "turned out to be false." Instead, the NSS declared China to be a "rival" aiming to "shape a world antithetical to US values and interests" by seeking "to displace the United States in the Indo-Pacific region, expand the reaches of its state-driven economic model, and reorder the region in its favor." The NDS similarly stated, "As China continues its economic and military ascendance, asserting power through an all-of-nation long-term strategy, Beijing will continue to pursue a military modernization program that seeks Indo-Pacific regional hegemony in the near-term and displacement of the United States to achieve global preeminence in the future." To prevent this outcome, it warned, "We must remain the preeminent military power in the world." Together, these two strategic documents described the reemergence of "long-term, strategic competition" with China as the "central challenge to US prosperity and security." Then senior director for Asia on the National Security Council, Matt Pottinger, added for the press, "In the United States, competition is not a four-letter word. We at the Trump administration have updated our China policy to bring the concept of competition to the forefront. . . . It's right there at the top of the president's national security strategy." Although more an attitude than any concrete concept, strategic competition quickly became the defining moniker of the Trump administration's approach to China and later came to guide that of the Biden administration as well.

Meanwhile, the USTR's January 2018 report castigated China's record on implementing the raft of structural economic reforms that had been pledged as part of China's accession to the WTO. Instead, the report accused it of having maintained practices "incompatible with the international trading system." It concluded, in addition, that "it seems clear that the United States erred in supporting China's entry into the WTO." Moreover, as it was "now clear that the WTO rules were not sufficient to constrain China's market-distorting behavior," the report recommended the White House implement strong trade tariffs on national security grounds. The stage was set for the type of trade war that came to define much of the first three years of US-China relations under the Trump administration.

Act II: From Trade War to Tech War

President Trump entered office determined to change America's approach to trade, and trade with China in particular. Viewing national trade deficits as an unmitigated harm and a sign of American weakness, he campaigned against the Washington establishment's alleged failures in dealing with a China that was "killing us economically." He declared early in his 2016 campaign that "we have made China a rich country because of our bad trade deals," and "China is sucking us dry. They're taking our money. They're taking our jobs. We have rebuilt China with what they've taken out." But, he told the crowds, "we have tremendous economic power over China. We have tremendous power. And that's the power of trade."

This was not a new view for Trump. Unlike the many political and cultural issues on which the mercurial Trump had more than once switched his public position and party registration over the years, his stance on trade with China remained remarkably consistent for decades. "If we're going to make America number one again, we've got to have a president who knows how to get tough with China, how to out-negotiate the Chinese, and how to keep them from screwing us at every turn," he had written in his 2011 book *Time to Get Tough*. Even back in 2000, Trump had argued that China was triumphing over American diplomats because "the game has changed" since the Cold War: "The day of the chess player is over. Foreign policy has to be put in the hands of a dealmaker."

Therefore, it was not surprising that despite a warm first visit by Xi to Mar-a-Lago in April 2017, at which Trump's granddaughter recited a poem to Xi in Chinese, causing the Chinese internet to lose its collective mind, followed by a "state visit-plus" by Trump to Beijing that November, by the spring of the following year, Trump, nonetheless, followed up his earlier preelection threats to launch a full-scale trade war against China. In March 2018, immediately following the publication of the USTR's report on China's trade practices, Trump ordered USTR to begin the process by imposing a 25 percent tariff on all steel imports and a 10 percent tariff on all aluminum imports into the United States, as well as $50 billion in tariffs on a further list of Chinese goods. "When a country [USA] is losing many billions of dollars on trade with virtually every country it does business with, trade wars are good, and easy to win," Trump tweeted confidently. Trump, as on so many other things, was wrong.

In ordering the imposition of tariffs, Trump disregarded the advice of his director of the National Economic Council, Gary Cohn; secretary of the Treasury, Steven Mnuchin; and secretary of state, Rex Tillerson, as well as his business advisory council made up of prominent CEOs, such as JPMorgan Chase's Jamie Dimon, Intel's Brian Krzanich, and Tesla's Elon Musk. Instead, Trump listened to a supportive faction of officials and advisors who were much more hawkish on China in particular and skeptical of globalization, open markets, and free trade in general. This group included USTR Bob Lighthizer, director of the White House Office of Trade and Manufacturing Policy Peter Navarro, secretary of commerce Wilbur Ross, and the then director of the CIA, Mike Pompeo (who later replaced Tillerson as secretary of state). They argued, in Lighthizer's words, that "the sheer scale of China's coordinated efforts to develop their economy, to subsidize, to create national champions, to force technology transfer, and to distort markets in China and throughout the world" was an "unprecedented" threat to the United States that justified drastic action.

China retaliated with tariffs of its own, and as a result, the trade war quickly escalated, preventing the quick and easy win Trump had promised. The two sides eventually began formal negotiations to reach a cease-fire in late 2018, crafting a 150-page draft trade agreement by the spring of 2019. However, in May of that year, the prospective deal collapsed after it was rejected by the Chinese Politburo. With talks continuing to languish over the summer of 2019, the trade war soon resumed. And by the fall, the majority of all US-China trade was under tariffs. At this point, the scale of the trade war was impacting Chinese, American, and global economic growth. Even Trump admitted to the media that he was having some "second thoughts" about the tariffs, while China's chief negotiator Liu He appealed for calm and a return to negotiations.

Finally, by October 2019, the two sides announced agreement on a phase-one trade deal, which was signed on January 15, 2020. I attended the signing ceremony at the White House at the invitation of both delegations. We had done some modest work as the Asia Society Policy Institute think tank in New York, seeking to identify ways through these difficult and protracted negotiations that had gone on for nearly two years. But the White House ceremony was a surreal moment. The first news of the COVID outbreak in China was reaching America. The Chinese delegation, led by Vice Premier Liu He (Xi's trusted economic lieutenant) was putting on the bravest possible face for the occasion—one that received virtually no coverage on Chinese state television back in Beijing for fear that the agreement would be interpreted as a humiliating backdown. The Chinese did not speak at the ceremony. USTR Lighthizer delivered a courteous and gracious speech. Trump also spoke, but neither courtesy nor grace passed his lips, as he sought to turn the occasion into an unbridled exercise in political triumphalism targeted at his domestic political audience. Trump's conduct that day soured an already problematic relationship well before the unfolding political dynamic of the pandemic later turned the entire US-China relationship into a tailspin. In the agreement itself, China undertook to purchase $200 billion in additional US goods, including $78 billion in manufactured goods, $54 billion in energy, $32 billion in agricultural products, and $38 billion in services imports, in exchange for the US removing some of its tariffs while a broader phase-two deal was explored. Trump lauded his "victory" as a big win for American farmers and factories, heralding it as a "momentous" and "transformative deal that will bring tremendous benefits to both countries."

However, the phase-one trade deal secured none of the significant concessions on Chinese structural economic reform that Trump administration officials originally hoped to achieve, although it did contain some concessions on intellectual property rights and technology transfer. Even the commitments China made to purchase US agricultural and energy products were severely delayed by the outbreak of the COVID-19 pandemic. More importantly, Trump's trade war failed to put a dent in China's trade dominance. In 2016, the US trade deficit with China was $347 billion; despite all the tariffs, in 2019 it had declined only to $345 billion. And by August of 2020 (eight months after the phase-one deal), China's global exports had already surged 9.5 percent and lifted China's global market share of world exports to a record 17.2 percent—up from 13.9 percent in 2019. By the time Biden assumed office at the start of 2021, the US trade deficit still stood at $310 billion, despite a significant slowdown in global trade from the pandemic.

By 2020, the final year of the Trump administration, apart from the USTR, it seemed that few in the White House were paying much attention to trade at all. What they were thinking about instead was technology. As noted in previous chapters, the 2015 launch of China's "Made in China 2025" plan (MIC 2025) to upgrade Chinese industry and achieve global technological leadership in emerging technologies had caused serious alarm in Washington. Technological supremacy has always been central to both American national identity and the reality of American power— from NASA to the internet to the high-tech firepower that has characterized the American way of war. Americans had always assumed that their technological lead would never be seriously challenged. With MIC 2025, China openly asserted its intention to do just that.

This threat coincided with an impression of a China completely comfortable with forced technology transfer, intellectual property theft, and commercial cyberespionage. This sense of China being engaged in a long-running strategy of stealing its way to technological parity was reinforced by a brazen series of mass cyberattacks throughout the Obama administration that succeeded in stealing large quantities of data from US companies and government agencies. These were traced back to China, including to Chinese military intelligence units, such as PLA Unit 61398, which had already been indicted by the US government in 2014 for multiple cyberthefts that "blatantly sought to use cyberespionage to obtain economic advantage." These concerns were heightened by China's stated policy of "military-civil fusion" and the legal requirement that private Chinese companies and institutions must automatically share technologies potentially beneficial to China's national security with the PLA. US leaders feared that a vast stream of American technological data, innovation, and commercial and military secrets was flowing into China via private-sector sales, foreign direct investment, research collaboration, or simple theft to help modernize the Chinese military. These fears were not new. In 2012, the Obama administration banned Huawei from US government contracts over cybersecurity concerns. But any focus on Chinese technology companies was initially overshadowed by the Trump administration's preoccupation with the trade deficit and low-tech industries, such as steel, manufacturing, and agricultural production.

This changed suddenly in April 2018, when the US Commerce Department banned all US companies from doing business with Chinese telecom company ZTE, having concluded that ZTE violated US sanctions on Iran and North Korea. With supply of nearly all of the company's components cut off, analysts described the ban as a commercial "death sentence" for ZTE. But in a dramatic turnaround reflecting his continuing preoccupation with negotiating a trade deal with China to reduce the bilateral trade deficit, one month later Trump unilaterally instructed the

Commerce Department to reverse the ban, tweeting that "President Xi of China, and I, are working together to give massive Chinese phone company, ZTE, a way to get back into business, fast. Too many jobs in China lost." By June, ZTE had agreed to a $1.4 billion settlement to avoid the ban. China hawks in Trump's White House and the US Congress were horrified, with a bipartisan group of lawmakers attempting unsuccessfully to restore penalties on ZTE.

As the trade war dragged on into 2019, however, a frustrated Trump became increasingly open to targeting Chinese technology companies as negotiating leverage with Beijing. Days after negotiations on the bilateral trade deal collapsed in May 2019, Trump signed an executive order banning Huawei from US networks. As discussed previously, the US Commerce Department placed Huawei on its entity list, effectively banning US companies from selling to it without government approval. Although in practice the Commerce Department continued to grant licenses allowing US companies to keep doing business with Huawei on a transaction-by-transaction basis, pressure on China's tech sector escalated. Five more Chinese technology companies that were leaders in semiconductors and supercomputing were added to the blacklist. This was followed by dozens of Huawei affiliates. With the accomplishment of the phase-one trade deal at the end of 2019, it looked like these restrictions might—like those on ZTE—be scaled back, having served their purpose as negotiating cards in Trump's trade war. Instead, they morphed into something more—a full-blown tech war—as the extraordinary events that unfolded in 2020 pushed the US-China relationship toward a precipice.

Act III: COVID-19 and the New Great Divide

The COVID-19 pandemic transformed Trump's relationship with China. Throughout his first three years in office—and even during the height of the trade war—Trump prioritized his relationship with his "very, very good friend" Xi Jinping, viewing personal bonds as the key to getting things done both in business and diplomacy. It was this perceived need that often stayed Trump's hand, as with the case of ZTE. As of January 2020, when the phase-one trade deal was finally signed, Trump still hoped to reach an even larger phase-two deal with Xi. Therefore, when COVID-19 first appeared in Wuhan around the end of 2019 and spread globally in January 2020, Trump initially downplayed the virus and repeatedly expressed confidence in Xi's ability to handle the crisis confronting his country. "China has been working very hard to contain the Coronavirus," he tweeted in January, adding that "the United States greatly appreciates their efforts and transparency. It will all work out well. In particular, on behalf of the American people, I want to thank President Xi!" Even as the coronavirus continued to spread in February, including to the United States, he tweeted that Xi was "strong, sharp and powerfully focused on leading the counterattack on the Coronavirus." As late as March 2020, Trump still insisted his relationship with Xi remained "really good" and praised close cooperation with China.

However, when the pandemic spread rapidly within the United States during the spring of 2020—with Americans rushing to stockpile supplies and the S&P 500 crashing by nearly a third of its value—Trump's tone changed quickly. "I wish they could have told us earlier about it because we could have come up with a solution," he complained. "It could have been stopped in its tracks," Trump said at a briefing at the White House on March 19. "Unfortunately, they didn't decide to make it public. But the whole world is suffering because of it." He pointedly referred to COVID-19 as the "China virus," using the expression more than twenty times between March 16 and March 30 alone. For his part, Secretary of State Mike Pompeo preferred the term "Wuhan Virus," using it six times in one press briefing. Both men were infuriated by China's leading wolf warrior, Foreign Ministry Deputy-Spokesman Zhao Lijian, who had accused the US Army of bringing the virus to Wuhan. By April, Trump had also turned his ire on the World Health Organization (WHO), saying the virus could have been contained "had the WHO done its job to get medical experts into China," but "instead the WHO willingly took China's assurances at face value." The administration announced it was halting US funding to the WHO. Pompeo accused the institution and its leader of having been "bought by the Chinese government." By May, the US announced it would withdraw from the WHO entirely.

Trump administration officials then publicly speculated that the virus had been unintentionally released from a virology lab in Wuhan or even been created as a bioweapon. Trump pressed US intelligence agencies to investigate and told the press that "we have people looking at it very, very strongly" as a possibility. "China will do anything they can to have me lose" the 2020 election, he added. Trump's special relationship with Xi was finally over. "Right now, I don't want to speak to him," Trump told an interviewer. Xi "should never have let this happen," he said. "I make a great trade deal and . . . the ink was barely dry and the plague came over. And it doesn't feel the same to me." By that stage, the majority of advocates for maintaining engagement with China were gone from the administration, including Gary Cohn, Rex Tillerson, and Defense Secretary James Mattis. Only Steven Mnuchin and Jared Kushner remained, along with Robert Lighthizer, who, having achieved the phase-one trade deal, became something of a stabilizing force as he fought to keep that agreement from falling apart as the divide between Washington and Beijing widened dramatically.

The White House faction in favor of decoupling was in control of policy making. With Trump finally on their side, these decouplers were determined to take on Beijing on every front, implementing what FBI director Christopher Wray described as a "whole of society" approach to confronting China. Their decoupling manifesto had effectively been launched more than a year before the arrival of the COVID pandemic in a seminal October 2018 speech by Vice President Mike Pence. Listing a litany of American complaints about Chinese overt and covert economic, military, technological, political, diplomatic, and media behavior, Pence used the speech to signal a shift toward a more general policy of decoupling. He called on business leaders to think twice "before diving into the Chinese market" and "turning over their intellectual property or abetting Beijing's oppression." Attorney General Bill Barr went further, accusing China of an "economic blitzkrieg," saying, "The ultimate ambition of China's rulers isn't to trade with the United States, it is to raid the United States." Accusing them of "bowing to Beijing," he warned corporate leaders that "appeasing the PRC may bring short-term rewards. But in the end, the PRC's goal is to replace you."

But Pompeo, with his eye already on the 2024 Republican presidential nomination, went the furthest. In a July 2020 speech, he slammed those "insisting that we preserve the model of dialogue for dialogue's sake," deriding the "old paradigm of blind engagement with China." Instead, Pompeo advocated a full-spectrum approach to "strategic competition" with China, hinted at the desirability of overthrowing the Chinese Communist Party itself, and declared, "Xi is not destined to tyrannize inside and outside of China forever, unless we allow it." He concluded with a call for "every leader of every nation to start by doing what America has done."

In April, with the decouplers firmly in charge, the US Commerce Department expanded export controls to prevent companies in China from purchasing US technology that could be used for military or surveillance applications "under civilian pretenses." More significantly, in May, the US Commerce Department moved to cut off Huawei from its global supply of semiconductors by requiring licenses for any sales to the company of chips made abroad that drew on US technology. This immediately put the survival of the company's flagship smartphone business in jeopardy. In August, the administration added thirty-eight additional Huawei affiliates to its entity list, then an additional twenty-eight Chinese companies that it alleged were active in island reclamation activity in the South China Sea. Also in August, Pompeo announced the Clean Network program, an expansion of American efforts to "ensure untrusted People's Republic of China (PRC) carriers were not connected with US telecommunications networks." Under this program, US allies and partners were to shut Huawei and other Chinese technology firms out of their telecom networks. Pompeo threatened that the US might be forced to "disconnect" even its closest allies from intelligence sharing if they failed to do so. Meanwhile, Trump signed executive orders banning Chinese-owned apps TikTok and WeChat from distribution in the US, although legal challenges subsequently forced their suspension. Then, in September, the US escalated again—imposing licensing requirements on exports to China's largest chip maker (the Semiconductor Manufacturing International Corporation or SMIC), directly threatening China's supply of advanced microchips.

Simultaneously, the administration used its final months to launch a sustained campaign to induce multinational companies to relocate their manufacturing supply chains outside of China. The State Department announced it was "turbocharging" an initiative to create an "Economic Prosperity Network" of "trusted partners" to host manufacturers under common US-led standards. Pompeo launched discussions with regional countries, including Australia, India, Japan, New Zealand, South Korea, and Vietnam to "move the global economy forward" with a conversation on "how we restructure . . . supply chains to prevent something like [trade war and pandemic-related trade disruptions] from ever happening again." In particular, the US and Taiwan agreed to expand cooperation on relocating supply chains to the island. In exchange, the Taiwan Semiconductor Manufacturing Company (TMSC)—the world's largest chip maker— agreed to build a $12 billion manufacturing plant inside the United States in order to supply chips for sensitive US industries.

Opening up a third front in the offensive, the Trump administration also took steps toward a decoupling of the US and Chinese financial sectors. In May 2020, Trump ordered America's $600 billion federal government pension fund to abandon plans to invest in a stock index containing Chinese companies. Then in August, the administration urged regulators to pass new restrictions that would kick Chinese companies off US stock exchanges if they didn't comply with US auditing rules. And in November, Trump signed an executive order prohibiting US investors from holding shares in thirty-five Chinese companies designated by the Pentagon as having ties to China's military, including a number of companies listed on US exchanges as part of emerging market funds. However, for the time being, these moves had little effect in stemming the flow of investment into China, as private American investors concluded that, irrespective of geopolitical tensions, the sheer size of the Chinese domestic market meant it was too big an economic opportunity to miss.

In the summer of 2020, the Trump administration expanded its retaliatory measures against Beijing by imposing widespread visa and financial sanctions on Chinese officials and their families, beginning with those reportedly involved in human rights abuses in Xinjiang. For the first time, this list included sanctions on a CCP Politburo member, Chen Quanguo, the party secretary of Xinjiang. The sanctions followed Trump's signing the Uyghur Human Rights Policy Act of 2020, passed by the US Congress in June with only a single no vote, which called for the sanctioning of Chinese officials responsible for denying the "right to life, liberty, or the security" of Muslim minorities in Xinjiang. The administration weighed sanctions against individual officials in 2018. However, back then, the proposal was shot down by Trump as incompatible with his trade negotiating strategy. But following evidence that China had detained up to one million Uyghur Muslims in a large number of reeducation camps across the Xinjiang Autonomous Region, this sanctions policy was revisited. These actions against the Uyghur were portrayed by Beijing as counterterrorism measures, but they were accompanied by a crackdown on religious liberty across China, including both Muslims and Christians. As a result, the Trump administration strengthened its international political messaging and collective policy action on Chinese human rights abuses.

Following China's imposition of new national security legislation in Hong Kong in 2020, which ended freedom of speech and freedom of assembly in the territory, the administration also issued sanctions on ten mainland and Hong Kong officials involved in China's crackdown on prodemocratic protests and political dissent in the city. This included Hong Kong chief executive Carrie Lam. Four more Hong Kong officials were added in November 2020, followed by fourteen members of the Standing Committee of China's National People's Congress in December. Those sanctions were implemented under the auspices of two acts of Congress passed in 2019–2020. First, the Hong Kong Human Rights and Democracy Act—passed nearly unanimously by Congress and signed by Trump at the end of 2019 after protests engulfed the city—which mandated an annual review of the city's autonomy and called on the president to impose sanctions against mainland and Hong Kong officials responsible for human rights abuses in Hong Kong. Second, the Hong Kong Autonomy Act—passed unanimously in July 2020—which required mandatory sanctions against individuals, entities, and financial institutions responsible for undermining Hong Kong's autonomy from the mainland. Several other Chinese officials were also targeted in September 2020 for their role in island "reclamation" in the South China Sea.

Concurrently, the Trump administration limited people-to-people contacts between China and the United States. In response to the earlier harassment and expulsion of US journalists from China, Washington reduced the number of Chinese journalists granted visas to report from the US; cut the number of Chinese students receiving study visas; imposed new restrictions on Chinese diplomats, including barring them from visiting universities or meeting with local American government officials without prior approval; and banned anyone with CCP membership from immigration to the United States (though in practice this was impossible to enforce, given the sheer size of the party's membership at ninety-five million members). Most dramatically, the administration ordered the closure of China's consulate in Houston, Texas, accusing diplomats there of engaging in widespread economic espionage. In retaliation, China ordered the closure of the US consulate in Chengdu. Chinese nationalist demonstrators booing as American diplomats departed the building got sufficiently out of hand that police had to move in to keep control of the crowd.

Finally, during 2020, the Trump administration intensified its diplomatic and military pressure on both the South China Sea and Taiwan. The administration stepped up the tempo of freedom-of-navigation operations (FONOPs) by US warships challenging China's territorial claims in the South China Sea. The US carried out six such operations in 2017, five in 2018, before escalating to nine amid growing tensions in 2019. That escalation continued in 2020, with the Trump administration swiftly conducting as many FONOPs in the first six months as Obama had authorized in his entire second term. With nine FONOPs conducted in 2020, the Trump administration appears to have set a new annual record in the quantity of such patrols, although it is also possible that the Trump administration simply publicized its operations more vocally than Obama. Trump certainly appeared to increase the pace and intensity of US operations, including scheduling back-to-back FONOPs over two days in April 2020 as the US Navy sought to increase the unpredictability of its challenges to China. These operations led to several near misses, as US and Chinese maritime forces came into close contact, including an incident in April 2020 in which Chinese vessels reportedly came within one hundred meters of a US guided-missile destroyer while chasing it out of waters near the Paracel Islands. That incident echoed a near miss in 2018, when a Chinese warship almost collided with another destroyer, coming within forty meters and forcing it to take evasive maneuvers.

In July 2020, Pompeo also announced that the US was, for the first time, changing its diplomatic stance on the South China Sea, directly describing China's maritime claims as illegal, illegitimate, and infringing on the rights of China's Southeast Asian neighbors. This was a significant shift, given that Washington had previously avoided taking any formal position on any of the claims in the South China Sea dispute. The administration then set out increasing the frequency and intensity of other naval exercises and maneuvers in the region, including, at one point, deploying three of its nine carrier strike groups simultaneously. They also announced the administration's intention to eventually establish a new expeditionary First Fleet, to be based somewhere in Southeast Asia.

Meanwhile, the administration sent a growing number of warships to transit the Taiwan Strait as it intensified its security cooperation with Taipei, with a record ten transits in 2020. Beginning with a record-breaking $8 billion sale of sixty-six F-16 fighter jets at the end of 2019, the administration embarked on a surge in arms sales to Taiwan. This included another $5 billion in missiles, torpedoes, drones, and other weapons systems over the course of 2020, bringing the total figure for the Trump era to over $17 billion—outstripping most of Trump's predecessors. The administration then moved beyond more traditional forms of military cooperation through arms sales to combined exercises between the US and Taiwanese special forces, including the US Marine Corps openly engaging in training exercises with the Taiwanese military for the first time in forty years. A US surveillance plane also reportedly made a stopover in Taipei. Under Trump, the pattern of growing US military contact with Taiwan and naval operations in the Taiwan Strait was a stark departure from the past.

However, most provocative from Beijing's perspective was the steady stream of US government officials that visited Taipei in 2020. This began with a large delegation of former officials and ambassadors who attended President Tsai Ing-wen's inauguration for a second term in May 2020. Pompeo also delivered a laudatory official congratulatory message, becoming the first secretary of state to do so. Then, in August 2020, US Secretary of Health and Human Services Alex Azar made a groundbreaking trip to meet with Tsai in Taipei—making him the highest-ranking US official to visit Taiwan in forty years. This prompted China to dispatch fighter jets across the center line of the Taiwan Strait during the course of Azar's meetings with Taiwanese officials. In September, the Trump administration followed up with a trip by US undersecretary of state Keith Krach, the highest-level State Department official to visit the island in decades. Simultaneously, US ambassador to the United Nations Kelly Craft held an unprecedented meeting with Taipei's top official in New York. Finally, the top military intelligence official at US Indo-Pacific Command, two-star Rear Admiral Michael Studeman, made an unannounced visit to Taiwan in November. With each visit, Beijing reacted with increasing anger, warning that the Trump administration was drawing closer and closer to its redline on Taiwan.

Trump to Biden

When President Biden took office in January 2021, he quickly set about fulfilling his campaign promise to reverse or dismantle nearly every Trump administration political priority—except for his China policy. Rather, the

Biden administration demonstrated striking continuity in upholding both the strategic thrust and many of the details of its predecessor's approach to China. Indeed, while Biden's team moved quickly to moderate the rhetorical tone of the US-China relationship and, most significantly, launched a diplomatic offensive to reassure US allies and multilateral partners around the world that the US was back and still reliable, Washington's operational approach to China continued to harden.

The Biden administration—sensitive to any form of domestic political criticism for being "soft on China"—did not take any immediate steps to scale back the tariffs, technology and financial restrictions, visa limits, or sanctions imposed by the Trump administration. Quizzed by senators during his confirmation hearing, new secretary of state Antony Blinken confirmed that the Biden administration would not only keep such measures but also agreed with an official designation made during the final days of the Trump administration that China's human rights abuses in Xinjiang constituted genocide. Moreover, Blinken confirmed that the Biden administration would only make slight adjustments to the rules previously issued under Secretary Pompeo that encouraged greater contact between US government officials and Taipei.

As the weeks wore on after Biden's inauguration, Beijing's initial hopes that he would institute a reset of the relationship proved unfounded. The Biden team studiously ignored entreaties by Beijing to quickly resume high-level dialogue, instead focusing on the diplomacy required to build a multilateral coalition to balance America's position against China. As outlined in chapter 10, the new administration moved rapidly to further revive the Quad, including with a landmark leaders-level summit in March 2021, and to bring the "China issue" to the heart of relations with the G7, NATO, the EU, and the Five Eyes intelligence alliance. Soon Biden was speaking openly of a new global "battle between the utility of democracies in the twenty-first century and autocracies."

When the US and China finally held a high-level diplomatic meeting in Anchorage, Alaska, in March 2021, it became clear that relations were likely to remain in the freezer for the foreseeable future. Both sides used the meeting to launch public denunciations of the other, with the US side—led by Blinken and National Security Advisor Jake Sullivan—expressing its "deep concerns with actions by China, including in Xinjiang, Hong Kong, Taiwan, cyberattacks on the United States, and economic coercion toward our allies," and directly threatening "the rules-based order that maintains global stability." They noted, "We do not seek conflict, but we welcome stiff competition." Speaking just ahead of the meeting, Blinken summed up the administration's overall posture toward China with what became an almost standard three-part formulation: "Our relationship with China will be competitive when it should be, collaborative when it can be, and adversarial when it must be."

The Chinese side, led by Director of the Central Foreign Affairs Commission Office Yang Jiechi, was particularly outraged by the imposition of new Hong Kong–related sanctions on Chinese and Hong Kong officials by Washington just two days before the Anchorage meeting. They attacked the US for having "exercised long-arm jurisdiction and suppression"; reminded them that "the US does not represent the world"; and accused the US government of "deep-seated" human rights violations against minorities at home, citing Black Lives Matter. Finally, Yang demonstrated his fealty to Xi Jinping's nationalist slogan that the "East is rising, the West declining" by declaring, "The United States does not have the qualification to say that it can now speak to China from a position of strength."

Conclusion

The confrontation in Anchorage was not a turning point in the relationship. However, it provided final confirmation that the US-China relationship was on a radically different course compared to the period prior to 2017, regardless of which party was now in power in Washington. In November 2021 Biden and Xi held their first (virtual) summit, with both sides voicing a desire to restore dialogue and establish "guardrails" to better manage the relationship. Only time will tell, however, whether this can lead to a breakthrough in the relationship, given the fundamental dynamics driving the two countries into competition.

As Biden rallied US allies to Washington's side using language reminiscent of the Cold War, in March 2021, Xi Jinping delivered a speech to the Central Party School in Beijing in which he warned the party, "We must rely on struggle to win the future." Soon after, at the annual meeting of the National People's Congress the same month, he warned military delegates that "the current security situation of our country is largely uncertain and unstable" and that the military must, therefore, enhance its combat readiness. At the same meeting, Defense Minister Wei Fenghe responded affirmatively that strategic confrontation with the US had entered a period in which "containment and countercontainment will be the main theme of bilateral ties in the long term." Meanwhile, General Xu Qiliang, the vice chair of the Central Military Commission, stated (for the first time in public by a military official), "In the face of Thucydides's Trap . . . the military must accelerate further the increase in its capacity"— implying that military conflict with the US was a serious possibility in the face of continuing structural tension. This emerging sentiment of political and military resolve was underlined in an unprecedentedly hard-line speech delivered to the Central Party School on September 1, 2021, when Xi Jinping himself declared:

> *The risks and challenges we face have obviously increased. It is unrealistic to always want to live a peaceful life and not want to fight. [We] need to discard wishful thinking, be brave to fight, and refuse to give way to even one inch on matters of principles. [We] need to safeguard our nation's sovereignty, security, and development interests with unprecedented will and character. [Our] communists, at all times, will maintain the spirit, integrity, and boldness, to not be taken in by fallacies, not to be afraid of ghosts, and not to be weak-kneed cowards.*

Beijing has concluded that the changes in Washington's strategy toward China are deep, enduring, and fundamentally a Thucydidean structural response to China's rise. It is in this environment of rock-bottom strategic mistrust and escalating competition across the policy spectrum that the Biden administration will continue to develop its own strategy toward China, having come a long way indeed from nearly four decades of strategic engagement. As of late 2021, the administration's interagency review process of its overall China strategy had not reached its conclusion. But all public indications to date suggest that the overall response will be as hard-line as the Trump administration's—but unlike Trump's, it is likely to be systematically rather than episodically hard-line. This does not mean that America's strategy for dealing with China through the 2020s is set in concrete or is doomed to move in only one direction. There is still considerable scope for policy creativity within the limits of strategic realism, just as there are likely to be opportunities for collaboration with China in areas of common concern. Indeed, if Xi Jinping were to chart a different strategic course for China's future—beyond the usual tactical adjustments that China brings to the table to accommodate the arrival of any new administration in Washington—the United States would adjust its own strategy accordingly. At present, however, it isn't clear that either is willing to deviate from the strategic race that stretches before them.

15

★ ★ ★ ★ ★

Xi Jinping's China in the 2020s: The Politics of the Twentieth Party Congress

So where does all this leave Chinese politics at the dawn of this "decade of living dangerously"? As we have seen in previous chapters, understanding the changing contours of Xi Jinping's worldview is important—including how these differ from those of his predecessors—particularly as Xi pushes Chinese politics, economics, and society to the left while taking Chinese nationalism further to the right, thereby politically turbocharging China's new assertiveness in the world at large. It has also been important to understand how America, under both the Trump and Biden presidencies, have read the Xi phenomenon so far—and how they have responded to it—causing the US body politic to conclude that Xi Jinping's China represents the single largest threat to American global and regional power since the Cold War.

But before we try to map the dangerous shoals of the coming decade, including how they could play out and what could credibly be done to avoid crisis, conflict, and war, it is important to take stock of where Chinese politics stands right now, at the dawn of the decade. It is particularly important to delve inside the opaque world of internal party politics in the lead-up to the Twentieth Party Congress scheduled for late 2022. The reason for this is straightforward: the politics of the Politburo, the Central Committee, the military, security, and intelligence apparatus—and, to some extent, the distilled opinions of China's elder statesmen—will shape the outcome of the congress on three consequential questions. Will Xi Jinping secure reappointment for a record third term through to 2027? If so, what does that mean for him continuing as China's paramount leader beyond 2027? Will his future powers be increasingly untrammeled as a result?

My argument, based on the evidence to date, is that the answer to all three of these questions is, with some caveats, yes.

Xi, the Master Politician

Xi Jinping's political modus operandi, when confronted with a challenge—either foreign or domestic—is to double down: to either crash through or crash. Unlike most of his recent predecessors, Xi is a calculated, albeit not a reckless, risk taker. His critical skill is to identify a political or policy vacuum and to fill it before others do. He is a master tactician in building political momentum across the cumbersome internal machinery of the CCP by deploying key personnel to critical positions; mobilizing the party's propaganda apparatus; and anchoring his worldview in a single, all-encompassing ideological framework in order to convince the party and the country that they are critical parts of a historical, righteous, and "correct" cause. Xi is also his own master class in internal party politics, possessing a ruthlessness not seen since Mao in dealing with political opponents. For these reasons, there is no credible competitor of comparable political stature left standing in the inner sanctums of Chinese party politics—or, at least, none that we know of.

Xi has broken the norms of post–Cultural Revolution politics. After that disaster, party elites, led by Deng Xiaoping, agreed that there would be no more political purges of the type that Mao had specialized in for more than thirty years. Leaders would be jailed only for rank corruption, not for political crimes. Under Xi, more senior Chinese leaders have been imprisoned than under the rest of his post-Mao predecessors combined. But in doing so, Xi has been careful to use his party-wide anticorruption campaign to bring his adversaries down on the grounds of financial impropriety rather than politics alone (although, over time, he has more directly hinted at the existence of "antiparty cliques" that needed—and still need—to be dealt with). The anticorruption campaign he launched in 2013 has rumbled on for more than eight years, with hundreds of thousands of party cadres at all levels formally investigated and punished. But in case his opponents had concluded it had run its course, Xi recently doubled down again. In 2020, he launched a formal party rectification campaign of the type Mao used at his guerrilla base in Yan'an during the Anti-Japanese War in 1942. This was when Mao physically eliminated or politically purged thousands of party cadres suspected of being disloyal to him. It is not coincidental that this particular campaign is being conducted by Xi's closest political supporters in the two years leading right up to the Twentieth Party Congress. In the bloody history of the CCP, rectification campaigns certainly focus the mind. And Xi Jinping plays for keeps.

However, it is important to understand that the reason Xi continues to resort to these harsh measures is because he is acutely aware that the radical changes he has brought about in China's overall political and policy direction have earned him a powerful group of enemies. Each of the leaders who has been purged has an extensive network of friends, family, and supporters. Although Xi has, in the main, been meticulous in taking out his enemies' protégés and camp followers or intimidating them into silence, or at least inertia, they nonetheless make up an informal network of the politically alienated. These have been joined by the ranks of disaffected officers from within the PLA. Large-scale purges, radical restructuring, and massive troop reductions in the PLA, conducted without providing adequate pensions, have also left a large legion of deeply alienated former military personnel. Furthermore, within the political, judicial, and intelligence apparatus of the party, Xi has long suspected active opposition to his power and position. For example, the purges within the Ministry of Public Security alone have been forensic. The MPS is just one of a number of agencies within the so-called legal and political affairs machinery that became the explicit target of Xi's most recent rectification campaign. Similarly, Xi's early decision to bring the People's Armed Police under direct party control (rather than having it continue to sit under the administrative apparatus of the state council) reflects his legitimate paranoia about this paramilitary force being deployed against him—as was reportedly almost the case just prior to him taking over the party leadership in 2012, when he faced down powerful internal rivals, such as Bo Xilai and Zhou Yongkang. Finally, there are the former party leaders themselves—including the ancients Jiang Zemin and Zhu Rongji and the rapidly aging Hu Jintao and Wen Jiabao—whose collective disdain for Xi's continuing repudiation of their policy legacy is evident from a number of sources. However, the problem with all these groups is that there is no single figure around whom political resistance could effectively coalesce. From time to time, the current vice president of the People's Republic, Wang Qishan, is mentioned, given his continuing stature in the party and signs of his recent political estrangement from Xi. There has also been some recent evidence of estrangement between Wang (once Xi's trusted companion but now rarely in public view) and Xi, including the purging of Wang's former aide Dong Hong. But were Wang to even begin contemplating a move against Xi, it would be career terminating in the extreme.

For any political opposition to effectively mobilize against Xi Jinping's reappointment in late 2022, there would need to be a series of catalytic and catastrophic events. These events could take a number of different forms. The most credible would be any self-inflicted economic crisis, decline, or even financial collapse. The party has only relatively recently rebuilt its domestic credibility and political legitimacy in China following the country's near economic collapse of the Great Leap Forward and, later, the Culture Revolution. That's because in the decades after 1978, the party finally lifted people's living standards in what had long been an impoverished socialist paradise. To undo the unspoken social contract between party and people (i.e., political control in exchange for economic prosperity) in any way would rebound badly on Xi.

Second, natural calamities (including pandemics) also have the potential to destabilize the party's leadership (as they have throughout Chinese history, in which disasters were commonly taken to mean leaders had lost the "mandate of heaven"). This is why the internal politics of China became particularly intense in the first half of 2020 following the eruption of COVID-19 in Wuhan and the leadership's initially tepid response. It also underscores the party's acute response to any foreign attacks regarding the Chinese origins of the virus for fear this would become part of the country's internal discourse, in addition to an international loss of face. In Xi's case in particular, the critique was that because of his feared status as an unforgiving and dictatorial leader, senior provincial officials hid the news of the pandemic from Beijing in its early and most critical weeks, hoping to contain it locally rather than following long-agreed protocols mandating immediate national and global notification.

A third cataclysmic event would be a military defeat, large or small, at the hands of either the United States or Japan. Xi's national political narrative about "the rise of the East and the decline of the West" carries with it the assumption that China would prevail in any direct contest. This has been furthered by Xi's decision to militarize his presidency (wearing battle fatigues, undertaking frequent troop reviews, and his constant public references to China's ever-growing comprehensive national power) to the extent that an inability to win an outright victory in any armed confrontation with the US or its allies would be politically lethal. It would be doubly so if this occurred in any scenario over Taiwan, which Xi has vowed to return to Beijing's control as part of the China Dream.

Xi has therefore adopted a generally cautious approach to these significant strategic risks, in contrast to his approach to tactical politics, where he has (as noted earlier) been much more agile and audacious. In the case of the pandemic, he quashed all domestic dissent and adopted a zero-tolerance strategy toward the virus itself—all the while deploying the party's propaganda apparatus to ensure that any international criticism is aggressively rebutted through his global team of wolf warrior diplomats, even seeking to sow doubt as to whether the virus actually originated in

China in the first place. On potential military crises, as noted in previous chapters, Xi may be forward leaning in dealing with US and Japanese naval and air incursions into what he describes as Chinese territory. But he is unlikely to allow any incidents to escalate to a point of no return—unless convinced that there is no risk that Chinese forces would not prevail or that the domestic political cost of blinking and backing down is simply too great.

Xi's real political vulnerability lies with the economy. As noted in previous chapters, the economy is not his policy strong suit. He has limited feel for financial markets or the complexities of macroeconomic management. Therefore, his recent major adjustments to China's domestic economic growth model outlined in chapter 6, including the reemphasis of the state over the market, and his new restrictions on the Chinese private sector pose a real political danger to his leadership if growth, employment, or living standards were to stall. This, in my judgment, is Xi's greatest liability, particularly given that his critics in the party leadership elite have previously championed a different economic policy strategy for China's future.

Xi Jinping's efforts to secure long-term control over the party have not been limited to coercive means. His efforts have also been directed at developing a personality cult elevating himself as the "indispensable core leader" in the eyes of the party's mass membership and the wider Chinese public. He has been accorded symbolically significant new titles, including leader (*lingxiu*) and the helmsman piloting the country's future—both designations previously reserved for Mao alone. But, most spectacularly, Xi has also become the author of the entire body of an eponymous Xi Jinping Thought that—after only a single term in office—has been incorporated into both the party and state constitutions. An official assessment of history, passed at party's Sixth Plenum in November 2021, declared its "decisive significance," codifying Xi Jinping Thought as the pliable new ideological orthodoxy for the party during this new era that has officially replaced the previous decades defined by Deng Xiaoping. Xi Jinping Thought is designed to navigate the party and the country along a new course that will deal with the "imbalances," "inadequacies," and "inequalities" of that previous era of unrestrained capitalist growth. Indeed, Xi Jinping Thought is specifically designed to provide a theoretical justification for Xi's reorientation of political, economic, and social policy in a new pro-party state interventionist direction across the board. Xi Jinping Thought has also extended its reach into foreign and military policy guidance, where it lays out the new path for China to follow in assuming its newfound great power status, along with new principles and frameworks (already discussed in chapter 13) for a new, more Sino-centric international order.

For those seeking to locate any particular theoretical coherence across the many tomes of Xi Jinping Thought that have emerged so far or any new interpretation of twenty-first-century Marxism, that is not the point. Xi Jinping Thought has been designed to be politically elastic: to expand and contract to absorb new political and policy developments as they arise and, as a result, ideologically legitimize them by attaching the Xi Jinping Thought mantra to them. That is not to say that Xi Jinping Thought is devoid of substantive content. But it is largely limited to three core propositions: (1) Chinese ideological orthodoxy is to be an amalgam of Marxism-Leninism, Chinese tradition, and Chinese nationalism—with the precise weighting of the amalgam to be defined by the party leadership from time to time depending on the need. (2) This orthodoxy embraces the current move toward the left on politics and the economy and to the right on nationalism. (3) Beyond intellectual cognition and moral legitimization, this new ideology legitimizes struggle as a necessary means of practical action for realizing progress, both at home and abroad. Importantly, *struggle*, in the Chinese Communist political vernacular, can take many forms—including both nonviolent and violent.

For all these reasons, Xi's domestic political position as he approaches the Twentieth Party Congress in late 2022 is relatively robust. There is no apparent challenger. He would also fear that if he did step down, he would become powerless in the face of the many he had purged or marginalized, who would then seek revenge. Furthermore, Xi's party-rectification movement has reduced any would-be opponents to a state of anxiety, terror, and, above all, silence. Moreover, since 2013, he has placed key supporters in critical positions across the entire party and military apparatus. The likelihood of a large-scale destabilizing internal or external event is therefore limited, although we should always keep a close weather eye on what could flow politically from the economy's performance in the future during 2022. Most importantly, Xi has seized the "commanding heights" of the party ideologically, which in the CCP remains critically important as a means of handling normative discourse across its ninety-five million members. Here, Xi has become (like Mao) the party's "ideologist in chief"—so much so that there is a Xi Jinping Thought textbook available for compulsory study for every school student, printed under the snappy subtitle *Happiness Only Comes Through Struggle*.

But should Marxism-Leninism falter in its capacity to offer a convincing narrative for explaining the significant changes he has already introduced and, more importantly, should the economy fail, Xi could still harness the ancient alchemy of Chinese nationalism as the ultimate legitimizing force behind his leadership. Xi's public language is littered with his concerns with both black swan and gray rhino events, reflecting his deep preoccupation with those forces that could bring him down. But at this stage, it would take a combination of both swans and rhinos for him to fail being reappointed as paramount leader at the 2022 Party Congress. It is a separate question what his official designation might be after that occurs, including whether, for example, he resumes Mao's old title of party chairman. But based on what we know, his material power is likely to continue to hold up into the future. It would, therefore, be prudent for American presidents to assume that Xi will be their opponent for much, and likely all, of the decade ahead, barring, of course, an early natural demise.

Xi Jinping and the Chinese Economy During the 2020s

As noted throughout this book, the possibility of economic failure represents the most pressing political threat hanging over Xi Jinping's head in the critical decade ahead—the decade likely to determine the future balance of power between China and the United States. Xi's most recent gambit to pivot to public on the economy is fundamentally a political one. All the primary elements of Xi's New Development Concept (as described in chapter 6) are meant to strengthen both his and the party's grip on power. These include the focus on common prosperity by reducing income inequality, achieving national technological self-reliance, and, most importantly, embracing state leadership over the market at most levels of the economy. In Xi's vision, this will simultaneously win over the people to his side, reduce China's vulnerability to external pressures, and provide a robust new driver for the sustainable growth of China's "real economy" far into the future. This is, however, highly optimistic. Casting aside the proven growth engine of China's recent economic transformation—the private sector—in favor of more centralized control of the economy risks stunting China's growth momentum at the most critical time. Indeed, private fixed capital investment is already lagging, reflecting declining levels of private-sector confidence.

Already, China's economic growth is slowing. While Chinese GDP posted a strong 18.3 percent early recovery from the pandemic in the first quarter of 2021, growth slowed to 7.9 percent in the second quarter and then only 4.9 percent in the third—well below expectations. Additionally, industrial production growth fell to 8.9 percent in the second quarter and then only 3.1 percent in the third, marking a significant drop from the 24.5 percent logged in the first. The slowdown signaled a halt to a hoped-for V-shaped recovery from the COVID-19 pandemic and hinted at the underlying structural challenges lying beneath China's economic growth prospects for the decade ahead.

Much of China's economic growth during 2021 was powered by the long-standing growth drivers of net exports, manufacturing, and government investment. Exports, however, are unlikely to persist as a major growth driver because of disruptions related to the pandemic, the US-China trade war, and global supply chains. Indeed, much of the growth in 2020 came on the back of industrial production, driven in large part by policy-driven public-sector investment. Despite this, much of Xi's strategy for future growth hangs on domestic consumption, innovation, and productivity growth. But in each of these areas, major policy problems loom that, on balance, are likely to impede growth rather than enhance it.

Under Xi's new development model, domestic *consumer demand* is also meant to drive much of China's economic growth for the coming decade. But while private consumption has proven to be relatively resilient so far, it is still limited by the country's culture of high household saving rates. In general, the future outlook for China's consumer demand is problematic. With the income and spending gap between China's rich and poor widening significantly during the pandemic, it is far from certain that China's overall consumption growth can maintain previous momentum. What consumer spending growth there has been is expected to moderate once pent-up demand from the pandemic dissipates. And while e-commerce has seen relatively strong growth during the pandemic and immediate postpandemic period, this is precisely the sector where Xi's antimonopoly campaign is cracking down hard with as yet unknown consequences for growth. Consumer demand is also likely to be undermined by persistent problems with unemployment. As of the time of writing, the latest official unemployment figures show that China's surveyed urban unemployment rate stood at around 5 percent. While this is not high (though some analysts speculate the real rate is much higher), it covers up more specific concerns—namely, the unemployment rate for sixteen- to twenty-four-year-olds, which even on the official numbers rose to 13.8 percent in July 2021. Xi's crackdown on China's private sector, which provides for about 90 percent of new employment growth, will only dim their employment prospects even further.

Xi has also focused on state-led *innovation* through initiatives such as the "Made in China 2025" policy and its various successor policies. But with China's access to foreign technologies becoming increasingly constrained because of geopolitical tensions, this is becoming an increasingly difficult prospect. Beijing has since launched massive state research, development, and innovation funds across ten priority industry sectors of the future (led by semiconductors)—treating these investments as large-scale venture-capital funds with equally massive anticipated losses—but also with some expectation that major breakthroughs will still occur. It remains to be seen whether this Beijing variation of the Chinese military and industrial complex will succeed, like its American antecedents in the 1950s, or whether it will only exacerbate China's existing inefficiencies in allocation of capital.

However, it is in overall *productivity growth* where China's economy is weakest and faces the greatest challenge in Xi Jinping's new economic era. Since 2008, China's total factor productivity (TFP) has grown by just 1.1 percent annually, less than a third the rate of the previous three decades, according to the World Bank. During the 2009–2018 period following the global financial crisis, aggregate labor productivity in China weakened to 7.4 percent per year, down from 9.0 percent in the 1999–2008 period before the crisis. Moreover, of all the sectors that have experienced slowdowns in the past few years, it has been the services sector—precisely the sector Xi is counting on powering the economy—that has been hit the hardest, with productivity falling from 8.1 percent to 4.6 percent over the last decade. That downward trend has persisted as the overall pace of reform has slowed. Comparatively, China's economy does not yet come close to measuring up against the economies of other advanced countries. China's economy is still only 30 percent as productive as the US, Japanese, or German economies. Most economists' evaluation of the reasons for this is clear: the continued size, influence, and unproductive investment of the state sector. While the IMF evaluates productivity at Chinese state-owned enterprises to be only about 80 percent that of private firms, state firms enjoy preferential access to capital from banks. Prior to 2015, Xi pledged to kill off zombie SOEs that were kept alive only by state funds. That effort has slowed considerably, reinforced by Xi's resolve under the new development concept to not only sustain but also expand the state-owned sector. This is bad news for long-term productivity growth. By contrast, economists argue that major state-sector reform to clean out low-productivity firms could more than double annual productivity growth over the next five years, from 0.6 percent to about 1.4 percent. This 0.8 percent improvement would also lift overall GDP growth by the same level (e.g., from the IMF's 5.7 percent projection for 2022 to 6.5 percent). Xi, however, shows little interest in moving in this direction.

These various trends came to a head in the second half of 2021, when Evergrande Group, a Chinese property behemoth with $300 billion in debts, began defaulting on bond payments. It was followed by other smaller property developers who also began to default. With an estimated 41 percent of China's approximately $45 trillion in banking-sector assets exposed in one way or another to the property market, this immediately raised fears that China might experience its Lehman Brothers moment, triggering a broader financial crisis. At time of writing it appears that the Evergrande problem is likely to be resolved by Beijing through an orderly distribution of its assets to a mix of private and state buyers, and most analysts are confident that, as the IMF put it, "China has the tools and the policy space to prevent this turning into a systemic crisis." But avoiding this immediate crisis will not solve the significant longer-term problem facing Xi. As of the end of 2020, the property sector represented approximately 29 percent of Chinese GDP, 41 percent of all Chinese bank loans, and 78 percent of the wealth invested by urban Chinese. Yet China's obsessive focus on growth powered by investment into infrastructure and property, along with slow progress on deleveraging, meant that in 2020, there was already enough empty property in China to house more than ninety million people—more than the entire population of Germany—according to an estimate by the Rhodium Group. Evergrande therefore effectively marked the end of the Chinese economy's ability to continue running primarily on the same investment-led model. Instead, a reckoning in the vast property sector, managed or otherwise, is likely to become a significant further drag on China's GDP growth, just as Xi's pivot away from the private sector presents deep uncertainties about the efficiency and effectiveness of China's future economic performance.

For all these reasons, while China is likely to reach its year-end target of 6 percent economic growth in 2021, the era of high growth in China is over. Even ahead of Xi's crackdown on the private sector and the Evergrande crisis, a consensus had emerged among global economists that China's economic growth will probably slow to around 4 percent by 2025. This forecast deceleration also reflects China's aging population, declining workforce, weak productivity growth, a negative trade environment, and high levels of official debt. Added to this is the as yet unknown impact of Xi's macro pivot to public across the overall political economy at the potential expense of China's hitherto remarkable culture of private-sector dynamism. Private-sector investment, both domestic and from foreign sources, is likely to slow further—stranded in a period of great uncertainty between Xi's common prosperity campaign at home and the threat of US-China decoupling abroad.

For years, economists have warned that only increases in total factor productivity can ultimately save China from the middle-income trap and that this increase can only come from an economy with less state involvement, not more. The next decade is likely to determine once and for all whether this hard-won collective wisdom proves still to be true—or whether China really is sui generis in the future efficacy of its new, but still unfolding, economic model. If Xi Jinping is fully aware of the economic policy gamble he is taking by changing the model in the midst of unfolding geopolitical risk, it may induce a level of caution about adding further risks to his overall strategic calculus. But if he is unaware, which may be the case because of his reported intolerance of official doubt, caution, and negativity, compounded by his lack of familiarity with the technical granularity of the economic policy brief, then China may embark on a decade of growing international assertiveness at a time when its domestic economy is weakening.

Xi Jinping and the Imposition of New Social Controls

Even if we accept that Xi's position is likely to be secure within Chinese *elite* politics through the 2020s, what about broader Chinese society? Are there social movements brewing that could cause his leadership to be derailed, or at least change course? This is even harder to predict because the data is more difficult to come by. There are, nonetheless, a number of social trends unfolding across China that need to be watched carefully. Party leaders recall that no one—either within China or among professional China watchers abroad—predicted the Tiananmen protests of 1989. The party, of course, now monitors social developments carefully. It does so through a number of different mechanisms—including opinion poll research, social attitude surveys, the infamous social credit score system, and government algorithmic control. It became adept at identifying any negative trends that might disrupt political stability or otherwise threaten the continued rule of the party and, where necessary, at intervening quickly to either prevent or disrupt those trends.

One growing problem the party has recently confronted is the emerging social movement that has grown active around environmental protection, including on air quality, land contamination, and water pollution as well as food-quality standards. In the case of air pollution, what was noteworthy was Xi Jinping's early intervention to change policy course once he concluded that popular discontent was gaining momentum, including demands for governmental action. This became particularly acute with air-quality standards in China's major cities (most particularly Beijing) as more and more people became concerned for their physical well-being and that of their children. Rather than simply suppressing this popular movement, Xi's response was to signal policy change. Despite this, however, the party has maintained close monitoring and surveillance of any environmental NGOs with any predisposition to develop a policy agenda outside the authority structures of the CCP. Nonetheless, the party's actions to date on environmental sustainability reflect Xi's desire to remain ahead of this particular curve rather than behind it—let alone being consumed by a deepening social movement that escapes his control altogether.

The second area where Xi Jinping faces real challenges, as noted previously, lies with China's private entrepreneurial class. The movement to suppress China's billionaire elite (most dramatically through his common prosperity campaign) has been popular across mainstream Chinese society, given that even Premier Li Keqiang admitted that as many as six hundred million Chinese are still surviving on salaries of less than 1,000 yuan ($155 dollars) per month. At the same time, Xi's crackdown on wealth has sent a chilling message across the Chinese private sector. The reality Xi has confronted is that, given the lack of secure, well-paying positions available in traditional jobs, such as with SOEs, it is common for China's university graduates to seek employment in China's gig economy and, in time, set up their own small businesses. The open question is whether the actions taken now against China's most successful entrepreneurs (until recently held up as exemplars for young Chinese seeking to get ahead) will generate a much wider reaction from across China's vast entrepreneurial class. There are also particular provinces (for example, Zhejiang) where historically there has been a limited state-owned economic sector and private firms have been dominant in the overall economic structure. Therefore, what may appear to be a politically sensible course of action from Beijing's position of reducing social inequality may end up generating an equal and opposite reaction from China's existing and emerging entrepreneurial class across the provinces.

A third important area of real, emerging social opposition is religion. This applies not only to the practice of Islam in Xinjiang, Gansu, Ningxia, and other parts of the country but also in particular to the practice of Christianity, especially Protestant Christianity (as discussed in chapters 2 and 4). Xi has initiated a wide range of new repressive measures to bring religious observance under much more direct state control. Xi's much-publicized bulldozing of unauthorized church structures in Zhejiang's cities of Wenzhou and Ningbo became symbolic of a much wider repression of religious institutions, which has met with often fierce resistance by church groups across the country. This has been compounded by the arrest of a large number of Protestant pastors operating outside the framework of the Chinese patriotic church. The overall number of Christians, by some estimates, rivals the number of members of the party itself—nearing one hundred million. For these reasons, Xi Jinping is likely to continue his hard-line repressive approach. What remains to be seen is the extent to which this, in turn, generates a broader social movement, demanding more fundamental political and policy change while increasingly directing its wrath at Xi himself as the architect of these recent oppressive religious policy changes.

Xi has also introduced China's first national NGO law, explicitly designed to bring both foreign-funded and domestic NGOs under much tighter control by both the party and the security apparatus. Xi has indicated his deep concern about the capacity of NGOs to act as agents of influence of foreign powers seeking to subvert the domestic political rule of the Chinese Communist Party. Given the absolute centrality of the party to Xi's overall vision for the future of Chinese politics, it is a vision that offers limited room for future NGO activities in China. Prior to Xi becoming leader and passing China's NGO law, there were more than seven thousand foreign NGOs and as many as one million domestic NGOs and social organizations spread across the country and engaged in every form of philanthropic activity. The fact that much of this activity has been brought to a shuddering halt will—as a matter of course—also add to this growing league of the politically disaffected.

A similar repressive approach has occurred across Chinese universities, where there has been a determined effort to reduce academic freedom. There has been not only a reemphasis on courses on Marxist-Leninist ideology but also new restrictions on what subjects can be taught and the curriculum material than can be relied on. More fundamentally, academics—particularly those who are foreign trained—have become the subject of much greater classroom surveillance and, in some cases, dismissal if any element of party or political orthodoxy is challenged in the classroom. While academics themselves don't represent a political challenge to Xi, he and his colleagues are acutely conscious that the universities gave rise to the protest movements of 1989. Once again, the open question is what reactions will emerge across China's university campuses given these most recent changes.

Parallel to these efforts, the party's propaganda department has moved to rein in unauthorized media activities across China. Local newspapers, which had sprung up as independent "champions of truth," have been quietly—and in some cases noisily—closed down. State-owned media has also been subjected to new restrictions on adhering to political and party orthodoxy in reporting, analysis, and opinion. Xi (from the publicly released transcripts of the speeches to the party's propaganda work conferences) has indicated that a Western-style media, along with NGOs and undisciplined academics, represents a fundamental threat to the authority of the CCP. However, what remains unknown is the extent to which this form of media repression will result in a countermovement against his administration and encourage even more creative searches for alternative sources of information. The problem for Xi's party is that despite his efforts to create a firewall between Chinese students and the internet, those students—and others—remain innovative in their abilities to break through the firewall and secure information from sources from around the world.

Another group to feel the brunt of Xi Jinping's increasingly repressive policies has been the legal profession. An infamous case early in Xi's rule saw hundreds of activist defense lawyers arrested and, in many cases, sentenced to prison because of their vigorous campaigns in support of criminal law reform and broader constitutional reform in China. In fact, Xi has taken a leading role in opposing efforts from the legal profession and the academic community supporting new forms of constitutionalism that would have the effect of making the party subordinate to the state constitution and to China's national parliament. This movement had gained considerable momentum over the twenty-three years of Jiang Zemin's and Hu Jintao's rule. Once again, however, Xi has brought this to an abrupt stop. All debate on constitutional reform has been banned. And the party has decreed that the only legal reform that is necessary is to ensure that the courts, the People's Procuratorate system, and defense lawyers are *all* subject to the will of the party. The capacity of the legal profession to constitute a general movement for a change within the CCP—or against Xi Jinping's personal leadership—would appear to be remote. But Xi's crackdown within the legal system after decades of incremental reform nevertheless builds collective resentment on the part of an articulate and activist profession.

Finally, Xi Jinping's regime has adopted a new policy toward young people that could produce a much more widespread unintended reaction. Recent restrictions on the amount of gaming time permitted for school-age children have given rise to massive negative reaction from young people across the internet. This has accentuated the generational divide between Xi's generation of party elders and younger Chinese, who have very different ideas about how they like to spend their spare time. Chinese millennials have become digital natives (albeit within China's generally restrictive system), and gaming in China has become even more popular than in most countries in the West. That does not mean that Chinese gamers are all closet nascent liberal reformers. Quite the reverse: the nature of games played often appeals directly to the crudest nationalist sentiments. But making young people the enemy by banning one of the few creative outlets available to students in a highly stressful and competitive school examination system is perhaps not the wisest of moves. Furthermore, attacks by officials from the Xi administration on young men of the rising generation being "insufficiently manly" and, in some cases, "downright sissy" is also treading on dangerous ground. This has been reinforced by reports that have emerged of a quiet crackdown on China's LGBT community—or at least new restrictions on their organizing of public events on Chinese university campuses and on the internet. And all this at a time when primers on Xi Jinping Thought are appearing across the school and university systems, encouraging China's youth to emulate the revolutionary achievements of their forebears.

None of these repressive measures individually is going to result in Xi Jinping being brought down. However, in the event of some other catalytic event—particularly in relationship to the economy, natural disasters, or national security—the fact that so many different social groupings across China are disaffected from Xi Jinping's chosen political direction could become problematic for the regime. Indeed, they *could* coalesce around a single major event or a series of events that catches the regime by surprise. That is why Xi, an acute observer of social developments, will be relying not only on rolling social attitudes surveys but also on the surveillance reports of his vast security intelligence apparatus to monitor any emerging threats from one or a number of these movements. Given Xi's history, he is also likely to be tactically agile in adopting forceful measures early in order to decapitate any such movement before it can become a real problem.

Xi Jinping's Nationalism

For these reasons, the balance of probabilities suggests that Xi Jinping will be reappointed comfortably in late 2022. At the same time, we would be foolish to ignore the political headwinds that are still being generated: among the political class who have been disenfranchised, in the economy as a result of Xi's new pressure on the Chinese private sector, and among young people and in a latent civil society due to his crackdown against a large number of social movements that he is determined to bring back under tighter party control. As noted above, Xi's political methodology for dealing with such headwinds is to push back hard against them, threatening the introduction of even more intense restrictions coupled with individual retribution against those whom the system happily calls troublemakers.

However, there is another significant quiver to Xi Jinping's bow in dealing with political and social unrest around him: his ability to call on the deep reserves of Chinese nationalism to reconsolidate his political position by harnessing populist opinion to his cause. Indeed, nationalism is becoming a core pillar of both the party's and Xi's personal political legitimacy and has become a central focus of the party's vast propaganda apparatus. Nationalism therefore becomes a dangerous additive to the already dangerous decade that lies ahead. So as we think about the China of the 2020s, beyond the internal dynamics of the 2022 Party Congress and Xi Jinping's reelection, the fluctuations in its economy, and the greater controls imposed on Chinese society, we also need to understand that Xi's China will be increasingly nationalist. This will also have profound implications for how Beijing navigates its already complex external relationships, particularly with the United States.

Nationalism in recent Chinese history has often proven to be a double-edged sword. The party sometimes authorized the expression of nationalist public opinion to send messages to foreign governments by arguing that "we Chinese have to manage domestic political opinion too." At the same time, it has sometimes proven difficult to put the nationalist genie back into the bottle after having released it. This problem has become progressively larger under Xi Jinping, as nationalist appeals have moved from the margins to the center of the Chinese propaganda apparatus across the board. Pride in China's national achievements is redolent across every news bulletin: not just Olympic achievements but also the international space race, the size of the Chinese economy, and the new capabilities of the Chinese military, to name just a few. All of these have become cause célèbre for officially endorsed nationalist celebrations.

It is, of course, difficult to measure the extent to which nationalist sentiment in 2022 will be stronger than it has been in previous years in China. Although their methodology is a point of academic debate, some social attitude surveys find a strengthening of national sentiment over time in China, especially among young people. But whatever the real feelings of average Chinese citizens might be, we can safely conclude that the party constantly makes greater recourse to nationalist themes as a conscious political and propaganda tool, and it would not be doing so if it did not work in enhancing the party's legitimacy. This new emphasis on nationalism has resulted from clear directions from Xi at the party's central propaganda work conferences, which state that the party's central mission is to cause the people to be proud of its achievements and to conclude that China could only have become wealthy and strong under the CCP's leadership. Furthermore, associating the country's strength with Xi's personal leadership becomes an effective means of further consolidating Xi's political position—particularly at a time when other parts of Xi's political, economic, and social projects may be encountering resistance.

Of course, the principal foil against which national sentiment is deployed in China is the United States. Japan has performed that function historically—particularly given Japanese atrocities against China in World

War II. But since the Korean War, and more recently since the implosion in US-China relations under both the Trump and Biden administrations, the United States has become acceptable cannon fodder within China's nationalist debate. At one level, Chinese nationalist positions reinforce some of the analysis put forward by the party, claiming that American national power is, by and large, spent. Chinese news coverage in recent years has focused on the dysfunctionality of the American democracy, the inability to contain COVID-19 (especially under the Trump administration), and other recent manifestations of declining American power, including the fall of Kabul in August 2021. In the Chinese nationalist take, all of these are indicative of the overall decline of the West, which is China's accepted political code language to refer to the decline of the United States. This line of substantive analysis and public presentation by the Chinese propaganda apparatus is likely to continue into the future, although with varying degrees of intensity to accommodate the political circumstances of the time. But in doing so, the regime's principal audience is domestic, and its principal objective is its political legitimacy.

If we accept that official nationalism will be allowed to wax and wane as needed in Xi Jinping's China, the question arises whether Chinese nationalism will also become a more potent force in pushing the party toward more hard-line policy positions toward the United States that the party would not normally take. There is no evidence that this has happened in the past. This is because the official bureaucratic class in China has historically been strong enough to resist any such domestic political impulse. But China's traditional foreign policy establishment is weaker than ever before, as the locus of international policy decision-making (as with all areas of policy) has been progressively relocated to the party center and Xi's powerful personal office. Therefore, nationalist sentiment as a tool of domestic political legitimacy building is also likely to play a larger role in strategic decision-making—often in defiance of classical foreign policy logic—than has been the case in the past. It is perhaps too crude to say that Chinese foreign policy is simply becoming the prosecution of Chinese domestic politics by other means. But there is increasing resonance in that proposition on the critical question of the foreign policy consequences of the party's continued quest for domestic political legitimacy through increasingly atavistic appeals to underlying nationalist sentiment, representing a new dynamic in Chinese foreign policy formulation.

As argued previously, three fundamental sources of political legitimacy remain for the CCP: Marxist-Leninist ideology, economic prosperity, and Chinese nationalism (the latter also incorporating selective extractions from the Chinese classical tradition). If all three work together seamlessly, the party's overall legitimacy will be high. But the truth is, despite the party's concerted efforts, they don't. First, however powerful a tool Marxism-Leninism may be as a legitimizing and disciplining force *within* the party, such ideology will not of itself provide a sufficiently legitimizing force within the broader body politic to comfortably sustain either the party's or the leader's long-term political standing. Second, if, for whatever reason, economic prosperity falters during the decade ahead, Xi would have no alternative but to revert to the coercive instruments of party power to maintain political and social control. Third, if both the ideological and economic underpinnings of party legitimacy become unstuck, nationalism, if effectively harnessed, could potentially become the most important legitimizing force in Chinese politics for the future. Furthermore, from the regime's perspective, it could reduce (but not remove) the need for purely coercive measures to maintain effective political control.

For these reasons, if Xi or the broader CCP leadership were to come under serious domestic pressure as a result of a failing economy, compounded by a failing ideology that had led Xi toward decisions that brought about that economic decline in the first place (through a return to greater party control), nationalism would become the only political card left to play in the party's legitimacy pack. We do not know if the Chinese economy is going to falter. On the balance of probabilities and given the historical experience of Xi's economic team in dealing with previous crises (in both 2008 and 2015), they will likely manage their way through. But contending with a leader as politically powerful and as ideologically determined as Xi Jinping under such circumstances may become more problematic than in the past. And the nationalist card would always be there for him to play.

These, then, are the dynamics that present themselves for the decade ahead. Nationalism is likely to add a new and potentially more volatile dynamic in the way that Chinese political elites respond to the United States in the future. Chinese foreign policy will therefore not be as rational in American eyes as it has been in the past (i.e., in rational pursuit of what the West would define as China's abiding national interests). And it may not be as predictable as in the past. Chinese nationalism, therefore, looms as a new and potentially dangerous wild card for the wider management of the US-China relationship during the 2020s.

Conclusion

As we look forward through the 2020s, Xi Jinping—barring an act of nature—will likely be with us as China's paramount leader throughout 2027 and probably beyond. It is also likely that, despite political opposition, uncertainties with the economy, and a range of potentially problematic social movements, Xi will continue to prevail by using the tools of ideological and coercive control. Failing that, Chinese nationalism remains a potent propaganda tool to be used to bolster Xi's hold on political power.

As we have already seen, however, nationalism already looms as an emerging new problem in the overall management of the US-China relationship. For example, it was to this nationalist audience that China's most senior foreign policy advisor, Yang Jiechi, addressed his public remarks during his meeting with Biden administration officials in Anchorage in March 2021. Yang's fiery lecture to Secretary of State Antony Blinken was not designed for an American audience. It was designed for a Chinese domestic audience. More specifically, it was designed to deal with the nationalist dynamic that has been enlivened in Chinese politics under Xi Jinping.

It remains to examine how all the factors we have examined so far in this book come together in the real-world geopolitical dynamics of US-China relations during the 2020s. This means integrating their complex history, their deep perceptions of each other's politics and foreign policy, Xi Jinping's transformation of the CCP's official worldview, Washington's strategic responses to Xi so far, and the likely state of Chinese politics and the economy in the decade ahead. The next chapter outlines a number of specific scenarios that provide us with a framework for understanding which way the decade might unfold. This is followed by a final chapter dealing with the practical challenge that faces us all: given the increasing risk of crisis and armed conflict between China and the United States, how we can best devise a joint strategic framework (of what I term managed strategic competition) between the two countries that is capable of reducing the possibility of a catastrophic war.

16

★ ★ ★ ★ ★

The Decade of Living Dangerously: Alternative Futures for US-China Relations

So what is likely to happen in this decade of living dangerously? The fixed factors at work in the US-China relationship, including China's expanding military, the broad contours of Xi Jinping's long-term strategy, and the growing intensity of strategic competition, may be relatively clear. But the variables are still vast. The most important of these include the content, continuity, and implementation of American strategy under Biden and its long-term political sustainability through the 2024 and 2028 presidential elections. There is also the question of how effective this strategy will be in rebuilding US military and economic power at home and in reconsolidating America's alliances abroad after the trauma that was Trump.

Then there are the unpredictable third-country variables that are also at play—for example, the decision by the European Commission to forge a new investment treaty with China in the dying days of the Trump administration in January 2021. This also followed the decision by America's principal Asian allies in October 2020 to join with China in RCEP, while both America and India remained outside. Both developments indicate that America will still have a difficult task on its hands against the long-term lure of the Chinese economy. Even before the Biden administration was sworn in, the global gravitational pull of the great Chinese economic juggernaut was—as Xi Jinping had predicted—beginning to look irresistible. On the other hand, the European Parliament's decision in May 2021 to suspend ratification of the investment treaty with China (because of Beijing's intimidatory tactics against parliamentary members of the European Parliament who had opposed Chinese policies in Xinjiang) demonstrates just how politically volatile diplomatic and economic relationships with Beijing have become. Then there are the problems unfolding in China's domestic growth model, referred to throughout this book, as Xi seeks to reassert party control over the private sector, depressing Chinese business confidence with as yet unknown consequences for long-term economic growth—and with some potential to unravel the fundamental domestic economic underpinnings of China's long-term claim to global geopolitical power.

It is hazardous, therefore, to attempt any single, authoritative forecast of what the US-China relationship will look like by 2030. The best way to envisage the future is to instead outline a range of potential scenarios based on different assumptions, providing some indication of the consequences that are likely to flow from each of them in the years ahead. This may at least provide a cautionary guide to policy makers today as they seek to navigate the dangerous shoals that lie ahead.

Scenario 1: China Succeeds in Taking Taiwan by Force as the US Decides Against Military Intervention— America's Munich Moment

Under this scenario, Xi Jinping—with or without provocation from independentists in Taipei—decides to bring about a military solution to the Taiwan question before this decade's end. The political motivation for such a course of action could include a radical turn in Taiwanese domestic politics following the 2024 Taiwanese presidential elections, a desire by Xi in the years leading up to the Twenty-First or Twenty-Second Party

Congresses (in 2027 and 2032, respectively) to secure his ongoing position as paramount leader, and/or a conclusion that American domestic politics were in such structural disarray that the risk of US armed intervention was minimal.

The military or paramilitary tactics Chinese action could take against Taiwan would be consistent with the patterns of Chinese war-gaming over recent years. They could include one or more of the following: organizing domestic insurrection within Taiwan (though unlikely to succeed alone, given largely negative Taiwanese public sentiment toward the PRC); a massive cyberattack against Taiwan's civilian or military infrastructure; the military occupation of one or a number of Taiwan's offshore islands as a warning for Taipei to seek terms; an economic blockade of the island; a preemptive long-range attack against the Taiwanese armed forces; or a full-scale air and amphibious assault on Taiwan itself.

This scenario assumes that the US military response will be nominal and that of its allies nonexistent. The Western response will, in this case, consist of the usual array of trade, investment, and financial sanctions, although these have already been factored into Chinese scenario planning with relevant contingency planning already put in place to mitigate their impact. This would include preparing China's financial system to withstand any assault from what would then be a weakened US dollar and a weakened US capacity to mobilize the dollar-denominated international financial system to impose punitive financial sanctions. Chinese leaders feared this would happen over Hong Kong in 2020, but it failed to materialize. The UN will be silent, as China will have secured its position both in the Security Council and the General Assembly through a growing array of compliant member states, including a number from the developed world. The UN will conclude that the Taiwan issue is an internal matter for the Chinese people to resolve. The EU as an institution will likely remain neutral, particularly in the UK's absence and the ultimate geopolitical ambivalence of Germany and France on China-Taiwan.

The geostrategic standing and international moral authority of the United States would then collapse due to America's failure to defend a

334 | THE AVOIDABLE WAR

small but vibrant democracy with whom it had been a de facto ally for three-quarters of a century. American treaty allies' confidence in the credibility of US security guarantees would be undermined. It would likely be seen globally as America's Munich moment, much as the original effectively saw the end of the United Kingdom as a global great power.

However, the problem for China under this scenario would be the brutality of the military occupation that would be necessary to control an island with a mountainous geography, home to twenty-five million people with sophisticated skill sets, weapons, and a deep and widespread animosity to the Chinese Communist Party. China's occupation of Taiwan would make the violence inflicted on Tibet and the measures taken in Xinjiang look peaceful by comparison. Taiwan would become a gaping wound in China's side in the court of international public opinion for the remainder of the twenty-first century. It would also collapse whatever moral authority China had by that stage in the eyes of the international community. The world would brace itself for a return to an earlier atavistic age in which might made right, effective international institutions were little more than dreams, and the global rules-based order lay in tatters.

Scenario 2: The United States Defeats a Chinese Military Action Against Taiwan—A Second Midway

Beijing believes the likelihood of a full US military, economic, and cyber response to an attack on Taiwan is less probable than not. But its sense of strategic caution means this scenario remains the subject of active planning by the PLA. Based on public reporting of both American and Chinese war-gaming, the prospect that the US could actually decisively "win" such a war is also less likely than the alternative. But this scenario leaves aside the question of how any such "win" should be credibly defined. It could mean the "defeat" of all Chinese naval, air, and missile assets deployed across the Taiwan Strait; the cessation of Chinese military and paramilitary action against Taiwan; the withdrawal of any Chinese forces from Taiwan; the collapse of Xi Jinping's rule; or the collapse of the CCP regime itself as a result of the total loss of domestic political legitimacy that would flow from such a dramatic military failure.

Each of these possibilities brings up a further range of contingencies, such as how the US could possibly defeat Chinese forces committed to attacking Taiwan without also disabling the core of the Chinese command, control, and communications systems coordinating that attack. That would mean at least partially disabling the line of communication with the Central Military Commission in Beijing—thereby risking rapid and near-total escalation. This brings us to the impossible question, almost too ugly to contemplate, of escalation to a larger-scale conventional war with China, including the threat of nuclear confrontation.

The bottom line of this scenario is that given that the domestic political stakes in Beijing to secure victory would be higher than at any time since 1949 and given that the party's number-one priority has always been to remain in power, it is more likely than not that Xi Jinping would be predisposed to escalating a military conflict with America once one has begun in order to retain nationalist support. China is also deeply aware of the American public's limited appetite for foreign wars, having observed closely the impact of public opinion on US military engagements in Korea, Vietnam, Iraq, Syria, and Afghanistan. Xi in particular is a keen student of the Chinese action against American forces in Korea, where Washington preferred to leave in stalemate rather than commit US ground forces to fight in China. Xi would therefore likely use whatever means are at China's disposal to make a war with the US over the Taiwan Strait as long and as costly as possible, enabling him to develop and deploy an effective domestic political narrative that would rally nationalist sentiment and help mask any military defeats in the field. Xi is sufficiently realistic in his worldview to understand that an American victory in response to Chinese military aggression against Taiwan, or even a stalemate that left Taiwan out of Beijing's hands, would be terminal for his leadership. That is because returning Taiwan to Chinese sovereignty has occupied a bigger part of Xi Jinping's political mission and mandate than any of his post-Mao predecessors. A failure would, therefore, carry a high political price indeed.

Scenario 3: China Defeats US Forces Intervening Against a Chinese Military Action to Take Taiwan—An American Waterloo

As indicated above, based on the current balance of forces and published reports of the most recent war-gaming by both sides, an American loss, at present, represents the most probable outcome of a full-scale US conventional military intervention in support of Taiwan in the event of a Chinese armed attack on the island. According to military analysts that run regular simulations for the Pentagon (including the RAND Corporation), most scenarios would begin with a massive barrage of Chinese missiles targeting Taiwanese and American aircraft, ships, and infrastructure in Taiwan, Okinawa, and Guam, overwhelming American missile defenses. RAND analysts describe projected American losses as "staggering" and say the destruction of basing infrastructure would make it "exponentially more difficult to project power" into the region. While American attack submarines near enough to Taiwan to respond would have an advantage, they would only be able to sink a limited number of ships in China's amphibious invasion fleet, which would aim to land a PLA standing force of some 220,000 soldiers and marines at fifteen to twenty different beachheads on the island following lightning attacks by Chinese airborne and helicopter troops. The result: "Team Blue" would have "its ass handed to it for years," according to David Ochmanek, a former US deputy assistant secretary of defense, now at RAND. With the Taiwanese army generally considered to be undertrained, under-armed, and poorly organized, the US would likely only have a matter of one to two weeks to rush significant forces to Taiwan's defense and would find defending the island especially difficult without striking the Chinese mainland. The results of recent war-gaming underline Beijing's significant strategic success over the last two decades in closing the military capabilities gap in the theater with the US, China's growing numerical advantage in weapons systems most relevant to Taiwan scenarios, and the overwhelming value of immediate geographic proximity—as opposed to fighting the war from Guam, Honolulu, and Washington.

But this scenario also presents real risks for China. Military success could only be guaranteed by taking out critical American bases—including Guam—which would constitute an attack on the sovereign territory of the United States. This, in turn, would trigger the likelihood of large-scale military escalation by the United States, turning a Taiwan conflict into a general war in the western Pacific, with the possible participation of America's Asian treaty allies, including Japan (especially given that US forces in Okinawa would also likely be struck).

While the US has not committed to a no-first-use nuclear doctrine (which would not permit the use, or even the threatened use, of US nuclear forces even in the event of likely conventional military defeat), in practice—given historical evidence—the US would be extremely unlikely to respond with nuclear force. If the US declined to use nuclear weapons in Korea, Vietnam, and the Taiwan Strait crises of the 1950s when there was negligible risk of any form of nuclear retaliation, the US would not do so over Taiwan in the 2020s, when the escalation risks are much greater.

Under this scenario, whatever form a Chinese military defeat of the United States might take, the bottom line is that it would signal the end of the American Century—not just in Asia but for the rest of the world. America's treaty allies and security partners would then likely seek varying levels of strategic accommodation with Beijing, as governments across the world would conclude that US military power no longer offered effective protection against the next global superpower. Xi Jinping would be further emboldened to prosecute China's remaining outstanding territorial claims in the East China Sea, the South China Sea, and against India. Europe— historically predisposed toward maximizing its economic interests in China while regarding China's security challenges as an Asian rather than a European concern—would quickly return to its long-running strategic drift toward Beijing. Indeed, Europe may see China as its best long-term strategic leverage against Russia, given that Beijing sees Berlin, Paris, and Brussels—not Moscow—as major economic, trade, and investment partners. Moscow would likely become anxious at that point that a bold and confident China might even try to reclaim what was once Chinese territory lost to the Russian Far East during the czarist period. Beyond treaty allies and partners, the world under this scenario would gravitate quickly toward a global order anchored in Beijing, with global institutions increasingly compliant with Chinese foreign policy interests and Chinese values. A US military defeat by China over Taiwan would likely—over time—come to be seen as an American Waterloo, heralding the beginning of a new and uncertain Chinese Century.

Scenario 4: Chinese and American Military Stalemate over Taiwan—A New Korean Stalemate

This is a possible extension of scenario 2 above and is drawn from the lessons of the Korean War, which involved more than three years of protracted, seesawing military conflict with large-scale casualties and losses. It is difficult to project what such a stalemate would look like, given that China's military strategy of air-sea denial against US forces would probably tend toward more decisive outcomes in the maritime domain. But some military theorists suggest that if the US continues to invest in similar standoff area denial weapons (such as long-range anti-ship and antiair missiles), this could lead to the region's ocean surface and airspace becoming a no-man's-land, creating something similar to a maritime version of World War I's trench warfare.

Nonetheless, the political imperatives of survival for the Communist Party would never allow any formal concession of defeat. The party's deep experience as a revolutionary army, which faced near extinction at various times during its century-long history, would cause it to regroup and continue the fight once strategic circumstances changed. Additionally, its army grew up on guerrilla warfare, in which major battlefield wins are not required to prevail, only wearing down the enemy over time in what Mao called "protracted war." Therefore, for China, a military stalemate is an acceptable—albeit not a desirable—outcome. But it would be difficult to see Xi Jinping surviving for long under such circumstances, even if the party itself did. The same cannot be said for the United States, whose political system and culture is more predisposed toward final resolution and less tolerant of rolling ambiguity or drawn-out conflict, especially after the experiences of Afghanistan and Iraq. Still, American military commanders are likely to have options at their disposal for long-term, lower-level military engagement (such as a blockade on crucial Chinese shipping) that would also be capable of denying China a clean victory.

Scenario 5: Washington and Taipei Together Succeed in Deterring Beijing from the Use of Force Against Taiwan—Washington's Best-Case Scenario

In the best-case scenario for both Washington and the current government in Taipei, it is possible that the United States and Taiwan, through combined economic and technological strength, military preparedness, and diplomacy, successfully deter China from seeking to take Taiwan by force for the duration of Xi's period as China's paramount leader. This would depend on the US rebuilding its national economic power in the post-COVID period and sufficiently funding the US military to reassert American dominance in the air-sea gap across the Taiwan Strait. It would also require Taiwan to intelligently upgrade its military weaponry and training (supported, where necessary, by US arms sales) and cyber and civilian defenses in order to present a credible national deterrent against attack or internal subversion by the mainland.

Such a scenario would require Taiwanese diplomacy toward the mainland to become more dexterous than in the recent past, capable of exploring new forms of long-term political accommodation with Beijing while preserving Taiwan's democratic system and absolute political autonomy. It would also be premised on Beijing becoming more conscious of its constraints in the use of its national hard power. Such constraints might include any weakening of Chinese economic growth, new budgetary limitations on the future growth of Chinese military spending because of competing domestic spending priorities deemed necessary to preserve social harmony, or a failure to keep pace with critical new game-changing military technologies developed by the United States.

However, there is another possibility: that the US and Taiwan might succeed in deterring a Chinese military assault but fail to prevent a comprehensive cyberattack that disables much of Taiwan's critical infrastructure. This, in turn, would pose the question of how Washington and Taipei might retaliate in such a scenario while avoiding escalation into a general war. Therefore, a successful deterrence strategy under this scenario would need to prevent the full range of military and paramilitary actions by China and against Taiwan—not just physical armed attack, amphibious assault, invasion, and occupation.

Scenario 6: China and the United States Engage in a Limited War in the South China Sea—Another Gulf of Tonkin

Perhaps one of the most likely—albeit unintentional—scenarios would arise from a collision between Chinese and American naval vessels in the South China Sea. There have been a number of near misses in recent years, as Chinese naval commanders have maneuvered within yards of US destroyers at full speed. In each of these cases, the US vessel changed course to avoid a collision. This will not necessarily prevent collisions in the future. While there are bilateral military protocols effective from the Obama period aimed at both avoiding and managing incidents at sea, future collisions (particularly those involving the sinking of a vessel or the loss of life) could result in a general escalation between combatants within the wider area.

A second possibility could also involve Chinese vessels deliberately ramming or otherwise attacking non-US allied naval vessels conducting freedom-of-navigation operations in the South China Sea. China's unofficial media, such as the *Global Times*, have already threatened that this could happen to Australian naval vessels. While such an attack would likely trigger the mutual assistance provisions of America's formal defense treaties with its Asian treaty allies, China might regard this as a lesser risk than a direct assault on an American naval vessel. Besides, such an attack could be carried out with enough ambiguity that the struck vessel would not be able to prove it was not an accident (nor might they want to, given the balance of possibilities for escalation), making it more difficult for the US to retaliate. A similar situation could arise in the air, with Chinese military aircraft colliding with American or allied planes (as happened with the EP-3 incident in the South China Sea in 2001), although this would much more likely be a genuine accident.

The proliferation of Chinese coast guard, customs, fisheries, and intelligence vessels engaged in gray-zone activities to consolidate Chinese territorial and maritime claims across the South China Sea presents a growing number of possibilities for future incidents at sea. There are several hundred Chinese vessels engaged in such activities in the region at any one time, meaning the probability of incidents at sea continues to rise exponentially. These could also involve US treaty allies such as the Philippines, which has, together with Vietnam, the largest conflicting territorial and maritime claims against China (for these countries, the importance of these claims is not just theoretical, as they often center on areas crucial to their local fishing industries). Philippine vessels' response to Chinese actions would be less likely to adhere to the level of restraint adopted by the US Navy, which has standing encounters-at-sea protocols in place with their PLAN counterparts. If an anti-China populist wins the 2022 Philippine presidential election to replace the more China-friendly Duterte, who in 2021 announced his intention to retire, such confrontations between Manila and Beijing could easily escalate.

One further set of possibilities arises if China resumes its efforts to reclaim further "islands" in the South China Sea or to further militarize the seven it has already built. China's last reclamation exercise began under President Obama when Biden was vice president, and Beijing was delighted it was able to succeed without any real form of US military resistance. China may be inclined to push the envelope once more. But given the radical change in the political environment toward China in Washington since that time, it is much more probable that the US would provide a military response.

The critical factor in all of these subscenarios is that their trajectories and outcomes, beyond the immediate triggering incidents themselves, are all uncertain. It was in an effort to deal with these uncertainties that the Obama administration negotiated protocols with China on the management of both air and naval collisions referred to above. However, that was possible at a time when the bilateral political relationship, while fraught, was still stable. That is no longer the case. Furthermore, if any of these incidents did result in escalation, including the deployment of weapons systems, while it might be possible to quarantine any ensuing military exchange to combatants operating within the South China Sea, the integrated theater command structures governing both the Chinese and US militaries would make fighting a strictly limited war very difficult. All the political and military variables at play, including the nationalist sentiment that would come into force in both countries, would likely push in the direction of escalating rather than containing any such conflict.

Scenario 7: Conflict with Japan and the United States over Claims in the East China Sea

Under this scenario, the immediate combatants would be the two claimant states to the Senkaku / Diaoyu Dao Islands, located in the East China Sea: China and Japan. However, in the event of a conflict over the Senkaku Islands, Washington has already publicly declared that its mutual defense treaty with Japan would apply. This makes any incident involving the collision of Chinese and Japanese vessels and aircraft particularly dangerous. The risk of escalation is both real and immediate. If the US failed to militarily back Japan in any such conflict against China, it would automatically herald the demise of the US-Japan defense treaty and could trigger a new debate in Tokyo on the need for Japan to rapidly increase its relatively constrained military expenditure or even acquire its own nuclear deterrent as the only effective long-term security guarantee against China.

China is, nonetheless, wary of Japan's current military capabilities, particularly its naval capabilities, even in the absence of US intervention—as it would be politically catastrophic for the CCP to find itself in a war with its old foe Japan and not win decisively. Given the historical role Japan and its navy played in China's Century of Humiliation, to fail again would destroy the party's legitimacy in the eyes of the people, especially given the decades of triumphalist propaganda that China has been revived as a strong great power. Japan's expanding naval and air capabilities, combined with the real risk of American military intervention under the terms of their mutual defense treaty, are, therefore, likely to continue to act as an effective deterrent against any preemptive Chinese military action in this theater.

Despite this, the scope and intensity of Chinese and Japanese naval, air force, coast guard, and other deployments have been increasing and are considerably greater than those between China and the US in the South China Sea. China has ramped up the pace and scale of its incursions near the Senkaku / Diaoyu Dao Islands, with a total of eighty-eight Chinese vessels entering Japanese territorial waters in 2020, up from sixty-seven in 2018 and virtually zero before 2012. By November 2020, Chinese coast guard vessels entered and operated inside Japan's contiguous zone for a total of 283 straight days in 2020, setting a new annual record. Japanese officials emphasize that this pattern of behavior continued to accelerate, oblivious to the state of diplomatic engagement between Beijing and Tokyo at any given time.

Moreover, while Chinese strategists may regard the East China Sea as only the third-most important of its territorial claims, after Taiwan and the South China Sea, Senkaku / Diaoyu Dao is still referred to in Chinese strategic literature as one of China's core interests. In an ideal world, at least from Beijing's perspective, the East China Sea problem with Japan could wait until after China demonstrated the finite limits of American power over Taiwan and the South China Sea, on the assumption that American strategic failures in those two theaters would lessen Japanese political resolve to fight over the third. However, the history of international relations tells us that crises are rarely resolved in such a neat and linear sequence.

Chinese strategic thought normally cautions against provoking incidents across several fronts simultaneously, but China's decision in 2020 to increase the tempo of its activities across all its disputed boundaries (the East China Sea, the South China Sea, the Taiwan Strait, and the Indian border) as well as domestically (in Xinjiang, Inner Mongolia, and Hong Kong) provides a cautionary tale to us all. Indeed, the experience of 2020 points to a more fundamental factor at play in Chinese politics and geopolitics: that if the party believes it is under threat at home (as it did in the first half of 2020 due to COVID-19), its default instinct is to demonstrate resolute strength abroad in order to convey a global message that Chinese strategic resolve will not falter despite any internal political pressures.

History also suggests that any incident in Sino-Japanese relations is capable of rapid political escalation, given that the previous toxicity of the relationship dating from much of the twentieth century is still capable of triggering raw, nationalist responses on both sides. The bottom line under this scenario is that while the Sino-Japanese dispute over the East China Sea may receive less public attention in Washington and the West than Taiwan and the South China Sea simply because it is relatively well managed between Beijing and Tokyo at a diplomatic level, the East China Sea remains inherently volatile. And if war were to erupt over the East China Sea, given that it would likely involve the three largest economies in the world, the global consequences would be profound, potentially sending Asian economic growth into a tailspin for a decade.

Scenario 8: Conflict Between China and the United States over North Korea

This may seem a remote possibility, but the absence of sustained international media attention on the future of the North Korean nuclear program since President Trump's public relations–driven diplomacy at his 2018 Singapore summit with Kim Jong-un does not mean that the problem of North Korea has disappeared. It has not. Nor should we forget that the only time Chinese Communist forces have fought American troops was on the Korean Peninsula, when China judged that its immediate national security interests were at stake because of the presence of US forces near its land border. From Beijing's perspective, there are immutable principles of strategic geography to consider when it comes to the Korean Peninsula, including a deep neuralgia about any adversary being able to threaten its continental territorial integrity. These concerns are reinforced by China's historical view that Korea lies within the ancient Confucian world—and now within China's legitimate modern sphere of influence. For these reasons, Beijing likely retains a series of redlines regarding any new US strategy toward North Korea.

But now that Trump's rolling circus act with Kim Jong-un has come to an end, China may seek to help (or at least appear to help) the US apply further pressure on Pyongyang to dismantle its nuclear and/or missile program. However, if North Korea refuses, China will not apply any effective energy supply sanctions against the North to force any policy change. Beijing refused to do so in the past when Xi's relationship with Kim was in bad repair. And after several years of improved interpersonal relations between the two leaders, Xi will be even less likely to do anything dramatic that would worsen his hard-won relationship with Kim. Xi's bottom line is that as long as Kim does not point his missiles at China, his weapons program doesn't fundamentally harm China's wider national security interests. A North Korean nuclear capability would likely be exclusively targeted at China's strategic adversaries: the US, Japan, South Korea, and even Australia. Complicating these countries' threat environment may enhance China's overall interests rather than the reverse.

In particular, China is adamantly opposed to the idea of a unified Korean state on its borders. With the possible exception of Russia, Beijing does not see any of its other neighbors as sufficiently strong to be able to challenge China's national security, foreign policy, or economic interests. China has no interest in changing the political status quo on the peninsula, even if it resulted in a neutral Korea and certainly not if it involved a pro-American, unified Korea. China's view would be unlikely to change even if a unified Korea was no longer formally allied to the US. China may seek to position itself in the future as South Korea's best security guarantee against any nuclear threat from the North, with Beijing working to limit Pyongyang's nuclear expansion in exchange for continued economic support for the regime. Ironically, China, rather than the US, would then become South Korea's nuclear guarantor.

For these reasons, in the absence of any other negotiating leverage applied by the US toward Beijing or any political implosion in Pyongyang, the Biden administration will discover that, on the central question of the elimination of North Korea's existing nuclear arsenal and missile program, Xi Jinping is unlikely to be helpful. In fact, given the general deterioration in the US-China relationship since 2018, Xi may actively seek to hinder any progress through his newfound warmer relationship with Kim Jong-un. This would represent a further setback in the US-China relationship but in itself would be unlikely to result in any form of confrontation on the peninsula.

However, should Kim recommence his nuclear and/or long-range missile testing program, the US–North Korea relationship would immediately be thrust into a new crisis. The US would have to confront the reality of allowing North Korea to become a full-fledged nuclear weapons state, able to threaten nuclear blackmail against South Korea, Japan, Australia, and potentially other allies as well as the United States itself. This, in turn, would trigger regional debates across Asia on the need to develop independent nuclear deterrents in case the US nuclear umbrella proved insufficiently reliable—a different sort of strategic nightmare for China. Any such decision by the North could thus trigger several unforeseen consequences across Asia.

An alternative scenario would be for the US to militarily preempt any such effort by North Korea to secure a full-blown nuclear and missile capability. However, if this happened, it would likely result in large-scale military action by the North against the South, with the real risk of beginning a second Korean War. Once again, direct Chinese military engagement could result in support of the North against the South—including the South's principal ally, the United States. In 2020, such scenarios may seem fanciful, but that is based on the absence of a genuine North Korean effort to achieve a full nuclear break-out and produce nuclear-tipped missiles in large numbers. Any resumption of hard-line American diplomacy toward North Korea could prompt just that. Biden's imperative is therefore to convince Beijing to forestall any such action by Pyongyang.

Scenario 9: Xi Jinping's Regional and Global Strategy Succeeds in the Absence of Military Confrontation with the United States—Xi's Optimal Plan

Under this scenario, by decade's end and in the lead-up to the Twenty-Second Party Congress in 2032, Xi would have achieved—or come close to achieving—all his major domestic and foreign policy objectives to the point of establishing China's regional and global preeminence. This would be accomplished without China facing any major political or economic setbacks or having to fire a shot. This is certainly Xi Jinping's optimal plan. To achieve it, the United States and its Asian and European allies would need to conclude that the sheer critical mass of China's strategic, economic, and technological weight had given it unstoppable momentum and that to arrest or even slow down its ascension would require a crippling expenditure of blood and treasure.

What would Xi's definition of success be under this scenario? Certainly, Xi's political position would be as secure as Mao's had been during the latter's last decade in power, having "rectified" all his potential opponents within the party and having established a watertight surveillance state. Xi's economic model—while delivering suboptimal economic growth—would have still managed to stay sufficiently high, through rising private consumption and public investment, to narrowly avoid the middle-income trap and create the largest consumer market in history, drawing the rest of the world into its economic orbit. Xi's China would have achieved an early peak in carbon emissions by 2025 without upsetting domestic economic output and established a trajectory for reaching carbon neutrality as soon as 2050—becoming a leader and no longer a laggard on global climate-change action. Hong Kong would have been calmed and made compliant through the National Security Law, while its economy would have been absorbed as but one part of a Greater Bay Area economic zone incorporating Shenzhen and the rest of the Pearl River Delta. Xinjiang would also have been pacified, with no significant tangible response mustered by the West.

Taiwan would have concluded that the US would not defend it, and Taiwanese domestic politics would include those conducting secret negotiations with Beijing on some form of greater Chinese confederation in the face of a China prepared to make a decisive move to take the island before 2035. On the South China Sea, China would have concluded its code-of-conduct negotiations with ASEAN and operationalized its first major joint maritime resource extraction projects with individual Southeast Asian states, thus securing de facto, if not yet de jure, control of the South China Sea. China would also have declared an air defense identification zone over the South China Sea of the type it declared in the East China Sea in 2013. These combined actions would have increasingly rendered future FONOPS in the area futile in the eyes of regional states, as they became increasingly resigned to China's overall maritime and territorial claims. In the East China Sea, partly because of Japanese political and military resilience and despite the continued escalation in Chinese deployments to Senkaku / Diaoyu Dao, an uneasy status quo would have been maintained without conflict.

South Korea would have moved more into China's strategic and economic orbit, creating even deeper splits in South Korean politics between right and left, while Xi Jinping succeeded in persuading North Korea to refocus its military threats away from Seoul and toward Tokyo and Washington instead. North Korea would have achieved its independent nuclear deterrent without an American preemptive strike. Center-left governments in Seoul would also have requested a reduction in US forces on the peninsula. Xi would have cut a deal over the Sino-Indian border with India's then leader, perhaps leveraging the threat of full-scale military action to secure the border on China's terms. China would then turn India into a new mass consumer market for Chinese goods and services while opening the Chinese market to India through a new free trade agreement aimed at finally weaning Delhi away from its strategic engagement with the US, Japan, and Australia.

China would have become the largest economy in the world by a large margin, thereby accelerating international acceptance of the reality of China as the next global economic superpower. China would also have secured military dominance over the United States across East Asia and the western Pacific, having sustained the pace of its military modernization program, completed its regional reorganization, and sustained its naval expansion plan. More broadly, across Asia, China would have leveraged its influence to succeed in joining the CPTPP trade agreement, while the United States continued to languish on the outside due to continuing protectionist political sentiments. By decade's end, once the Chinese economy had surpassed that of the United States, Xi would also likely have given the green light to liberalize the Chinese capital account, including the floating of the RMB and the full and open circulation of the digital RMB globally, putting it on a path to become the preferred currency for global digital commerce. Xi would have scaled back the financial scope of the Belt and Road Initiative, turning it into a more sustainable infrastructure investment program while still harnessing it to bring BRI economies within the Chinese digital world.

In Europe, China would have built on its 2020 China-EU Investment Treaty (by then unfrozen and successfully ratified) with a comprehensive free trade agreement as it continued to peel the continent away from the United States on trade, investment, technology, capital markets, and ultimately digital commerce. As for the rest of the world, Africa would have progressively become China's long-term source of needed commodities and its next big consumer market after India. Brazil would be developed as China's long-term supplier of its iron-ore needs, Beijing having concluded that Australia was no longer secure because of its umbilical security relationship with the United States. Perhaps Afghanistan and central Asia, successfully kept stable, would also contribute their vast mineral reserves to the Chinese economic machine. And finally, in what remained of the UN and the Bretton Woods institutions, China would have become the single largest source of finance for much of the global multilateral system, which by this time would have become increasingly compliant to Chinese interests and values as a result. Consequently, the UN Human Rights Commission would have been redirected toward US and Western failures rather than examining the political excesses of authoritarian states, and China would have succeeded at entrenching its set of global human rights norms that privileged collective economic development over individual rights.

What is the likelihood of such a scenario coming to pass? On the balance of probabilities, Xi's current prospects for success appear reasonable. However, this outcome depends on three critical variables. First, the success or failure of Xi's adjustment of China's domestic economic model in generating sufficient long-term, sustainable growth while avoiding social instability and also funding China's large-scale military needs. Second, the success or failure of China's new national technology strategy in closing the gap between Beijing and Washington on the critical technologies of the future—particularly artificial intelligence, semiconductors, and quantum computing. And finally, the ability or inability of the US system of divided democratic government to successfully rebuild American power at home and harness the collective energies of American allies abroad in order to meet the China challenge.

The jury is still out on the first and second of these. On the third (at least at the time of writing), the odds appear to lie with China. America and much of the rest of the collective West appear to have lost confidence in themselves, their mission, and their future. The danger of this loss of common purpose is highlighted when contrasted with the ruthless discipline of China's Leninist state and the softening economic seduction of access to the world's largest market. In many respects, the greatest asset the CCP has is its ability to bluff the rest of the world into believing that China is much bigger, more powerful, and more fiscally solvent than it really is. In doing so, China successfully masked many of its domestic failures, weaknesses, and vulnerabilities from the rest of the world. To some extent, this masking strategy continues to succeed today, always capitalizing on a residual Western gullibility. Now, however, the gap between the image and the reality of Chinese power is much narrower than it was before, although a significant gap still exists.

Scenario 10: Xi Jinping Fails to Achieve His National, Regional, and Global Ambitions—A Defeated and Humiliated Xi

It would be easy to assume that this scenario is simply the reverse of the previous. To some extent, that is true. But it would also involve Xi being judged harshly for failing on a wider set of domestic and foreign policy objectives. This would include an outbreak of factionalism within the party as a reaction to the rolling series of party purges Xi has instigated since 2013. But more importantly, it would be defined by economic stagnation and static income levels, rising unemployment, and a once-vibrant entrepreneurial class now on a private investment strike. One further liability would be China's long-standing problem of the stability of its financial system, given a total debt-to-GDP ratio already standing at around 300 percent. Slowing growth would compound the problem of unsustainable corporate debt, and bank liquidity and the capacity of the system to sustain the collapse of individual financial institutions would be insufficient. This has long been the ticking time bomb within the Chinese financial system, fueled by debt-driven growth, threatening those whose projections for the future of the Chinese economy have always been naively bullish. Such a financial crisis—should it occur—would cause governments around the world to reappraise the scale and sustainability of the China economic miracle, on which a raft of foreign policy and security policy judgments are being made. Furthermore, if China's political leadership continued to balk at the prospect of liberalizing the capital account and allowing its currency to be freely traded before decade's end, it would undermine China's efforts to replace the United States as the recognized center of the global financial system. Another major blow to Xi Jinping would be a significant forced retrenchment of the BRI, were it to become financially unsustainable, given that it is one of Xi's longest-running signature personal projects.

In foreign and security policy, Xi's ambitions would fail as a result of the US delivering a substantive, comprehensive international strategy that responded effectively to Chinese pressure and included all America's major treaty allies and major economies, such as India, Indonesia, and Mexico—a situation that the Biden administration took a step closer to achieving in June 2021 with a closer alignment on China through the G7. Under those circumstances, Xi would be critiqued internally for having violated Deng Xiaoping's strategic wisdom by being too assertive too soon in China's development, thereby inducing a strategic reaction before China was able to prevail. Any movement to transform the Quad into a full-fledged quadripartite security treaty, resulting in Chinese strategic encirclement, would be criticized in the same terms among Chinese political elites. But as disastrous as that would be, any rapprochement between Russia and the US would create the very greatest levels of alarm in Beijing, given that China's freedom of strategic maneuver has, for decades, been predicated on the security of its long northern border.

On human rights, failure would come from China being indicted before international tribunals for its treatment of its many ethnic minorities but particularly in Xinjiang. This would be seen as a major loss of face for both the party and the country. Further failure would result from large-scale protests in Hong Kong or elsewhere and any bloody repression of such unrest. Chinese leadership legitimacy will also be affected by international reactions to the 2022 Beijing Winter Olympics. China's political memory of the Beijing 2008 Olympics was that it was an outstanding success as the country's global coming-out party as a respected great power. Global political controversy surrounding the 2022 Beijing Winter Olympics will be compared and contrasted with the success of 2008. Negative international political reaction against Xi Jinping's policies that generates international boycott activity will be used as part of the internal critique of Xi for having unnecessarily damaged China's international reputation compared to 2008.

But the ultimate failure for Xi Jinping, as noted above, would arise from a military crisis with the United States that resulted in any form of Chinese defeat. This would be especially terminal if it occurred over Taiwan, as Xi's colleagues and competitors would round on him for producing a political and strategic catastrophe. The same would in all likelihood apply over any disastrous escalation of a crisis in the South China Sea. That is why any decision by China to escalate would likely be deeply calibrated against the probability of Chinese success and/or American retreat. The consequences for Xi for any serious miscalculation in this regard would be career-ending—or worse. It is impossible to attach any degree of probability to this Xi-Jinping-fails hypothesis; there are multiple permutations and combinations of what such a failure might consist of. And at this stage, comprehensive failure would appear to be more of a possibility than a probability. It is, nonetheless, one that haunts all Chinese political leaders, given the stark consequences that flow from perceived failure.

Conclusion

None of these scenarios seeks to be definitive. It is not possible to predict which of these scenarios—or which combination of them—may come to pass during the decade ahead. There are simply too many moving parts in the overall strategic equation. But if there is no *sustained* counterstrategy from the United States over the next several US administrations that effectively rebuilds American power, reenergizes US alliances, and creates a credible global economic alternative to the long-term gravitational pull of the Chinese market, the overall trend lines appear to favor Xi Jinping's China.

However, of all the moving parts at play in these scenarios, there are four in particular that should be analyzed most closely: three domestic economic factors and one external, where the policy settings lie largely in Chinese rather than American hands. The first remains the long-term sustainability of the emerging Chinese economic growth model, given Xi's move to the left on Chinese economic policy, and the uncertain effects this will have on private-sector business confidence. The second is the extent to which China's rapid demographic decline brings about earlier-than-anticipated impacts on domestic consumption, labor market cost, and government finances. The third is whether China can succeed in closing the semiconductor manufacturing gap between itself and the US and its allies, given that silicon chips underpin the future drivers of the global digital economy and military technology, including the unfolding artificial intelligence revolution. Finally, it remains to be seen how China will resolve its current internal dispute between its rising wolf warrior generation and its older traditional cadre of professional diplomats on how Chinese diplomacy should be conducted. How this is answered will determine whether Beijing continues to unite the liberal-democratic world against it or whether a return to an earlier, more positive pattern of global diplomatic engagement will allow China to fracture that coalition. Taken together with the most critical variable of all—the future trajectory of US strategy toward China—these five factors will do much to determine the outcome of the great strategic race between Washington and Beijing over the course of the next decade.

The problem for all of us—Americans, Chinese, and the rest of the world—is that five of the ten scenarios outlined above involve one form or another of major armed conflict. Wars radically change the course of human history, often in radically unpredictable directions—for example, the collapse of three global empires with world war and the rise of fascism and Bolshevism as a result. The international anarchy of the interwar years came with the absence of any effective international system, leading ultimately to World War II and then the rise of the US-led rules-based international order following World War II and its triumph in the Cold War over the Soviet Union. International developments of this scale were not in any way predictable beforehand, determined instead by the chaos of the battlefield.

Such profound geopolitical and military unpredictability should therefore weigh heavily on the minds of decision makers in both Washington and Beijing. As should the unknowable human and financial costs of war.

As should the impact on global economic development as the world rapidly tilts toward being polarized into two camps and then crisis, conflict, and war, resulting in international business confidence being undermined, trade and investment flows halted, and global financial markets crashed—all with profound consequences for the real economy, employment, and living standards. For these reasons alone, it would be worthwhile for leaders to consider what measures might be available that could manage the deeply engrained competitive impulses of China and the United States, thereby maximizing the prospects for continued peace.

17

★ ★ ★ ★ ★

Navigating an Uncertain Future: The Case for Managed Strategic Competition

This book began as a letter to two friends: the Chinese and American peoples, not just the governments that led them at different points of time. Over nearly half a century, I have come to respect and admire both these nations—warts and all—including their history, technology, art, literature, aesthetics, and contributions to the wider world of ideas, philosophy, and human spirituality. Foreigners can never claim to know another country intimately. But they can *begin* to do so if they put both their hearts and minds to the task, seek to understand the language and culture of the other, and spend time living and working among them. In my case, I have spent half a decade in near full-time study of Chinese language and history. I lived in mainland China, Hong Kong, and Taiwan for three years earlier in my career and in America for the last seven. I have also engaged with both these countries in multiple capacities over the years—through diplomacy, business, politics, scholarship, and, of course, many, many personal friendships. I believe I have been received in both capitals over the years as an honest, forthright, and constructive interlocutor. My views have not always been welcomed, but on many occasions, they have been. And they may have helped at the margins in navigating shared futures between these two great countries on some of the bilateral differences that have emerged between them. As I said in my speech at Peking University all those years ago, I have sought to act as a *zhengyou* (an honest friend, prepared to speak his mind privately while not seeking to humiliate publicly) to both sides in this most important and impossible of relationships.

My experience of China and America has not resulted in political capture by either, although my critics have attacked me at different times for being an apologist for each. Australians, at their best, have about them a gritty independence. We are psychologically incapable of bending the knee to any higher authority—perhaps the cumulative impact of our convict heritage and our abiding disrespect for our English jailors. And while I may not have been the best of Australians, the record demonstrates I have from time to time been deeply critical of both China and America, particularly during their periodic lurches toward the political extreme. My view of China's and America's futures are not shaped by some misty-eyed view of what these countries might once have been but rather by their contemporary and imperfect realities. Even less is my view of Washington and Beijing the product of some artificially constructed symmetry, let alone synthesis between mythical or manufactured conceptions of East and West. International political reality is more complex than that.

Instead, my views are based on a lifetime of observation and experience of these two radically different cultures whose peoples nonetheless aspire to remarkably similar futures: prosperity for their families, the best education for their children, the opportunity to build their businesses with a minimum of government interference, respect from others for their extraordinary individual and national achievements, and a desire to live in reasonable peace with their neighbors.

Neither country has any long-standing tradition of having vast overseas empires that the Europeans perfected over five hundred years and that left the rest of the world variously traumatized, arbitrarily divided, or on the continuing verge of civil war. For two great powers such as China and the United States—which, at different periods in their histories, have been the most powerful on earth—the fact that they chose not to colonize the world beyond their shores but instead to simply trade with it is no small thing. Certainly, they expanded their continental peripheries, often violently. And both have been determined to have around them neighboring states that are as compliant to their core national interests as possible. But, by and large, both China and the United States have been big enough, vast enough, and complex enough to absorb most of their political and economic energies within their national boundaries rather than dreaming of a larger territorial empire beyond.

Yet despite these similarities between the *peoples* and *nations* these two governments represent, I also have a realistic view of the difficulties that lie ahead in forging any common strategic future between them. Whatever strategic trust may have existed in the relationship in the past is long gone. And the reasons for this are not whimsical, ephemeral, or even entirely about the personal influence of Xi Jinping on China. They are deeply structural.

A Clash of Strategic Perceptions

For Americans, Xi Jinping's leadership represents a radical change in China's official strategic approach to the world. It was willful blindness that kept them from understanding that the idea that China was headed for an American-style democracy was always a Western fantasy. What Xi has done is to make clear that the CCP has no intention of ever transforming China into a more liberal democratic state. Instead, as we have seen, he is adopting a model of authoritarian capitalism that is more tightly controlled, less market-driven, and more mercantilist than his recent predecessors'. Beyond all this, Xi has fanned the flames of an aggrieved Chinese nationalism that is increasingly explicitly anti-American. Americans see a Chinese leader determined to alter the strategic and territorial status quo in the western Pacific, establish a Chinese sphere of influence across the Eastern Hemisphere, and dilute—and eventually remove—America's military presence from the wider region.

Across the wider world, Washington has concluded that Xi is exporting his domestic political model to developing countries and leveraging the global gravitational pull of the Chinese economy to maximize China's political and foreign policy influence across every region. In the process, they see China building support for a future international system that is more accommodating of Chinese national interests and values and more hostile to the West. They also see these changes in China's international behavior being underpinned by an economically, militarily, and technologically powerful Chinese state capable of accomplishing Xi Jinping's China Dream of returning China to global superpower status. In other words, in the American view, Xi Jinping's China is on a self-selected collision course with the United States. This means that Washington, as a matter of strategic logic, must either submit to Chinese interests, accommodate them, or actively seek to resist and—if possible—defeat them.

The view from Beijing is, of course, radically different: that there is nothing wrong with China's political-economic model and that while Beijing offers it to others in the developing world to emulate, it is not "forcing" it on any other state. By contrast, China points to the considerable failings of Western democracies in dealing with core challenges, such as the pandemic, political polarization, and the gathering momentum of anti-globalization. Beijing argues that China has modernized its military only to secure its self-defense and that this naturally includes its long-standing territorial claims, most particularly including over Taiwan. Beijing makes no apology for using the gravitational power of the Chinese economy to advance its national interests across the board. Nor does it apologize for using its newfound global power to rewrite the rules of the international system and the institutions that comprise it, arguing that this is precisely what a victorious America did after World War II.

And while strategic caution is warranted from Beijing's perspective for the decade ahead, as the regional and global balance of power gradually shifts in China's favor, there will be increasing opportunities for China to push the envelope against the United States and its allies without risking the uncertain outcomes of security crises, clashes, or even war. Xi Jinping, while impatient for progress, nonetheless believes that time and momentum are on Beijing's side, as the correlation of forces becomes increasingly advantageous to China. This means that Xi can achieve his objectives without China firing a shot. Or if military action is ultimately required, engage only when victory is assured.

The Death of Strategic Trust

Clearly, strategic trust cannot magically be conjured up, let alone reconstructed between the US and China. This is because the two countries' core national interests and values are in direct conflict with each other. Political and diplomatic urging by well-intentioned third parties for Washington and Beijing to resume previous patterns of communication and engagement established back in the Bush and Obama periods will fall on deaf ears. Pious hopes that greater dialogue between the two sides will somehow remove continuing misunderstandings concerning each other's capabilities, intentions, and actions are simply naive. The bottom line is that fifty years after the resumption of high-level political and diplomatic contact between China and the United States, each side has already adopted a hard-baked view of the other side's strategic intentions—one that is not swayed by anything the other might say in public but only by the concrete actions they can physically observe being taken. These conclusions will not be massaged away by a cocktail of summits, press statements, or even new diplomatic communiqués. None of these can any longer mask the fundamental dynamics of a relationship that remains anchored in the hard calculus of the balance of power and a brutal assessment of how far the other party is willing to go to change it.

There is an enduring view in Washington that all Chinese diplomacy is based on deception. In this view, any protocols Beijing might agree to in order to stabilize strategic or economic tensions with Washington would ultimately prove to be worthless. China's party-state, backed by a Chinese military that answers directly to Xi, is, in this view, embarked on a long-term strategy from which it is not about to change course—and certainly not because of some new understanding reached between the Chinese Foreign Ministry and the US State Department. Such things are assumed to be designed for cosmetic, or at most tactical, purposes. American hawks point to the CCP's long history of broken agreements with various domestic and foreign partners, extending back to the party's assurances to Washington about power-sharing with the nationalists in 1946, just prior to unleashing a second and successful civil war in 1947. Such deceptions are seen as the institutional hallmarks of a Leninist party for whom lying to class enemies at home or abroad is not only normal but also laudatory. High-minded calls to rebuild strategic trust will therefore have negligible impact on *real* decisions about strategy to be made in either capital.

Hard Policy Choices

The burden of this book so far has been to identify the difficult policy choices faced by each side in what has become a profoundly dangerous, competitive strategic relationship—choices that will either push these countries closer to crisis, conflict, or war or, alternatively, steer them away from the abyss. The book's purpose is to identify what minimum strategic framework might still be established between the two countries to prevent war. I call this overall framework managed strategic competition. It is anchored in three core propositions:

- First, the United States and China must both develop a clear understanding of the other's irreducible strategic redlines in order to help prevent conflict through miscalculation. Each side must be persuaded to conclude that enhancing strategic predictability advantages both countries, strategic deception is futile, and strategic surprise is just plain dangerous.
- Second, the two sides would then channel the burden of strategic rivalry into a competitive race to enhance their military, economic, and technological capabilities. Properly constrained, such competition aims to deter armed conflict rather than tempt either side to risk all by prosecuting what would become a dangerous and bloody war with deeply unpredictable results. Such strategic competition

would also enable both sides to maximize their political, economic, and ideological appeal to the rest of the world. Its strategic rationale would be that the most competitive power would ultimately prevail by becoming (or remaining) the world's foremost power—with Armageddon avoided.

- Third, this framework would create the political space necessary for the two countries to continue to engage in strategic cooperation in a number of defined areas where both their global *and* national interests would be enhanced by such collaboration—and indeed undermined by the absence of an agreed, collaborative approach.

Of course, it is important to be realistic. No joint strategic framework can, in itself, prevent war. But properly constructed and based on clarity, transparency, and most importantly credible deterrence, it may significantly reduce the risk of it. Such a framework would also keep alive the possibility of political change, the evolution of each side's worldviews, or the emergence of new ways of thinking about old problems (both conceptual and even technological) and better managing great power relations in the complex world of the twenty-first century. Most importantly, it may cause both China and the United States to conclude that after more than 150 years of one form of political engagement or another, they are not destined for war.

The Concept of Managed Strategic Competition

Many doubt that US and Chinese leaders can find their way to a framework to manage their diplomatic relations, military operations, and activities in cyberspace within agreed parameters that would maximize stability, avoid accidental escalation, and make room for both competitive and collaborative dynamics in the relationship. But I argue that the two countries need to consider something akin to the procedures and mechanisms that the United States and the Soviet Union put in place to govern their relations after the Cuban Missile Crisis. In the case of the US and China, however, it would be preferable if this conclusion could be reached without first going through the near-death experience of a barely avoided war. Managed strategic competition would obviously involve establishing certain hard limits on each country's security policies. It would also allow for full and open competition in the diplomatic, economic, and ideological realms. It would also make it possible for Washington and Beijing to cooperate in certain areas, through bilateral arrangements and also multilateral forums. Such a framework would be difficult to construct, but not impossible. More importantly, the alternatives are more likely to be catastrophic.

The real question for both Washington and Beijing is whether they can conduct this high level of strategic competition within agreed-on parameters that would reduce the risk of a crisis and armed conflict. In theory, it is possible, but in practice, the near-complete erosion of trust between the two has radically increased the degree of difficulty. Indeed, as noted earlier, many in the US national security community believe that the CCP has no compunction about lying or hiding its true intentions in order to deceive its adversaries. In this view, Chinese diplomacy aims only to tie opponents' hands in order to buy time for Beijing's military, security, and intelligence machinery to achieve superiority and establish new facts on the ground. To win broad support from US foreign policy elites, therefore, any concept of managed strategic competition will need to include a stipulation by both parties to base any new rules of the road on a reciprocal practice of verification.

The idea of managed strategic competition is anchored in a deeply realist view of the global order. It accepts that states will continue to seek security by building a balance of power in their favor while recognizing that, in doing so, they are likely to create security dilemmas for other states whose fundamental interests may be disadvantaged by their actions. The trick in this case is to reduce these risks as competition intensifies by jointly crafting a limited number of rules of the road that can help prevent war. The rules would enable each side to compete vigorously across all policy and geographical domains. But if either side breaches the rules, then all bets are off, and it's back to all the hazardous uncertainties of the law of the strategic jungle.

Strategic Redlines

The first step to building such a framework would be to identify a number of immediate steps that each side can take for substantive dialogue to proceed and then agree to a limited number of hard limits. For example, both sides could abstain from cyberattacks targeting critical infrastructure. Washington could return to strictly adhering to the One-China policy, especially by ending the Trump administration's provocative and unnecessary high-level visits to Taipei. For its part, Beijing could dial back its recent pattern of provocative military exercises, deployments, and maneuvers in the Taiwan Strait. In the South China Sea, Beijing could undertake to not reclaim or militarize any more islands and commit to respecting full freedom of navigation and overflight. For its part, the United States and its allies could then (and only then) reduce the number of operations they carry out in the area. Similarly, China and Japan could cut back their military deployments in the East China Sea by mutual agreement over time. These agreements would need to be developed through private diplomacy rather than public declarations. The objective is for each side, over time, to have a clear idea internally of what the other side's irreducible redlines are in these four critical security domains and—most critically—to understand that if these redlines are breached, large-scale retaliatory action would likely ensue. While it may seem counterintuitive to some, there should be no doctrinal statement that seeks to publicly define what these redlines might be. To do so would be self-limiting, self-defeating, and yield far too much influence to the court of domestic political opinion within each country, either real or contrived, on whether a breach had occurred.

Strategic Competition

If both sides could agree on those stipulations, each would then have to accept that the other will still try to maximize its advantages while stopping short of breaching the agreed strategic guardrails. Washington and Beijing would continue to compete for strategic and economic influence across the various regions of the world. They would keep seeking reciprocal access to each other's markets and would still take retaliatory measures when such access was denied. They would still compete in foreign investment markets, technology markets, capital markets, and currency markets. And they would likely carry out a global contest for hearts and minds—with Washington stressing the importance of democracy, open economies, and human rights and Beijing highlighting the advantages of authoritarian capitalism and what it calls the China development model.

Strategic Cooperation

However, even amid escalating competition, there would still be political space for cooperation in a number of critical areas. This occurred even between the United States and the Soviet Union at the height of the Cold War. It should certainly be possible between the United States and China when the stakes, at least at this stage, are not nearly as high. Aside from collaborating on climate change, the two countries could conduct bilateral nuclear arms control negotiations, including on mutual ratification of the Comprehensive Nuclear Test Ban Treaty, and work toward an agreement on the acceptable military applications of artificial intelligence. They could cooperate on North Korean nuclear disarmament and on preventing Iran from acquiring nuclear weapons. They could undertake a series of confidence-building measures across the Indo-Pacific region, such as coordinated natural disaster response and humanitarian missions. They could also work together to improve global financial stability, especially by agreeing to reschedule the debts of developing countries hit hard by natural or medical disasters. And they could jointly build a better system for distributing future vaccines to the developing world.

Diplomatic Machinery to Make Managed Strategic Competition Work

These lists of possible redlines and potential areas for competition and cooperation are far from exhaustive. But the strategic rationale for each of these three sets of agendas is the same: it is better for both countries to operate within a joint framework of managed competition than to have unmanaged competition with no rules at all. The framework would need to be negotiated between a designated and trusted high-level representative of Biden and a Chinese counterpart close to Xi. Only a direct, high-level channel of that sort could lead to confidential understandings that could be respected by both sides. These two people would also become the points of contact when violations occurred (as they are bound to from time to time) and the ones to direct the enforcement of consequences for any such breaches. Over time, a minimum level of strategic trust may reemerge from this minimum level of predictability. Both sides may then discover that the benefits of continued collaboration on common planetary challenges, such as climate change, could then inspire the confidence necessary to tackle more difficult areas of the relationship.

There will be many who will criticize this approach as naive. However, their responsibility is to come up with something better. I am yet to see one. Both the United States and China, whatever their governments may say publicly, are currently in search of a formula to manage their relationship for the dangerous years ahead. The hard truth is that no relationship can ever be managed unless there is a basic agreement between the parties on the terms of that management.

Measures of Success—or Failure—Under a Managed Strategic Competition Framework

What would be the measures of success (or failure) for such a joint strategic framework? One sign of success would be if by 2030, the US and China have avoided a military crisis or conflict across the Taiwan Strait or a debilitating cyberattack. A convention banning various forms of robotic warfare would be a clear victory, as would their acting immediately together—and with the World Health Organization—to combat the next pandemic. But perhaps the most important sign of success would be an open and vigorous campaign by each for global support for the ideas, values, and problem-solving approaches that their respective systems offer—without ever trying to impose those systems by force.

The most demonstrable example of a failed approach to managed strategic competition would be over Taiwan. If Xi were to calculate that he could call Washington's bluff by unilaterally breaking out of whatever agreement had been privately reached with Washington, the world would find itself in a world of pain. In one fell swoop, such a crisis would rewrite the future of the global order.

How Could China Navigate Its US Relationship Under Managed Strategic Competition?

So how might China respond to a framework of managed strategic competition? The short answer is "with some difficulty." This would be particularly the case with the first element of the framework: dealing with China's strategic redlines, including the new constraints such a framework could impose on Chinese operational behavior concerning Taiwan, the South and East China Seas, and cyber. Beijing has long deployed gray-zone tactics writ large in these various security domains, where the PLA (or its paramilitary surrogates) have pressured and probed American, Taiwanese, Japanese, and other allied patterns of response over time. This has been designed to serve three sets of objectives. First, to provide active training for Chinese maritime forces, given that the Chinese navy has had no war-fighting experience since the birth of the People's Republic. Second, to establish how China's potential adversaries would likely act and react in the event of a real-world crisis or conflict. And third, in the case of China's multiple territorial disputes, to continue to adjust realities on the ground to legitimize Chinese territorial and maritime claims on a de facto, rather than de jure, basis. China will never submit to any form of international arbitration on these disputes. Therefore, changing both the perceived and accepted "reality" over the long term has long been China's operational approach to advancing its claims. China also wishes to convey the impression that, as time passes, it will have overwhelming resources to deploy against each of these targets (for example, by the massing of its fishery militia fleets in disputed waters in the South China Sea), ultimately causing its opponents to conclude that resistance is pointless.

Moreover, within its system of government, China has become habituated to the near-complete bifurcation of its diplomatic and its military/paramilitary operations. The function of this is for China to appear to be as reasonable as possible in the management of its overall bilateral and regional political relationships while, at the same time, allowing its military to do whatever is deemed operationally necessary to advance Beijing's national security objectives on the ground. In reality, given Chinese internal decision-making processes, China's most senior Foreign Ministry officials are relatively powerless to constrain—let alone direct—what Central Military Commission staff do. By and large, these are seen as two discrete universes: one military, and the other diplomatic, brought together only within the ultimate decision-making center of Xi Jinping's personal office.

Chinese Concerns: Managed Strategic Competition Ties China's Hands with Only a Limited Possibility of Real Strategic Gain

Given all these factors, what possible advantage would there be for China to tie its hands on any of these fronts through the constraints of a managed strategic competition framework? This would depend in large part on China's net assessment of future risks arising from its current, increasingly *unconstrained* patterns of behavior. On questions of military tactics and training, the PLA, like the US military, does not like its operational freedoms impaired by the interventions of well-meaning diplomats. Nonetheless, neither the Chinese leadership nor the PLA want to trigger a premature armed conflict with the United States in any of the maritime theaters of direct concern to it—not unless and until Beijing is certain that China is in an unassailable military position. As of now, that is not the case, and the risks are still judged as being too high. It is this factor—reinforced by any potential change in American and Japanese operational responses to Chinese military deployments—that creates a possible opening for Beijing to honestly consider adopting a more restrictive set of mutual limitations for ships and aircraft for the foreseeable future.

It is difficult to speculate as to what that might mean in detail for Taiwan, the South China Sea, and the East China Sea. China's current patterns of behavior differ significantly across all three theaters, as do American and (in the case of the East China Sea) Japanese responses. But the bottom line is that a mutually agreed-upon framework of managed strategic competition offers some potential to reduce the temperature levels in these highly volatile theaters of operation—where, at present, there are very few, if any, rules of the road. Absent any such guardrails, the frequency and intensity of naval and air operations across all three will continue to increase. This means that it is less and less a question of *if* Beijing will have to handle the operational and diplomatic consequences of an unintended collision between Chinese, American, or Japanese military vessels or aircraft in the future, but *when*.

Cybersecurity and cyberattacks present a different set of security risks, challenges, and opportunities for China. This is shaped by the extent to which China currently resorts to state-based attacks on US government, commercial, and private citizen targets—and those of US allies around the world—and the benefits it derives from those attacks. It is also shaped by the extent to which the US resorts to the same against Chinese targets, whether Chinese countermeasures are deemed by Beijing to be sufficient, and whether therefore this is of significant concern to the Chinese leadership. These questions are the murkiest and most opaque aspects of the US-China security relationship.

There have been many reported Chinese attacks on US targets over the last ten years. The most spectacular of these was the 2013 penetration of the US government personnel records system discussed earlier, including confidential files on all employees and the details they had divulged to apply for security clearances. The Obama administration had already raised with the Chinese leadership additional US concerns about Chinese cyberattacks on American private corporations. Efforts were made to reach an agreement that all commercial cyberattacks would cease. However, according to the Americans, these undertakings only held for several months before cyberattacks were resumed in force. Earlier second-track efforts were made through American academic institutions to engage Chinese counterpart institutions on mutual cybersecurity protocols, but these also met with limited success.

Given this background, the questions once again arise: What benefit would China derive from agreeing to any binding arrangements with the Biden administration to limit or eliminate cyberattacks, and would they have any interest in adhering to them? After all, many in Beijing would argue that current arrangements (or the lack thereof) have benefitted China greatly as a form of asymmetric warfare, particularly given that American cybersystems offer a large number of soft and easily penetrable targets. Beijing, however, will have its own sense of vulnerability to American cyberattack, including of its critical public infrastructure. Beijing will be even more mindful of the potential exposure of its major state and private corporations to external cyber penetration, given the expanding scope of China's indigenous innovation programs. And the party, in particular, will be deeply conscious of the potential for damaging information about its central leadership, such as the extent of their personal wealth, to be stolen and leaked into the public domain. For these reasons, there is likely to be a debate within the Chinese system about the merits of a renewed discussion with their American counterparts on a possible cyber protocol between them.

Managed Strategic Competition and a Return to Chinese Economic Priorities

As for the other aspects of a managed strategic competition framework that could be relevant to Beijing's overall calculus, we should never forget that China's underlying interests continue to lie in the long-term growth of its economy. In the eyes of the leadership, it is the growing size, sophistication, and strength of the Chinese economy that remains fundamental to all other elements of Chinese national power. For nearly twenty years, successive Chinese administrations defined the current era as a period of strategic opportunity, when the absence of significant international conflict meant that China could focus almost exclusively on its national economic development task. While the party has not yet formally changed this net assessment of its current international circumstances, it may do so at the Twentieth Party Congress in November 2022.

As of 2021, despite the rhetorical positioning the Chinese leadership has adopted domestically and internationally, China does *not* at this stage welcome the adversarial strategic environment in which it finds itself. On balance, the Chinese political establishment would have preferred to avoid the new, sharp edges of America's post-2017 strategic response to Xi Jinping's China. This has already been evidenced by repeated Chinese calls to the Biden administration to resume previous regular channels of high-level political dialogue in the hope of restabilizing the overall bilateral relationship. There is therefore an appetite within the Chinese political system for some level of restabilization of the US-China relationship that would enable the Chinese leadership to return to its principle focus on the long-term transformation of its economic model. But Beijing is sufficiently pragmatic to recognize that returning the US relationship to the *status quo ante* is simply not possible. Too much has happened since the 2018–2019 trade war and the 2020 pandemic—and the increasingly hard-wired policy settings of the Biden administration since the start of 2021—for all of the damage to the relationship to be repaired overnight. But that does not mean that Beijing would not have an interest in preventing the relationship from becoming even worse (even though that is its current expectation), given the regime's acute understanding of its internal vulnerabilities and the time it still needs to overcome them.

Therefore, from Beijing's perspective, a framework of managed strategic competition able to manage down the growing array of security and foreign policy tensions and simmering crises that currently dominate its relationship with the United States would, on balance, be welcome. China's long game has always been to triumph on the back of economic power and technology. In Beijing's calculus, managed strategic competition might enable China to continue consolidating these strengths until its comprehensive national power is sufficient to deploy for other national security and foreign policy objectives. In the meantime, managed strategic competition might—from Beijing's perspective—help take the strategic temperature down.

Managed Strategic Competition and Chinese Foreign Policy Interests

At the same time, a framework of managed strategic competition would not prevent Beijing from competing vigorously with the US for regional and global foreign policy influence. Indeed, some could argue that, if managed strategic competition were able to reduce overall security policy tensions for the decade ahead, it would make it less problematic for China to extend its foreign policy influence—particularly if other countries no longer felt the need to take an acute binary decision in their overall relationships with Washington and Beijing on fundamental national security grounds. In fact, in the eyes of some in the Chinese leadership, if Chinese foreign policy returned to being the servant of its successful economic development policy seen over the last several decades rather than having its wolf warriors ripping other states into line for offending Chinese sensibilities on Taiwan, the South China Sea, and Xinjiang, then China's net political position in the eyes of the world would probably be enhanced. This would not preclude China, if it so chose, from continuing to wage its ongoing ideological war against the US, the West, and the rest of the democratic world by defending and championing its China development model. Indeed, if China is convinced of the superiority of its system, as its domestic propaganda apparatus argues, then it should be encouraged to do so. Given some of the more spectacular failures of the liberal-capitalist system in recent decades (for example, the 2008 global financial crisis and its initial mismanagement of the 2020 COVID-19 pandemic response), China may judge that there are significant systemic vulnerabilities to exploit within what was once seen as an all-conquering Washington Consensus. It would be for China to judge whether doing so would help its overall ideological cause or hinder it. But ideological and ideational competition would, in many respects, lie at the heart of a managed strategic competition framework. As I have argued elsewhere, in the world of ideas, systems, and governance, may the best team win.

Chinese Multilateral Diplomacy Under Managed Strategic Competition

A managed strategic competition framework would also provide scope for continued cooperation with the United States in defined areas of deep mutual interest. There are several policy domains where China would see its national interests being served by working collaboratively with Americans, especially in the decade ahead. These include the maintenance of global financial stability through the G20, the Financial Stability Board, the Basel Committee, and the International Monetary Fund, where both China and the US are already active members. China has no interest in a repeat of recent international financial crises, as another such crisis could potentially derail China's long-term economic trajectory, including its domestic political stability. Furthermore, given the injection of unprecedented sovereign debt levels into global bond markets following the 2020 recession, China will have a significant interest in avoiding the risk of sovereign defaults that could trigger a wider financial crisis. China's 2021 negotiations with the Paris Club on the need for Chinese debt rescheduling for its creditor states (which have grown rapidly in number under the Belt and Road Initiative) further underline the importance of international cooperation on this complex and delicate task of maintaining global financial stability.

On climate change, China's national economic and environmental interests mandate global collaboration. Although China is the largest global emitter of greenhouse gases, and its national emission reduction targets are critical to global climate outcomes, they will ultimately be ineffective unless this is done in tandem with the US, Europe, Japan, and especially India in the decade ahead. In other words, on climate, there is no option for Beijing other than to work with Washington to drive global solutions.

Then there are the ongoing risks of global nuclear proliferation. Iran and North Korea represent the greatest dangers on this account. While neither country is likely to ever target China, Beijing does have an interest in preventing retaliatory proliferation by other states (for example, Japan) seeking to maintain their own security against future nuclear threats from Tehran and Pyongyang. Once again, a Chinese national interest is at stake in collaborating with the United States in maintaining the integrity of the existing multilateral nonproliferation regime.

For all of these reasons, managed strategic competition may offer China an acceptable alternative strategic framework to govern its overall relationship with the United States for the decade ahead. The Chinese think tank community is currently in search of a new organizing principle for the relationship, given the post-2017 US strategic reality it confronts. There is no possibility, as noted previously, of returning to an era of what successive American administrations called strategic engagement—or what China used to routinely refer to as the principles of win-win cooperation. There has already been too much water under the bridge for that. The critical question for Beijing will be whether there is sufficient leeway to work with under a concept of managed strategic competition from the perspective of its national interests, values, and strategy to justify the constraints that such a framework would impose. I do not know the answer to that question—but it would be worth asking.

US Policy Toward China Within a Framework of Managed Strategic Competition

What about the other side of the strategic equation: How would American policy makers accommodate the evolution of US-China strategy within a framework of managed strategic competition? Would it help or hinder

America? American military strategists (like their Chinese counterparts) would not want their hands unnecessarily tied by what they would see as foreign policy abstractions—especially abstractions that got in the road of the hard business of military preparedness, including naval exercises and aerial surveillance missions. The Pentagon could argue that the problem with managed strategic competition is that it would deliver the Chinese an effective strategic "leave pass" for much of the decade ahead, enabling China to continue strengthening its economy in the absence of any imminent military threat while also continuing to expand its military capabilities. This would place China in an even more advantageous position if it then suddenly decided to change its policy course toward the end of the decade and bring its more powerful military capability to bear against Taiwan or other targets. Moreover, the US intelligence establishment could argue that whatever security policy protocols China might agree to (on Taiwan, the East and South China Seas, and cyber), such a framework would, in reality, prove worthless because, based on past practice, at a military operational level, Beijing would fail to comply with its commitments. As evidence, they might point to the Obama administration's previous experience with Xi Jinping on their short-lived cyber protocol—and Xi's undertakings not to militarize its reclaimed islands in the South China Sea.

Managed Strategic Competition, the Balance of Power, and Deterrence

There are a number of answers to these objections. From an American perspective, having another decade to rebuild or strengthen US economic, military, and technological power, thereby improving the balance of power against China in each of these domains, is no small thing. In this sense, time may be America's friend—and not its enemy—despite the fact that the Chinese might argue the same from their perspective. From the perspective of an American military planner, the critical question would become whether they believe they would be in a better or worse position to deter a Chinese military push in a decade's time.

On the question of China "cheating," it is true, as noted previously, that Beijing has zero reservations about using deception as a normal feature of diplomatic and military tactics and strategy—particularly against capitalist and imperialist adversaries who (in Beijing's perspective) humiliated China during much of the previous two centuries. However, China does not have a monopoly on the question of deception. This brings into sharp relief the importance of *mutual verification* of any agreements entered into. In the case of the four most relevant operational theaters in the US-China security relationship (a fifth would include space-based systems, given the risks of strategic blinding through antisatellite warfare), the verification of strategic undertakings, along with associated confidence and security building measures, is, by and large, technically achievable. In other words, given the nature of the measures that would be most relevant to the specific security scenarios that are the most dangerous in US-China relations, the opportunity to cheat at scale on the implementation of these measures (such as building more islands in the South China Sea) is more limited. As Ronald Reagan reminded us, in a different era but not in dissimilar circumstances, verification is also key to the rebuilding of any level of future political, diplomatic, and strategic trust.

Apart from the complex challenges that these practical considerations would present to both sides in operationalizing a concept of managed strategic competition, the overwhelming advantage for the United States would be to simply reduce the overall risk of armed conflict with China—either by accident or design—over the coming decade. America does not want a war. The uncertainty of the outcome is too great. The possibility of escalation is too dangerous. In many ways, America has the most to lose as the world's foremost power. There is at present too great a risk that America could lose—in a single epoque-defining event—its global leadership. And the sheer destructive force of such a conflagration for both the American military and economy is beyond imagining. Unsurprisingly, these concerns mostly mirror those currently felt by the Chinese leadership in Beijing. For this reason alone, there is an overwhelming case to take all necessary precautionary measures now to significantly reduce the risk of war. That is where managed strategic competition comes in.

Some American and Chinese nationalist politicians, along with the strategic policy über-realists who advise them, might argue that all this does is kick the can down the road. There is much truth in this, but that does not make it wrong. I would argue that there is nothing wrong, let alone cowardly, with kicking this particular can (i.e., war) a long way down the road. Some might even attack such an approach rhetorically as a form of appeasement, but the essence of appeasement in Europe lay in watching one piece of territory after another be annexed without response, which is the exact reverse of what is proposed here because of the clearly defined nature of the enforceable strategic redlines being contemplated here. Seeking to resolve the underlying political confrontation in the US-China relationship by contemplating a more immediate limited war is a fool's errand. This was one of the national psychological delusions at play in a number of European capitals at the outbreak of World War I. History tends not to believe in limited wars. Instead, history tells us that wars are far more likely to escalate out of control. By contrast, kicking the can down the road creates political space—space that over time can accommodate changing diplomatic sentiment that, in turn, may be capable of bringing about a long-term, peaceful resolution to the all-encompassing strategic competition currently engulfing these two great powers of the twenty-first century. Such a resolution may currently be beyond our political capacity to imagine, but it may become possible with the passage of time. However, that possibility is lost altogether as soon as war breaks out. Once we hear the drumbeats of war and respond to them, reason is suspended as worst-case scenario planning comes to the fore, brute force enters in, and any prospect of a peaceful resolution disappears forever. Then the collective political and personal futures of both the Chinese and American leaderships will be determined by a very bloody feat of arms. Managed strategic competition is not a fail-safe mechanism to prevent such a war, but it would provide the best possible chance.

Managed Strategic Competition and US Strategic Interests in Taiwan and the South and East China Seas

So how might managed strategic competition impact America's core strategic redlines over Taiwan, the South China Sea, and the East China Sea? The answer for the US—as it is for China—would be a mixture of opportunity and constraint. On Taiwan, there is already sufficient flexibility available to provide the Biden administration all it needs to support Taiwan's security. The June 2021 reaffirmation by the administration of the long-standing US policy of strategic ambiguity has also been stabilizing for relations with Beijing, notwithstanding the apparently unequivocal language of President Biden on this question the following October. Under strategic ambiguity, the US has left open the question of whether and to what extent it would intervene militarily in any potential Taiwan scenario. This ambiguity has two objectives. The first is to deter China from contemplating an attack because China could never assume that the US would not intervene in support of Taiwan. The second is to deter future Taiwanese governments from becoming reckless on the question of Taiwan's formal independence from China, as Washington might then decline to support such a move—as this would almost certainly provoke Chinese military action.

However, managed strategic competition would likely mandate much greater American vigilance on long-standing Chinese political sensitivities about adherence to the One-China policy. This would preclude future high-level US official contact with the Taiwanese government, including direct military collaboration with the Taiwanese armed forces of the kind we saw increase under the Trump administration and continue under Biden. But if the overriding US strategic objective for Taiwan is to deter future Chinese coercive military action against the island, then securing that objective does not require any violation of these long-standing pillars of the One-China policy. What it would require is for the United States to restore the wider military balance of power with China across the East Asian theater by redressing gaps and vulnerabilities in its current force structure and capabilities. It would also require the Taiwanese to take seriously their military deficiencies, which have accumulated over several decades and which neither side of Taiwanese politics has so far demonstrated sufficient determination to resolve. The US, Japan, and Taiwan would also need to work together with other partners, friends, and allies to build greater long-term economic resilience for the Taiwanese economy against the risk of future Chinese economic coercion. However, none of these measures would be impeded by a broader American understanding with Beijing that the fundamental architecture of the One-China policy remained intact. Indeed, to fool around with the operational or declaratory terms of the One-China policy would be an exercise in US political self-indulgence and strategic folly rather than a hard-headed advancement of US national security policy. The former may make for good domestic politics in some parts of the US, but the latter requires a focus on the more fundamental objective of preserving the strategic status quo over Taiwan—as has successfully been achieved by previous administrations over the last half century.

In the South China Sea, any quantitative or qualitative limits on the PLA's current pattern of gray-zone operations within a wider framework of managed strategic competition would be welcome from an American perspective. Securing Chinese agreement that there would be no further island reclamations would be a helpful start, although China would under no circumstances agree to withdraw its military forces from the seven "islands" it has already created, despite earlier assurances to the United States that these would never be militarized in the first place. China might, however, be pushed on preventing further militarization of other existing land features in the South China Sea. Given the swarming of Chinese coast guard, customs, maritime research, and fisheries vessels in the region in recent years, any limits that could be agreed on regarding the number of Chinese maritime deployments would constitute a positive, stabilizing measure. This might be reciprocated by the US, with an appropriate, proportionate, and calibrated regularization of US-led freedom-of-navigation operations (FONOPS) in the South China Sea in the future. The alternative could be an explicit warning to China that the continued escalation

NAVIGATING AN UNCERTAIN FUTURE | 381

of Chinese gray-zone operations would result in a corresponding increase in the frequency, intensity, and extent of both FONOPS and US military flights above the South China Sea.

However, beyond all these possible measures, an agreement with China not to use its military and paramilitary assets to assert further territorial and maritime claims against the Philippines (the only US treaty ally with a disputed claim with China in the South China Sea) would be the most important potential arrangement within a framework of managed strategic competition. Of course, China is likely to resist this. But given the Biden administration's recent reaffirmation of the integrity of its treaty obligations with the Philippines and the fact that the 2022 Philippine presidential elections may bring to power a much less China-friendly administration than Duterte's, it may be within the scope of China's interests to scale back its hitherto forward-leaning military strategy that is pushing its territorial claims against Manila to the brink.

Strategic circumstances in the East China Sea are vastly different to the South China Sea. As discussed earlier in the book, of the three maritime theaters important to Beijing, Taiwan is the most vital to Chinese interests, and the South China Sea (where the size of China's disputed claims is massive and where it finds itself directly arrayed against the US) comes second, while the East China Sea is of lesser but still real importance. Furthermore, direct US air and naval deployments to the contested areas in the East China Sea have always been limited, with all responses to Chinese air and maritime incursions in the two-hundred-nautical-mile exclusive economic zone claimed by Japan around Senkaku / Diaoyu Dao Islands having been carried out by the Japanese Self-Defense Force. Nonetheless, China's gray-zone activities against Japan have exhibited some similarities with the South China Sea. This is clear from the steady and sustained increase in Chinese maritime and air sorties designed to test Japanese response patterns while also, over time, exhausting Japanese defense assets' capacity to respond effectively to every individual incident.

Despite this, China could still have some structural interest in de-escalating its overall political relationship with Japan for much of the decade ahead within a framework of managed strategic competition rather than continuing to drive Tokyo and Washington even closer together. For example, China has become concerned that the Quad (linking the US, Japan, India, and Australia) is evolving more rapidly into a multilateral security and foreign policy mechanism than Beijing originally thought. Beijing has also become concerned more generally by the emerging hostility toward China across many Asian and European democracies in response to China's sustained experiment in wolf warrior diplomacy and its increasingly confrontational approach. Moreover, as with the Philippines, the Biden administration has also reaffirmed the applicability of its bilateral defense treaty to the Japanese-controlled Senkaku Islands. This means that clashes or collisions involving Chinese and Japanese vessels or aircraft carry the rolling risk of immediate escalation with the United States. If recent trends in the numbers of Chinese sorties continue, then it follows that the likelihood of incidents will increase over time. For these reasons, the United States may find that China might have an interest in lowering the temperature of its overall relationship with Japan.

China, in more normal circumstances, does not want to be fighting on multiple diplomatic fronts at once. Nor does it wish to risk an early and unnecessary armed conflict with Japan and the United States in a less critical, albeit still important, theater. And China knows there is only one way of substantively reducing tensions with Japan—reductions in the frequency and intensity of its challenges to the Japanese-claimed exclusive economic zone. For these reasons, within a wider framework of managed strategic competition, it may be possible for China to reduce its overall levels of military and paramilitary activity against Japan. At least for the next several years, such an outcome would be beneficial to both Tokyo and Washington. If China refused, other options could be considered, including the beginning of direct US deployments in and around the disputed islands to respond more effectively to the increasing pace and intensity of Chinese incursions. This would not be seen in Beijing as a welcome development. Indeed, the risk of it might provide Beijing with an even greater incentive to embrace a more moderate approach as part of keeping strategic competition with the US within more manageable political and military parameters.

Managed Strategic Competition and US National Interests in Cyber and Space

As for cyber and space, there is some room for both the US and China to take practical measures that would enhance longer-term strategic stability. As noted previously, for the United States, cyber is a double-edged sword in terms of both Chinese and American capabilities. But if Washington were able to conclude an enforceable cybersecurity protocol with Beijing to limit Chinese cyberattacks on private corporations (particularly technology firms) and critical public infrastructure, it would enhance overall US national security interests. If that proves not to be a possibility, an alternative American approach could be a full-scale US cyberassault on Chinese corporations and demonstration attacks against critical elements of Chinese infrastructure. This would greatly raise the stakes in the unfolding US-China cyberconflict but may force the parties to the table to reconsider a bilateral protocol. Russian cyber proficiency, combined with the rapidly developing Russia-China security relationship, adds another level to long-standing American concerns about this new form of asymmetric warfare. While the extent to which Russia and China share both raw and distilled intelligence product gathered from the US and its allies remains unknown, the trajectory of this relationship has been unrelenting since 2014. Therefore, to be effective, cyber protocols with Beijing would need to be followed with a similar arrangement with Moscow. Unfortunately, the need to include Russia may further reduce the prospects of bringing about overall progress with China on cyber for the foreseeable future.

There are a number of parallels between these cyber-related challenges in the US-China relationship and what is unfolding with both countries' space-based systems. Consistent with its general strategy, China's current policy (as described in chapter 5) has been to overcome as rapidly as possible the vulnerabilities it has in space-based intelligence, tracking and surveillance systems, satellite navigation networks, and antisatellite warfare. Bringing China to the negotiating table in any of these areas before they have achieved parity with the US remains unlikely. The one exception may be in antisatellite warfare, which, like cyberattacks on critical communications infrastructure on the ground, would have the effect of blinding both sides at a time of major security crisis. This could, in turn, trigger preemptive military action by one side or the other for fear that they may be under attack. This is recognized in Beijing, Washington, and Moscow alike as inherently destabilizing, which may create the grounds for modest progress in this area.

China and Russia have submitted to the UN their proposed treaty framework called the Treaty on the Prevention of the Placement of Weapons in Outer Space, the Threat or Use of Force Against Outer Space Objects (PPWT). This would commit signatories "not to place any weapons in outer space" or "resort to the threat or use of force against outer space objects." However, US negotiators and policy makers have little to no trust in the treaty, noting that both countries have repeatedly tested dual-use systems that they claim are for peaceful purposes but can be used as antisatellite weapons (such as laser systems or "scavenger" satellites with robotic arms capable of intercepting larger satellites). They also note that both China and Russia were among only twelve countries who refused to sign a December 2020 UN resolution urging new steps on "reducing space threats through norms, rules, and principles of responsible behaviors" in space. Still, it is possible that a more limited and specific bilateral or trilateral agreement on the use of antisatellite weapons could be reached as a first step or, at the very least, that a dialogue mechanism to discuss such steps could be established. However, antisatellite systems aside, there appear to be limited prospects for significant progress in limiting the expansion and growing military potential of Chinese space-based systems overall. This is likely to continue to be the case so long as China remains in a competitive race without any constraints to close the large capabilities gap that still exists in this area between itself and the United States.

Managed Strategic Competition and America's Ability to Compete with China During the 2020s

However, the principal benefit to the United States from an extended period of managed strategic competition would lie in the economic, foreign policy, and human rights dimensions of its relationship with China. An ability to contain the underlying security redlines in the relationship within reasonable, manageable, and stable strategic guardrails would enable the US to focus on the long-term fundamentals of American national power. This would be based on three overarching priorities. One is the revival and reengineering of the American economy, particularly in next-generation infrastructure, technology, research, and development funding and education investment. Another priority is the rebuilding of US diplomatic, trade, investment, technology, and security policy ties with friends, partners, and allies around the world as part of a broad-based, politically sustainable international coalition. The third priority is likely the launch of a new ideological offensive, both at home and abroad, based on democratic resilience and renewal, the universality of individual freedom, and the long-term effectiveness of liberal-democratic forms of governance—as opposed to what the US would define as the oppressiveness, brittleness, and corruption of the authoritarian alternative. As noted earlier in this chapter, in these three critical areas, America needs time. Indeed, for America to succeed with an effective national China strategy, it will need sufficient buy-in across both sides of American politics so that the 2020s becomes a *decade* of rebuilding American power, no matter which party holds political office. This will require unprecedented bipartisan consensus to guarantee strategic continuity across administrations rather than limiting US strategy to something that is truncated every time there is a change in the White House.

Once Again: It's the Economy, Stupid

The engine room of America's global power remains its economy—its size, its innovation, its efficiency, its competitiveness, its influence on international standard-setting, its impact on global trade and investment, the depth of its capital markets, and the continuing global status of the US dollar. None of these historical economic strengths are set in stone, and all are now being challenged. For example, to compete effectively with China, America would need to reform and resume large-scale immigration to continue to grow its domestic market, just as it would need to expand its international markets through a new approach to regional and global trade liberalization. American innovation would need to be supported by a new combination of tax, industry, higher education, and innovation policy. American competitiveness would require that a careful new balance be struck on tax policy, with ideological zeal from both the left and the right prevented from undermining one of the traditional cornerstones of US global economic success. And American efficiency demands that federal and state governments finally crack the nut on modernizing the country's crumbling infrastructure. America would need to regain a place at the forefront of the fintech revolution sweeping global financial markets. The US Federal Reserve would need to manage the privileged international status of the US dollar, avoiding its further weaponization for political and foreign policy purposes and responding effectively to emerging digital and broader alternative currency challenges. And, above all, the United States would need to sustain sufficient domestic political support for this longer-term economic reform program by strengthening the American middle class and reducing the current gross levels of income inequality present across much of the country. All this is a tall order for any government. It would therefore require continued, and in some cases radical, domestic-policy surgery in order to succeed. And all this would require time. This would, needless to say, become more achievable if potentially ruinous major conflicts or war can be avoided for the decade ahead.

However, this is not just a domestic economic policy challenge. It is equally an international economic policy challenge involving trade policy, the digital commerce revolution, and global digital governance. This would arguably be the most difficult component of any future US national China strategy: the greater opening of the American economy to its major strategic partners around the world. America has long prided itself on being one of the most open and globalized economies in the world. The truth is that it is not. Even before Trump's orgy of protectionism, this was not the case. The tariff and nontariff barriers to free trade, investment, capital, technology, and talent markets are still formidable—even for America's closest allies. The core truth is this: if the United States wishes to remain the center of the free world, then creating an increasingly seamless international market across the national boundaries of its major North American, European, and Asian strategic partners and allies is essential. This could also apply, in time, to America's major Middle Eastern, Latin American, and African partners. To ask these countries to simply ignore their core economic interests with China (already their largest trading partner) and instead pledge their enduring political fealty to the American cause in an increasingly binary world, for no comparable economic benefit, will be increasingly seen as foreign policy folly. Of course, such an agenda runs headlong into the political hornet's nest of domestic protectionist impulses across America that Trump masterfully exploited through his populist demagoguery. Navigating these domestic political shoals through a divided Congress presents an almost impossible degree of difficulty. Nonetheless, Biden's great challenge is to guide American accession to comprehensive transatlantic and transpacific free-trade agreements that, together with NAFTA, create, over time, a mega–free market across much of the world. Failing that, the "gravitational pull" of China's vast authoritarian capitalist market is likely to prevail, just as Xi Jinping intends, as economics eventually triumphs over politics and values despite the compromises to freedom and security that would entail for many countries around the world.

Just as Xi's political success depends on keeping China's citizens content, the corollary for the United States of any such trade liberalization agenda must be expanding the tent of economic equality and opportunity for all Americans at home. Working families will not support any trade and investment liberalization agenda unless they see advantages for themselves through lower prices, good jobs, better wages, and radically improved universal education, health care, and environmental standards. During the halcyon days of American global power in decades past, the unwritten social contract between employers and employees was as striking as it was strong. In recent decades, that has unraveled as the ranks of the working poor have swollen, wealth has been highly concentrated, social trust has declined, racial divides have worsened, and the environment has been ravaged. All of these together are tearing away at the social fabric that ultimately underpins the body politic. Therefore, any effective national strategy to sustain American national power through the twenty-first century will require repair not just of the fundamentals of US domestic economic strength but also of the social contract. And, once again, that requires time.

Managed Strategic Competition and US Foreign Policy Interests

While the foundations of America's global and regional response to China will depend on the economy, and specifically whether the US government will rise to the breadth of the economic policy challenges it faces, classical foreign policy engagement would also be critical. The core strategic principle at play in the foreign policy stakes for the United States is that practically all American friends, partners, and allies are neuralgic about the consequences for them of an increasingly binary world. For economic and—in some cases—security policy reasons, most of these countries do not want to be forced to make a final choice between Washington and Beijing. Certainly, they do not want to be forced to do so overtly. Africa, in many respects, has already made its strategic choice in support of China. But the same pressures are also evident across Europe, East Asia, Southeast Asia, large parts of South Asia, the Middle East, and Latin America. If a framework of managed strategic competition can reduce the geopolitical temperature in the US-China relationship for the 2020s, then—combined with the absence of the polarizing impact of the Trump administration— this is likely to create a more conducive environment for American bilateral and multilateral diplomatic reengagement.

Managed strategic competition will not impede the future evolution of the Quad as a form of foreign and security policy coordination in the

Indo-Pacific region. Nor will it, in itself, impede any future expansion of the Quad to include Korea or perhaps even Indonesia. Nor will it undermine US efforts to make China into a common challenge on the formal foreign and security policy agendas of NATO and the European Union. Indeed, China has already succeeded in doing so through its efforts in recent years. Cyberattacks, human rights, a recent history of divide and conquer between the countries of eastern Europe and western Europe, and trade restrictions against Australia have all generated international and not just national reactions against Beijing. And as a result, countries have sought to *rebalance* their interests with Washington to afford themselves greater leverage against the possibility of future Chinese economic coercion. Nor will managed strategic competition prevent the proposed emergence of a D10 (or a grouping of ten major democracies) over time as a natural evolution of the G7. Indeed, the inclusion of India, Korea, Australia, and South Africa in its number (possibly expanding it to a D12 if Indonesia and Mexico are also ultimately included) would result in the effective globalization of the original G7 beyond its European origins. Of course, China will, through its global diplomacy, push in exactly the reverse direction to fragment any such effort. But foreign policy competition for influence is an essential component of the overall concept of managed strategic competition.

The natural instincts of the Biden administration have been to bring America back to the wider multilateral table. The administration has already embarked on a strategy to reinvigorate its traditional patterns of multilateral engagement. None of this would in any way be undermined or impeded by a commitment to the principles of managed strategic competition. Once again, it is more likely to enhance it by reducing a number of the binary security policy tensions between China and the United States. American reengagement will apply not only to the UN but also to the World Bank, the IMF, the WTO, APEC, the East Asian Summit, and the G20 (China's only natural ally on the G20 will be Russia, although Argentina, Brazil, and Turkey remain potential partners in certain defined areas). Most of the world would welcome this, not least in the context of the trail of diplomatic wreckage still left behind by the Trump administration across human rights, sustainable development, nuclear security, trade, and climate. The damage to brand America in the eyes of the world has been extensive, as for four long years, the United States wrought havoc across the very multilateral institutions that it painstakingly created as the essential machinery of the postwar international order.

As noted earlier, all of this cannot be repaired overnight. It will take time. It will also take leadership possessed with an intelligent humility that has rarely been seen in the past. The reform of the WTO disputes resolution machinery, the rejoining of the Paris Agreement on climate change, and the further capitalization of both the World Bank and the IMF (as alternative mechanisms for developing economies to the Asian Infrastructure and Investment Bank and the Belt and Road Initiative) all loom as major priorities. Similarly, the refunding of the UN's critical agencies where China has already become the second-largest source of financial support. As for the G20, the US—rather than ignoring yet another institution of its own creation—could use it in partnership with others to break the political and policy logjams that have undermined the historical effectiveness of the formal institutions of multilateral governance. These are not just instruments of American (or Chinese) soft power; they contain within them the potential for negotiations that materially affect the future of American hard power—for example, on North Korea, Iran, nuclear proliferation, autonomous weapons systems, and other areas of arms control. Unless the US steps up to the plate on the future of the multilateral system, the UN will increasingly become a Chinese satrapy driven by Chinese finance, personnel, and the sheer voting power it can mobilize right across the G-77. Once again, a framework of managed strategic competition between Washington and Beijing not only accommodates a renewed American commitment to multilateralism but also actively encourages it.

The Battle for Hearts and Minds

At its core, managed strategic competition is also a fundamental contest of ideas and of the efficacy of systems. It is a contest between two conflicting worldviews: one based on the principles and institutions of liberal-democratic capitalism and ultimately anchored in the geostrategic power of the United States, and the other in the ideology of Marxism-Leninism, authoritarian governance, and the driving force of Chinese nationalism. Liberal-capitalism, and the American-led order that underpins it, offers a concept of universal human freedoms best expressed in the UN Universal Declaration of Human Rights of 1948. China, under Xi Jinping, offers a different development model to the world, one where the suppression of political freedoms is justified because of the collective imperatives of economic growth and political security. In Beijing's eyes, this model has developed a new international legitimacy because of China's formidable record of economic achievement over the last forty years. These competing narratives lie at the center of the ideological debate between China and the US-led liberal-democratic world. That much has been made clear by Xi Jinping's repeated statements on the centrality of China's struggle over international order and the future of global governance.

Since the Nineteenth Party Congress in 2017, China's global propaganda apparatus has been fully engaged in this unfolding global ideological debate. This is a debate that the United States and its liberal-democratic allies have belatedly joined. Nonetheless, the advantage of a framework of managed strategic competition would be that, if it succeeds in reducing the immediate intensity of the military flash points across the US-China relationship, it may be possible for this global ideological contest to unfold relatively peacefully—that is, without the risk of an ideological struggle erupting into an armed struggle or the type of destabilizing proxy wars that we saw between the US and the Soviet Union during the long history of the Cold War. Indeed, if the outcome of this global contest of ideas is to be determined on the basis of their intrinsic merits, their different track records of achievement, and their levels of popular support across the peoples of the world, then may the best system win. In fact, the liberal-democratic-capitalist world should have every confidence that it can. Xi Jinping certainly exhibits the same confidence for his system.

A Global Perspective—The Advantages of Continued US-China Strategic Cooperation

The great strength of managed strategic competition as a framework for the US-China relationship is that it would also accommodate continued international collaboration between the two countries when it is in their national interests to do so. This would not be possible if we were already in the depths of a new Cold War. In fact, a bilateral framework that continues to actively embrace defined areas of cooperation may be the best means of arresting, or perhaps preventing altogether, a slide into a full-on cold war.

In the case of the US and China, there is a wide range of areas where both countries, and the international community more generally, will continue to have an interest in working together. This will be the case in both the bilateral relationship and in their engagement in multilateral policy and regulatory institutions. For example, the engagement between the US Federal Reserve, the US Treasury, and the People's Bank of China is critical for the smooth functioning of global currency, debt, and equities markets. The sheer scale of American and Chinese financial markets, the scope of their current interaction (notwithstanding the bilateral political implosions of the last several years), and the prospects for still further growth in each other's jurisdictions means that the two countries' regulators have a major interest in working closely together. In the likely event that the relationship becomes more politically problematic in the future, this level of collaboration will likely become even more important. This is particularly the case now that the US and China have imposed targeted financial sanctions against designated individuals, institutions, and corporations in each other's countries. This is entrenched in a formalized set of laws on both sides that are in effect, including the United States' detailed entity list of export controls and China's Antiforeign Sanctions Law.

Furthermore, multilateral financial collaboration through the G20 finance ministers, the Financial Stability Board, and the Basel Committee will become more important rather than less over time, given China's and America's shared interests in the future stability of global debt markets and their common desire to avoid another financial crisis triggered by sovereign or corporate defaults. Therefore, in global finance, there is an emerging degree of mutually assured destruction between Washington and Beijing that renders the complete unscrambling of this $5 trillion combined capital engagement extremely difficult—and, indeed, potentially dangerous. For these reasons, whatever may happen in any future decoupling of US-China global supply chains in goods, any parallel decoupling between their financial services industries will be much more problematic.

US-China collaboration on climate change is also in both countries' national interests. Both Xi Jinping's regime and the Biden administration recognize the domestic political, environmental, and economic importance of global greenhouse-gas reductions into the future. They also understand that without significant reductions by both of them, global temperature increases this century will reach dangerous and potentially irreversible levels. For these reasons, the two countries have little alternative but to collaborate on climate in the future, given that they are the world's two largest emitters and will remain as such until well into the 2030s. It will be in Washington's interests to maximize its bilateral engagement with Beijing on climate to leverage greater Chinese emissions reductions at home and less support for coal abroad—and to work with China through the UN Framework Convention on Climate Change to pressure other major emitters (such as India) to do much, much more. A managed strategic competition framework makes such collaboration possible.

Financial market stability and combined climate change action therefore represent two important areas of continued strategic cooperation between the two countries. This collaboration advances both US and Chinese national interests. It also advances the combined interests of the wider international community. There are many other such areas in the relationship, including bilateral nuclear arms control, nuclear nonproliferation, the deployment of artificial intelligence systems in warfare, counterterrorism, narcotics, future pandemic management, quarantine, routine elements of trade law, and civil aviation. Indeed, a failure to collaborate with China in these and other areas in the future would be potentially injurious to

American interests. It would therefore be foolish to have a future strategic framework for the US-China relationship that does not recognize and embrace the potential upsides for America through continued cooperation in a number of critical domains. It may also be that under different geopolitical circumstances, decisions made now to retain collaborative frameworks in a number of defined areas of the relationship may provide the stepping-stones necessary to move toward rebuilding bilateral political and diplomatic capital in the future.

Conclusion

The underpinning logic of this concept of managed strategic competition may appear to some to be contradictory, in that a mutually agreed managed strategic competition framework provides *both* China *and* the United States with an opportunity to advance their respective regional and global objectives. But that is the essential point. For any such framework to be effective in reducing the risk of armed conflict in the midst of high-octane strategic competition between the two countries, it must have some chance of being accepted, or at least recognized, in both capitals. Otherwise, it would be little more than the sound of one hand clapping and of limited strategic use in stabilizing the overall relationship. Therefore, to achieve its central purpose, managed strategic competition must offer a balanced framework. It cannot be weighted entirely in one direction or the other. Were that to be the case, there would be no chance of it ever being adopted or acknowledged as a common approach. It would then simply be yet another unilateral formula left to mold away on the shelf as the relationship headed for disaster.

As for the particular joint framework offered here, Chinese critics will argue that it is still too weighted in favor of American interests, most particularly in maintaining the status quo over Taiwan. This is anathema to fundamental Chinese articles of faith. But the strategic reality is that to do anything other than maintain stability over Taiwan would automatically trigger equally assertive American and Taiwanese objections. On the other hand, a number of American critics will attack the proposed managed strategic competition formula as naive because it assumes that China would automatically adhere to the rules once they are agreed upon, when much of the post-1949 history of Chinese international relations suggests that the CCP does not regard agreements with the West as binding them to anything. However, the equal strategic reality here is that there is little that has been recommended under a managed strategic competition framework that cannot readily be monitored and verified. Trust is therefore not a prerequisite.

The critical logic of managed strategic competition is to allow maximum competition across the full breadth of the foreign policy, economic, and security relationship while doing this within fixed political guardrails that minimize the risk of crisis, conflict, and war. Therefore, for the terms of such a framework to be mutually acceptable and enforceable, each side would need to have some level of confidence that it could still effectively compete and prosper within it. Of course, their individual capacities to advance their interests through such competition, within its agreed parameters, would depend entirely on the effectiveness of their policies: a combination of economic success, political resilience, diplomatic skill, technological advance, and the robustness and global appeal of the competing ideational frameworks each side puts forward.

This approach is far from perfect. But for those who disagree with it, I repeat my challenge: the responsibility lies with critics to come up with a credible alternative. It is easy to come up with *unilateral* options for the future—that is, advice to either side on how they might militarily prevail against the other. But it is much harder to think through a *joint* framework for the future that preserves the peace without undermining each other's fundamental national interests. The reality is that in this new age of strategic competition between China and the United States, there are, as a matter of logic, only two alternatives: managed competition, with some rules of the road and some prospect of preserving the peace, or unmanaged competition, with the loss of all strategic guardrails and the growing risk of crisis, conflict, or war.

★ ★ ★ ★ ★

Epilogue

The reason for this book is that armed conflict between China and the United States over the next decade, while not yet probable, has become a real possibility. In part, this is because the balance of economic, military, and technological power between the two countries is changing rapidly. In part, it is because back in 2014, Xi Jinping changed China's grand strategy from an essentially defensive posture to a more activist policy seeking to advance Chinese interests and values across the region and the world. It is also because, since 2017, in response to China's newfound national power and policy assertiveness, the United States has embraced an entirely new China strategy in what both the Trump and Biden administrations have called this new age of strategic competition. These three factors combined have put both China and the United States on a collision course in the decade ahead. Of course, there are many other factors at play in the relationship as well—including the cumulative impact of history, race, culture, identity, and ideology. On top of this heady mix, there is also an enduring tradition of what has been described to me by a former Chinese vice foreign minister as a deeply entrenched tradition of mutually assured misunderstanding between Washington and Beijing.

Taking all these factors and forces together, we are at a point in the long, historical evolution of the US-China relationship when serious analysts and commentators in both Beijing and Washington increasingly assume that some form of crisis, conflict, or even war is inevitable. This thinking is dangerous. The advantage of diplomatic history—if we study it seriously—is that the risk of talking ourselves into a crisis is real. The discourse of inevitability takes hold; mutual demonization increases; and the public policy response, ever so subtly, moves from war prevention to war preparation. The sleepwalking of the nations of Europe into war in 1914 should remain a salutary lesson for us all.

It is for these reasons that I have entitled this book *The Avoidable War*. Its purpose is threefold: to explain, for a mainly American audience, how the worldviews now dominant in China and the United States are pushing the two countries toward war; to outline how such a war could be sparked, what it could actually look like, and what unintended world-changing consequences could flow from it; and to consider what could be done, in realistic terms, to prevent it.

I doubt that many of the armchair strategists commenting on the coming conflict between China and the United States have thought through how many Chinese, American, and Taiwanese service members and civilians would be killed. They may not have imagined the extent to which the Chinese Communist Party would see itself as fighting for its very survival in such a war or understood how a conventional war could thus easily escalate into one involving weapons of mass destruction if Chinese forces began to lose. These are the sort of real-world considerations that should inform public debate in both China and the United States on the so-called inevitability of war. Indeed, a retired American three-star general recently told me that the Australian novel (and later movie) *On the Beach*, which describes the real-world consequences of nuclear Armageddon, had a bracing impact on allied field commanders dealing with critical political-military decisions at the height of Cold War tensions with the Soviet Union. Perhaps we need just such a book or movie today, but this time one set against the perils of an escalating real-world conflict with China. We must never become inured to the inevitability of war. To do so is a form of collective learned helplessness.

There is also no guarantee that any war can remain a limited one. In a time of real crisis, the political and military incentives in favor of either preemption or rapid escalation could prove irresistible. The geographical scope, kinetic intensity, and duration of any such conflict are all difficult to model. But neither side could politically afford to lose. If China did not prevail militarily, it is likely that Xi Jinping would fall, given that the overwhelming political psychology of the CCP is that blame must be attributed to the person held responsible for the crisis. If the military defeat was comprehensive enough, popular reaction against the regime itself would be widespread, as its political legitimacy crumbled under the weight of defeat, particularly given the gap between public expectations of Chinese victory, fed by more than a decade of nationalist propaganda pumping up Chinese military prowess, and the cold hard battlefield reality began to hit home. And if the regime fell, it would also be impossible to predict what—for better or worse—would replace it. Meanwhile, if the US was militarily defeated by China, it would likely mark the end of three-quarters of a century of American regional military dominance. East Asia would move definitively into China's strategic orbit. And beyond the Asia-Pacific, power would, at best, become contested between China, Russia, Europe, India, and a seriously diminished America before China, in time, assumed a new position of unchallenged global leadership.

In other words, any regional war between China and the United States could trigger truly seismic geopolitical shifts around the world. The profound uncertainty about the consequences of that should give all political leaders pause to reflect on the wisdom of the first line of Sun Tzu's *The Art of War*: "The art of war is of vital importance to the State. It is a matter of life and death, a road either to safety or to ruin."

This should cause us all to carefully analyze how war could be avoided in the first place. At one level, this may appear to be an impossible question to answer, given the complexity of the variables involved. However, at a different level, the best way forward may be relatively simple: a mutually agreed strategic framework for avoiding war while preserving a principled peace, and one that would need to be robust enough to provide clear-cut strategic guidance for *both* the political and military leadership of each country for the decade ahead. At the same time, it would need to be sufficiently flexible to deal with multiple contingencies as they arose. This is the essential strategic rationale for the concept of managed strategic competition.

This approach, as I have argued already, is deeply realist. It accepts current strategic realities for what they are rather than wishing they did not exist. It does not rely on any expectations that strategic behaviors will somehow magically improve because of the goodness in people's hearts, better strategic communication, or perfect understanding of strategic intentions. Therefore, what I call managed strategic competition does not rely on any level of strategic trust. It relies instead on a framework that sets minimum rules of the road, with clear guidance and a rolling process of monitoring, reporting, and verification.

Nevertheless, managed strategic competition does leave open another possibility: that, over time, if it delivers the strategic stability that is sought, new levels of trust may indeed emerge through experience. In time, it may be that new modes of thinking (*siwei*) about each other develop. Common global challenges—for example, on combatting climate change—may assume a greater importance for all governments as more classical forms of interstate rivalry subside within our overall political priorities and a new, more globalized generation of networked political leaders, comfortable with this way of thinking, take on the leadership positions of the future and guide us into the decades that lie beyond this most dangerous decade of the 2020s. But for that to happen, we must first get through this one.

Acknowledgments

This book is the product of a thousand conversations over half a lifetime. In truth, the genesis of this book comes from an Australian newspaper headline my mother handed to me when I was a fourteen-year-old kid in rural Australia in October 1971 that proclaimed, "The People's Republic of China Joins the United Nations." It was this moment and her encouragement that sparked in me a lifelong fascination with China and, in particular, its relationship with the United States—a country in which I have also lived and worked over many years and, despite its many faults, have come to admire.

Indeed, it was during my time at Harvard University in 2014, immediately following my second term as prime minister of Australia, that the idea of this book really took root. It was there, alongside colleagues and friends like Graham Allison, who was busy writing his seminal book *Destined for War: Can America and China Escape Thucydides's Trap?*, that I began to reflect on the lessons of decades in the practitioner's trenches—first as an Australian diplomat in Beijing and then as Australia's prime minister and foreign minister. In many ways this book builds on a Harvard paper I produced the following year with the less-than-snappy title "U.S.-China 21: The Future of U.S.-China Relations Under Xi Jinping—Toward a New Framework of Constructive Realism for a Common Purpose."

Besides Graham, I also want to acknowledge many current and former Harvard colleagues, including Tony Saich, Joe Nye, Nick Burns, Iain Johnston, Bob Zoellick, Larry Summers, and Mark Elliot, for their ideas, debate, and counsel, which helped inform this book, as well as two great

Harvard Sinologists, Ezra Vogel and Rod MacFarquhar, who have since left us.

In the world of US-China relations, Henry Kissinger remains a giant. No single individual has had more of an impact on US-China relations over the course of the last half century than Henry—other than perhaps Mao, Deng, and Xi Jinping, albeit for very different reasons. I'm grateful to Henry for the many and regular conversations we've had over a number of years, especially his encouragement of my own creative thinking on what can be done to better manage the relationship between these two giant powers of the future.

My special thanks also go to Rana Mitter and Paul Irwin-Crookes, who have supervised my Oxford DPhil on *Xi Jinping's Worldview*, which I have slaved over these last several years in parallel to this project, *The Avoidable War*. My Oxford thesis has been an academic accompaniment to this book as I grappled with Xi's writings, speeches, and decisions over his term in office. I hope it has deepened the analysis underpinning my conclusions on what I describe as a future concept of managed strategic competition between the US and China.

Other friends—including Geremie Barmé, Linda Jaivin, Barclay Shoemaker, and my Asia Society colleague Orville Schell—also helped review and provide advice on early versions of the text, for which I am deeply grateful. Additionally, I am especially grateful for the support of a handful of others, such as Ray Dalio, Steve Schwarzman, Joe Tsai, Jim Stavridis, and Rick Niu, and to many others for their earlier encouragement and advice, including the great Sinologist Pierre Ryckmanns, who was one of my undergraduate lecturers at the Australian National University (where I began learning Mandarin), and former Australian diplomats Dick Woolcott, Dennis Richardson, and David Irvine.

My staff at the Asia Society have labored intensively over this book with me for several years, especially my tireless China advisors, Nathan Levine and Qian Jing (who has been with me on this journey since Harvard), and my chief of staff, Thom Woodroofe, as well as Jared Owens in my Australian office. Special thanks also go to my Asia Society Policy

Institute senior colleagues Danny Russel and Wendy Cutler—two first-class former US senior officials—for their continuing intellectual rigor, alongside Debra Eisenman for her help in managing this book project. I also want to thank the many research assistants who have contributed in some way to this project and worked to establish the Asia Society Policy Institute as one of the leading global and US-based foreign policy think tanks, especially on China. This includes Danny Li, Betty Wang, Mike Pilger, Joshua Gottesman, Virgilio Bisio, Chris Vassallo, Karson Elmgren, Harrison Wang, Chen Wang, Ben Guggenheim, and Joshua Park, who all helped provide research papers in support of this book.

No book can succeed without a first-class publishing team. For this I thank my literary agent Michael Carlisle of Inkwell Management, Geoffrey Shandler, Thomas Dunne, and PublicAffairs publisher Clive Priddle, plus the entire editorial and design team. Like its subject, this project has been challenging; I remain grateful for their commitment and insights.

Finally, I want to thank my family—especially my wife of forty years, Thérèse; our three kids, Jessica, Nick, and Marcus; and now our three little grandkids, Josie, Mackie, and Scarlett. Family is everything in public life. They have been with me every step of the way, including on our many and regular travels and sojourns in both China and the United States. I owe them so much. I hope this book goes some way to helping peacefully navigate the complex shoals of the twenty-first century, where I pray my grandchildren will be able to live in harmony with the grandchildren of my many Chinese and American colleagues who have also become very dear friends.

The Honorable Kevin Rudd, AC

Index

414 | INDEX

New York Stock Exchange, 109
New Zealand, 31, 206, 214
NGOs, 61, 92, 320, 322
Nixon, Richard, 31–33, 73
Non-Aligned Movement, 81
North America Free Trade Agreement
(NAFTA), 258
North Atlantic Treaty Organization
(NATO), 211, 243–244, 265, 302, 389
Northeast Passage, 260
North Korea, 49, 161, 168, 192–193, 344–348,
375
Norway, 241

Obama administration: approach to
China of, 48–52, 285–286; Chinese
cyberattacks and, 164, 292; Chinese theft
of technology and, 292; climate change
work with China and, 143; negotiations
with Xi of, 73; "pivot to Asia" of, 54–55;
Trans-Pacific Partnership (TPP) and,
54; US freedom-of-navigation operations
(FONOPs) and, 300
Obama, Barack, 48–49
Ochmanek, David, 336
oil, 231–232, 260
Olympics in Beijing (2008), 47–48
Olympics in Beijing (2022), 352
Opium Wars, 22, 201
Orbán, Victor, 246

Pacific Island Forum, 217
Pakistan, 185, 225–227, 229–230, 257
Palau, 215, 216
Palestine, 234
Panama, 254
Papua New Guinea, 215
Paraguay, 254
Paris Climate Agreement (2015), 143–144,
269–270, 270
Paris Peace Conference, 25, 60
Paulson, Hank, 46, 50
Pearl Harbor, 28
Pence, Mike, 295
People's Bank of China, 115, 136
People's Liberation Army (PLA): A2/
AD strategy and, 158–159; African
security and, 250; in a managed
strategic competition framework,

368–369; artificial intelligence and, 128;
assessment of balance with US military,
152, 172–177; ballistic missiles and, 169,
171; Century of Humiliation and, 152–153;
"counterspace" capabilities and, 166;
cyberwarfare capabilities and, 161–165;
Djibouti naval base, 160; forward defense
strategy, 156; gray-zone pressure and, 157,
181; importance of in Xi's view, 152–155;
informationized warfare strategy and,
155–156; institutional respect for US
military and, 64–65; integrated joint
operations and, 155, 159; internal use and,
153; and international Chinese workforce,
160; maritime theater structure and,
155–156, 159; modernization of ground
forces, 158; naval power and, 8, 154,
156–158, 160–161; nuclear submarines
and, 169; nuclear weapons and, 167–172;
as part of China Dream, 151; People's
Armed Police and, 175, 310; PLA Air
Force and, 158; planned naval bases and
ports, 160; PLA Rocket Force (PLARF)
and, 158–159; PLA Strategic Support
Force (PLASSF), 159; port facilities
and, 228–230; public opinion and, 175;
purges of, 309; space superiority goals of,
165–167; Strategic Support Force (SSF),
166; Taiwan and, 98, 153–155; undersea
operations in Pacific, 215; US alliances
and, 152; US sanctions on arms sales and,
38; Xi's core principle of modernizing,
79, 159–160, 177; Xi's focus on, 152–155;
Xi's reforms of, 151–152
Philippines: Chinese claims to South
China Sea and, 53, 197, 199; effect
of possible-future scenarios on,
341; managed strategic competition
framework and, 381; post-war alliance
with US and, 31; under Duterte, 196–197;
US alliance with, 197; US defense
commitments and, 8, 173; US military
presence in, 202
Pinduoduo, 115–116
Polar Research Institute of China, 261
Pompeo, Mike, 289, 295–297,
300–301
Pottinger, Matt, 287
private schooling/education, 92, 110

Kevin Rudd is the global president and CEO of Asia Society and has been president of the Asia Society Policy Institute since January 2015. He served as Australia's twenty-sixth prime minister from 2007 to 2010 and then as its foreign minister from 2010 to 2012 before returning as prime minister in 2013. Rudd graduated from the Australian National University with honors in Chinese studies and is fluent in Mandarin. He also studied at the National Taiwan Normal University in Taipei. In 2023, he became the twenty-third ambassador of Australia to the United States.

PublicAffairs is a publishing house founded in 1997. It is a tribute to the standards, values, and flair of three persons who have served as mentors to countless reporters, writers, editors, and book people of all kinds, including me.

I. F. STONE, proprietor of *I. F. Stone's Weekly*, combined a commitment to the First Amendment with entrepreneurial zeal and reporting skill and became one of the great independent journalists in American history. At the age of eighty, Izzy published *The Trial of Socrates*, which was a national bestseller. He wrote the book after he taught himself ancient Greek.

BENJAMIN C. BRADLEE was for nearly thirty years the charismatic editorial leader of *The Washington Post*. It was Ben who gave the *Post* the range and courage to pursue such historic issues as Watergate. He supported his reporters with a tenacity that made them fearless and it is no accident that so many became authors of influential, best-selling books.

ROBERT L. BERNSTEIN, the chief executive of Random House for more than a quarter century, guided one of the nation's premier publishing houses. Bob was personally responsible for many books of political dissent and argument that challenged tyranny around the globe. He is also the founder and longtime chair of Human Rights Watch, one of the most respected human rights organizations in the world.

·   ·   ·

For fifty years, the banner of Public Affairs Press was carried by its owner Morris B. Schnapper, who published Gandhi, Nasser, Toynbee, Truman, and about 1,500 other authors. In 1983, Schnapper was described by *The Washington Post* as "a redoubtable gadfly." His legacy will endure in the books to come.

Peter Osnos, *Founder*